AGE OF ATROCITY

FROM SOME REVIEWS OF THE HARDBACK

'[A] fascinating book with impeccable insights and scholarship, read it; use it; learn from it.'
Martyn Bennett, *Scottish Historical Review*

'[R]eveals the true nature and extent of violence and atrocity in the sixteenth and seventeenth centuries as a conquering England gains territorial supremacy.'
William J. Smyth, *Irish Times* Books of the Year 2007

'The collection offers some thirteen contributions all of which are in themselves of considerable interest and value ... in their several ways these essays add considerably to our knowledge and our understanding of the place of political violence in Irish history in the sixteenth and seventeenth centuries ... this is a pioneering effort in Irish history, ... this promises to be the source of much exciting work to come.'
Ciaran Brady, *Irish Economic and Social History*

'In the troubled history of Ireland, the early modern period stands out as one of the bloodiest ... The fourteen chapters in this book re-examine this period with reference to acts of violence, and, specifically, to atrocities executed against unarmed civilians or captured soldiers.'
Patrick Little, *English Historical Review*

'Given its detailing of such a variety of savagery, it is not always an easy or pleasant read. But it is an important, even required one.'
Brendan Kane, *Renaissance Quarterly*

'This is an exciting and challenging volume that should encourage historians of Ireland and Britain to engage more effectively with their violent pasts. The essays, and in particular the introduction, make a significant contribution to a severely under-developed field and will help readers to understand the violent history of early modern Ireland.'
Rhys Morgan, *Welsh History Review*

Age of Atrocity

Violence and political conflict in early modern Ireland

David Edwards, Pádraig Lenihan
& Clodagh Tait

EDITORS

FOUR COURTS PRESS

Typeset in 10.5pt on 12.5pt EhrhardtMt by
Carrigboy Typesetting Services for
FOUR COURTS PRESS LTD
7 Malpas Street, Dublin 8, Ireland
e-mail: info@fourcourtspress.ie
and in North America for
FOUR COURTS PRESS
c/o ISBS, 920 N.E. 58th Avenue, Suite 300, Portland, OR 97213.

First published 2007
First paperback edition 2010
© the various authors and Four Courts Press 2010

A catalogue record for this title is available
from the British Library.

ISBN 978–1–84682–267–4

All rights reserved.
Without limiting the rights under copyright
reserved alone, no part of this publication may be
reproduced, stored in or introduced into a retrieval system,
or transmitted, in any form or by any means (electronic, mechanical,
photocopying, recording or otherwise), without the prior
written permission of both the copyright owner and
publisher of this book.

Printed in England by
Antony Rowe Ltd., Chippenham, Wilts.

Contents

ACKNOWLEDGMENTS 7

1 Early modern Ireland: a history of violence 9
   Clodagh Tait, David Edwards & Pádraig Lenihan

2 The escalation of violence in sixteenth-century Ireland 34
   David Edwards

3 Atrocity and history: Grey, Spenser and the slaughter at Smerwick (1580) 79
   Vincent P. Carey

4 'Slán Dé fút go hoíche': Hugh O'Neill's murders 95
   Hiram Morgan

5 The pacification of Ulster, 1600–3 119
   John McGurk

6 'The just vengeance of God': reporting the violent deaths of persecutors in early modern Ireland 130
   Clodagh Tait

7 Religious violence against settlers in south Ulster, 1641–2 154
   Brian Mac Cuarta

8 The other massacre: English killings of Irish, 1641–3 176
   Kenneth Nicholls

9 Archaeology of massacre: the Carrickmines mass grave and the siege of March 1642 192
   Mark Clinton, Linda Fibiger & Damian Shiels

10 Inventing an Irish Protestant icon: the strange death of Sir Charles Coote, 1642 204
   Kevin Forkan

11 'Escaping massacre': refugees in Scotland in the aftermath
   of the 1641 Ulster Rebellion   219
   John R. Young

12 The Drogheda massacre in Cromwellian context   242
   John Morrill

13 Propaganda, rumour and myth: Oliver Cromwell and the
   massacre at Drogheda   266
   Micheál Ó Siochrú

14 The laws of war in seventeenth-century Europe and their
   application during the Jacobite War in Ireland, 1688–91   283
   John Childs

NOTES ON CONTRIBUTORS   301

INDEX   305

Acknowledgments

This volume emerged from two conferences, 'Violent Death in Early Modern Ireland', held at Collins Barracks, Dublin, on 20 April 2002, and 'The Moral Context of War: Early Modern Ireland', held at the University of Limerick on 6 May 2004. The editors wish to thank all of the speakers at these conferences, and all of those who attended, for their enthusiasm and interest. The financial and other support offered on those occasions by the Department of History, National University of Ireland Maynooth, the Department of History, University College Cork, and the Historical Research Centre, University of Limerick, is gratefully acknowledged.

1 Map of Ireland (P. Lenihan).

Early modern Ireland: a history of violence

CLODAGH TAIT, DAVID EDWARDS
& PÁDRAIG LENIHAN

When Archbishop William King concluded that 'either they or we must be ruined' he was referring specifically to natives and newcomers in the reign of James II (1685–91).[1] But the grim mindset expressed could as easily have applied any time across that period from 1534 to 1691 that historians call early modernity. It was during these years that the forces of political and social change overcame those of continuity and Ireland was completely transformed. In one sense, change was inevitable. Shifting patterns of trade, accompanied by the expansion of towns, the development of markets, and the growth of commercialized farming, would naturally have been followed by changes in diet, settlement, class structure; perhaps even language and religion. But in Ireland, early modern developments were exceptionally abrupt and exceptionally extensive. They also entailed a considerable degree of violence and destruction.

At the outset the country was a largely autonomous zone on the periphery of Europe, under the heel of independent military lords. In just a few generations it became a subject kingdom of the English, or 'British', triple monarchy, and the first colony of the fledgling British empire. In 1534 Ireland was ostensibly a land of 'two nations', notionally divided between 'the Irishry' and the medieval 'Englishry'. By 1691 the population of English or Scottish stock had grown from virtually nothing to over one quarter: a dramatic transformation of ethnic composition by any European yardstick. The proportion of land (the surest index of wealth and power in an agrarian society) owned by newcomers increased to over four-fifths through confiscation from native landowners, a project that simply would never have been seriously considered in early modern England or even in lowland Scotland. Rather than work in cooperation with local elites, therefore, the crown displaced them and drove a radical course of colonisation, trying to reshape Irish society, in government, language and culture, as a replica of England. Immigration meant that Ireland became a religiously mixed land too. From about 1570 Anglican-style Protestantism became the official religion of state, albeit with little effective

---

1 W. King, *The state of the Protestants of Ireland* (London, 1692), p. 270.

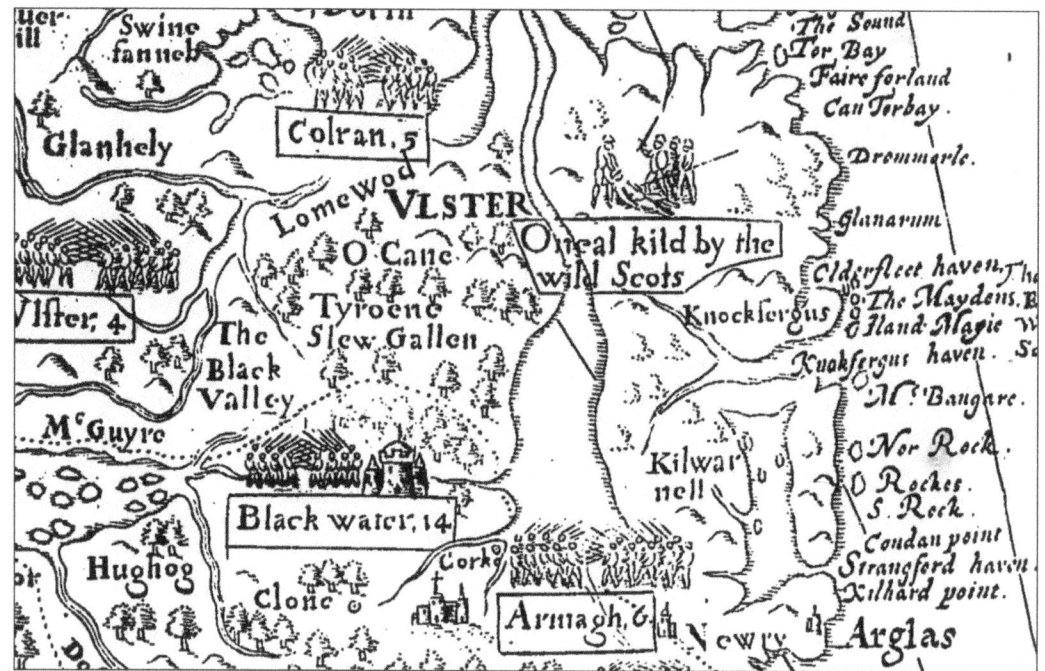

2 Shane O'Neill 'kild by the wild Scots', from John Speed, *A description of the civill warres of England* (London, 1601).

attempt at evangelization or conversion of the largely Catholic population. After 1600 those who held power, controlling the courts and the legislature, and, increasingly, owning most of the land, were Protestants, while the majority of the island's inhabitants remained Catholic, despite growing disadvantage.

Such change could only have been driven through by violence. Five major wars punctuate the period, the Kildare Revolt and the Geraldine League (1534–40); the second Desmond Rising (1579–1583); Tyrone's Rebellion (1594–1603); the Confederate and Cromwellian wars (1641–53); and the War of the Two Kings (1689–91). But violence also pervaded the intervening years. Antagonized by growing royal power and alienated by the antics of the crown's garrisons, few of the military lordships that dominated the country in the early sixteenth century retreated before the growing influence of the English state without recourse to armed conflict. From 1534 onwards the reduction of the local lords impelled the English Tudor monarchy towards a policy of bloody conquest as well as negotiated settlement. The so-called 'Flight of the Earls' in 1607 retrospectively confirmed the Tudor conquest and cleared the way for the Stuarts to finally dismember the Gaelic lordships by plantation. But even after 1607 the new Stuart line of kings allowed the neutralization of the lordships to be continued by decidedly heavy-handed measures. The brief assertion of Irish independence by the Confederate Catholics in the 1640s arose out of violent revolt and fell amid the carnage of the Cromwellian re-conquest (1649–52). The total overshadowing of the old native nobility and the triumph of British Protestant power were finally sealed on the killing fields of Aughrim, on 12 July 1691.

The dispossession and removal of the majority of existing native owners invited resistance and required considerable use of coercion. In many instances even the purchase of land led directly to violence, with the new owners and their followers often confronted either by native tenants and peasants forced off estates to make way for them, or else by impoverished relatives of the former owners. Notoriously, the 1641 Depositions – the collected testimonies of 'British' settlers who in late 1641 and early 1642 became refugees following the outbreak of a countrywide rebellion – contain numerous lurid accounts of acts perpetrated by insurgents against the newcomers, especially in heavily-settled Ulster. Yet they are not the only evidence of this type. Tales of conflict shape the narrative of the very first state colony, commenced in 1549, the Laois–Offaly Plantation, and can be found scattered across a range of sources, including Gaelic annals, English state papers, and contemporary histories written by both English and Irish authors. The greatest colonial project of all, the Cromwellian settlement of the 1650s, was only possible because an exceptionally bitter and destructive conquest offered the English Commonwealth and Protectorate an apparently blank sheet.

Ethnic and cultural change both consolidated and deepened the causes of violence, providing ideological justification for intolerance and bloodshed. From their sixteenth-century beginnings, English plans to take greater control of Ireland also had a cultural dimension, with observers advocating that the Irish be Anglicized and the Gaelicized descendants of the medieval English colonists, the Anglo-Irish or Old English, be re-Anglicized. The Gaelic Irish were repeatedly stereotyped as wild and backward, even as savages, a quarrelsome, tribal people enslaved to their history and lineage, much given to drink and licentiousness, and as unreliable and dishonest, hopelessly lazy, content to live in nit-picking poverty. The Irish too resorted to abusive cultural stereotypes to comfort them in adversity and rationalize their position. Equating respectability with antiquity, they often characterized the New English colonists as low-born 'bodaigh' and boors, addicted to vice and brutality, who lacked the only true sign of gentility, a long genealogy.

Religious alterations added much to the volatility, resulting in constant underlying sectarian tension and occasional outright sectarian conflict, the stubborn legacies of which are still identifiable today. Religion gave Irish affairs a dangerous international dimension that served only to exacerbate existing tensions. Rebellions by Irish lords increasingly succeeded in exciting European interest by playing the religious card (though the extent to which their followers conceived of such conflicts in a religious light is still hotly debated). Thus the Desmond Rising was aided by a combined papal-Spanish force that landed on the Kerry coast in autumn 1580, the Tyrone Rebellion reached its zenith with the arrival of Spanish forces at Kinsale in late 1601, and the Pope proved the most open-handed supporter of the Confederate insurrection (1642–9), which was for a time controlled and manipulated by an Italian archbishop serving as papal nuncio. The growing Protestantism of officials and settlers after about 1570, coinciding with the first appearance in the country of new European-schooled Catholic clergy specifically trained to combat Protestantism, meant that the various conflicts between native lords and crown officers further poisoned a deepening well of religious unrest. Ireland became one of the battlefields of Reformation and Counter-Reformation Europe, and the chief battlefield on which, before 1553, the English monarchy had to defend its religious independence of Rome and, after 1558, its increasing commitment to outright Protestantism.

ACKNOWLEDGING THE VIOLENT HISTORY OF EARLY MODERN IRELAND

The violence of the sixteenth and seventeenth centuries was a very visible element of Victorian and early twentieth-century histories of Ireland. The energetic promotion of highly partisan and selective Catholic history-writing focussed in particular on the persecution of that community in the past. Publications like M. O'Reilly's *Memorials of those who suffered for the Catholic faith in Ireland* (1868), and P.F. Moran's *Historical sketch of the persecutions suffered by the Catholics of Ireland under the rule of Cromwell and the Puritans* (1907), reflected the nationalistic spirit of the age, concentrating on depicting the Irish as the innocent, bemused and thoroughly Catholic victims of an unprovoked onslaught by Protestant forces. They also aimed to promote a positive image of the contemporary Irish Catholic church – both Moran, who became Cardinal Archbishop of Sydney, and his uncle, Cardinal Cullen, were convinced of the value of such works in counteracting the effects of 'light literature' and promoting devotion. Concurrent attempts to procure the canonisation of a number of prominent Catholics killed during the early modern period further help explain the focus on suffering and martyrdom.[2]

---

2 These aims are mentioned on a number of occasions in Cullen's letters. See, for example, Dublin Diocesan Archives, Cullen papers, 40/4. Many thanks to Colin Barr, who is editing the documents for publication, for providing access to transcripts of them. M. O'Reilly, *Memorials of those who suffered for the Catholic faith in Ireland in the 16th, 17th and 18th centuries* (London, 1868); P.F. Moran, *Historical sketch of the persecutions suffered by the Catholics of Ireland under the rule of Cromwell and the puritans* (Dublin, 1907).

Meanwhile, accounts of Protestant tribulations took a long time to pass out of political discourse, being revived in later periods when that community felt embattled and threatened.³ The horrors of the 1641 rebellion formed a central theme. A tract published by the Long Parliament in 1642 claimed that the Irish massacred no fewer than 154,000 Protestants between October 1641 and March 1642.⁴ Sir John Temple's *Irish Rebellion*, first published in 1646, laid claim to scholarly credibility by liberal citation from a documentary source, the depositions. Temple's volume proved an authoritative source for a black legend of 'barbarous cruelties and bloody massacres' that was little shaken by the counter-narratives of Catholic apologists.⁵ In the eighteenth century, David Hume's *History of England* slavishly followed Temple in depicting an unprovoked and unexpected 'universal massacre',⁶ and nineteenth-century Irish Catholics found themselves again charged with collective guilt in J.A. Froude's popular history *The English in Ireland* (1874) and in his introduction to Mary Hickson's two-volume selection of 1641 depositions.⁷ In riposte, W.E.H. Lecky, Froude's old adversary, dismissed the entire historical tradition from Temple to Froude as nothing more than 'garbled accounts from untrustworthy documents', while Robert Dunlop critiqued the depositions even more trenchantly as 'worthless',

---

3 J. Hill, 'Popery and Protestantism, civil and religious liberty: the disputed lessons of Irish history, 1690–1812', *Past and Present*, 118 (1988), 96–129; J. Hill, '1641 and the quest for Catholic emancipation, 1691–1829', in B. MacCuarta (ed.), *Ulster 1641: aspects of the rising* (Belfast, 1997), pp 159–71; T.C. Barnard, 'The uses of 23 October 1641 and Irish Protestant celebrations', *English Historical Review*, 106 (1991), 889–920; James Kelly, '"The glorious and immortal memory": commemoration and Protestant identity in Ireland, 1660–1800', *Proceedings of the Royal Irish Academy*, 94 (1994), 25–52; B. Walker, *Dancing to history's tune: history, myth and politics in Ireland* (Belfast, 1996), pp 1–14. A few extreme Protestant groups still highlight 1641 as a plot directed from Rome 'to seize Ireland', for example, http://www.ianpaisley.org/article.asp?ArtKey=deliverance7, accessed 11 January 2007. 4 H. Jones, *A remonstrance of divers remarkable passages concerning the church and kingdome of Ireland* (London, 1642). 5 J.T. Temple, *History of the Irish rebellion* (London, 1646); R.S., *A collection of some of the murthers and massacres committed on the Irish in Ireland* (London, 1662); *Good news from Ireland* (London 1642), cited in T. Bartlett, '*The academy of warre*': *Military affairs in Ireland 1600 to 1800* (Dublin, 2003) p. 25; D. O'Hara, *English newsbooks and Irish rebellion, 1641–1649* (Dublin, 2006) p. 77; N. Canny, *Making Ireland British, 1580–1650* (Oxford, 2001) pp 462–3; T.C. Barnard, '1641: a bibliographical essay', in MacCuarta, *Ulster 1641*, pp 174, 178–80. 6 David Hume, *The history of England, from the invasion of Julius Caesar to the revolution of 1688* (6 vols, London, 1874) 5, p. 62. For other views, see R.E. Ward, 'A letter from Ireland: a little-known attack on David Hume's *History of England*', in A. Carpenter (ed.), *Eighteenth-century Ireland* (Dublin, 1987), p. 197. Barnard, '1641: a bibliographical essay', p. 182; J. Liechty, 'Testing the depth of Catholic/Protestant conflict: the case of Thomas Leland's *History of Ireland*', *Archivium Hibernicum*, 42 (1987), 19–22; J. Curry, *Historical memoirs of the Irish rebellion in the year 1641* (London, 1765). 7 J.A. Froude, *The English in Ireland in the eighteenth century* (London, 1874), pp 21–4; M.A. Hickson, *Ireland in the seventeenth century: or, The Irish massacres of 1641–2, their causes and results* (2 vols, London, 1884).

J.T Gilbert called them 'utterly untrustworthy and invalid', and Thomas Fitzpatrick and others ridiculed their imaginative excesses.[8] So effective were attacks on the credibility of these sources that only in the late twentieth century were the depositions rehabilitated by historians who began slowly to engage with what actually happened in 1641.[9]

Given the established traditions that highlighted conflict and suffering, it is strange that for much of the twentieth century Irish historians had little or nothing to say about the violence that characterized early modern Ireland. Even though warfare is ubiquitous in narratives of the sixteenth and seventeenth centuries, the true nature and extent of the violence of the period has been consistently elided, even evaded. *Irish Historical Studies (IHS)*, the main professional journal of Irish historians, first appeared nearly 70 years ago, in 1938. Founded by two early modernists, it is hardly surprising that it gave generous coverage to some of the main developments in sixteenth- and seventeenth-century Ireland, publishing articles, for instance, about the expansion of English government under the Tudors and Stuarts, the onset of the plantations and planter society, and the political strategies and military tactics employed by the opposing sides during the Elizabethan, Confederate and Williamite Wars. Significantly, however, it was not until forty years had elapsed, and both founding editors had resigned, before an article appeared in the pages of *IHS* that directly addressed the violence and bloodshed, the bigotry and atrocity, of early modern times. The article in question, a groundbreaking examination of the outbreak of the 1641 rebellion that considered the significance of the Irish slaughter of Scottish prisoners near Augher, Co. Tyrone,[10] did not signal a new departure. For many more years the early modern content of the journal continued more or less as before. A trenchant critique appeared in 1989, in which five massacres perpetrated by English forces during the sixteenth century were briefly cited as the sort of history not usually covered by the journal.[11] Even then, it was not until 1993 that *IHS* included a piece that explored the violent military culture of the early modern Irish borderlands,[12] and only in its sixty-first year of existence, in 1999, did a sustained study of a particular atrocity appear, Carey's treatment of the government massacre of Gaelic clansmen on Mullaghmast hill in Co. Kildare during the reign of Elizabeth I.[13]

8 W.E.H. Lecky, *A history of Ireland in the eighteenth century* (5 vols, London, 1892) 1, p. 80; J.M. Read, 'Atrocity propaganda and the Irish rebellion', *The Public Opinion Quarterly*, 2 (1938), 229–44; Barnard, '1641: a bibliographical essay', pp 184–5; Thomas Fitzpatrick, *The bloody bridge and other papers relating to the insurrection of 1641* (Dublin, 1903), pp 105–62, 193. 9 Canny, *Making Ireland British*, p. 464. 10 M. Perceval-Maxwell, 'The Ulster rising of 1641, and the depositions', *IHS*, 21 (1978), 144–67, especially 157–9. 11 B. Bradshaw, 'Nationalism and historical scholarship in Ireland', *IHS*, 26 (1989), 329–51. 12 David Edwards, 'The Butler revolt of 1569', *IHS*, 28 (1993), 227–55. This essay also contains a short discussion of the Irish massacre of civilians at Enniscorthy, Co. Wexford (at p. 250). 13 V. Carey, 'John Derricke's

The prolonged neglect of early modern violence in the pages of *IHS* would not greatly matter had historians published investigations of the subject elsewhere. However, in the years immediately following the establishment of *IHS*, bloodshed and brutality were likewise ignored in Irish academic studies of the sixteenth and seventeenth centuries. Other periodicals, old and new, including stalwarts such as the *Irish Sword* and the *Journal of the Royal Society of Antiquaries in Ireland*, were equally reticent. Books published after 1938 ploughed much the same furrow – a remarkable fact, given that two monographs that explored early modern bloodshed in great detail, Hayes-McCoy's history of the Scottish galloglasses[14] and O'Rahilly's study of the massacre of Smerwick,[15] had appeared in 1937 and 1938 respectively, and might have been expected to serve as a platform for further studies. For nearly forty years thereafter, only one academic book on sixteenth-century Ireland emphasized the notable violence of the period, D.B. Quinn's study of Elizabethan colonialism. Containing a chapter called 'Horror Story', this revealed more about the centrality of violence and atrocity in the English pursuit of colonial expansion than the work of any previous writer.[16]

It was only in the early 1970s that the violence of the sixteenth century began to be acknowledged again, chiefly in the work of Nicholas Canny.[17] Even then, the extraordinary violence of the following century remained unexplored. Significantly, when the early modern volume of the *New History of Ireland* series appeared in 1976, it was the soft-focus view that prevailed, with the main narrative remaining studiously evasive about killing and atrocity. Discussion of religion and religious conflict was minimal, peculiar in a volume designed to cover the period of the Reformation and Counter-Reformation and to place events in Ireland in their broader European context. The sanitizing effect continued through to the narrative chapters; for example, Hayes-McCoy, in treating of massacres in Ulster in 1574 and 1575, spoke of the earl of Essex's 'lessons in frightfulness' and mentioned in passing acts of 'sadism', 'treachery' and 'savagery', but none of these incidents was treated in detail, and the overall focus was on the overarching political developments of the Elizabethan period.[18]

Image of Irelande, Sir Henry Sidney, and the massacre at Mullaghmast, 1578', *IHS*, 31 (1999), 305–27.   **14** G.A. Hayes-McCoy, *Scots mercenary forces in Ireland, 1565–1603* (Dublin 1937; rep. Dublin, 1996).   **15** A. O'Rahilly, *The massacre at Smerwick, 1580* (Cork, 1938).   **16** D.B. Quinn, *The Elizabethans and the Irish* (New York, 1966), chapter 10. Cyril Falls, *Elizabeth's Irish wars* (London, 1950), provided a good general history of its subject, but tiptoed around atrocity.   **17** Nicholas Canny, 'The ideology of English colonisation: from Ireland to America', *William & Mary Quarterly*, 30 (1973); *The Elizabethan conquest of Ireland: a pattern established, 1565–1576* (Hassocks, 1976).   **18** T.W. Moody, F.X. Martin and F.J. Byrne (eds), *A new history of Ireland, iii: early modern Ireland, 1534–1691* (Oxford, 1976). The minimal coverage of atrocity in the wider historiography after 1976 is best demonstrated in A. Clarke, R. Gillespie & James McGuire, *A new history of Ireland: bibliographical supplement, 1534–1691* (Oxford, 1991).

Though such oversights might seem strange now, at the time many historians had good reason to feel they were acting in the best interests of Irish history by attempting to counter the traditional manipulation of the past for political and confessional ends. In the nineteenth century, the subject of history in schools and universities was a contentious issue, its potential as a 'political weapon' and a means of shaping ideologies was acutely recognized, so much so that the Irish hierarchy was reluctant that Catholics be exposed to the study of history at third level, for fear of them absorbing unorthodox or 'unsafe' (i.e. non-Catholic, non-nationalist) interpretations of the past.[19] After Partition in 1920 the dominant forces of the two Irelands, the majority Protestant unionist state of Northern Ireland and the majority Catholic nationalist Free State (and later Republic) in the south, continued to attempt to manipulate the past to give a sense of historical legitimacy to the present. For example, in Northern Ireland, rather than learning Irish history, pupils in state schools were taught a version of British history that celebrated colonialism and imperialism. In contrast, in the Irish Free State/Republic the history syllabus was heavily influenced by what Gabriel Doherty terms 'the belief in an inner spirituality of the Irish people, demonstrated by their abiding fidelity to the twin ideals of Catholicism and political freedom'. Likewise, other narratives of the Irish past (the 'alternative curriculum', in the words of Lawrence McBride) continued to be presented as a catalogue of wrongs suffered, structured and punctuated by outbreaks of physical-force nationalism. The diverse contexts of events such as the revolts of the sixteenth and seventeenth centuries, 1798, Robert Emmett's rising, 1848, the Fenian revolt, and 1916 were elided to give a sense of a continuous tradition of struggle against malevolent forces.[20] To ensure the very survival of Irish history as an independent intellectual discipline, free from political manipulation in the rhetoric of nation-building, those involved in *Irish Historical Studies* and other publications realized that it was vital for historians to rise above contemporary political and confessional allegiances to embrace a broader, more diverse understanding of the country's past. Some brilliant work was done, chiefly in the area of constitutional and administrative history and, in lesser volume, in economic and social history, but even so progress was far from even. Moreover, their determination to avoid the trap of writing history that might lend weight to either Catholic nationalism or Protestant unionism meant that scholars avoided the study of key aspects of the country's past, in particular political and colonial violence and religious discord. In doing so, they have often

---

19 C. Barr, 'University education, history, and the hierarchy'; L.W. McBride, 'Young readers and the learning and teaching of Irish history, 1870–1922', in McBride, *Reading Irish histories: texts, contexts, and memory in modern Ireland* (Dublin, 2003), pp 62–117.   20 G. Doherty, 'National identity and the study of Irish history', *English Historical Review*, 111 (1996), 324–49; S. Howe, 'The politics of historical "revisionism": comparing Ireland and Israel/Palestine', *Past and Present*, 168 (2000), 227–53; McBride, 'Young readers', pp 80–117.

favoured empiricist narrative over the introduction of the newer theoretical frameworks that have given historians new questions to ask old sources and expanded understandings of the worldviews of past peoples elsewhere.[21]

Coverage of the early modern period was probably most seriously affected. Because so much of Ireland's twentieth-century conflict could be traced back to early modern origins, a special effort was made to decouple early modern history from current affairs by minimizing or passing over the political and religious violence of the period. Evasion is never a good choice for historians. For one thing, the myths surrounding early modern events, especially 1641, Cromwell, and the Battle of the Boyne, had lost little of their power, continuing to feed political and sectarian conflict. For another, many of the general public failed to be convinced by the historians' bloodless representation of sixteenth- and seventeenth-century Ireland. Critics questioned the 'revisionist' ethos of many professional academic historians which was seen to concentrate on certain aspects of the past (some of which had undeniably been neglected hitherto) while ignoring others. Far from saving Irish history from abuse, therefore, by their persistent evasion of disturbing events historians risked being identified among its abusers.

This was certainly the attitude taken by two early modernists who aligned themselves with nationalist politics. Brendan Bradshaw and Willy Maley, in 1989 and 1999 respectively, penned strongly-worded critiques of what was described as the 'value-free' school of historical interpretation ('value-free' seems to have been a mischievous choice of term that implied an attempted but impossible neutrality, while also inferring a grave degree of ideological and imaginative impoverishment – indeed, Bradshaw accused his targets of stylistic dullness as well). Bradshaw castigated what he saw as 'blatant' evasion in recent histories of the 'unprecedented ruthlessness of the crown's reaction to dissent in Ireland' from the 1530s and their 'perfunctory' treatment of 'the phenomenon of catastrophic violence' during the Elizabethan reconquest. Maley felt that the Northern Irish Troubles had led to a situation where violence was 'decried rather than described', and accused historians of being 'concerned as much with concealing as with healing the wounds of Irish history, with dissolving conflict into consensus'. Though their arguments contain excesses and inconsistencies, Bradshaw and Maley do effectively take historians to task for 'burying' and 'suppressing' historical violence.[22]

---

21 See C. Brady (ed.), *Interpreting Irish history: the debate on historical revisionism 1938–1994* (Dublin, 1994); G. Boyce and A. O'Day (eds), *The making of modern Irish history: revisionism and the revisionist controversy* (London, 1996); S.F. Moran, 'History, memory and education: teaching the Irish story', in McBride, *Reading Irish histories*, pp 212–19.   22 Bradshaw, 'Nationalism and historical scholarship', especially 336–43; W. Maley, 'Nationalism and revisionism: ambiviolences and dissensus', in S. Brewster et al. (eds), *Ireland in proximity: history, gender, space* (London, 1999), pp 12–25.

The editors of this volume agree that the best way for historians to prevent history being misused is to provide an accurate record of the past in all its aspects, warts and all – and Ireland's past has sometimes been very warty indeed. Moreover, by recovering uncomfortable historical evidence historians can play a small role in peacemaking through preparing communities for the process of reconciliation by encouraging them to confront historic wrongs perpetrated in their names, bridging gaps in popular historical consciousnesses, and promoting a more nuanced understanding of historical events and processes. Focusing on ancient violence should not mean revicitimizing or manipulating its casualties: truth lies not in the voyeuristic rehearsal of their sufferings, nor in the harnessing of those tribulations to modern grievances, but in the acknowledgement of the nastiness of the past in its own terms.[23]

Some progress has already been achieved in the fields of literary, religious and political history, less as a result of Bradshaw and Maley's comments than because of other theoretical and methodological advances. It is scholars trained in literary criticism who from the early 1990s have made the greatest strides towards incorporating violence into the Irish historical record. In their investigation of the flowering of English literature from the later sixteenth century, it was found that figures as celebrated as Spenser and Shakespeare, as well as a host of lesser-known writers, had rather a lot to say about Ireland, much of it inflammatory.[24] The rhetoric of ideological justification of violence and atrocity is further considered in this volume. Historians of early modern religion have similarly begun to tackle the subjects of religious violence, martyrdom, and sectarianism, and attempts have been made to understand the religious component of conflict in Ireland within a wider European context, paying attention to toleration as well as persecution.[25] Meanwhile, David Edwards' work on the

---

23 Howe, 'The politics of historical "revisionism"', 252. S. Radstone, 'Reconceiving binaries: the limits of memory', *History Workshop Journal*, 39 (2005), 134–50, talks convincingly about the limitations of 'victim politics'. A remarkable article by Anne Dolan on the killing of supposed English spies in Dublin on 'Bloody Sunday' in 1920 is a model for the ways in which an unflinching consideration of violent events and their actors can expand our understanding: 'Killing and Bloody Sunday, November 1920', *Historical Journal*, 49 (2006), 789–810. 24 Work by Hadfield, Carey, Maley, and others is cited elsewhere in this volume. See also, for example, P. Coughlan (ed.), *Spenser and Ireland: an interdisciplinary perspective* (Cork, 1990); C. Carroll, *Circe's cup: cultural transformations in early modern Ireland* (Cork, 2002); P. Palmer, '"An headlesse ladie" and "a horses loade of heades": writing the beheading', *Renaissance Quarterly*, 60 (2007), 25–57. 25 A. Ford and J. McCafferty (eds), *Sectarianism in early modern Ireland* (Cambridge 2005); A. Ford, 'Martyrdom, history and memory in early modern Ireland', in I. McBride (ed.), *History and memory in modern Ireland* (Cambridge, 2001); C. Lennon, 'Taking sides: the emergence of Irish Catholic ideology', in V. Carey and U. Lotz-Heumann (eds), *Taking sides: colonial and confessional mentalités in early modern Ireland* (Dublin, 2003); C. Tait, 'Adored for saints: Catholic martyrs and the Counter-Reformation in Ireland, c.1560–1655', *Journal of Early Modern History*, 5 (2001); Tait, 'Persecution and toleration in early modern Ireland', in V. Carey (ed.), *Voices for tolerance in*

tactics used by English military commanders in times of ostensible peace as well as during warfare is beginning to clarify just how widespread, and how shockingly extreme, was the use of martial law in Tudor and Stuart Ireland.[26]

This collection of essays goes further. It is, in essence, a book about killing. By foregrounding the violence and brutality of early modern Ireland it takes a large step towards restoring killing and conflict to their proper place in the historical record. These essays confront that most uncomfortable of subjects, atrocity. They do so not merely to place it on record, but also to determine its causes and effects, and to establish its contemporary meanings by examining the rhetoric of justification and condemnation. By dwelling on some of the very ugliest events of the early modern period, how they were justified, and how they were perceived, it is hoped that what follows will not only facilitate a deeper appreciation of the lasting importance of the sixteenth and seventeenth centuries, but will also give a greater sense of balance to its coverage by examining both the perpetrators and victims of atrocity, and trying to place their experiences in their proper context.

DEFINING AND CONTEXTUALISING ATROCITY

Some clarifications and definitions are initially necessary, especially in regard to the issues of atrocity and violence. The concept of 'atrocity' in particular threatens to overwhelm historians' pretensions to be dispassionate recorders of events. Historians are supposed to report and attempt to understand the past on its own terms, but to define an incident as an atrocity is implicitly to lay blame on one side or another. The problem, however, is that to substitute some other term for atrocity is to detract from the impact of bloodshed, to ignore some of its most important effects, such as horror and outrage, and generally to water it down. A reluctance to apportion blame largely explains the concerns of those historical texts which have drawn back from engaging with the true scale of the violence that occurred in early modern Ireland. But not to acknowledge atrocity, to leave it unnoticed or dismiss it as just part of the 'ugly reality' of life long ago, is to fall into a fatal trap – that of choosing simplification and even falsification over more messy and complicated truths.

The idea of atrocity has long served as one means of separating the illegitimate use of violence from the legitimate. After all, this was an age when

---

an age of persecution (Washington, 2004). 26 D. Edwards, 'Beyond reform: martial law and the reconquest of Tudor Ireland', *History Ireland*, 5 (1997), 16–21; 'Ideology and experience: Spenser's *View* and martial law in Ireland', in H. Morgan (ed.), *Political ideology in Ireland, 1541–1641* (Dublin, 1999), pp 127–57; 'Two fools and a martial law commissioner: cultural conflict at the Limerick assize of 1606', in Edwards (ed.), *Regions and rulers in Ireland, 1100–1650* (Dublin 2004), pp 237–65.

many violent acts – the making of war, the execution, mutilation and torture of criminals, and the 'lawful correction' of subordinates such as wives, children, and servants – were considered to be entirely acceptable. Their significance, P.C. Maddern points out, hinged on 'the motives of the actors, and the context'. People believed that God himself 'supported the violent in righteous action', and that the way to peace might be through the violence of the just towards the wicked.[27] Susan Amussen speaks of the 'moral economy' of violence. Violence was one means of 'claiming power', but acceptance of the legitimacy of violent acts 'depended on both the context and the adherence by participants to a certain set of rules and limits'. Breaches of these rules and limits and abuses of power could lead onlookers to contest their rationale.[28] In Ireland, there was less than usual agreement about rules, limits, and even objectives.

Atrocities differ in scale. In the past as today, an attack causing minor injuries could as equally be defined as extreme and unforgiveable as one that caused massive loss of life. This was even more the case when those who bore the brunt of the attack were seen to be innocent of any provocation, or to be especially vulnerable in some way (civilians, women and children, the elderly, and other non-combatants, including clerics). As discussed in this volume by Clodagh Tait and Brian MacCuarta (chapters 6 and 7), assaults on places and things as well as people might similarly draw charges of excessive violence, especially if those places and things held special symbolic importance. The stripping and humiliation of Protestants in 1641 was taken as evidence enough of the inhumanity of Irish rebels. Instances abound of symbolic violence against places and items with special resonance for an enemy. In this volume, for example, we find the O'Neill inauguration chair at Tullyhogue being smashed by Mountjoy. In the 1640s in Ulster, Protestant churches were put to base uses, and bibles and pulpits were ill-treated and destroyed, while legend accused Charles Coote and Henry Brouncker of destroying Catholic religious symbols. These were more than acts of wanton vandalism. Just as the destruction of buildings and fortifications was intended to lessen the power of one's opponents, the power of the O'Neills was implicitly eroded by the loss of the traditional symbol of their entitlement to rule. Attacks on the words and houses of the Protestant God denied the legitimacy of Protestant belief and practice and removed the pollution they were believed to have introduced to the community, while

---

[27] P.C. Maddern, *Violence and social order: East Anglia 1422–1442* (Oxford, 1992). [28] S.D. Amussen, 'Punishment, discipline and power: the social meanings of violence in early modern England', *Journal of British Studies*, 34 (1995), 1–34; '"Being stirred to much unquietness": violence and domestic violence in early modern England', *Journal of Women's History*, 6 (1994), 70–89. See also J.C. Wood, *Violence and crime in nineteenth-century England: the shadow of our refinement* (London, 2004), especially chapter 1; D. Riches, 'The phenomenon of violence', in Riches (ed.), *The anthropology of violence* (Oxford, 1986), pp 1–27; A. Blok, *Honour and violence* (Basingstoke, 2001), especially pp 103–14.

Brouncker and Coote's actions demonstrated their contempt for Catholic devotion to the saints. The killing of things mimicked, paralleled and provoked the killing of people.

Meanwhile, the infliction of ritual 'multiple deaths' on certain individuals carried further the humiliation and punishment of the other side. Assaults on the bodies of dead Protestants, and refusals to bury them, again demonstrated the need to remove them totally from the community of the just.[29] The mutilation of bodies was a time-honoured tradition in Ireland. John McGurk comments (chapter 5) on the headhunting and display of trophies that characterized the Elizabethan wars. Patricia Palmer has recently revealed the extent to which all sides used beheading in early modern Ireland as a terror tactic designed to symbolize the criminality and eternal damnation of the victims. In English literature, Irish beheadings were presented as yet more evidence for Irish inhumanity, while the heads of rebels spoke to confess their misdemeanours.[30] But beheading was not merely a mark of ethnic conflict: as John Morrill notes in chapter 12, it was the heads of English rather than Irish officers which were displayed by Cromwell after Drogheda, since their perfidy was perceived as being particularly great, while Edwards (chapter 2) gives examples of occasions where the sixteenth-century Irish beheaded enemies even from their own families.

Atrocity could be seen to have desirable results, and could be excused as a necessary evil or a just response to provocation. In England itself during the 1640s, when quite strong emphasis was placed on the laws of war, '[r]eprisal offered a particularly useful justification for appalling actions, matching atrocity for atrocity': in both England and Ireland in this period, the Irish were liable to harsher treatment as a result of beliefs about what had transpired during the early stages of the 1641 rebellion (the Welsh and Cornish also might be especially denigrated).[31] Those who committed atrocities could also play them down to minimize their psychological impact (witness wording like the 'many inhabitants' killed at Drogheda, casually tacked on at the end of the casualty list), while those groups who suffered them played them up, the prime example being the exaggerated tallies of those Protestants killed in 1641/2.

---

29 See C. Tait, *Death, burial and commemoration in Ireland, c.1550–1650* (Basingstoke, 2002), pp 81–3, 93–6. On French parallels, see N.Z. Davis, 'The rites of violence', in *Society and culture in early modern France* (Stanford, 1975), pp 152–87; K. Luria, *Sacred boundaries: religious coexistence and conflict in early modern France* (Washington, 2005).   30 Palmer, 'Writing the beheading'.   31 B. Donagan, 'Atrocity, war crime, and treason in the English Civil War', *American Historical Review*, 99 (1994), 1137–66; Donagan, 'Codes and conduct in the English Civil War', *Past and Present*, 118 (1988), 65–95; M. Stoyle, 'Caricaturing Cymru: Images of the Welsh in the London press, 1642–6', in D. Dunn (ed.), *War and society in medieval and early modern Britain* (Liverpool, 2000), pp 162–79; Stoyle, 'English "nationalism", Celtic particularism, and the English Civil War', *Historical Journal*, 43 (2000); Stoyle, *West Britons: Cornish identities and the early modern British state* (Exeter, 2002).

We need therefore to consider the potential disjuncture between our definitions of atrocity and those accepted by people at the time. John Childs points out in his chapter (14) on the early modern laws of war that the killing of soldiers fleeing a battlefield 'is not an atrocity'. He cites the pursuit after the Battle of Aughrim; another engagement mentioned in this volume was the slaughter of the Irish forces after the battle of Dungan's Hill in 1647. Our contributors agree that the deaths at Drogheda in 1649, and at Smerwick in 1580 were killings in cold blood, but acknowledge that the blood at Wexford was rather hotter, and consider the niceties, sometimes opaque to us, of terms such as 'quarter' and 'mercy'. Kenneth Nicholls (chapter 8), for example, distinguishes between the slaughter of soldiers 'taken in arms' and those killed despite having been promised quarter. This all serves as a reminder that what clearly seems an atrocity to modern eyes might not have been so defined by many contemporaries. They did not need to be self-delusional to hold such positions.

The randomness of many acts of violence and atrocities presents another challenge entirely: why did they issue from some incidents rather than others? It is sometimes tempting to dismiss such occasions as irrational and inexplicable acts by perpetrators who were mad or bad or both, or as a stroke of rotten luck for victims in the wrong place at the wrong time. Violence is rarely, if ever, 'senseless', but in the past, just as in the present, many were perplexed by excesses of brutality.[32] Early modern people themselves put forward the idea of 'fury', a sort of psychosis gripping those, like Charles Coote the elder, who engaged in extreme violence. Increasingly from the 1570s, as the religious element of war began to emerge, this was often understood to be provoked by the Devil. Yet, significantly, it was also possible for extreme violence and atrocity to be excused as an expression of the zeal of soldiers in the heat of battle, or as a reaction to the privations they had suffered, as this volume shows in relation to massacres at Smerwick, Wexford and elsewhere. Atrocity could be seen, then, as an unfortunate but not entirely unexpected result of justifiable or uncontrollable rage or passion.

A thorough examination of the sources reveals not only that soldiers and ordinary people were capable of terrible acts of cruelty, but also that such actions can only be understood in their proper context. English military strategy and tactics during the 1550s, early 1580s, and late 1590s, described by David Edwards, Vincent Carey, and John McGurk in chapters 2, 3 and 5 were not solely attributable to the character and beliefs of Elizabeth's officers. The previous failures of the royal army to pacify parts of Ireland were at least as important. Financial factors made brutality cost effective: killing prisoners obviated the need to feed them or to assign scarce troops to guard duties and ensured that suspects could never again become involved in anti-government

---

32 Blok, *Honour and violence*, pp 9–10, 103–14.

activities; famine caused by scorched earth, as Edwards comments, was the 'fast route to lasting impact'. The temptation to resort to extreme security measures (or turn a blind eye to them) was enormously increased by the growing links between Irish rebels and England's Catholic enemies on the continent, with fears on this issue influencing crown activities as early as the 1540s. Those whom Raleigh and Grey massacred at Smerwick included continental invaders as well as Irish troops: their presence had realized fears of England's vulnerability to attacks launched via Ireland. Writing on the atrocities of the 1640s, Brian MacCuarta demonstrates that the Irish Catholic dispossession and murder of British Protestants in 1641–2 in part was a culmination of resentments about the previous loss of land and anxieties about indebtedness, and was fuelled by rumours of moves against Catholics in England and the fear that similar tactics would soon be introduced in Ireland also. Meanwhile, Hiram Morgan (chapter 4) demonstrates the hard-headed political rationale for massacres and assassinations carried out at the behest of Hugh O'Neill, and his careful justification of them in Dublin and London.

The chapters in this volume demonstrate a level of violence in Ireland that was more intense and vicious than elsewhere in the Tudor and Stuart kingdoms. Morrill points out that the massacres at Drogheda and Wexford were unparalleled in the four nations during the 1640s, though he also suggests that the gulf between actions in Britain and Ireland was not as wide as has been painted. McGurk proposes some European and Scottish parallels for the events of the Elizabethan wars in Ireland, but notes that such measures were 'comparatively new in Irish warfare', and that those usually spared in warfare – women and children – might be targeted specifically in Ireland in attempts to root out those who succoured rebels. Childs convincingly demonstrates that the conduct of the War of the Two Kings was 'neither outstandingly ferocious nor especially benign'. On the Irish side, Morgan and Edwards demonstrate a level of violence carried out by native nobles and gentry within their own territories that would not have been possible in many other European states. Ironically, government acceptance of excuses by Hugh O'Neill and others for their actions meant that local lords were enabled to increase their own influence, frequently to the state's distinct disadvantage.

In a myriad of ways in these chapters we can trace the self-perpetuating nature of violence: atrocity begat atrocity as little acts of violence escalated into bigger ones. Discussing the human remains unearthed at Carrickmines Castle in south Co. Dublin, the archaeologists Mark Clinton, Linda Fibiger and Damien Shiels (chapter 9) note that prior to slaughtering the Irish at the castle in March 1642 the English troops responsible had been subjected to attacks by the Irish of Wicklow. Having followed their attackers to Carrickmines, they were driven to 'fury' by the loss of their commander, Sir Simon Harcourt. Carrickmines thus emerges as an important example of the poisonous dynamic of escalation that characterized 1641–3. Similarly, Oliver Cromwell's harshness in Ireland in 1649–50 drew from his past experiences of the Civil Wars in England. After Cromwell departed things got a lot worse as junior officers, previously restrained, committed more of the sort of excesses that Cromwell had tried to avoid.

Desire for revenge and related ideological factors escalated conflict. Childs talks of the mechanics of the early modern laws of war, pointing out that 'reciprocity, the fear of reprisals, has always been the basic coercion obliging soldiers, civilians and politicians to follow codes of conduct in the fighting of wars.' Did some of the nastiness of the Irish wars result from the fact that the idea of reciprocity was muddied? In the sixteenth century, English commanders in Ireland, and many of their troops, were recent arrivals in Ireland, with few ties to the local areas in which they operated or to the people whom they fought: their own loved ones were in little danger of immediate revenge attacks. After the destruction of the Munster plantation in the 1590s, and as an increasing body of settlers arrived in the country in the early 1600s, the potential for reciprocal violence increased.[33] Ideology further fuelled the drive for, and justification of, revenge. Both Tait and Morrill note the participation of seventeenth-century actors in a world view where the spilling of 'innocent' blood justified vengeance; blood-guilt was, in the words of Patricia Crawford, 'more than a moral justification for action. It was an incentive for action.'[34]

Yet most commanders in Ireland were fairly convinced (or claimed to be convinced) of the undesirability of extreme violence. Disembarking in Ireland, Cromwell expressed the hope of winning 'the hearts and minds of the local population'. But he could also rationalize and defend the massacre at Drogheda as preventing 'the effusion of blood for the future': a prophecy that would have caused much cynicism amongst the people of Wexford. One hundred years earlier 'The Gunner' Skeffington had justified the massacre of prisoners at Maynooth as being 'for the dread and example of others'.[35] Herein lies a central reason for atrocity. As well as getting rid of troublesome enemies, the use of massacre, murder and martial law communicated messages of strength and intent. Terror could have positive results if it intimidated effectively, especially at crucial junctures. After all, Carter Wood notes that violence 'speaks', people 'communicate with their violence', while the anthropologist David Riches labels violence as a form of 'performance' that carries both practical and symbolic messages.

Riches also talks of the role of 'tactical pre-emption' in violent actions, suggesting that even acts of vengeance are in essence pre-emptive, since they seek to undermine the capacity of the opposition to respond, though such

---

33 Riches, 'The phenomenon of violence', p. 12. 34 P. Crawford, 'Charles Stuart, that man of blood', *Journal of British Studies*, 16 (1977), 41–61. 35 See Morrill and Edwards, chapters 2 and 12.

purposes are concealed by the rhetoric of retribution.[36] Indeed, Childs points out in this volume that a literary tradition dating back to Roman times had justified 'exaggerated action', including scorched earth tactics, that 'might save lives in the long term'. MacCuarta, for example, argues that Irish violence against British settlers in Ulster in 1641–2 was justified primarily as a means of pre-empting similar violence expected from the 'heretics'. The Franciscans were particularly responsible for whipping up anti-Protestant sentiment. On the government side, many of the incidents delineated in this volume seem to indicate particular brutality at points where commanders were trying to consolidate their authority: Lord Deputy Grey, like Cromwell, was a recent arrival in the country when the massacre at Smerwick occurred. McGurk demonstrates that the predominant view at the end of the Nine Years War was that reduction of the country was necessary before reform could be effected, pointing to financial imperatives for harsh measures aimed at ending the war quickly. His description of Chichester and Mountjoy's 'scorched earth' tactics in Ulster suggest, however, that scorched earth might go far beyond usual definitions in Ireland. The victims of the Carrickmines massacre were likewise pawns in attempts to pacify the still unstable Wicklow frontier following the alarming incidents of the early stages of the 1641 rebellion. Meanwhile, Kenneth Nicholls carefully teases out the broader sequence of events during this period, showing that 'indiscriminate and bloody repression' by government forces in Leinster in response to the killing of Ulster Protestants in turn led to reprisals perpetrated on local Protestant populations. In a world where politics was highly personal and the stakes were constantly shifting, tough actions set a seal on the reputations of military commanders. By shooting up the saloon, the sheriffs sought (and sometimes found) a bit of respect, or at least respite.

In one sense, then, the methods used in Ireland, though extreme, can be seen as logical given local conditions. Local leaders had long been accustomed to aggression expressed in raids, counter-raids, skirmishes, assassination and destruction of resources. Pitched battles were rare, though they became more of a usual part of warfare in the seventeenth century. The patchwork of lordships and ever-shifting alliances and enmities meant that the English in Ireland faced elusive opponents who were difficult to defeat in traditional-style warfare. The situation was magnified by the problem noticed by Childs: often 'negotiated peace settlements ... contained the seedlings of the next war'. The differing concerns of different lordships and their internal factions in Ireland made peace settlements all that much more unstable. No wonder some commentators like Edmund Spenser advocated drastic measures in Ireland. The wide distribution of commissions of martial law, as well as the lack of adequate funding or close supervision of the actions of English officers, made viciousness

---

36 Wood, *Violence and crime*, p. 9; Riches, 'The phenomenon of violence', pp 4–7, 12–13.

cost-effective and unlikely to be punished. Under such circumstances, it was easy to rationalize actions by reference to expected (but ill-defined) future consequences, just as modern terrorists – and state terrorists (securocrats) – excuse their methods by reference to the broader public good that they feel will be gained as a result. That many Irish towns promptly surrendered on the approach of the Cromwellian army may have convinced parliamentarians that the massacres at Wexford and Drogheda, however unsavoury, had yielded results. The fact that on the demise of Charles Coote (whose brutality is noted by Tait and Kevin Forkan in chapters 6 and 10) one onlooker lamented 'we have lost him whose name was their terror' reminds us that bystanders were aware of the potential rewards of tough policies.

DESCRIBING ATROCITY

The ways in which violent events are reported are also vital to our understanding of them and their wider context and impact. Accounts of atrocities circulated in written form in letters and pamphlets, and also by word of mouth, both immediately after the events and in local oral tradition subsequently. Historians have in the past concentrated on the confident statements of official sources like the State Papers. Increasingly, however, we are beginning to discern a babble of voices – report, opinion, lies, rumour, poetry, legend – emerging from people of all kinds, not just those involved in the governance of early modern Ireland. Silence too is revealing: the 'and many inhabitants' at the end of the Drogheda casualty lists implicitly denies their importance, and reveals an attempt to avoid awkward questions that might humanise the victims of a civilian massacre. We need to endeavour to understand the dynamics and messages of different types of sources, and rival attempts to encode events with meaning. What many of the chapters in this volume show is that the meanings invested in actions and events might be contested.[37]

Governors and military captains in Ireland, including Hugh O'Neill; Cromwell and his supporters; and the native leaders of the insurrection in 1641 were all quick to justify their actions, and to paint them as legitimate and appropriate responses to the circumstances of the times and to the character of the enemy which they faced. The reportage is more often blusteringly confident than shamefaced. For example, McGurk records one of Mountjoy's captains exulting that 'we killed man, woman, child, horse, beast, and whatever we found'. A printed despatch praising the services of Sir Frederick Hamilton at Manorhamilton, Co. Leitrim, to the English parliament is a vainglorious recitation of similar indiscriminate killings.[38] Pamphleteers and poets alike,

[37] See Riches, 'The phenomenon of violence', pp 11, 14. [38] Anon, *Another extract of several letters from Ireland* (London, 1643), p. 26.

including figures like Edmund Spenser, Barnaby Rich, John Milton and Anthony Monday, willingly wrote in support and praise of the aims and methods of commanders in Ireland. Phillip O'Sullivan Beare, John Lynch, Nicholas French and Dominic O'Daly on the Catholic side wrote to convince audiences in Ireland and on the Continent of exactly the opposite. Long after the 1640s, the actions of the Irish were rehearsed as evidence for the need of the government to maintain vigilance and control the country with a heavy hand. In face to face contacts, as demonstrated by John Young (chapter 11), the family tragedies rehearsed by Protestant refugees in Scotland both spread news of Irish atrocities, and facilitated the search for sympathy and relief. Conquest and resistance in Ireland involved words as well as swords.

One of the deepest common strands running through the papers in this volume concerns the language used in oral communications and in letters and print, on the one hand to justify, and on the other to condemn, execution, murder, massacres and other forms of mayhem. Dehumanization of members of the other side by attacking their characters and beliefs is a common feature of this. Derogatory naming allowed each side to set opponents apart and 'remove them from the moral community'.[39] McGurk and Carey rehearse the long literary tradition in which the Irish were characterized as barbarians, and Micheál Ó Siochrú (chapter 13) cites Thomas Waring's claim that the Irish were savages and cannibals with whom no détente could be reached. For some, the Irish were not merely culturally backward, many were also 'churls', a term that referenced both their allegedly graceless behaviour and their low social standing. Did the characterization of the Irish as plebeians influence their treatment as much as their ethnicity and religion? After all, Childs points out that, throughout Europe, peasants might not be accorded the courtesies due under the older customs of war to 'chivalrous gentlemen and aristocrats', and in civil law the violence of inferiors towards their betters was especially denounced and severely punished.[40] According to Nicholls, the Irish themselves seem to have treated individuals of higher and lower status differently. But it was not only the Irish who suffered charges of barbarism, untrustworthiness and inferiority. Royalists, for example, described the Cromwellian forces' actions in Ireland as 'inhuman' and 'barbarous', and their commanders as 'men of blood'. Irish Catholic writers presented English officers as duplicitous murderers, while Irish rebels denounced English settlers as dogs and, predictably and repeatedly, as churls.

It is impossible to ignore sectarianism. Religion had a large part in the language of justification. People in all ages are eager to believe that some sort of natural justice exists, that 'what goes around comes around'. In the early

---

[39] Blok, *Honour and violence*, p. 109; Tait, *Death, burial and commemoration*, pp 137–8; N. Sanford and C. Comstock, *Sanctions for evil: sources of social destructiveness* (San Francisco, 1971). [40] Maddern, *Violence and social order*, p. 228.

modern period the punishment for bad lives, bad faith and bad religion could only be destruction and death, and God was believed to have a very personal interest in meting out justice to those who disobeyed his laws and oppressed his chosen people. The providentialist interpretation of English triumphs and the justification of the excesses of campaigns in Ireland features time and again. Mountjoy described the Irish as 'little better than devils', while other military captains compared Irish leaders with the primary non-Christian bogeymen of early modern Western Europe – the Turks and Tartars. The massacre at Smerwick could be explained as God's intervention on the righteous and godly side over the 'Antichriste' himself. Meanwhile, Catholics in Ireland likewise attributed their own successes and the accidents that befell their opponents to the interventions of a God who was undoubtedly working in their favour. As Tait's essay shows, the deaths of Lords Justice Drury and Ireton, Lord President Brounker and Sir Charles Coote ('the devil, or the son of a devil'), all served for Catholics as vindications of their position. Individuals whose polices were interpreted as corrupt, violent and insane were believed to have come to stinking, painful and raving ends: divine justice was nothing if not poetic. Against such powerful propaganda, those who sought to present alternative versions of these men's deaths struggled for their less engaging and dramatic accounts to be heard.

The descent into sectarian justification for atrocities was, of course, most nakedly seen in the 1640s. MacCuarta demonstrates the nastiness of the attacks on English and Scots settlers and Irish Protestants in Ulster, particularly ministers of the Church of Ireland and their tithe-proctors, during this period. Allegations of imminent threats to Catholicism were seized on as justification for mob actions, but deep-rooted sectarianism informed much of the violence, with Protestants being described as heretics, dogs and followers of the devil, and coerced to attend mass. Safe in Dublin, Scotland and England, those dispossessed in 1641–2 comforted themselves with pamphlets that cited their attackers as purveyors of superstition, as un-Christian and inhuman – in the early modern period, the two terms meant much the same thing. Cromwell and his generals drew on the rhetoric of vengeance for 1641 to justify their intervention in Ireland, though, as Morrill points out, in general the Lord Protector was 'not amongst the most anti-Irish of Englishmen' and 'short of strong anti-Catholic rhetoric'. His ire was directed in particular at those Irish Catholic clerics whom he believed had been instrumental in the 'most unheard of and barbarous massacre' of Protestants in 1641–2. MacCuarta confirms that priests were active in fomenting antipathy against Protestantism, though they occasionally tried to curb excesses against individual Protestants – clerical involvement in rebellion can also be traced as far back as the Desmond Revolt and Nine Years War, as demonstrated by Tait, and McGurk. Nevertheless, Cromwell could also justify the slaughter of civilians in the course of his work, claiming that God was on his side 'in prosecuting just and righteous causes' and that death was 'just judgment' for resistance.

The issue of rumour is an important one, since word of mouth was difficult to control or contradict. As well as considering the official reports that have long been at the core of investigation of early modern Ireland, the papers in this collection also hint at the voices speaking behind the scenes. We hear echoes of the conversations and rumours that spread out from the epicentres of violent actions – soldiers, sailors and politicians talking about Drogheda, refugee Protestants of all occupations and degrees talking about 1641, continental Catholics wooed with tales of the sufferings of their co-religionists in Ireland. Each conversation recreated each violent event in different ways. Reputations could be permanently destroyed: Cromwell's has never recovered; 'Grey's faith' was a byword for treachery; Walter Raleigh, part-time Renaissance poet, part-time executioner, became a bogeyman in the Smerwick area. Even those not involved in acts of violence might find their reputations damaged. According to Ó Siochrú, Ormond suffered some of the blame for Drogheda, being castigated for not having come to the town's assistance. When pressed he rather churlishly attempted to turn the recriminations on the town's defenders, the inhabitants and the Catholic clergy. To use modern terminology, the perpetrators of acts of atrocity may have seen them as 'surgical strikes' but in fact they are the most unreliable of weapons, sending shrapnel in all directions.

Influenced by the anthropologist James C. Scott, many historians have recently begun to look at the potential for resistance to domination and persecution in everyday life. By looks, gestures, dissimulation, and passive unhelpfulness, subordinate groups have some small means of demonstrating their displeasure with, and of implicitly thwarting, the ruling order. Of course, in acts of atrocity we catch the moments where resistance of any type was entirely bulldozed aside. But in rumour and legend we see the practical aspects of how people received word of incidents and how they reacted to news, as well as how dominant interpretations of events could be undermined, how they could be searched by certain groups for meanings that were very different. These forms of communication should not be seen as 'idle talk'. As Ó Siochrú points out, in early modern society rumours 'often represented the only source of uncensored news'. Historians have noted that rumours flourish 'in times of social unrest and tension', and can constitute 'an attempt at collective conversation by people who wish to enter their sentiments into a public discourse'. Steve A. Smith comments that their capacity to 'generate collective action' can be limited.[41] But in the face of tragedy the narratives told by defeated groups

41 J.C. Scott, *Domination and the arts of resistance* (New Haven, 1990), especially pp xii–xiii; A.A. Yang, 'A conversation of rumors: the language of popular *mentalités* in late nineteenth-century colonial India', *Journal of Social History*, 20 (1987), 485–506; S.A. Smith, 'Talking toads and chinless ghosts: the politics of "superstitious" rumors in the People's Republic of

could, at the very least, restore a sense of purpose and pride. Rumour and legends comforted the oppressed, for example turning the clerics seen by Cromwell, Brounker and others as fomenters of disorder into omnipotent martyr-heroes, uniquely connected to God and possessed of powers of prophecy. Likewise, the martyred Protestant leader, Sir Charles Coote, became an example of decisive and righteous action for certain factions in the Dublin government in the anxiety-ridden early 1640s.

In print and in folklore, atrocities might live on for a long time after their occurrence serving to legitimize feelings of grievance and to stoke later hostilities.[42] The commemoration of atrocity in print could be informed by the awareness of an audience and the propaganda needs of a new generation. The revisiting of 1641 into the eighteenth century served to stir Protestant fears of another rebellion, and justified legislation to protect themselves from their Catholic neighbours. Meanwhile, folk histories similarly sought to make sense of the past for the purposes of the present. Tait's chapter demonstrates that folklore accounts of the supposed deeds of sixteenth- and seventeenth-century persecutors continued to be told into the 1900s. Likewise, the Schools Folklore Collection from Drogheda in the 1930s preserves narratives of deaths of civilians, soldiers and priests during the massacre there, as well as of Cromwellian ghosts, and placenames allegedly linked with the massacre such as 'Cromwell's Mount', 'Gallows Hill', 'Graves Lane', 'Scarlet Street' and 'Bloody Street' (from the blood running along them).[43] The folk memory of violent events could be a long one, and even if the accounts that were preserved bear little relation to what actually occurred, they certainly give a sense of how people have understood and interpreted Ireland's violent past in the longer term.[44]

CONCLUSION

While this volume makes a start, much further research on violence and atrocity remains to be done. The destructiveness of war needs to be measured: how was social and economic life affected by military action, how large were casualty

China, 1961–1965', *American Historical Review*, 111 (2006), 405–27; E.H. Shagan, 'Rumours and popular politics in the reign of Henry VIII', in T. Harris (ed.), *The politics of the excluded, c.1500–1850* (Basingstoke, 2001), pp 30–66. 42 See Read, 'Atrocity propaganda', for the uses of atrocity stories, p. 230. 43 Irish Folklore Commission, Schools Folklore Collection, volumes 679, 680. 44 A burgeoning literature has increasingly focussed on the memory of events such as 1798, 1916, the War of Independence and the Civil War, as well as the neglect shown to the dead of the two World Wars. See Tait, *Death, burial and commemoration*, pp 210–11, nn 14–19; A. Dolan, *Commemorating the Irish Civil War: history and memory 1923–2000* (Cambridge, 2000). G. Beiner, 'The decline and rebirth of "folk memory": remembering "the year of the French" in the late twentieth century', *Éire-Ireland*, 38 (2003), 7–32, is a good example of the less commonly considered issue of commemoration in folklore.

levels, and how often were casualties exaggerated or underestimated? Can we explicate further the structures and values within Gaelic society that promoted military readiness as an element of masculine identities, facilitated the creation of alliances between families and territories for the purposes of both peace and war, and aimed at maintaining ties between lords and subjects? Recent work by Fiona Fitzsimons, Clodagh Tait and the anthropologist Peter Parkes, for example, has begun to illuminate the importance of ties created through institutions like fosterage and 'gossiprid' (Morgan's paper here notes the role of O'Neill's fosterbrothers as advisors and hitmen), while Elizabeth FitzPatrick has looked at the functions and sites of local assemblies and kingly inauguration.[45] More also needs to be learned about the wider-scale banditry perpetrated by (or attributed to) groups like the 'tories' of the later seventeenth century, and the earlier kern.[46] The ritual aspects of atrocity and what Blok calls the 'spatial formations of violence' also need to be addressed – where and when was violence most likely to occur, and how did time and place shape violent actions?[47] How were concepts like 'anger' and 'revenge' conceptualized and justified, and how did ideas about 'honour' (above and beyond the concept of honourable prosecution of warfare) tie in with violent actions?[48] What else can we say about the mobilization of the rhetoric of atrocity and memories of the violence of the early modern period in subsequent generations? Further efforts to promote interactions between the disciplines of history, literary criticism, historical geography, sociology, anthropology and archaeology (conflict archaeology is a growing field), and greater openness to approaching the sixteenth and seventeenth centuries from the points of view of society and culture as well as of politics, will certainly be necessary.

What, also, of alternative forms of violence? In other countries, investigation of the true extent and nature of violence of early modern society has gained pace since the 1970s. It is not just that early modern Ireland was more violent than has previously been acknowledged: it is also the case that other societies were less peaceful. In England, for example, historians using court and other records have increasingly pointed to the conflicts that pervaded (but did not

---

[45] F. Fitzsimons, 'Fosterage and gossiprid in late medieval Ireland: some new evidence', in P. Duffy, D. Edwards, and FitzPatrick (eds), *Gaelic Ireland, c.1250–c.1650* (Dublin, 2001), pp 138–9; P. Parkes, 'Celtic fosterage: adoptive kinship and clientage in northwest Europe', *Comparative Studies in Society and History*, 28 (2006), 359–95. C. Tait, 'Spiritual bonds, social bonds: baptism and godparenthood in Ireland, 1530–1690', *Cultural and Social History*, 2 (2005), 301–27; E. FitzPatrick, 'Parley sites of Ó Néill and Ó Domhnaill in late sixteenth-century Ireland', in Edwards, *Regions and rulers*, pp 201–16; 'Assembly and inauguration places of the Burkes in late medieval Connaught', in Duffy et al., *Gaelic Ireland*, pp 357–74. [46] É. Ó Ciardha, 'Toryism in Cromwellian Ireland (1650–60)', *Irish Sword*, 19 (1993–5), 290–305. On bandits, see Blok, *Honour and violence*. [47] Blok, *Honour and violence*, pp 109, 112. [48] D.L. Smail, 'Hatred as a social institution in late-medieval society', *Speculum*, 76 (2001), 90–126; W. Palmer, 'That "insolent liberty": honor, rites of power, and persuasion in sixteenth-century Ireland', *Renaissance Quarterly*, 46 (1993), 308–27.

necessarily compromise) local communities.[49] Quite apart from the political, religious and social tensions that led to a number of small-scale rebellions in the sixteenth century and, more seriously, to the Civil Wars of the seventeenth (better understood now they are usually placed in a wider 'Three Kingdoms' context), a truer picture has emerged of neighbourhood squabbles and brawls,[50] sexual assaults,[51] murders,[52] domestic violence,[53] cruelty to wildlife,[54] and criminal activities going on behind the scenes. We are hearing an increasing amount too about those occasions when violence and riot could have metaphorical as well as prosaic causes and meanings,[55] about symbolic violence directed at images, publications, property, and animals,[56] and about fears that harm could be caused by magical means.[57] There is much too about how resistances might

[49] Amussen, 'Being stirred to much unquietness'; idem, 'Punishment, discipline and power'; A. Macfarlane, *The Justice and the mare's ale* (Oxford, 1981); L. Stone, 'Interpersonal violence in English society, 1300–1980', *Past and Present*, 101 (1983), 22–33; J.A. Sharpe, 'The history of violence in England: some observations', *Past and Present*, 108 (1985), 206–15; L. Stone, 'The history of violence in England: some observations: a rejoinder', *Past and Present*, 108 (1985), 216–24.   [50] B. Capp, *When gossips meet: women, family and neighbourhood in early modern England* (Oxford, 2003).   [51] M. Chaytor, 'Husband(ry): narratives of rape in the seventeenth century', *Gender and History*, 7 (1995), 378–407; G. Walker, 'Rereading rape and sexual violence in early modern England', *Gender and History*, 10 (1998), 1–25; M. Ingram, 'Child sexual abuse in early modern England', in M. Braddick and J. Walter (eds), *Negotiating power in early modern society* (Cambridge, 2001), pp 63–84.   [52] M. Gaskill, *Crime and mentalities in early modern England* (Cambridge, 2000); 'Reporting murder: fiction and the archives in early modern England', *Social History*, 23 (1998), 1–30.   [53] E. Foyster, 'Male honour, social control and wife beating in late Stuart England', *Transactions of the Royal Historical Society*, 6 (1996), 215–24; Foyster, 'A laughing matter? Marital discord and gender control in seventeenth-century England', *Rural History*, 4 (1993), 5–21; A. Shepard, *Meanings of manhood in early modern England* (Oxford, 2003), pp 181–95; F.E. Dolan, *Dangerous familiars: representations of domestic crime in England, 1550–1700* (Ithaca, NY, 1994); L. Gowing, *Domestic dangers: women, words, and sex in early modern London* (Oxford, 1998), pp 206–29; J.A. Sharpe, 'Domestic homicide in early modern England', *Historical Journal*, 24 (1981), 29–48; C.B. Herrup, *A house in gross disorder: sex, law, and the 2nd earl of Castlehaven* (Oxford, 1999).   [54] K. Thomas, *Man and the natural world: changing attitudes in England, 1500–1800* (Oxford, 1996).   [55] See especially the work of E.P. Thompson, John Walter, Andy Wood, and David Underdown.   [56] For example, see D. Cressy, 'Different kinds of speaking: symbolic violence and secular iconoclasm in early modern England', in M. McClendon, J.P. Ward, M. MacDonald (eds), *Protestant identities: religions, society and self-fashioning in post-Reformation England* (Stanford, 1999), pp 19–42; J. Walter, 'Popular iconoclasm and the politics of the parish in eastern England, 1640–1642', *Historical Journal*, 47 (2004), 261–90; '"Abolishing superstition with sedition?" the politics of popular iconoclasm in England, 1640–1642', *Past and Present*, 183 (2004), 79–123; D. Beaver, 'The great deer massacre: animals, honor, and communication in early modern England', *Journal of British Studies*, 38 (1999), 187–216; Beaver, '"Bragging and daring words": honour, property and the symbolism of the hunt in Stowe, 1590–1642', in Braddick and Walter, *Negotiating power*, pp 149–65.   [57] S. Clark (ed.), *Languages of witchcraft: narrative, ideology and meaning in early modern culture* (Basingstoke, 2001); J.A. Sharpe, *Witchcraft in early modern England* (Harlow, 1999); J. Goodare (ed.), *The Scottish witch-hunt in context* (Manchester, 2002).

take other forms: for example, strategies such as satire threatened to stir disorder and often provoked violent reprisal.[58] One historian of medieval Ireland, drawing on studies of England and Europe, has considered the ways in which verbal attacks might be regarded as having effects as devastating as physical assaults and there is much that could be said about these topics as regards the early modern period as well.[59] On the other hand, we are also learning about the degree to which the church and civil court systems successfully managed to contain violence and mediate in conflicts by providing an outlet for grievances: mediation was often also carried on in more informal ways. The 'lower-level' manifestations of interpersonal antagonism and symbolic violence have been, predictably, largely omitted from the historiography of early modern Ireland, as have issues such as violent crime and its punishment. It is our ambition that further volumes in the present series will begin to tackle these issues too, thereby helping to give a more nuanced picture. The kind of violence considered here may seem either less or more exceptional when we see it as part of a continuum, part of a range of violent actions perpetrated and endured by men and women, adults and children, rich and poor, as well as by natives and newcomers.

---

58 For one example, see S. Hindle, 'Custom, festival and protest in early modern England: the Little Budworth wakes, St Peter's Day, 1596', *Rural History*, 6 (1995), 155–78.   59 D. Hall, 'Words as weapons: speech, violence and gender in late medieval Ireland', *Éire-Ireland*, 41 (2006), 122–41. Recent works on slander include R. Suggett, 'Slander in early modern Wales', *Bulletin of the Board of Celtic Studies*, 39 (1992), 119–53; Gowing, *Domestic dangers*, pp 59–138; M. Todd, *The culture of Protestantism in early modern Scotland* (New Haven, 2002), pp 235–49; J.H. Dickenson, and J.A. Sharpe, 'Courts, crime and litigation in the Isle of Man, 1580–1700', *Historical Research*, 72 (1999); M.L. Kaplan, *The culture of slander in early modern England* (Cambridge, 1997).

The escalation of violence in sixteenth-century Ireland

DAVID EDWARDS

Atrocity punctuates the history of sixteenth-century Ireland. Countrywide, from the time of the Kildare rebellions until the end of the Nine Years War, there was a tendency for military and political conflict to spiral wildly out of control. Combatants committed the worst excesses: multiple murders, summary executions, the mass slaughter of unarmed civilians (women and children included), dismemberment, even famine inducement, all became widespread in the course of one of the bloodiest and nastiest epochs in Irish history. Large-scale group killings, or massacres, occurred in many places, at Maynooth (1535), Belfast (1574), Rathlin Island (1575), Mullaghmast (1577), Smerwick (1580), and Dunboy (1602), to name just some of the most notorious instances. As this list of massacres indicates, levels of violence appear to have escalated as the century advanced, with conditions especially bad from the 1570s. The killings climaxed at century's end with the scorched-earth operations carried out by the forces of the English Tudor monarchy before and after the battle of Kinsale. As those responsible intended, the native population was starved and terrorized into submission. Many thousands died, and much of the country was destroyed, made wasteland.[1] In the words of David Quinn, when peace came at last, in March 1603, it was 'the peace of death and exhaustion'.[2]

Given the disturbing nature of these developments, it might be expected that they would feature prominently in the historiography of sixteenth-century Ireland. The sixteenth century was also a time of terrible bloodshed in France and the Netherlands, and over the years historians of these countries have engaged in a wide-ranging debate about the scale and overall pattern of violence that occurred there. By examining various episodes of atrocity such as the St Bartholomew's Day massacre in Paris in 1572 and the 12 July massacre in Haarlem in 1573 they have succeeded in greatly improving understanding of the

---

1 For detailed assessments of the devastation of the years 1594–1603 see especially Vincent Carey, '"What pen can paint or tears atone"? Mountjoy's scorched earth campaign', in Hiram Morgan (ed.), *The battle of Kinsale* (Dublin, 2004), pp 205–14, and the essay by John McGurk, 'The pacification of Ulster, 1601–3', in this volume. 2 D.B. Quinn, *The Elizabethans and the Irish* (Ithaca, NY, 1966), p. 140.

political and religious conflicts of the period and the forces that shaped them.[3] In contrast, historians of sixteenth-century Ireland have followed a somewhat different path. Recognizing that many of the atrocities that occurred were associated with the Tudor re-conquest of the country, they have noted them as proof of the ugliness of the conquest, which was characterized by 'horrific suffering' and 'cruelty and injustice'.[4] Otherwise, however, they have said little, with few modern scholars prepared to dwell long upon the violence. In the past twenty years no fewer than four textbooks have been published about Tudor Ireland, but in none of them has the level of bloodshed received more than just a few lines.[5]

This tendency to acknowledge the carnage, only to bypass it, is due partly to the fact that interpretations of the Tudor era have changed profoundly since the 1960s. Inspired by English Tudor scholars (chiefly G.R. Elton) whose writings had transformed understanding of the making of the Tudor state in England and Wales, some Irish Tudor historians abandoned the traditional military narrative of the sixteenth century to explore the lesser-known areas of administrative, intellectual and constitutional history. Poring over such diverse source material as council minute books and parliamentary records, government financial accounts, treatises, and official memoirs, they explored in exemplary detail the workings of the English colonial executive in Dublin Castle and the range of ideas that underpinned certain aspects of crown policy. A new view of Tudor rule in Ireland emerged, one in which military conflict and the putting down of rebellions was not nearly as central as once it had been. Instead of crude military subjugation, it was revealed, the central aim of Tudor government in Ireland was the political and legal 'reform' of the country, through a series of

---

[3] E.g., Mack P. Holt, *The French Wars of Religion, 1562–1629* (Cambridge, 1995); J.H.M. Salmon, *Society in crisis: France in the sixteenth century* (London, 1975); Philip Benedict, 'The Saint Bartholomew's Massacres in the provinces', *Historical Journal*, 21 (1978); Barbara Diefendorf, *Beneath the cross: Catholics and Huguenots in sixteenth-century Paris* (Oxford, 1991); Emmanuel Le Roy Ladurie, *Carnival in Romans: a people's uprising, 1579–1580* (London, 1979); Jonathan Israel, *The Dutch Republic: its rise, greatness and fall, 1477–1806* (corrected edn, Oxford, 1998), ch. 6–10; Geoffrey Parker, *The Dutch Revolt* (revised ed., London, 1985); Alaistair Duke, *Reformation and revolt in the Low Countries* (London, 1990); Henry Kamen, *The Duke of Alba* (New Haven, 2004). [4] Ciaran Brady, *The chief governors: the rise and fall of reform government in Tudor Ireland, 1536–1588* (Cambridge, 1994), Preface, p. xv. [5] Steven G. Ellis, *Tudor Ireland: crown, community and the conflict of cultures, 1470–1603* (London, 1985); Nicholas Canny, *From Reformation to Restoration: Ireland, 1534–1660* (Dublin, 1987); Colm Lennon, *Sixteenth-century Ireland: the incomplete conquest* (Dublin, 1994); and Steven G. Ellis, *Ireland in the age of the Tudors: English expansion and the end of Gaelic rule* (London, 1998). However, Professor Canny has dealt in detail with the violence in two other books: Nicholas Canny, *The Elizabethan conquest of Ireland: a pattern established, 1565–76* (Hassocks, 1976), esp. ch. 6, and idem, *Making Ireland British, 1580–1650* (Oxford, 2001), ch. 2.

local settlements that rested on negotiation and persuasion as well as on force, and sought at least a modicum of native consent.[6]

Regarding the wars and violence of the sixteenth century, the insights into English policy achieved by this reform-centred school of historians necessitated that old explanations be revised. Given that the Tudors apparently hoped to extend crown authority by reform rather than by conquest, it no longer seemed sufficient to emphasize the bloodshed through a narrative of English military engagements. Such slaughter as occurred was not, we were told, predestined, an unavoidable result of Tudor policy. Rather, it was 'inadvertent', an unfortunate outcome of 'relatively benign' initiatives that either backfired or failed to take hold.[7] At a stroke the violence was pushed from the foreground of sixteenth-century studies to the margins. To explain the period by its rebellions and battles, its massacres and executions – by its trail of dead – was to invest in a 'venerable' tradition of military history that was, supposedly, outmoded. The historical importance of the bloodshed was still further diminished when even the very notion of the Tudor re-conquest was placed in doubt, with some historians writing of a 'so called Tudor conquest', or referring to 'conquest' only in parentheses.[8]

Of course, most reform-centred scholars still accept that a conquest of sorts occurred, and that it produced atrocities and led to major loss of life, but nonetheless their study of Tudor administrative records has persuaded them both to minimise and wholly redefine it. There has been growing agreement that it was a delayed development, commencing sometime after 1579,[9] or 1583,[10] or 1588,[11]

---

6 As well as works cited above, the most important publications associated with this trend include: Steven G. Ellis, *Reform & revival: English government in Ireland, 1470–1534* (Woodbridge, 1986); Ciaran Brady, 'Court, castle and country: the framework of government in Tudor Ireland', in Ciaran Brady & Raymond Gillespie (eds), *Natives & newcomers: the making of Irish colonial society* (Dublin, 1986); idem, 'Sixteenth-century Ulster and the failure of Tudor reform', in Ciaran Brady, Mary O'Dowd & Brian Walker (eds), *Ulster: an illustrated history* (London, 1989); idem, 'The road to the *View*: On the decline of reform thought in Tudor Ireland', in Patricia Coughlan (ed.), *Spenser & Ireland: an interdisciplinary perspective* (Cork, 1989); Victor Treadwell, 'The Irish parliament of 1569–71', *PRIA* 66 C (1966–7); idem, 'Sir John Perrot and the Irish parliament of 1585–6', *PRIA* 85 C (1985); Bernadette Cunningham, 'The composition of Connacht in the lordships of Clanricard and Thomond, 1577–1641', *IHS*, 24 (1984); Jon G. Crawford, *Anglicising the government of Ireland: the Irish privy council and the expansion of Tudor rule, 1556–1578* (Dublin, 1993).   7 Brady, *The chief governors*, pp xii–xiv, 166.   8 E.g., Crawford, *Anglicising the government*, pp 1, 14–16, 242n, 281, 286, 326, 414; Bernadette Cunningham, 'Natives and newcomers in Mayo, 1560–1603', in Raymond Gillespie and Gerard Moran (eds), *A various country: essays in Mayo history, 1500–1900* (Westport, 1987).   9 Ellis, *Tudor Ireland*, p. 274; idem, *Ireland*, p. 311. 10 Canny, *From Reformation to Restoration*, pp 106–7. Previously, he favoured the late 1560s as the watershed period (idem, *The Elizabethan conquest*, passim).   11 Brady, *The chief governors*, on the grounds that the downfall of Perrot marked the final abandonment of reform government.

or 1594[12] – in other words, that there was not so much a 'Tudor' re-conquest, but rather an Elizabethan one, and a *late* Elizabethan one at that. Aside from Henry VIII in the mid-1530s, it has been contended that until the later years of Elizabeth I no Tudor monarch authorized the formation of a royal army large enough to undertake the military reduction of the country. Even then, troop numbers remained high only in response to major emergencies such as the Desmond and Tyrone rebellions, and/or the threat of a foreign invasion. Crucially, none of the various other wars fought by the crown in Ireland are now afforded any real consequence. Dubbed 'little wars', these other engagements have been relegated to the status of mere local encounters that lasted a short time, involved minimum English forces, and cost the English crown very little money.[13] (The cost of the 'little wars' to the local communities that suffered them has not been considered.)[14]

As the story of English re-conquest has shrunk, another explanation for the rise in violence in sixteenth-century Ireland has begun tentatively to emerge. It has been suggested that, far from being the product of aggressive English expansion, the terrible violence of the period may be attributed mainly to the behaviour of the Irish lords. According to some reform-centred scholars, it was the military culture of the native warlords, not the English government, which contributed most to the growing bloodshed. Thus it has been asserted that, while the crown was content mainly to police the country, and rarely instigated wars, in contrast the local Gaelic Irish and Anglo-Irish rulers were frequent aggressors, responsible for what has been described as a 'chronic level of violence'. Retaining private armies, attacking neighbours and foes at will, the lords insured Ireland was rarely a land of peace. Worse, it has been claimed, their antics played a decisive role in the escalation of violence and slaughter in the sixteenth century.[15] Early in the Tudor intervention, in the 1530s, the crown forces had to be ruthless 'because warfare as practised by Gaelic forces differed from English perceptions of what was permissible'.[16] By the last quarter of the sixteenth century the inability of the Irish lords to renounce violence – indeed, their very addiction to warfare – had forced the government's hand and compelled it towards conquest, on the pessimistic presumption that native society could not be reformed.[17]

This new line of interpretation has not been based on any close examination of the evidence for native aristocratic violence across the sixteenth century. Instead, it has been extrapolated largely from the work of historians of late

---

12 Idem, 'The captains' games', pp 138–9.   13 Ibid., p. 139.   14 This is beginning to change through the growth of local studies; see n.19 below.   15 Brady, 'The captains' games', pp 138–9; Crawford, *Anglicising the government*, p. 325n.   16 Steven G. Ellis, 'The Tudors and the origins of the modern Irish states: a standing army', in T. Bartlett and K. Jeffery (eds), *A military history of Ireland* (Cambridge, 2006), pp 130–1.   17 Brady, 'Sixteenth-century Ulster', p. 81.

medieval Gaelic and Anglo-Ireland that had stressed the highly militarized nature of the indigenous order in the fourteenth, fifteenth and early sixteenth centuries. The following essay attempts to put this new interpretation to the test by examining the military history of both the native lordships and the English crown forces in the period 1500–70. By focusing on the hard edge of military action – that is, on Irish and English strategies of violence and their relative impact on the population – it is hoped that it will help bring the study of war in sixteenth-century Ireland more into line with the treatment of the subject as it is currently practiced by historians of early modern Europe and the Americas. Instead of marginalizing episodes of killing and atrocity the essay will highlight them and seek to place them in their correct chronological and cultural contexts, the better to identify the patterns of violence evident in Ireland during the 1500s and to compare and contrast native aristocratic warfare with English colonial warfare. Above all, it will try to determine the extent to which the conduct of fighting worsened across the century, when this occurred, and why. In pursuing these and other related questions, it will be necessary to take a fresh look at the Tudor re-conquest. If what follows joins with a growing number of studies in challenging part of the reform-centred view of sixteenth-century Ireland, this is unavoidable.[18]

I

When referring to the terrible violence of the sixteenth century the reform-centred scholars are, of course, right to assert that the military culture of the native lords and chieftains contributed considerably to the situation. It should be noted from the outset that the fact that the Irish lords were warlords,

---

18 David Edwards, 'Beyond reform: Martial Law and the Tudor reconquest of Ireland', *History Ireland*, 5:2 (Summer 1997); idem, 'Ideology and experience: Spenser's *View* and Martial Law in Ireland', in Hiram Morgan (ed.), *Political ideology in Ireland, 1541–1641* (Dublin, 1999); idem, *The Ormond Lordship in County Kilkenny, 1515–1642: the rise and fall of Butler feudal power* (Dublin, 2003), pp 166–7, 174–5, 191, 194, 201–2, 215–28, 237–45; idem, 'Collaboration without Anglicisation: the MacGiollapadraig lordship and Tudor reform', in Patrick J. Duffy, David Edwards & Elizabeth FitzPatrick (eds), *Gaelic Ireland: land, lordship and settlement, c.1250–c.1650* (Dublin 2001); Brian Donovan, 'Tudor Rule in Gaelic Leinster and the rise of Feagh McHugh O'Byrne', in Conor O'Brien (ed.), *Feagh McHugh O'Byrne: the Wicklow firebrand* (Rathdrum Historical Soc., 1998); Vincent Carey, 'John Derricke's *Image of Irelande*, Sir Henry Sidney, and the massacre at Mullaghmast', *IHS*, 31 (1999), 305–27; Hiram Morgan, '"Overmighty officers": the Irish lord deputyship in the early modern British state', *History Ireland*, 7:4 (Winter 1999); idem, '"Never any realm worse governed": Queen Elizabeth and Ireland', *Transactions of the Royal Historical Society*, 6th series 14 (2004). For sharp criticism of the 'reform' school and its treatment of official sources from a textual and literary perspective see Willy Maley, 'Apology for Sidney: making a virtue of a Viceroy', *The Sidney Journal*, 20:1 (2002).

responsible for all manner of violent deeds, is not in dispute. What is disputed, however, is both the nature and level of violence attributed to the native order, the chronological point at which this violence deteriorated, and also the implied suggestion that it was at least as terrible as the sort of violence perpetrated by English soldiers after the mid-1530s, as gradually Tudor power spread across the country. The better to expose the reform-centred scholars' misunderstanding of the native lords, in this and also in the next section of the essay the extent and character of war as it was practiced in Ireland on the eve of English expansion will be examined in detail. (English military conduct will be dealt with in sections III and IV). Though the dispute between historians has so far hinged very much on the interpretation of events in the later years of the sixteenth century, only by examining the entire century is it possible to gain a clear impression of the underlying patterns of violence afflicting the country, and to gain the proper chronological perspective needed to identify major changes within those patterns. Moreover, close scrutiny of native military behaviour in the decades before 1550 has the added advantage of revealing for the first time the roots and character of the opening *native* phase of the sixteenth-century escalation of violence, a phase that has been only casually acknowledged.

In the opening years of the sixteenth century all parts of the country – even the English Pale around Dublin – were dominated by a number of Gaelic and Anglo-Irish aristocratic lineages that controlled patches of the country as independent or semi-independent fiefdoms known as lordships. The lordships were military as well as political units. They owed their origins to war, and their continued vitality rested entirely upon the ability of their rulers to defend and, if possible, extend their frontiers by anticipating and countering hostile incursions, or attacking and intimidating neighbours/enemies when the opportunity arose.[19] One only has to glance at the surviving Gaelic annals to perceive the

---

19 There is, at last, a growing literature on the world of the lordships. For their military environment, classic works such as G.A. Hayes-McCoy, *Scots mercenary forces in Ireland, 1565–1603* (Dublin, 1937) and Kenneth Nicholls, *Gaelic and Gaelicized Ireland in the Middle Ages* (Dublin, 1972, 2nd ed. Dublin 2003), ch. 1, 4, have been augmented by Hiram Morgan, *Tyrone's Rebellion: the outbreak of the Nine Years War in Tudor Ireland* (Dublin, 1993); David Edwards, 'The Butler revolt of 1569', *IHS*, 28:111 (May 1993); idem, *The Ormond Lordship*; idem, 'The MacGiollapadraigs (Fitzpatricks) of Upper Ossory, 1532–1641', in P. Lane and W. Nolan (eds), *Laois: history & society* (Dublin, 1999); Ciaran Brady, *Shane O'Neill* (Dundalk 1996); Katharine Simms, 'Gaelic warfare in the Middle Ages', in Bartlett and Jeffery, *A military history*; Anthony McCormack, 'Internecine warfare and the decline of the house of Desmond, *c*.1510–1541', *IHS*, 30:120 (Nov. 1997); Fiona Fitzsimons, 'The lordship of O'Connor Faly, 1520–70', in W. Nolan and T.P. O'Neill (eds), *Offaly: history & society* (Dublin 1998); Vincent Carey, 'The end of the Gaelic political order: the O'More lordship of Laois, 1536–1603' in Lane & Nolan, *Laois*; Christopher Maginn, *'Civilizing' Gaelic Leinster: the extension of Tudor rule in the O'Byrne and O'Toole lordships* (Dublin, 2005).

extent of native aristocratic aggression. The Annals of the Four Masters, for instance, record just two years during the fifty-year period 1501–50 during which there was no war (in the form of incursions, battles, or sieges) anywhere in Ireland – 1529 and 1550.[20] Even then, neither year was entirely without military violence: in 1529 the two east Ulster lords, Cormac MacQuillan of the Route and Brian Ballagh O'Neill, on leaving Carrickfergus together, came to blows, resulting in O'Neill's death, while in Donegal the O'Donnell chieftain dispatched a troublesome Scottish vassal 'with one stroke of a sword', and two of the MacSweeneys were assassinated by a kinsman.[21] Similarly in 1550, when more trouble among the MacSweeneys gave rise to the plunder of Killybegs, followed by the punitive killing of the plunderer.[22]

Table 1: Native military incursions, 1501–50

Period	Total	Scorched earth
1501–10	13	6
1511–20	26	11
1521–30	20	13
1531–40	14	11
1541–50	22	17

Source: AFM

By any yardstick military conflict was endemic. To take the most common feature of Irish warfare, the armed incursion or invasion, during the same fifty-year period the Four Masters record no fewer than 95 incursions by one native lord into the territory of another: that is, very nearly two a year (see Table 1). The real figure was certainly much higher. Though it is the best set of annals to have survived, the Four Masters, compiled in a hurry by clerics in the early seventeenth century, is far from complete.[23] Thus, despite providing fairly good coverage of events in the northern half of the country, especially across central and west Ulster and north Connacht, it deals with Leinster and Munster in a haphazard fashion. Other sources clearly show that military incursions were no less widespread across the south of the country. According to English government documents – the well-known 'presentments' of 1537–8 – even the

---

20 *AFM*, s.a. 1501–1550 passim. The Annals of Ulster and the Annals of Thady Dowling record no wars in 1529, but the Annals of Loch Cé note a bloody encounter in Elfin between O'Connor Ruadh and MacDermott Ruadh; regarding 1550, both Dowling and Loch Cé agree there was no war that year (the Annals of Ulster end in 1540).   21 *AFM*, s.a. 1529.   22 Ibid., s.a. 1550.   23 A.T. Lucas, *Cattle in ancient Ireland* (Kilkenny, 1989), pp 148–50; Kenneth Nicholls, 'Introduction' to the reprint of John O'Donovan (ed.), *Annála rioghachta Éireann: annals of the kingdom of Ireland, by the Four Masters* (Dublin, 1990), 1, pp i–vi.

most stable and prosperous areas of the south, such as Co. Wexford, had to contend with near-constant external menace. Along Wexford's northern frontier the MacMurrough Kavanaghs made regular incursions throughout the 1510s, '20s and '30s, penetrating as far south as the town of Fethard-on-Sea in 1532;[24] while on its western border, along the banks of the River Barrow, the Butlers of Ormond were equally active, attempting to impose *de facto* overlordship from their base in Co. Kilkenny.[25] If there was any discernible difference in the pattern of incursions around the country it was probably that pastoral districts were targeted more often than arable ones, partly because the *creach* or cattle raid (and horse and sheep raid) was the surest way to capture easily moveable wealth, but also because arable areas, being more heavily settled, tended to be much better defended.

The main reason why incursions and *creaca* were commonplace was because the martial culture of the Irish lordships demanded that rulers demonstrate their ability to rule by feat of arms and successful plundering. Invading a neighbour allowed a lord to display his prowess, satisfy his followers, and impress his subjects; accordingly, for prospective new rulers anxious to advertise their leadership potential, the incursion was a sort of rite of passage, something that had to be done to confirm their eligibility to become lord. A poem by the Munster bard Loghlin Oge O'Daly expressed this well. Written about 1550, it celebrated the emergence of three young O'Brien warriors who seemed to possess the necessary attributes to one day assume power in Thomond. All they had to do was prove their mettle through military action by leading incursions and engaging in combat: 'Soon shall their javelins be fighting in Conn's Half [that is, throughout Munster] as bright and blood-red spears of valour'.[26] Indeed, incursions were so central to Irish notions of nobility and political legitimacy that a special form of literature existed to record them, the *caithréim*. Usually composed late in the life of the reigning lord, this provided a list of the various raids and military triumphs that he had carried out during his rule.[27]

Traditional enmities, nurtured over scores or even hundreds of years, fed the flames of conflict in every part of the country. At a regional level, in Ulster the O'Neills and O'Donnells had renewed their struggle for provincial dominance late in the fifteenth century, while the affairs of Leinster and Munster were no less determined by the historical antagonism of, most famously, the Butlers and Fitzgeralds, but also the O'Briens, MacCarthys, and Fitzgeralds.[28] Much of the

[24] Herbert Hore and James Graves (eds), *Social state of south-east Ireland in the sixteenth century* (Royal Historical & Archaeological Society of Ireland, Dublin, 1870), pp 41, 43, 45–6, 48–9, 50, 63, 66–7, 68–9.   [25] Ibid., pp 39, 40, 45–6, 69–70.   [26] Osborn Bergin, *Irish bardic poetry* (Dublin, 1970), no. 18, st. 12.   [27] For example, T. Ó Raghaillaigh (ed. & trans.), 'Seanchas na mBúrcach: History of the Burkes', *JGHAS*, 13 (1924–7), 50–60, 101–38; ibid., 14 (1928–9), 30–51, 142–67; Michelle Ó Riordan, *The Gaelic mind and the collapse of the Gaelic world* (Cork 1990), pp 72–9.   [28] Nicholls, *Gaelic and Gaelicized Ireland*, ch. 7–10

3 Irish warfare, from John Derricke, *The image of Irelande* (London, 1581).

worst warfare of the early sixteenth century involved the armies of these greater lords, for in their determination to extend their power, or prevent a foe extending his, they dragged wide areas not immediately under their control into their contests and turned them into combat zones. Many of the smaller ruling lineages also fought regularly with traditional enemies. In Co. Waterford, for example, the Powers of Curraghmore feuded endlessly with the Fitzgeralds of the Decies, while in the Midlands, in present-day Co. Laois, relations between the MacGiollapadraigs and the O'Mores were rarely harmonious.[29]

Not that a history of animosity was necessary to trigger military action. Temporary weakness in a lordship, such as the ill health of a once-strong leader or the outbreak of a successional conflict following his death, was enough to provoke a violent attack. The annals are peppered with references to such opportunistic invasions, often purely predatory in character. Furthermore, as recent research has made clear, geographical factors like mountains, woodlands, and bogs contributed in no small way to the prevalence of incursions, ensuring that in many parts of the country the terrain hindered effective defence, and greatly favoured the surprise attack.[30]

provides the best guide to these and other rivalries. **29** D.B. Quinn & K.W. Nicholls, 'Ireland in 1534', *NHI*, 3, p. 9. **30** K.W. Nicholls, 'Woodland cover in pre-modern Ireland', in Duffy et al., *Gaelic Ireland*, pp 181–206, esp. 203 where it is noted that 'much of the woodland ... lay along the borders of the autonomous lordships'. See also the perceptive

Yet, endemic though warfare undoubtedly was, there is little evidence to support the suggestion by reform-centred scholars that it produced an especially high level of bloodshed. As historians of native society in sixteenth- and seventeenth-century North America have shown, endemic violence among tribal or lineage groups was actually *not* greatly destructive of life. Because warfare was a matter of raids and counter-raids, ambushes and skirmishes, combat mortality was usually low.[31] Irish warfare was similar. One of the objects of war was the capture of prisoners, in order to ransom them for money or cattle, or exchange them for other people.[32] By the same measure the bloodiest form of conflict, open battle between rival armies, was unusual. In the first two decades of the sixteenth century just one major battle took place between rival native armies, at Knockdoe, Co. Galway, in August 1504. To be sure, it was a huge confrontation, involving forces drawn from most parts of the country, and contemporary accounts agree that it was an extraordinarily bloody contest. Discounting the exaggerated claims of the victors, it is generally accepted that it resulted in the deaths of approximately 4,000 soldiers – a level of battlefield mortality not seen in Ireland previously (and that would not be seen again for another 180 years, until the 1690s).[33] But the sheer carnage of Knockdoe insured it was not repeated. Tellingly, the leader of the victorious coalition, Garret Mór Fitzgerald, the 'Great Earl' of Kildare, was never able subsequently to assemble a force of comparable strength from among his allies, many of whom probably regretted allowing so many of their men to be sacrificed in his name. It is therefore difficult to entirely accept the suggestion of one historian that Knockdoe signalled the 'growing bellicosity of Irish life in the early sixteenth century';[34] in a sense, it signalled the opposite, as afterwards for a significant number of years lords seem to have stepped back from further involvement in costly pitched battles. The next battle of any real size did not occur until September 1520, when the new earl of Desmond and his enemies came to blows in south-west Munster.[35] In the intervening period such 'battles' as took place were often little more than glorified skirmishes. Table 2 (below)

comments of Seán Ó Domhnaill, 'Warfare in sixteenth-century Ireland', *IHS*, 5 (1946–7), 39–40. 31 Helen Rountree, *The Powhatan Indians of Virginia* (Norman, Ok 1989), ch. 7; Daniel Richter, *Facing east from Indian Country: a native history of early America* (Cambridge, MA, 2001), pp 62–7. 32 *AFM*, s.a. 1507, when Niall O'Neill was ransomed for 16 people, and s.a. 1518, when Hugh Balbh O'Neill was ransomed for 15 horses (by his brother!); *AC*, s.a. 1514, when the slioght Airt sept of the O'Neills suffered 'a great capture' by O'Neill of Tyrone, and s.a. 1516, when Butler of Cahir seized many of Piers Butler's men in Tipperary. 33 O Domhnaill, 'Warfare', 32; G.A. Hayes McCoy, *Irish battles: a military history of Ireland* (Belfast, 1990), pp 48–67; Donal O'Carroll, 'The Battle of Knockdoe', *JGHAS*, 56 (2004). 34 Lennon, *Sixteenth-century Ireland*, p. 66. Elsewhere, however, Professor Lennon observes that the nature of most Irish warfare in the early sixteenth century was 'small-scale, if persistent' (ibid., p. 58). 35 Anthony McCormack, *The earldom of Desmond 1463–1583: the decline and crisis of feudal lordship* (Dublin, 2005), pp 50, 64–5.

shows how each battle that was noticed by the Four Masters for the years 1505–20 involved casualties of at most 100 men, and usually much fewer.[36] The most striking feature of the table, however, is what it suggests about the general frequency of battles: for 10 of the 16 years covered, the annalists noted no battles at all. This apparent decline of battles after Knockdoe contrasts markedly with the record of incursions outlined in Table 1 (above), which shows that the number noticed by the annalists more than doubled after the bloodbath of 1504. Evidently, if Irish society was getting more bellicose in the early 1500s, its rulers appear to have set about it in a decidedly cautious fashion. Limited combat, in the form of raiding and ambushing, was the order of the day. From the viewpoint of the aggressor lord it involved both minimum risk of military casualties and a higher probability of success; in short, it was the most effective way to fight. For this reason it is not entirely accurate to describe all surviving *caithréimheanna* of the sixteenth century as 'battle rolls' or 'battle careers',[37] in that the armed encounters that they commemorate were mostly not battles, but violent affrays, and generally occurred during raids or as a result of a trap ('combat rolls' would be a far better description). A contemporaneous word that perhaps best encapsulates the true nature of warfare as it was practiced in Ireland, and that also reflects the cunning of the native military leaders, is 'stealth'. An equally suggestive word is 'prey'.

When noting the generally low mortality of Irish warfare at this time it is important to remember the two categories into which all casualties fell – direct (combatants) and indirect (non-combatants). While clearly the growing disinclination of the lords to battle-type confrontation and the corresponding extension of raiding-based warfare facilitated the survival of combatants, it is not clear that the same trend helped non-combatants to better endure military action. Raids and incursions were primarily economic forms of warfare, designed to enrich the attackers at the expense of those they attacked. At the highest social level, if carried out persistently, raids could so impoverish a lord or leader as to undermine his pretensions to autonomy and turn him into a vassal, but they could also have drastic consequences lower down the social ladder. More often than not it was the unfortunate tenant farmers and peasant labourers who bore the immediate impact of the raids, having their livestock (or the livestock in their care, and for which they were liable) or other moveable goods and possessions stolen by the raiding parties. With raids becoming apparently more numerous after 1504 it follows that many more among the lower orders may have been driven towards destitution, and faced serious malnourishment and even death from starvation, because of the military methods of their social superiors.[38] As suggested by Table 1 (above) their

---

36 When reporting the killing of thirty of the Maguires' soldiers by the O'Reillys the Annals of Connacht did so because it seemed such a high figure (*AC*, s.a. 1520). 37 For example, Ó Riordan, *The Gaelic mind*, p. 72; Simms, *From kings to warlords*, p. 172. 38 A similar

Table 2: After Knockdoe – Irish battles, 1505–20

Year	Place of Battle	Details of casualties
1505	None recorded	–
1506	The Route	MacQuillan, 9 of his chief supporters, and 17 other men
1507	None recorded	–
1508	Donagh Church, Monaghan	
1509	Lough Leaghaire, Tyrone	3 leaders
1510	Monabraher, beside Limerick	2 leaders and 'many other men of distinction'
1511	None recorded	–
1512	Bunowen, beside Lough Erne	1 leader, 9 men drowned, and others
1513	Killybegs	O'Malley, and c.100 others
1514	None recorded	–
1515	None recorded	–
1516	None recorded	–
1517	None recorded	–
1518	None recorded	–
1519	None recorded	–
1520	None recorded	–

Source: AFM

vulnerability was further exacerbated by the fact that the escalation of raids and incursions was apparently paralleled by an escalation of scorched-earth tactics by invaders. Between 1500 and 1510 approximately half of the incursions noted by the Four Masters were accompanied by land- and crop-burning; by 1550 scorched earth seems to have become a feature of almost every recorded incursion. While it would be unwise to place too much faith in this because of the stylized format of the annals, evidence among the English state papers tends to corroborate the impression of widespread and growing recourse to scorched earth.[39]

Predictably, the worst mortality occurred when scorched earth coincided with natural disaster. For instance, the Annals of Ulster record that in 1496 a combined campaign by the O'Donnells and MacMahons against the O'Reillys had unusually severe consequences for the population in East Breifne (modern Co. Cavan): the burning and devastation of the land that was carried out by the invaders followed a period of prolonged bad weather, which had destroyed crops in the area, and also overlapped with a serious outbreak of cattle disease. There was famine after the invaders' departure.[40]

conclusion is reached in Kenneth Nicholls, 'Gaelic society and economy', in NHI, 2, p. 410. **39** For example, see Piers Butler's charges against Kildare and Desmond of 1525 (TCD MS 842), and the mid-century writings of the archbishop of Armagh (PRO, SP 62/2/44–5), discussed below. **40** AU, s.a. 1496, 1497. See also AFM, s.a. 1541 for food shortages in

While thousands of non-combatants must inevitably have been casualties of Irish warfare in the early sixteenth century, it should be nevertheless recognized that for the most part they were *indirect* casualties. As a rule, native armies did not look to slaughter the common people. On the contrary, killing peasants and other non-combatants may actually have been considered dishonourable, partly because they were property-less 'churls', and as such were not worth killing, but partly also because they were defenceless. An entry in the Annals of Ulster criticizes the sons of Donough Maguire for having slain 'two inoffensive farmers' during a raid, an occurrence that the annalists saw as an unprovoked and apparently unprecedented outrage that had offended not only human society, but God, and invoked divine wrath upon Fermanagh.[41] Similarly, the Four Masters dwell on the grisly punishment meted out in a Midlands lordship to a group of displaced soldiers who had murdered a physician and six unarmed persons in the 1540s.[42] Ultimately, however, the fact that during wartime Irish armies chose not to slaughter the peasantry was more a matter of economics than ethics. People were a precious resource in early sixteenth-century Ireland. In most parts of the country, but especially in rural areas far from towns, population levels were low.[43] It was because of this that Irish lords and ruling lineages tended to measure power through lordship over people as much as lordship over territory, operating on the premise that land had little productive value without a labour force to work it. Accordingly in wartime it made more sense for a lord or chieftain to spare such peasants as he encountered on an incursion, and to take them into his protection, than to kill them; that way, he might add to his power and status, and the wealth and productivity of his 'country', by making them serve and enrich him instead of his foe. This situation needs to be better appreciated by reform-centred historians, who tend to base their assumptions about the violence of Irish life on hostile English accounts that were written to justify outside intervention, rather than native evidence. Though it is undeniable that the peasants' lot was generally harsh in the Gaelic and Anglo-Irish lordships, it was not so harsh that their lives were worthless; far from it. As Mary O'Dowd has observed, in many places the peasants were semi-itinerant, able each year to move from one lordship to another in search of more favourable conditions, and in return for their labour and tribute the lords were willing to offer them protection.[44]

Strikingly, it was largely among the higher ranks of society, not the lower, that violent death was concentrated. As shown in Table 3 (below), during the period 1501–40 over 160 members of the local ruling lineages were killed by members of another, enemy lineage – or approximately four a year –

Fermanagh caused by the O'Donnells. 41 *AU*, s.a. 1492. 42 *AFM*, s.a. 1548. 43 Nicholls, 'Gaelic society', pp 408–9. 44 Mary O'Dowd, 'Gaelic economy and society' in Brady and Gillespie, *Natives and newcomers*, pp 129–30.

occasionally in a battle, but usually as a result of an ambush or assassination. Likewise, atrocities and violent excesses were part of elite life. The annals contain many reports of horrifying acts of cruelty that were perpetrated by one Irish leader and his men on another. Maimings and mutilations were common: sometimes fatal, as when Donough O'Donnell, a claimant to the O'Donnell chieftainship, having been taken prisoner in 1503, was maimed (*scatad*: literally pruned, or his limbs lopped) by the son of the reigning chieftain before a crowd of onlookers, 'in consequence of which he died';[45] sometimes not, as when, the same year in neighbouring Derry Richard O'Cahan (O'Kane) was ritualistically maimed by his brother Donal.[46] A tradition of grisly trophy-taking, in the form of beheadings, existed in some regions. In Connacht one of the Clanricarde Burkes achieved renown as a decapitator of his adversaries, earning the nickname *Ulick-na-gceann*, Ulick of the heads.[47] Across the Shannon the Midlands warlord Kedagh O'Melaghlin gained the ultimate war memento when he beheaded his great enemy Seamus MacCoghlan in his own house.[48] A few years later the MacCoghlans fought a bitter civil war in which one segment of the lineage busied themselves in beheading 20 members of a rival segment after an encounter near Clonmacnoise. The heads were subsequently put on public display, 'elevated on sharp poles as trophies of victory'.[49]

Table 3: Causes of death of Irish rulers, 1501–40

Date	Died peacefully[50]	Died violently	
		Killed by kin	Killed by others
1501–10	68	27[51]	29
1511–20	60	14	64
1521–30	38	22	31
1531–40	32	31	40

Source: AFM

Yet the sheer brutality of life as it was lived by many of the Irish ruling elite is probably most plainly demonstrated by the remarkable frequency with which local lords and leaders met violent deaths at the hands of their own relatives.

45 *AFM*, s.a. 1503.   **46** Ibid.   **47** Ibid., s.a. 1536.   **48** Ibid., s.a. 1540.   **49** Ibid., s.a. 1548.   **50** This includes four who died accidentally, by drowning, in 1505.   **51** This excludes *c.* 360, 'eighteen score', killed in a civil war among the MacCarthys in 1508, partly because it is so removed from the norm, but also because the description by the Four Masters is vague, making it impossible to separate out MacCarthy leaders from their rank and file troops. Given the scale of the killing, it would of course be desirable to mention the conflict in the discussion of battles (above), but again, regrettably, the Four Masters do not mention any battle *per se*, but rather describe the unusually high casualties as resulting from a series of encounters that apparently commenced in 1508, and continued for some time subsequently.

Although the principle of primogeniture was widely accepted in the Anglo-Irish territories, and was in the process of becoming established in several Gaelic ones,[52] such was the potency of the martial ethos that within most ruling lineages succession was contested by rival 'strong men'. Competition for supremacy within a lordship, or part of a lordship, was seen as a source of strength. In the Gaelic lordships in particular, all senior members of the ruling bloodline (the *derbfine*) were theoretically entitled to stake their claim to rule by force, but by 1500 contested succession was also common in a growing number of Anglo-Irish lordships – so much so, indeed, that by 1513 even the earldom of Kildare was affected, when the new earl, Garret Óg, had to see off a challenge by his half-brother, Henry Fitzgerald, following the death of their father.[53] To paraphrase an authority on the subject, even the strongest lordships could be internally fragile, their ruling families existing in a near permanent state of hostility and division, with brothers, uncles and cousins constantly jostling for position, plotting the downfall of rivals.[54] Table 3 (above) shows that between 1501 and 1540 nearly 100 members of indigenous ruling families were recorded in the Four Masters as being murdered by near kinsmen. However, while such murders seem often to have formed part of a vicious retributive cycle of tit-for-tat killing between rival family members and sub-groups, they did not usually spill over into large-scale bloodshed, presumably because steps were taken by other lineage members to limit the violence.

But even if the native lords and their families managed to avoid large-scale slaughter, by far the greatest problem facing them early in the sixteenth century, and something which made their violent culture much more difficult to manage, was that increasingly from about 1520 the political order that had given a measure of equilibrium to Irish affairs since the mid-1400s[55] began, visibly, to come apart. It is from this date, not 1504, that the growing bellicosity of Irish life is most clearly detectable. Within barely twenty years, by the mid-1540s, a domino effect had set in as instability in the leading dynasties added hugely to the instability of the lesser ones, and lords and leaders everywhere struggled with growing desperation to create a new regional pecking order that would benefit them and not their enemies. Overall the period 1520–50 saw a general escalation of native violence that was discernible across all four provinces.

II

The origins of the escalation can be dated with a fair degree of precision to the second decade of the sixteenth century. In just nine years, from 1511 to 1520,

---

52 O'Dowd, 'Gaelic economy', p. 123. 53 *AFM*, s.a. 1514. 54 Nicholls, *Gaelic and Gaelicized Ireland*, pp 10–11. 55 Lennon, *Sixteenth-century Ireland*, pp 51–8; Seán Duffy, *Ireland in the Middle Ages* (Dublin 1997), ch. 6.

what might be called the native political establishment was rocked by a series of developments which, had they occurred one by one over a longer period of time, might have been easily withstood; however, occurring close together, they had a combined effect of undermining the existing lordship system. The crisis had three key elements: (i) the passing, in quick succession, of a generation of lords and chieftains who had ruled several of the greater lordships for many years (see Table 4); (ii) the inability of some of their successors to curb growing family disunity or prevent the partial break-up of their lordships; and (iii) the renewed assertiveness of once strong lineages that had been quiet for a number of years previously.[56]

Table 4: The passing of the old order, 1511–20

Ruler's name	Death	Title	Length of rule
Murrough Ballach Kavanagh	1511	king of Leinster	35 years
Cathair O'Connor Faly	1511	lord of Offaly	37 years
Niall Mór O'Neill	1512	lord of Clandeboy	30 years
Garret Mór Fitzgerald	1513	8th earl of Kildare	35 years
Rossa MacMahon	1513	lord of Oriel	16 years
Thomas Butler	1515	7th earl of Ormond	38 years
Phelim O'Connor Sligo	1519	lord of Carbry	24 years
Maurice Bacach Fitzgerald	1520	10th earl of Desmond	33 years

Among the first to be touched by these troubles were the MacMahons of Monaghan. Though not a dynasty of the first rank, they had for many years enjoyed considerable influence in northern affairs, and had been strong enough to collect a sizeable tribute from the Anglo-Irish community of Co. Louth. Following the death in 1513 of Rossa MacMahon, their lord for 16 years, they were unable to unite behind a single chieftain. A split soon followed, the main Oriel line unable to prevent the MacMahons of both Farney and Dartry breaking away, and the importance of their 'country' was seriously diminished by the prolonged in-fighting that ensued. Almost at once the disturbances in Monaghan were mirrored in Fermanagh, where a bitter civil war had erupted among rival segments of the Maguires. In this way, within a matter of months a power vacuum spread across much of southern Ulster; this in its turn further fuelled the great conflict that was then raging between the O'Neills and O'Donnells. War was no longer merely endemic; it was becoming acute.

---

56 Except where otherwise indicated, the best guides to developments in the lordships during these years are D.B. Quinn, '"Irish" Ireland and "English" Ireland', in *NHI*, 2, pp 621–36, and Nicholls, *Gaelic and Gaelicized Ireland*, ch. 7–10.

Simultaneously, very similar problems beset the most powerful dynasties in Leinster. As already noted, the greatest family in Ireland, the Fitzgeralds of Kildare, had to contend with a disputed succession following the death in September 1513, after 35 years of rule, of Garret Mór Fitzgerald, the 'Great' eighth earl of Kildare. While the Great earl's successor as ninth earl, Garret Óg, dealt swiftly with the problem, heading off the danger of further family division by capturing his rival in 1514,[57] developments in the Kavanagh country to the south demonstrated that further provincial instability, directly affecting the Fitzgeralds, was unavoidable. A few years earlier, in 1511, the last undisputed Gaelic king of Leinster, Murrough Ballach Kavanagh, had died after reigning for more than 30 years. Though a successor had emerged first in the person of Art Boy (d. 1517) and then Gerald (d. 1523), they were but 'kings with opposition'. Their claims to suzerainty were violently disputed by other members of the dynasty – consequently, having survived for centuries, the Kavanagh kingdom suddenly went into terminal decline as an effective institution, with the lineage dividing permanently into three rival warring chieftaincies.[58]

But it was in the Ormond country straddling the provinces of Leinster and Munster that the greatest change occurred, after August 1515. Hitherto, for 50 years, owing to the prolonged absenteeism in England of the Butler earls,[59] the earldom of Ormond had existed more in theory than practice. This was transformed by the death in London of the old seventh earl of Ormond, Thomas Butler, and the emergence of his Irish kinsman Piers Ruadh Butler of Pottlerath as his ruthlessly effective successor. Within two or three years Piers had managed to impose his authority across the vast Butler lordship, and also to outmanoeuvre Earl Thomas's heirs-general, his English-born daughters and their husbands. Piers's efforts signalled a political revolution throughout the southern half of the country: since 1485, he had been tied very closely to the Kildare Fitzgeralds; from 1516 he turned against them, with devastating effect. By the beginning of the 1520s his re-ignition of Ormond authority had begun to destroy the various local power arrangements that had become established in its absence – arrangements that formed the basis of what historians call the 'Kildare ascendancy'. Thereafter, until the final collapse of Kildare power in 1534–5, much of south Leinster, the Midlands, and north Munster was engulfed by a series of satellite wars among the Kavanaghs, O'Mores, O'Carrolls, O'Kennedys and others, as the Butlers and Fitzgeralds intervened in lordship after lordship, sowing division and facilitating conflict in their contest for regional dominance.[60]

---

57 *AFM*, s.a. 1514. 58 Donal Moore, 'English action, Irish reaction: the MacMurrough Kavanaghs, 1530–1630' (unpublished MA thesis, NUI Maynooth, 1985), pp 14–20, 23–9. 59 For Ormond absenteeism now see David Beresford, 'The Butlers in England and Ireland, 1404–1515', (unpublished PhD thesis, Trinity College, Dublin, 1999). 60 Edwards, *The Ormond Lordship*, pp 81–90, 147–9.

This growing breakdown of the established political order was subsequently confirmed at opposite ends of the country by the outbreak of major crises affecting two more of the greatest lordships. In Ulster the chaos engulfing the southern territories of the province had begun to spread to its centre by 1516 when the new O'Neill chieftain, Art Óg, is known to have been confronted by serious internal opposition, almost certainly stoked up by the O'Donnells. Efforts at mediation served only to delay the eruption of full-scale civil war until 1519, when the election of Con Bacach O'Neill as the new chieftain proved too much for the powerful Art Boy sept of western Tyrone. Immediately they went into violent secession to become a major supporter of O'Donnell ambitions. Had Con Bacach managed to retain the support of the Gaelic Scots settled in Antrim, the MacDonnells and their followers, he might have been able to draw upon them for military aid out of the Western Isles, and so fared better. However, having been preoccupied with Scottish affairs for many years, in the early 1520s the MacDonnells became active in Ulster again, seizing the opportunity to expand presented by the growing crisis in the province.[61] The power of the O'Neills began to dip significantly.[62]

Meanwhile, far away in Munster, it was the turn of the Fitzgerald earldom of Desmond. For 33 years Maurice Bacach Fitzgerald, the tenth earl of the line, had ruled the earldom, but in the final years of his life the re-emergence of Ormond power under Piers Butler had cast a shadow over his affairs. Shortly after his death in 1520 it engulfed his successor as eleventh earl, James Fitzgerald. Seizing upon opposition by the new earl's uncle, Thomas 'the Bald' Fitzgerald, and also on the resurgence of the MacCarthys, the Butlers connived at Desmond's ruin, and partly succeeded. At Earl James's death in 1529 the earldom continued to be crippled by internal disruption, and rival forces carried on fighting each other for years to come.[63]

Though precise statistics are not possible, an impression of at least some of the effects of this spiralling instability and warfare can be detected in surviving sources. After a hiatus of 16 years, the 1520s opened with two major battles, one in the south, near Mourne Abbey in MacCarthy country, in which the new earl of Desmond was heavily defeated,[64] the other in the north, at Knockboy, in which Con O'Neill and Burke of Clanricarde proved unable to stem O'Donnell

---

61 J. Michael Hill, *Fire and sword: Sorley Boy MacDonnell and the rise of Clan Ian Mor, 1538–90* (London 1993), pp 12–13, 15, 17–18; Simon Kingston, 'Delusions of Dál Riada: the co-ordinates of Mac Domhnaill power, 1461–1550', in Duffy et al., *Gaelic Ireland*, pp 110–11.   62 It is hard to accept the description of this period as 'the most stable era of O'Neill rule in Ulster' (Brady, *Shane O'Neill*, pp 17–18).   63 McCormack, 'Internecine warfare'.   64 *SP Henry VIII*, 2, no. 8. The site of the battle is recorded in the mid-seventeenth-century history of the Munster Fitzgeralds, a partisan and often inaccurate account written in Latin by the exiled cleric Dominic O'Daly; for a translation, see C.P. Meehan, *The rise, increase and exit of the Geraldines, earls of Desmond* (Dublin, 1878), ch. 9.

power. On both occasions casualties were unusually high, around 1,000 men falling at each battle.[65] Subsequently Irish lords seem again (as in 1504) to have turned away from war by battle to war by incursion – there are no more major battles recorded in the annals until the mid-1530s – but even so it appears that in general conflict was becoming noticeably more widespread and destructive. For instance, the power struggle between the Butlers and the Fitzgeralds intensified after 1522, when Piers Butler became briefly head of the royal government; it was marked by the burning of Dungarvan in Waterford, Arklow in Wicklow, Tullow in Carlow, and Levittstown in Kildare, besides other places, attacks which seem invariably to have resulted in the deaths of a number of non-combatants, mostly tenants and artisans.[66] The rising number of raids and the mounting frequency of scorched earth tactics, suggested above in Table 1, appear to have become more marked after 1530. Another contributory factor was the growing use of firearms.[67] Albeit not yet a major feature of Irish warfare, which remained essentially a matter of blade-fighting, nonetheless guns were becoming more available through the international arms trade. Even by the 1510s firearms were in limited use in all four provinces, and the dramatic deployment of artillery by the Fitzgeralds of Kildare and the Burkes of Clanricarde to destroy the fortresses of enemies served greatly to advertise their importance.[68] But most important by far was the bulging size of the private armies maintained by the Irish lords. Partly a response to the increased instability of the period, it was greatly aided by the growing availability – and affordability – of thousands of Scottish part-time mercenaries, the 'redshanks', who poured into the country in increasing numbers from the Western Isles at exactly this time.[69] To begin with, the Scots' presence was noticeable mainly in Ulster, but soon they were in Connacht, and within a decade they were being hired in Leinster and Munster too. Indeed, by the late 1520s a great gathering of Scottish troops occurred in Kilkenny and Tipperary, where for the first time in its history the army of the Ormond lordship was augmented by a force of galloglasses, more than 400-strong, specially imported from the Isles to bolster the Butlers' challenge to Fitzgerald influence.[70] (The Fitzgeralds, of course, had

---

[65] The only extant contemporary report of Desmond's defeat at Mourne Abbey is not an eye-witness account, but rather was written a few days later in Dublin, following excited reports of the battle sent from Kilkenny; the casualty figures it provides of 1,440 galloglasses and 480 horsemen seem highly improbable (*SP Henry VIII*, no. 8). [66] PRO, SP 60/1/34; *SP Henry VIII*, 2, no. 42. [67] Siobhán de hÓir, 'Guns in medieval and Tudor Ireland', *Irish Sword*, 15 (1982), 80–2. [68] E.g., *AFM*, s.a. 1503 (Belfast Castle destroyed by Kildare), 1504 (three O'Kelly castles destroyed by Burke), 1516 (Leap Castle destroyed by Kildare). [69] The Annals of Connacht draw explicit attention to the arrival of more Scots in 1522 (*AC*, s.a. 1522). An English report estimated there were 'above the number of two or three thousand of them' in Ulster in 1542 (Philip Wilson, *The beginnings of modern Ireland* (Dublin & London, 1914), p. 34 n.2). [70] Edwards, *The Ormond lordship*, p. 156.

many Scots of their own – probably far more, in fact – but unfortunately precise figures are impossible).[71]

III

This, disastrously, was the Ireland that the English encountered. It was in the years either side of 1520 that the government of Henry VIII decided to embark on the reassertion of royal authority over its weakened Irish dominion. As they arrived in Dublin to take charge of the process, everywhere the king's agents looked they found political and social turmoil. It is one of the great tragedies of the sixteenth century that had the English crown intervened even 15 years earlier – say, in 1506, when King Henry's father, Henry VII, briefly considered trying to re-conquer Ireland[72] – it would have faced a situation that was more settled, more manageable for its purposes. Or, for that matter, had it delayed for a further generation, until maybe 1550, conditions in the lordships might well have stabilized. By intervening when it did, just as the Irish lordships were spinning out of control, the English monarchy was destined to take the initiative at the very time its policies of centralization and Anglicization were probably most unworkable.

As recent research has revealed, one of the crown's main methods of initial intervention – 'affinity management', a form of cheap indirect rule – did little to improve the situation. Orchestrated by the king and Cardinal Wolsey between 1515 and 1530, it was intended to alter the balance of power in the country and achieve a *détente* that was more amenable to crown influence by playing the main Anglo-Irish lineages off against each other, advancing the re-emergent Butler interest at the expense of the long-established ascendancy of the Kildare Fitzgeralds.[73] Perhaps unaware of the growing dislocation then confronting the Fitzgeralds as the old order began to rupture, the government's meddling backfired spectacularly. Rather than confirming royal power it provoked its outright rejection, and after twice flirting with revolt, in 1528 and 1532, the

---

71 The usual source for the Desmond Fitzgerald army at this time is Liam Price (ed.), 'Armed forces of the Irish chiefs in the early sixteenth century', *JRSAI*, 62 (1932), 203, a late fifteenth-century document that claims the Desmonds had 3,000 galloglasses by *c*.1490. One of the more striking aspects of this source is the remarkable disparity it suggests between armies in the Pale and across the south-east (generally numbered in the low hundreds) and those in the north, west and south-west (numbered in the thousands). Clearly compiled by someone with detailed knowledge only of Leinster, the Midlands and east Munster, its figures for Desmond are almost certainly fanciful.   72 D.B. Quinn, 'The hegemony of the earls of Kildare, 1494–1520', *NHI*, 2, pp 653–4.   73 Fiona Fitzsimons, 'Wolsey, the native affinities, and the failure of Reform in Henrician Ireland', in D. Edwards (ed.), *Regions and rulers in Ireland, 1100–1650: essays for Kenneth Nicholls* (Dublin 2004), pp 78–121, is a major new study of the politics of English intervention.

Kildares entered into full-scale insurrection in 1534.[74] Their rebellion, as every student knows, was not without consequence.

Because the Fitzgeralds had hoped to capitalize on Henry VIII's growing international isolation following his break with Rome by daring to seek aid from the pope and the Holy Roman Emperor, they managed to transform English official attitudes to Ireland, greatly heightening the country's status as a potential security risk.[75] Immediately, King Henry abandoned his dependence on the great rival Anglo-Irish affinities and despatched a force of 2,300 English soldiers to the country under the command of an English-born viceroy, Sir William Skeffington, known in Ireland as 'The Gunner', and subsequently an English-born marshal (and Skeffington's eventual successor), the nobleman Lord Leonard Grey. Historians usually stress the importance of the arrival of 'The Gunner' and Grey for two reasons, one political, the other military: it was the harbinger of more than a century of direct rule from Whitehall in which the royal administration was controlled by English-born chief governors instead of Anglo-Irish magnates; and it signalled the establishment of a permanent English garrison, or army of occupation, something that was destined to become a key component of English rule in Ireland down to 1922.[76] There is, however, a third reason why the advent of Skeffington and Grey was of lasting significance: they and their army had a discernible impact on the conduct of war in Ireland, propelling the ongoing escalation of violence in the country into a dangerous second phase.

It was not just that they succeeded in destroying the Fitzgerald army, until then the greatest military force in the country, in just a few months of combat. Equally important was how they did it. Commanding the largest English force in Ireland for generations, first Skeffington and later Grey dealt with the rebels with unparalleled ruthlessness. Fearing that European interference was imminent in Ireland, and also that the rebellion might excite copycat uprisings in parts of England (where King Henry's religious innovations were far from popular), the Henrician regime determined to vanquish the Irish insurgents through a demonstration of unbridled state terror. Mere victory was insufficient. The leading rebels and their supporters were to be annihilated, to deter other prospective opponents from taking the field.

In fairness, the severity exhibited by the crown forces was to some extent aggravated by the alleged behaviour of the Fitzgeralds. Steven Ellis has contended that the army's ruthlessness was necessitated by the ruthlessness of the rebels.[77] This is difficult to accept in certain respects. Yes, the Geraldines

74 Ibid., pp 119–21.   75 Lawrence McCorristine, *The revolt of Silken Thomas: a challenge to Henry VIII* (Dublin, 1987), passim; Micheál Ó Siochrú, 'Foreign involvement in the revolt of Silken Thomas, 1534–5', *PRIA*, 96C (1996), 49–62.   76 Ellis, 'The Tudors', pp 131–2.   77 Ibid., pp 130–1.

fought a hard war, burning widely, pillaging, killing any who resisted them, yet they only fought traditionally. They seized many prisoners as hostages, sparing their lives to secure compliance (and, of course, for future ransom), and even in the government's charges against them, or the charges made by the Butlers, they appear to have committed no massacres.[78] Yet in one crucial regard Ellis is correct. In line with a series of measures intended to coerce the Pale population into supporting the rising, the Fitzgeralds ('Old English' by descent) seem to have committed a form of ethnic cleansing, as they were alleged to have ordered the summary execution of anyone who was English by birth. It is unclear whether these allegations were true or just exaggerated reportage of a handful of isolated killings of English people, such as the archbishop of Dublin, John Alen, murdered in June 1534;[79] however, there is no doubt that in London they were *believed* to be true. Within weeks of the insurrection, as King Henry began preparing his military response, it was even being reported at court that English women and children were among the Fitzgeralds' victims.[80]

The crown's vengeance, when it came, was terrible. Whatever killings of defenceless English people (and others) the Geraldines had perpetrated, the carnage done by Skeffington's royal army was of a different order. If extant sources can be trusted, his officers' execution of Geraldine military prisoners at Naas on Saturday 6 March 1535, 'to the number of a hundred', was the first definite massacre of the sixteenth century, insofar as it was the earliest recorded large-scale despatch of unarmed, or as here, disarmed, persons. On this occasion necessity was the official reason given for the slaughter. The English forces guarding the prisoners feared they were about to be attacked by other Geraldine elements in the vicinity, and so they killed their captives to prevent them being freed.[81]

But no such excuse applied to the second massacre of the period, the English slaughter of Geraldine prisoners taken at Maynooth Castle nearly three weeks later, on 25 March. As before the rebels were disarmed after their surrender,

---

78 When entering Butler country they besieged Tullow Castle, Co. Carlow, for 5 days, and killed the entire ward, but as the earl of Ossory's allegations indicate, this was a hot-blooded killing of soldiers by soldiers, not a cold-blooded slaughter of disarmed prisoners or ordinary people (*SP Henry VIII*, 2, no. 93). For the government's charges see Philomena Connolly (ed.), *Statute Rolls of the Irish Parliament, Richard III-Henry VIII* (Dublin 2002), pp 148–58. 79 The fact that the act of attainder against the Fitzgeralds and their adherents mentions their determination 'most cruelly to murder, put to death, and exile all those that were resident [in Ireland] ... born within the realm of England' tends both to confirm that murders of some English took place yet also to suggest that others were not killed, but banished: Connolly, *Statute Rolls*, pp 150–1.   80 Ellis, 'The Tudors', p. 128.   81 *LP Henry VIII*, 8, no. 382. The massacre is also mentioned in the contemporary English campaign journal, 'The feats of the English Army' (PRO, SP 60/2, f.97), an important source that has recently been published in full in Steven G. Ellis, 'Promoting "English Civility" in Tudor times', in *Tolerance, intolerance and state policy* (Pisa, 2002), pp 168–9.

then butchered, but unlike the earlier massacre there was no danger of their being rescued by comrades; rather, the fall of the castle signalled the collapse of the rebellion in the Pale, and the retreat of all remaining Geraldine forces deep into the Gaelic Midlands. The killing of the prisoners was statecraft, pure and simple. Though it followed a short but intensive siege (commenced on 14 March) it is difficult to accept it as a hot-blooded killing. According to Skeffington's own testimony, written the following day, the heat of battle had long receded[82] by the time he ordered the executions, which were carried out after all the prisoners had been interrogated and arraigned before the provost marshal of the English army in a specially convened court martial.[83] Moreover, the contemporary Gaelic annals, the Annals of Ulster, indicate that the prisoners were not the only ones killed in cold blood at the fortress. This was the case, apparently, even with many of the soldiers that defended it. Far from being killed in hand-to-hand fighting they were 'slain in their sleep' by the English after the constable, Christopher Paris, had secretly betrayed the castle to Skeffington in the hope of saving his own skin – and, probably, the lives of others too.[84] By Skeffington's estimate, 'about 60' Geraldine troops were killed when his men entered the castle; the northern annalists, usually well informed about Geraldine affairs, reckoned that 'the majority' of these died in their beds. The low number of English casualties – just seven men – lends weight to the annalists' account.[85] Yet it was not what happened during the taking of the castle, but afterwards, that most clearly constituted a massacre. Killing a sleeping enemy in the course of an assault is one thing; killing all prisoners, long after their capture, quite another.

The precise number and status of the executed prisoners is uncertain. In his letter Skeffington indicates that those put to death included five prominent ringleaders, including two clerics, the dean of Kildare and a priest named Walsh, and 37 others, who he said were all soldiers.[86] But another government source, 'The feats of the English Army', suggests the number of executed captives as closer to 50 or more, and describes the victims as mostly 'household servants' – that is, non-combatants.[87] It is an important distinction, to be sure. Either way, whether the majority of the Maynooth Castle prisoners had been combatants or non-combatants, it is clear that their killing served a single purpose – namely, to emphasize the English army's role as agent of royal retribution. In 'The Gunner's' own words, 'We thought it expedient ... to put [them] to execution for the dread and example of others'. To insure maximum impact, 25 of the prisoners were beheaded 'before the gates of the castle', their

---

[82] By more than 48 hours, in fact (see below). [83] *SP HVIII*, 2, no. 87. [84] *AU*, 3, s.a. 1535. [85] McCorristine, *The revolt*, p. 110. [86] *SP HVIII*, 2, no. 87. [87] PRO, SP 60/2, f. 97. Skeffington had a reputation for being less than truthful (McCorristine, *The revolt*, p. 111).

heads subsequently taken by crown troops and impaled on the castle's turrets – an act which, incidentally, made it the biggest episode of decapitation recorded for early sixteenth-century Ireland. The remnant appears to have been led away towards Dublin either to be executed there or in important places along the way.

The calculated nature of the massacre is most clearly revealed, however, by the date chosen to carry it out. Maynooth Castle had been in crown hands since about six o'clock in the morning of Tuesday 23 March, when Constable Paris had helped the royal troops to gain entrance. Skeffington could have proceeded with the executions later that day, or else the following day, but he waited until 25 March – the traditional New Year's Day in England and Ireland, and a major holy day, being the feast of the Annunciation.[88] By delaying the beheadings until then he broadcast a message that was universally intelligible: the New Year announced a new order achieved by the extermination of the old. The awful logic of the Tudor treason laws was also asserted; insurrection meant doom. By rebelling the rebels had forfeited all rights, so much so that even on a traditional holy day they could expect no mercy. This applied to their priests and servants as well as to their soldiers; the crown would stop at nothing to punish them all. (That 25 prisoners were decapitated on this, the twenty-fifth day, gave added symbolism to the message.)

Massacre, it has been suggested, is an impressive way to assert authority.[89] It is also, however, inflammatory, and as often as not leads to a rejection of the very authority it is designed to promote. In 1535 the willingness of the English army to kill all prisoners was probably enough to cause astonishment throughout Ireland. As noted above, one of the customary features of Irish warfare was the seizing of prisoners for ransom; to coldly put them to death *en masse*, long after hostilities had ceased, was unprecedented. The fact that clerics and other non-combatants were among the executed was equally shocking, the violation of another taboo – although, that said, the English were hardly innovators in this instance, considering the murder of the archbishop of Dublin by the Fitzgeralds' troops the previous summer. And then there was the question of bad faith. The treachery of Christopher Paris was not the only act of duplicity committed at Maynooth. Just as he betrayed the castle to Skeffington in the hope of being spared, so Skeffington betrayed him, having him killed with the rest of the prisoners. Indeed, the viceroy or his officers may have similarly duped other captives. It is recorded in the state papers that in the wake of the massacre English soldiers coined the expression 'the pardon of Maynooth' as a euphemism for Skeffington's emerging stratagem of obtaining surrenders through pretence of mercy. The phrase was pure gallows humour,

---

88 C.R. Cheney (ed.), *The handbook of dates for students of English history* (London, 1991), pp 4–5. 89 Brady, *The chief governors*, p. 276.

the subterfuge it celebrated (and its bloody consequences) a source of mirth, but behind the laughter lurked an unsettling fact: Sir William's fondness for deception was deeply alienating. The Irish were appalled. For them the fall of Maynooth and the slaughter that ensued was an example of 'Saxon' (English) perfidy, a dishonourable event that was characterized not by fierceness and indomitability – positive traits in Gaelic military culture – but rather by 'murder and foul treachery'. Hence Skeffington became the first English governor of the period to attract widespread Irish opprobrium.[90]

His successor, Leonard Grey, soon joined him. Whereas Skeffington would be forever associated with the 'pardon of Maynooth', Lord Leonard was destined to be remembered for 'Grey's pardon', another broken promise of mercy, this time involving the leader of the revolt, 'Silken' Thomas Fitzgerald, tenth earl of Kildare. The young earl was persuaded to surrender to Grey in August 1535 only to be arrested and taken to London, where he was later executed without trial despite Grey's guarantee – sworn as a holy oath, upon sacraments – that his grievances would receive a fair hearing. Ironically, Grey was not strictly responsible for the duping of Earl Thomas. That was essentially Henry VIII's doing. With the royal army victorious, the king had been irate that Lord Leonard had promised Kildare a full royal pardon to secure his surrender. An offer of clemency to such a major rebel made Henry look weak. To save face, the king eventually decided to treat Grey's promise as if it had never been made (Grey, understandably, acquiesced, and was handsomely rewarded).[91] Kildare was hanged and beheaded at Tyburn in February 1537, together with his five uncles, who as well as being hanged and beheaded were subjected to the full grisly routine of execution for treason, having their bodies torn apart, their bowels and genitals removed, before being drawn and quartered, 'their quarters with their heads set up about the city [of London]'.[92] In many parts of Ireland news of the executions was greeted with outrage, the cause of great 'lamentation'.[93] The Annals of Connacht cursed the English for their action: 'May you be worse in a year's time, you evil, false band … You have blinded us'.[94]

Although King Henry and his councillors at Whitehall were the true authors of the treachery behind 'Grey's pardon', it is understandable that the Irish blamed the new governor. Long before Kildare and his uncles were given over to the royal executioner and his implements – in fact, since Grey's arrival in Ireland in the summer of 1535 – Lord Leonard had been to the forefront in

---

[90] His notoriety was such that, when compiling the Four Masters early the next century, the Irish annalists confused Skeffington with Lord Grey, depicting the false pardon proffered by Grey to Kildare as Sir William's idea (*AFM*, s.a. 1535). Every reference to Skeffington in the Four Masters, dating back to 1530, reflects badly on him (ibid., s.a. 1530, 1532).
[91] McCorristine, *The revolt*, pp 117, 121–4.   [92] J.G. Nichols (ed.), *The chronicle of the Grey Friars of London* (Camden Society, 53, London, 1852), p. 39.   [93] *AFM*, s.a. 1537.   [94] *AC*, s.a. 1535.

attempts to capture the remaining Geraldines, through deception as much as military skill. Throughout Gaelic Ireland this final round-up of the Fitzgeralds was seen as entirely dishonourable. As the Four Masters later put it 'every one of the family who was apprehended, whether lay or ecclesiastical, was tortured and put to death'.[95]

Grey was also responsible for the third recorded massacre of the period, at Carrickogunell Castle, Co. Limerick, in August 1536. After bombarding and then storming the fortress, Grey duly executed the survivors, 46 in all. At first glance, Carrickogunnell might seem a standard act of war, for the defenders (doubtless mindful of events at Maynooth) had refused to surrender. However the killings went beyond usual practice in Ireland: as Grey noted in his own account, there were women and children among those he had killed.[96]

It is the very fact that he included this information in his report to London, deeming it a piece of service fit to be recorded, that pinpoints his significance in the military history of sixteenth-century Ireland. Traditionally, Irish warlords only rejoiced in the killing of soldiers, and passed over the killing of non-soldiers in silence. Grey (and other English officers of the time) saw *all* killing as virtuous, an achievement worthy of commemoration.

Lord Leonard Grey's bloody reputation has recently been revised by a leading reform-centred historian. Because Grey managed to win a series of victories while required by the king to cut costs and reduce the English army to barely 700 men, he has been identified, quite correctly, as a governor who overcame serious obstacles to impose royal authority in large parts of the country. His political achievements, long overlooked by nationalist writers, have also been afforded some overdue recognition.[97] Yet, for all that Grey achieved, it is hard to accept the suggestion that just because his army was reduced the administration he headed favoured 'the minimum of force'.[98] Such a radical refashioning of Grey rests on a fundamental misunderstanding of his military record, confusing the size of his army with the nature of its use. Grey, like Skeffington, was determined to inflict high casualties in Ireland: that is, to kill as many enemies of the crown as possible, whether armed or unarmed, and thereby to secure obedience to English rule *ad terrorem*. Accordingly, Carrickogunnell was just the first of a series of massacres that he and his smaller army committed. On capturing Brackland Castle in Offaly in June 1537, he allowed the commander to live, but 'all the residue had the pardon of Maynooth' – that is, death after promise of life.[99] The same fate awaited the defenders of Dangan Castle, where perhaps 40 O'Connor soldiers 'had the same grace and pardon which such men deserved'.[1] Even Grey's greatest military

---

95 *AFM*, s.a. 1537.   96 *SP Henry VIII*, 2, no. 145.   97 Brady, *The chief governors*, pp 13–25 passim.   98 Ibid., p. 22.   99 *SP Henry VIII*, 2, no. 169; *Cal. Carew MSS, 1515–74*, no. 100.
1 *SP Henry VIII*, 2, no. 170; see also *AFM*, s.a. 1536.

feat, his surprise attack and dispersal of the numerically far superior O'Neill forces at Bellahoe in 1539 appears, on closer inspection, to have had some of the characteristics of massacre. O'Neill having escaped unharmed with the bulk of his retainers, it was less the triumph of English arms that Grey later claimed than an exercise in slaying those who the annals emphasized were 'the common people', unarmed herdsmen and peasants trapped in the Monaghan countryside after O'Neill and his confederates had gone.² Grey's final year in office was marked by one of the worst atrocities committed by royal troops thus far – the beheading of the prior and other members of the Franciscan conventual community in Monaghan in 1540, an action that served no discernible object save to announce the government's disdain for the Franciscans, and perhaps also to humiliate MacMahon, the local chieftain, whose ancestors had founded the friary.³ Although it constitutes the one definite massacre to have occurred in Ireland during the Henrician dissolution of the monasteries, it has been consistently ignored by historians.⁴

Armies do not need to be big to have a major impact. By acting like 'The Gunner' Skeffington, albeit with a lesser force, Grey helped to insure that the intervention of the English army had a transformative effect on the conduct of war in Ireland. Its arrival signalled the introduction of a new set of standards concerning what constituted acceptable violence. Whether the royal army numbered in the hundreds or thousands its approach was essentially the same: to vanquish its foes through sheer, unbridled ferocity.

Instead of recognising the exceptional severity of English operations, or noting their significance in Ireland, reform-based historians have tended to depict crown policy as relatively moderate and to shrug off all the bloodshed associated with it as merely routine. For example, the glut of executions that occurred in and around the Pale in 1534–5, of which the massacres at Naas and Maynooth discussed above were just part, has been characterized as 'modest', 'moderate', even 'mild', and this on the dubious basis that the crown sanctioned more executions of rebels in England in 1536–7 during the suppression of the Pilgrimage of Grace.⁵ In fact, as an examination of the surviving evidence reveals, significantly more rebels were executed in Ireland in 1534–5 than pilgrims in England two years later.⁶

2 *AC*, s.a. 1539; *AFM*, s.a. 1539.   3 *AC*, s.a. 1540; *AFM*, s.a. 1540. The priory had been founded by Felim MacMahon in 1462.   4 Curiously, the only academic scholar to notice this massacre has poured doubt on its importance because it occurred during a royal military campaign! See R. Dudley Edwards, *Church and state in Tudor Ireland* (Dublin 1934), p. 110. 5 Ellis, *Ireland*, p. 142; idem, 'Promoting "English Civility"', p. 165; Crawford, *Anglicizing the government*, p. 254.   6 The total number put to death in northern England after December 1536 was somewhere between 137 and 153 (M.L. Bush and David Bownes, *The defeat of the Pilgrimage of Grace* (Hull, 1999), pp 411–12). The number of rebels executed in Ireland, following their surrender or capture, was at least as high as this. As already mentioned, proceeding by martial law the government forces had slain 100 prisoners at Naas

Equally misguided is the suggestion that the actions of the royal forces in Ireland from 1534 onwards should be seen less as aggressive acts of war and more as standard crown defence and counter-insurgency measures which, though harsh, were utilized as little as possible, as elsewhere in the Tudor state.[7] This contention is not just wrong, it is doubly wrong, being misinformed about the operation of counter-insurgency measures in England as well as misleading about the sort of measures adopted by the English government in Ireland. When confronted with insurrection in England Henry VIII (and his successors) usually exercised a degree of restraint, mindful that over-zealous prosecution of rebel districts might prove counter-productive.[8] This is why there were no massacres in Tudor England (not even in 1569, when very harsh measures were employed). It is also why the crown was reluctant to resort to scorched earth even in notoriously troublesome regions such as the far north, along the Anglo-Scottish border. In 1523 King Henry denied the commander of his forces permission to burn the lands of rebels there, stating that although the rebels were 'evil men' deserving punishment yet they were still royal subjects. As such 'We do rather desire their reformation than their utter destruction'. Later, in 1540, Henry again refused to sanction scorched earth in the north, this time explaining that such tactics were only permissible 'in extreme war between strange realms'.[9] He required no such restraint in Ireland. Although the inhabitants of Kildare, Meath and Westmeath, English by descent, were deemed subjects of the crown just like their counterparts in the north of England, subject status (and English lineage) did not have the same value in Ireland. When combating the Geraldine forces in 1534–5, instead of proceeding cautiously, the royal army set large parts of Kildare and Meath ablaze without hesitation. According to 'The feats of the English Army' the crown forces made a series of expeditions into Co. Kildare early in 1535, deliberately burning towns and villages in their path, and towards the end of February they managed to burn forty villages in a single day, thirty in Kildare, ten in Meath.[10] 'Much

---

on 6 March 1535 and at least 42 at Maynooth and places nearby on or after 25 March. In all likelihood, the total number executed was far higher. Months before the Naas massacre, in the autumn of 1534, detachments of the Geraldine army had been captured at Drogheda and Trim, of which at least one group, the company commanded by Captain Brodie – perhaps 50 men, or more – was 'put to execution' (PRO, SP 60/2, f.97). Additionally, an unknown number of rebels and rebel sympathizers were executed in Dublin after common law trial or by attainder.
7 Crawford, *Anglicizing the government*, pp 247, 322. So too the assertion that the government discriminated between Anglo-Irish and Gaelic Irish rebels when seeing to their punishment, using judicial proceedings against the Anglo-Irish prisoners because they were 'English by birth', and summary measures reserved only for the Gaels (Ellis, 'Promoting English "civility"', pp 165–6). Neither government nor Gaelic sources record any such policy.   8 Penry Williams, *The Tudor regime* (Oxford, 1979), pp 375–94; K.J. Kesselring, *Mercy and authority in the Tudor state* (Cambridge, 2003).   9 Ralph Robson, *The rise and fall of the English Highland clans: Tudor responses to a medieval problem* (Edinburgh, 1989), p. 149.   10 PRO, SP 60/2, f. 97.

burning and destruction' also marked an expedition into Westmeath in April, into the territories of the 'Old English' Daltons and the Tyrrells.[11] Nothing of the sort would have been contemplated in England.

Of course, scorched earth was hardly new to Irish warfare. Like most Irish warlords, the Fitzgerald rebels had utilized it during their own campaign. Even so, just as the English army's predisposition to commit massacres or to kill all prisoners broke new ground, so it set a new standard in scorched earth, burning more intensively, more systematically, than its Irish opponents. To achieve a better sense of the emerging patterns of violence in sixteenth-century Ireland it is necessary that this be acknowledged. By the same measure, the method of fighting favoured by the crown should be seen for what it was – colonial warfare.[12] Despite claiming sovereignty over the island, the English troops treated the country more as an enemy territory or 'strange realm' than a subject jurisdiction, a typical feature of colonial conflicts.[13]

This is not, of course, to absolve the Irish rebels from their share of responsibility for the devastation perpetrated during the 1530s conflicts. In August 1534 (just before harvest time) the Kildare army had paid special attention to the Butler lordship in Co. Kilkenny, twice laying waste to the shire, the second time breaking a truce to add to the level of destruction.[14] However, it was only after the English onslaught early in 1535 that the rebels' behaviour worsened. Before Maynooth fell the Geraldines had burned only selected areas of the Pale, but subsequently their forces burned more widely, apparently punishing their former underlings for not resisting the crown more, desperate to create a no-man's-land behind which they could re-group. The worst affected area was Co. Kildare itself. By late summer 1535 it was reported that, since the spring, owing partly to the actions of the Fitzgeralds as well the behaviour of the royal army, six of the eight baronies of the county were utterly destroyed and uninhabited; the situation in Meath was nearly as bad.[15] And yet there were limits to what they did. As the traditional overlords of the Pale, they could not afford to continue ravaging the places that they had until recently controlled, and some of which were bound to them by centuries of lordship and custom, without damaging their ability to rule. Indeed, it was primarily his desire to retain a basis for lordship, and to stop attacking the lands of the very people that might one day assist in his family's recovery, that persuaded 'Silken' Thomas to surrender to Grey on 24 August. The royal army was not constrained by such considerations.

11 *SP Henry VIII*, 2, no. 93.   12 Not for what, in theory, it should have been – the same as in England.   13 Accordingly, the Irish wars feature prominently in a useful new guide to English colonial warfare: Bruce Lenman, *England's colonial wars, 1550–1688* (London, 2001). See also Thomas Bartlett, *'The academy of warre': military affairs in Ireland, 1600–1800* (Dublin, 2002), p. 9.   14 Edwards, *The Ormond lordship*, pp 161–2.   15 *SP Henry VIII*, 2, no. 98.

IV

And so to the third and, in many respects, the most crucial phase of the growth in violence in sixteenth-century Ireland – the middle decades of the century, when the extension of English royal power became central to political developments in large parts of the country, and the conduct of war intensified dramatically.

Even without further action by government forces, already by the early 1540s conditions in many places had become more volatile because of the overthrow of the Geraldines and their supporters. The political vacuum that followed the Fitzgeralds' bloody removal served to increase the difficulties affecting the native order, with several of the main regional dynasties determined to grasp the opportunity to push forward into former Geraldine areas before others succeeded in annexing them. In the ensuing new wave of aristocratic wars the Butlers of Ormond took a leading part, expecting, as crown loyalists, to be the chief beneficiaries of their old enemies' fall. Their troops marauded through south Leinster, north Munster, and east Connacht,[16] but others such as the Kavanaghs (Wexford and the Carlow/Laois borderlands),[17] the MacCarthys (north Cork and Limerick),[18] and the O'Donnells and MacDonnells (north and east Ulster) were equally aggressive.[19]

Yet, destabilizing as these conflicts were, they were destined to be dwarfed by the Tudor government's decision of 1546 to begin implementing the 'reformation' of the country through a policy of limited conquest and colonization. Believing that the pace of political and social change needed to be speeded up to better assure England's control of Ireland, and prompted into action by the security implications of fresh conflict with France and Scotland, the monarchy took the military route to greater dominion. The policy had two interrelated objectives: first, to provide a much larger territorial base for English power by the creation of a cordon sanitaire around the Pale, re-peopling neighbouring Gaelic districts with people of English origin; and second, to reduce what was seen as the potentially dangerous autonomy of some of the strongest Gaelic lordships. Although it did not always pursue this policy consistently, it pursued it consistently enough, and over a long enough period – about 21 years – to achieve at least some of its objectives. Largely because of this development, warfare in Ireland was transformed.

---

16 *Cal. Carew MSS, 1515–74*, no. 185; HMC, *Haliday MSS*, p. 275; *AFM*, s.a. 1544; NLI, MS 7409. 17 Moore, 'English action, Irish reaction', ch. 2; R. Butler (ed.), *The Annals of Thady Dowling* (Dublin, 1849), p. 38. 18 PRO, SP 61/1/113. 19 Hill, *Fire and sword*, pp 28–30.

Table 5: Crown military operations in Ireland, 1546–66

1546	Spring: Wicklow Summer: Laois and Offaly Late Summer/Autumn: Kildare and Carlow
1547	Early Summer: Wicklow Summer: Laois and Offaly (twice)
1548	Early Summer: Laois and Offaly, Kildare borders High Summer: Cutting passes in Kildare, Laois, Offaly, and across the Shannon; occupying Athlone and forts in north Tipperary Ditto: occupying Armagh, Newry, Down Priory Autumn: throughout Midlands
1549	Spring: fort-building in Midlands Summer: Carlow, north Wexford, Shillelagh Summer: Central and east Ulster (Tyrone, Iveagh, Lecale, the Dufferin)
1550	Summer: Laois and Offaly (with surveyors) East and central Ulster
1551	High Summer: Progress through Munster and south Leinster Late Summer: north Wexford Autumn: Rathlin Island, east Ulster; re-occupation of Armagh Winter: east Ulster
1552	New Year: Laois and Offaly Summer: Ulster (twice)
1553	Summer: throughout Midlands Late summer: general hosting
1554 1555	Summer: progress through Limerick, Thomond, and Midlands Winter: Offaly Summer: Ulster
1556	Early Summer: Wicklow, Carlow, north Wexford Summer: Antrim coast, East Ulster (Clandeboy and the Route) Ditto: progress into Munster Winter: Laois and Offaly
1557	Spring: Laois and Offaly High Summer/Autumn: Antrim, the Glinns, Tyrone and central Ulster Winter: Laois and Offaly →

1558	Spring: Fercall Early Summer: Ulster Late Summer: North Munster, Ely, Midlands
1559	New Year: Wicklow Autumn: Ulster
1560	Summer: Wicklow Summer: Midlands and Longford Autumn: Tyrone and central Ulster
1561	Summer: Tyrone (twice)
1562	Late Winter: foray into Ulster
1563	Summer: Ulster
1564	Spring: Midlands Summer: Midlands
1565	New Year: Midlands High Summer: hosting towards Breifne
1566	Ulster

Sources: *AFM; Cal. Carew MSS, 1515–74; CSPI, 1509–73*; HMC, *Haliday MSS*; BL, Add. MS 4763, ff 231r–233v.

Here is not the place for a detailed discussion of the political circumstances underpinning the crown's embrace of expansion by conquest; given the excessive length of the present essay, that must await treatment elsewhere. Instead, it will have to suffice simply to notice the growth of royal military operations at this time. As shown in Table 5 above, for almost every one of the 21 years 1546–66 the royal army is recorded as out on campaign at least once, and usually twice or three times, per annum. The principal theatres in which it operated were the Midlands (as far west as Athlone and the Shannon), east and central Ulster, and Gaelic south Leinster, but there were also some occasional forays into north Munster. Considering the efforts made by some reform-centred historians to minimize the importance of English military activity in sixteenth-century Ireland, claiming that such expeditions as were undertaken by the crown prior to 1580 were few and far between, and limited in scope,[20] it is important to

---

20 See esp. Brady, 'The captains' games', pp 144–51, and also Crawford, *Anglicizing the*

acknowledge the frequency and scale of the mid-Tudor operations. Such prolonged and wide-ranging movement by a single army, affecting a territory approximating to half the total area of the country, was unprecedented.

The growing size of the royal army assured its impact on the pattern of warfare. Comprised of both 'English bands' and 'Irish bands' its numbers grew rapidly from an average of approximately 900 men during 1546–51, to 2,010 during 1551–6, before climbing to 2,200 during the ten-year-period 1556–65.[21] In no way was such a force small, as some maintain. For this to be the case, the military strength of such native armies as opposed it would have needed to be significantly higher than they were.[22] Although some of the major Irish lords could sometimes field similar-sized armies, unlike the crown they could not do so all year round, an important distinction; and while some of them undertook quite distant operations, no lord, no matter how powerful, had the capacity to continue long-range warfare year after year. The ampleness of the royal army was still further enhanced by the availability of large auxiliary forces raised by the loyalist Anglo-Irish of the Pale, by the Butlers of Ormond (and, for a time, the Fitzgeralds of Desmond) and their clients across the south, and by a rising number of compliant Gaelic lords anxious to secure the crown's friendship.[23]

Then there was the matter of weaponry. Simply put, the crown forces far surpassed the native armies in this area. The proportion of archers traditionally employed in the royal army began to decline in Ireland from the mid-1530s, replaced by gun-carrying infantry (called arquebusiers). Thereafter the transition to gun warfare – and, significantly, the higher combat mortality rates associated with it – proceeded steadily. Within 25 years, by 1559, the gunners in the government forces outnumbered the archers by as much as two-to-one. As early as 1566 they had replaced them almost entirely.[24] By that time the English bands usually contained between 400 and 700 gunners; in 1566–7, when the army swelled temporarily to over 4,000 troops in readiness for an invasion of Ulster, more than a quarter of its number – 1,140 men – were described as gunners.[25] No Irish lord could compete with such firepower. Though a royal monopoly of violence was still many years away, it is nonetheless the case that during the mid-Tudor period a major step was taken towards government military supremacy.

government, pp 323–4, although in general the latter provides one of the best discussions of the royal army in Ireland, from a structural viewpoint.   **21** For a detailed discussion of these and other figures see my forthcoming paper, 'Crown forces in Ireland, 1534–1575'.   **22** Ellis, *Ireland*, pp 248–50 is valuable on the limits of the native armies; for a different view, contending that the crown forces were weaker than the lords' private armies, see Brady, 'The captains' games', p. 146.   **23** For some of these besides the Butlers, see Edwards, 'The MacGiollapadraigs (Fitzpatricks)', p. 344; Maginn, *'Civilizing' Gaelic Leinster*, pp 74–5, 86–9; McCormack, *The earldom of Desmond*, p. 76.   **24** A.K. Longfield (ed.), *Fitzwilliam Accounts 1560–65* (IMC, Dublin, 1960), pp 70–1, 75–80.   **25** HMC, *De L'Isle & Dudley MSS*, 1, pp 389–402.

Perhaps if the royal army had conducted its affairs as some claim – 'by the same means that had brought peace and order to the outlying parts of England'[26] – its impact on the pattern of violence in Ireland would have been less noticeable. But as in the 1530s, government military conduct in Ireland continued to be unlike anything recorded in England. One of the most distinctive (and unsettling) features of the mid-Tudor Irish wars was the readiness of the crown to favour a disproportionate response to its problems with native lineages, and also its open embrace of pre-emptive strikes, its officers apparently encouraged even to provoke rebellion in order to subjugate territories that it considered important. When in the summer of 1546 the chief governor Sir William Brabazon attacked the increasingly compliant O'Mores and O'Connors he did so on the basis that 'disturbances' among them were a major threat to the Pale, and needed to be quelled.[27] In fact, the one recorded incursion into the Pale prior to Brabazon's response, a raid into Carbery, Co. Kildare by Donough O'Connor, was probably prompted by the introduction of an important new crown captain on the Kildare/Offaly frontier, Henry Cowley, who had taken up formal occupation of Carbery Castle after November 1544.[28] Had Brabazon responded more cautiously to Donough's incursion, and sought the support of biddable elements within the region, a general 'rebellion' might have been averted. However, he seems to have attacked indiscriminately, assaulting the O'Mores as well as the O'Connors, with predictable consequences. The O'Mores, hitherto preoccupied with a successional dispute,[29] re-united and entered into a strong alliance with the O'Connors (who previously had been their main local rivals), after which the crown carried on an 'extreme war' of expropriation against them both. The campaign was waged remorselessly, year after year, by a succession of chief governors, and laid the ground for the government's first great colonial project, the Laois/Offaly Plantation.[30]

Surrounding lineages were also treated roughly, with the O'Melaghlins, Mageoghegans, and O'Maddens all subjected to sudden attacks in the autumn of 1548.[31] But it was above all the crown's decision to instigate simultaneous hostilities against the O'Neills in Ulster that most clearly revealed the extent of its growing aggression. In 1548-9 the previously loyal first earl of Tyrone,

---

26 Brady, *The chief governors*, p. 70.   **27** For the crown's generally peaceful relations with these families before 1546, see Carey, 'The end', p. 218, and Fitzsimions, 'The lordship', pp 216–19.   **28** *Irish Fiants*, Henry VIII, no. 442.   **29** Carey, 'The end', p. 218.   **30** White, 'The reign', p. 199.   **31** PRO, SP 61/1/96, 109. The operations against 'the rebel Dillons' may also fit this pattern, as it is not clear whether the Dillons were in revolt before or after the crown campaign; moreover, the fact that the Nugents of Delvin were prominent in the royal forces strongly suggests that local factional issues played a role in determining the army's actions. For a completely different analysis see Brady, *The chief governors*, p. 50, where it is claimed that it was crown policy in 1548–9 to 'assure' and 'encourage' the Irish chiefs who bordered on Laois and Offaly.

Con Bacach O'Neill, was driven to the brink of rebellion by the harassment of newly established English military officials in East Ulster such as Nicholas Bagenal and Andrew Brereton. These repeatedly scoured the earl's country, roughing up his kin, pillaging, and seizing livestock. Brereton even went so far as to encourage the MacCartans to defy Earl Con's claims to overlordship; when Con sent his troops into Kinelarty to collect his tribute, the captain was waiting, and reputedly killed up to 140 of them, an enormous blow to the earl.[32] Soon afterwards the O'Neills fell into bitter civil war, thereby presenting Bagenal, Brereton and their co-officers with fresh opportunities for interference and the extension of their influence. It was out of these circumstances, with royal policy in Ulster increasingly the preserve of military adventurers, that the province became the centre of resistance to Tudor rule in the 1550s and '60s, following the rise of the fearsome warlord and 'arch-rebel', Shane O'Neill.

In Gaelic south Leinster, meanwhile, the Kavanaghs received like treatment. Goaded by the behaviour of other new officers stationed in and around their country they first flirted with rebellion in 1549–50, only to step back from the precipice,[33] but a renewal of official antagonism sometime after 1554 proved too much to bear. By spring 1556 the lineage commenced a major revolt, following which its leadership was destroyed by crown forces and its power greatly diminished.[34]

Plainly, the pre-emptive aggression displayed by the royal army in these and other areas of the country does not sit easily with the interpretation favoured by reform-centred historians, wherein the army officers are seen as little more than armed policemen whose primary role was the extension of English law and order into 'uncivil' frontier areas.[35] Considering their openly provocative conduct it is difficult to accept Bagenal, Brereton, and their ilk as all that concerned with law and order, still less the suggestion that their actions are best understood as defensive, or counter-insurgency, measures.[36] To qualify as *counter*-insurgency, the actions of such officers should necessarily have occurred *after* insurrection had broken out, a set of circumstances which demonstratively did not apply in these cases. The importance of this goes beyond mere academic point-scoring. It shows that when it came to starting wars the government, confident of its superiority, was not behindhand. Just as important, it also reveals the extent to which Tudor rule in Ireland was continuing to diverge from Tudor rule in England. Despite the growing conflict (and expense) incurred by the aggression of its military officers, the royal government refused to curb

---

32 PRO, SP 61/2/39, 41. 33 PRO, SP 61/1/17. Brian C. Donovan, 'A community in transition: the Royal liberty and county of Wexford, 1536–1603' (unpublished BA dissertation, Trinity College, Dublin, 1989), pp 67–8. 34 For the series of government agreements with the Kavanaghs between 1543 and 1554, see Moore, 'English action, Irish reaction', ch. 2. 35 Brady, 'The captains' games', p. 153. 36 Crawford, *Anglicising the government*, pp 286, 320, 322, 326.

their powers; quite the opposite. Following the appointment of Thomas Radcliffe, third earl of Sussex, as the new viceroy in 1556, the capacity of the military for starting wars was significantly amplified. In particular, new powers of martial law – hitherto a strictly *counter*-insurgency measure – were made available that permitted the government's officers to kill or otherwise punish, as though they were rebels, all such 'suspected enemies' of the crown as they deemed necessary. Henceforth, no proof of enmity would be needed to justify an attack or killing; mere suspicion, or the potential for resistance, would be enough. To make matters worse, according to the terms of the hundreds of martial law commissions that were subsequently issued over the following years, there was a financial inducement for royal officers to kill as many prospective 'enemies' as possible, because of their entitlement as commissioners to a third part of the goods and possessions of whoever was slain. Among the often-chronically underpaid officer class, demand for martial law commissions was high. As well as contributing to the bloodshed in the main theatres of government operations, the spread of martial law facilitated the emergence of a new type of conflict, smaller in scale, but politically highly destabilizing – semi-private and entrepreneurial warfare involving government representatives operating in the provinces, pursuing their own local interests in the name of state service. And so it was that the number of 'little wars' (as they have been dubbed by reform-centred scholars) also proliferated.[37]

The consequences for the overall level of violence in the country were very serious. Kenneth Nicholls' observation about sixteenth-century developments, namely that the crown's commitment to military intervention helped to change Ireland from a country suffering from an excess of violence into one utterly devoured by it,[38] makes particular sense from the mid-Tudor period onwards. As well as traditional wars between the local ruling lineages, which showed little sign of declining, from the late 1540s the population was forced to withstand the predations of a large and growing English army that entered the field two or three times a year either in response to a prevailing emergency (a rebellion or invasion scare), or else in pursuit of greater regional power and territory

---

[37] Edwards, 'Ideology and experience', pp 131–2. Having failed to notice the high incidence of martial law in Ireland after 1556, or its provocative pre-emptive character, Jon Crawford has accused the present writer of exaggerating its importance, maintaining the mantra of all reform-centred scholars that Tudor Ireland was governed the same as Tudor England (Jon Crawford, *A Star Chamber court in Ireland: the Court of Castle Chamber, 1571–1641* (Dublin, 2005), p. 43). The instruments of government may have had the same name, but in Ireland they could be – and often were – altered and extended to such an extent as to be barely recognizable. It should not be necessary to advise historians to look for divergence as well as convergence in the course of their research.   [38] K.W. Nicholls' introductory comments to a final year undergraduate seminar 'The Transformation of Irish Society' that he co-presented with the present writer in the Dept. of History, University College, Cork, in October 1994.

(conquest). But even if reform-centred scholars have underestimated the importance of English aggression, their insistence that the Irish lords made a significant contribution to the crisis is not wrong. In order to defend their territories against the gathering might of the royal army, many of those local rulers who either were driven to rebel, or else chose to do so, succeeded in putting up a more effective show of resistance than the crown had expected; hence the long duration of the mid-Tudor wars. Some of the rebel actions betrayed their desperation, others their growing resolve to match the crown raid for raid and, if possible, body for body. But while the Irish resorted to atrocities to an extent not previously recorded, their inclination in this regard was not matched by their capability. Accordingly, as in the 1530s, the scales of atrocity appear to have weighed heaviest on the government's side.

To examine the native 'rebel' violence first: in their various wars of resistance after 1546, insurgent Irish forces looked (as always) to spread terror by murder and wholesale destruction, but more noticeably than before they were inclined to target non-combatants. When the O'Connors and O'Mores responded to Governor Brabazon's invasion of their lands they attacked the town of Athy, Co. Kildare, where they are noted to have 'destroyed many persons, both English and Irish, both by burning and slaying'. The purpose of the attack was to discourage the local community from supporting the royal army, and perhaps also to prevent the town's use as a garrison base, but it seems few if any of their 'many' victims had a military vocation.[39] Accounts of Murrough Kavanagh's uprising of 1556 leave a similar impression, with contemporary and near-contemporary descriptions emphasising the mounting civilian cost of the rebels' actions, which fell mainly on poorly defended tenants and farmers 'in such sort as no man's life ... [was] safe within three miles of Dublin'.[40] Shane O'Neill was perhaps more ruthless again. According to an extraordinary denunciation of his behaviour among the state papers, in the three or four years before 1564 he had had his forces slaughter huge numbers of peasants in Donegal when waging war against the crown's main ally in Ulster, Calvagh O'Donnell. Given that the denunciation was written by Calvagh himself, who hoped thereby to excite Elizabeth I's indignation against O'Neill, the alleged scale of the killings was almost certainly exaggerated; but that Shane's victims included many peasants can probably be taken as fact.[41]

In the Midlands and parts of Leinster the commencement of plantations, with the introduction of English and Welsh colonists in Laois and Offaly, only

---

39 *AFM*, s.a. 1546. See also PRO, SP 62/2/44, where it is noted that when 'Dillon's son' was killed by O'Connor/O'More forces a few years later, they also killed 'divers persons and husbandmen'. 40 Wilson, *The beginnings*, pp 385–6. 41 PRO, SP 63/11/96. The reliability of this allegation is left entirely unquestioned in the standard modern biography of O'Neill (Brady, *Shane O'Neill*, p. 55); the need for greater caution is highlighted in a review of the book by Hiram Morgan, in *History Ireland*, 5:2 (1997), pp 58–9.

encouraged this trend, making legitimate targets of the new tenant farmers, artisans, and their families who arrived to occupy the forfeited lands of the O'Mores, O'Connors, and other local septs. Even so, initially at least, it is possible that a distinction may have been drawn between men on the one hand, and women and children on the other. While one observer, Bishop Bale of Ossory, later stated that several of his English tenants were deliberately slaughtered by local Gaelic and Anglo-Irish forces in 1553 when out working in a hayfield, he also recorded that an English woman driven out of Laois by the O'Mores was stripped but left alive.[42] Eventually, however, women and children appear to have become targets too. When the local Irish menfolk evacuated Shillelagh in anticipation of an attack by the dissident Anglo-Irish knight, Sir Edmund Butler, in 1568, they did so in the expectation that he would be content to set fire to their houses, and leave. They miscalculated. His position as a powerful border lord progressively threatened by a combination of new government and traditional local opponents, Butler was determined to hit his enemies hard; accordingly, he ordered the killing of the only people that his troops encountered, women and children.[43]

Butler's notoriety was secured a year later. In August 1569 his troops combined with those of the Munster rebels James Fitzmaurice Fitzgerald, Donal MacCarthy Mor, earl of Clancarty, and elements of the Kavanaghs, to descend on the north Wexford market town of Enniscorthy, where the crown had established a small military presence. His rebellion already a failure, having evoked little sympathy among the largely loyalist population of the south-east, Sir Edmund timed the attack to coincide with the annual fair, confident that his confederates' appetite for plunder would overcome any reservations they might have had about joining him in one last demonstration of their combined strength before returning to their respective territories. They put the town to the sword. Merchants and ordinary townsmen were hacked down where they stood, others were drowned in the Slaney, and their bodies left floating in the river, while the local women and girls were subjected to an orgy of rape before the whole town was set ablaze.[44]

The Enniscorthy massacre reveals just how bad Irish military conduct could get during the sixteenth century. Evidently, the deliberate butchery of large numbers of defenceless people was no longer deemed dishonourable. What is perhaps most remarkable about it, however, is the fact that nothing closely resembling it appears to have happened before. Prior to 1569, though

---

42 *The vocacyon of Johan Bale to the bishoprick of Ossorie in Ireland*, ed. Thomas Parke (Hareian Miscellany, 6, London, 1810), pp 415–17.   43 Bodleian Library, Carte MS 131, f.83.   44 *The Statutes at large passed in the parliaments held in Ireland* (London, 1786), 1, p. 371. For the political background to the massacre see David Edwards, 'The Butler revolt of 1569', *IHS*, 28:111 (1993).

increasingly more inclined to target civilians as part of their campaigns, none of the various Irish rebel armies that took to the field are recorded as having committed such a cold-blooded massacre of non-combatants. The most likely explanation for this is that the guerrilla-style methods typical of Irish warfare, contingent as they were on raiding and fast movement across wide areas, did not easily lend themselves to massacre, which usually entailed the employment of concentrated and overwhelming force on a fixed point over an extended period of time.[45] Had it not been for the great annual fair the rebels would probably not have attacked the town in such force, or stayed for so long; but the fact that they did, and were prepared to treat civilians so frightfully, showed that potentially the population had as much to fear from them as from the least restrained of the government's forces.[46]

That said, it was the government which overall seems to have committed most of the worst outrages of the mid-century. As well as the growing strength of the royal army it was its method of fighting – 'extreme war' – that made it the most notable contributor to the ferocity of the mid-Tudor years. Large-scale killing, for instance, was a regular feature of crown military operations. The slaughter of up to 200 O'More kerne by crown troops in 1547–8, after they had been located and surrounded, was most likely hot-blooded, the immediate result of combat,[47] as was Andrew Brereton's aforementioned killing of 140 O'Neills in 1549, and likewise the despatch of 200 MacDonnells by Lord Deputy Sussex and the 'black' earl of Ormond in July 1556,[48] but other incidents read much more like outright massacre. The battle of Three Castles in Wicklow, circa May 1547, saw the government forces (supported by the local Gaelic loyalist Brian O'Toole) inflict a crushing defeat on the Fitzgerald rebels, yet most of the reported victims seem to have been killed long after the battle, as prisoners, in cold blood.[49] Another example of cold-blooded butchery occurred in May 1556. Combining with sections of the previously co-operative O'Tooles who, like him, had had enough of government harassment, Murrough Kavanagh had begun his revolt, and sent part of his forces to Powerscourt Castle in Wicklow. Besieged by Sir George Stanley, the new marshal of the royal army, the Kavanaghs and O'Tooles agreed to surrender on a promise of mercy. Over the following two days, once they had been taken to Dublin, no fewer than 74 of them were put to death.[50] A year later, on the banks of the Shannon, Sussex had

---

[45] This, presumably, is why the only 'massacre' attributed to rebel Irish forces in the long and detailed writings of Archbishop Dowdall was one of combatants – 12 of Sir John Parker's English soldiers killed and beheaded by the O'Mores and O'Connors sometime before summer 1558 (PRO, SP 62/2/44). [46] The devastation done by the Butler, Fitzmaurice and Clancarty troops in Munster is described in Canny, *The Elizabethan conquest*, pp 144–5. [47] *AFM*, s.a. 1547. [48] Lambeth Palace Library MS 621, f. 17r; *AFM*, s.a. 1555. [49] Maginn, *'Civilizing' Gaelic Leinster*, pp 87–8. [50] Ibid., pp 100–1; Wilson, *The beginnings*, p. 386n.

4 A successful English reprisal, from Derricke, *The image of Irelande*.

the defenders of Meelick all killed after he had bombarded their castle, stormed it, and captured them.[51] Similarly, in the course of several campaigns against the MacDonnells in east Ulster neither Sussex nor his successor as governor, Sir Henry Sidney, were willing to offer the lineage much mercy;[52] indeed, the government was prepared to carry on killing the MacDonnells even when they were at peace with the state. One of the most notable atrocities of the period was the murder of 'divers' of the MacRanaldboy branch of the line at Ardglass by the general of Ulster, Andrew Brereton, in 1562. Having separated them from their leader, Alasdair, who he had earlier invited into his home, only to murder him, Brereton had the rank and file MacDonnell soldiers surrounded and killed in their sleep in the nearby town. Like his ambush of the O'Neills in 1549 these could hardly be classified as enemies of the crown, as shortly beforehand the MacRanaldboy sept had agreed to assist in the government's war effort in Ulster.[53]

51 *AFM*, s.a. 1557; HMC, *Haliday MSS*, pp 39–41. 52 Hill, *Fire and sword*, pp 42–56; Wilson, *The beginnings*, pp 424–5. 53 'The Complaints of Shane O'Neill', *Ulster Journal of Archaeology*, 1st series, 2 (1854), 222–3, corroborated by PRO, SP 63/8/36, a letter by Sussex of April 1563. The earl's letter helps to date the massacre, which must have occurred sometime after October 1562, when Alaisdair had written to him seeking government protection (British Library, Cotton MS Vesp. F XII, f.96). The massacre is misdated to 1551 in Hill, *Fire and sword*, p. 38.

Civilians, crucially, did not escape. One of the grimmer aspects of government activity during this period was the formal extension of military severity over large sections of the ordinary populace. Several factors contributed to this trend. In part it represented the application to Ireland of the repression of the 'troublesome poor' that was then already underway in England, where fears of social chaos caused by economic recession and rising unemployment produced a heavy-handed crackdown on lower order 'idleness' and vagrancy.[54] Yet it was also an intrinsic part of the crown's Irish reform policy, attempting to accelerate the Anglicization of the country by taming the ordinary Irish of some of the 'wilder' or 'ruder' aspects of their behaviour. The semi-nomadic nature of Irish peasant life, with its constant shifting from lordship to lordship and seasonal migrations from upland to lowland and back again, was considered especially intolerable, seeming to pose a threat to the establishment of an English-style sedentary society of permanent villages and manor houses.[55] Accordingly, the authority to execute wandering idlemen and women was annexed to the first new commissions of martial law issued by the earl of Sussex after his arrival in Dublin in 1556, and subsequently the punishment of 'vagabonds' became a routine function of government officials.[56] But ultimately, of course, the government adopted harsh measures against the most vulnerable elements of Irish society because it made military sense. Threatening the peasantry was a guaranteed way to sever the ties binding the broad mass of ordinary people to their traditional local rulers. Conscious that no Irish lord could hope to maintain a functioning private army without billeting his troops on the populace, the government effectively declared war on the ordinary subjects of whatever enemy lord it happened to be fighting by identifying all 'aiders and maintainers' of his army as abettors of treason – traitors in their own right. As the declaration of war against O'Connor Faly put it in February 1557, 'no person, of what[ever] degree or condition', daring to 'maintain or succour', 'in any wise', the said O'Connor, could hope to avoid the government's wrath, or 'the penalty that ... is ordered for the punishment of such as shall maintain traitors'.[57] In the course of the crown campaigns the killing of the low-born became widespread. It was even considered unremarkable. Returning from one of his outings Lord Deputy Sidney joked in a letter to Whitehall that he had killed so many Irish 'varlets', he had lost count.[58]

Far from being reluctant to employ scorched earth tactics because of the high civilian mortality that it wrought (as has been claimed elsewhere),[59] the

---

54 A.L. Beier, *Masterless men: the vagrancy problem in England, 1560–1640* (London, 1985); B.L. Beer, *Rebellion and riot: popular disorder in England during the reign of Edward VI* (Kent, OH, 1982). 55 Quinn, *The Elizabethans*, pp 32–3. 56 HMC, *Haliday MSS*, pp 20–1. 57 Ibid., p. 29. 58 *Cal. Carew MSS*, 2, no. 52. 59 Brady, 'The captains' games', p. 140, where, having acknowledged several examples of it from the 1560s, '70s and '80s, it is claimed that scorched earth 'was never advanced by governors as either a desirable or a necessary

government forces resorted to land- and crop-burning repeatedly during the mid-Tudor and early Elizabethan years, and did so precisely because it promised to wreak the most havoc, and kill the most people. In 1547 the second Midlands campaign waged by Lord Justice Brabazon was a textbook exercise in devastation. Whereas Irish warlords invariably moved quickly through enemy country, burning as they went,[60] Brabazon brought a specially enlarged force into Laois and Offaly and stayed in the region for a month. First he spent 15 days in O'Connor's country, 'plundering and spoiling it, burning churches and monasteries [the main settlements], and destroying crops and corn', before proceeding into O'More's country, where he repeated the exercise, spending another 15 days there with an even larger force. In response to Brabazon's coming the local rulers had managed to get most of their cattle away, but his desire to induce actual dearth was such that 'not long afterwards' he returned and took 'many thousands of cows' from *non*-rebel chieftains who had earlier submitted to him and agreed peace terms with the crown.[61]

The subsequent increase of the army and extension of the garrison system enabled the government to campaign just as destructively in more distant parts of the country, and also, more significantly, to do so in different regions simultaneously. Thus, while Lord Deputy Sussex ordered at least seven major hostings into Ulster between 1556 and 1563 – not three, as is sometimes claimed[62] – he was just as determined to impose his presence in the Midlands, and advance the plantations there. Towards this end he authorized several campaigns into Laois, Offaly, Ely O'Carroll, and the O'Molloys' country of Fercall.[63] As with Brabazon before, these Midlands campaigns were intended to destroy Gaelic power in the area by threatening to eliminate the Gaelic population unless their leaders submitted to dispossession and displacement. Scorched earth was the preferred method of persuasion. In 1557 the English commander in the Midlands, Sussex's brother Sir Henry Radcliffe, was specifically empowered to 'plague, punish and prosecute with sword and fire ... all Irishmen and their countries' who gave succour to the dispossessed rebel lords.[64] The destructiveness of the Midlands operations is noted in the Gaelic annals, where it is recorded that O'Molloy's country was singled out for special treatment in 1558, being invaded and set ablaze twice in quick succession by Sir Henry Sidney.[65] The refusal of the O'Mores and O'Connors to accept the forfeiture of their lands, maintaining a near-constant guerrilla war of resistance,

means of imposing English authority in Ireland'. 60 For example, AU, 3, s.a. 1536, where the annalists recorded a day and a night of burning by forces in Tyrone because it seemed longer, more sustained, than usual. 61 *AFM*, s.a. 1546. 62 The orders for the hostings are recorded in the Irish Council Book: HMC, *Haliday MSS*, pp 3–4 (1556), 36, 43 (1557), 54–5 (1558), 70, 73 (1559), 88–94 (1560), 122–3 (1561), 128 (1563). 63 Ibid., pp 22–3 (1556–7), 32–3, 44 (1557), 47, 63 (1558), 130–1 (1564). 64 Ibid., p. 42. 65 *AFM*, s.a. 1557. See HMC, *Haliday MSS*, p. 47 for the proper dating.

insured there was never any respite in the decidedly draconian measures adopted by the crown against them. As Elizabeth I insisted in her orders to Sidney in 1566, the stubbornness of the O'Mores and O'Connors should receive his full attention. In a chilling turn of phrase she stated that he must insure the royal forces stopped at nothing 'to cleanse' Laois and Offaly of all dissidents and 'disordered persons' whatsoever.[66]

The Ulster expeditions, meanwhile, being both more frequent and involving much larger forces, were similarly destructive; though considerations of cost and the problem of maintaining supplies over such a large area served to limit their impact to some extent. To head off a deluge of refugees, Sussex tried to minimize the degree of devastation on territories closest to the Pale. When contemplating the prosecution of the MacMahons of Farney, whose lands bordered Co. Louth, he issued orders to his troops specifying that they were 'to spare and preserve all corn and haggards', and refrain from burning houses;[67] however, his feelings were far less delicate towards territories further away. Once in Ulster's Gaelic heartland Sussex's army roved freely about, burning at will. Presumably because he could not linger in the province for as long as he would have liked, the earl prioritized the fastest route to a lasting impact: famine. Hence his ordering the slaughter of 4,000 captured cows in Tyrone;[68] likewise his sacking and burning of Armagh. Travelling straight to the little city, 'and finding there a great mass of butter, corn and other victuals ... [enough] for a whole year', he ordered his men to seize what they could carry and destroy everything else. Only two houses were left standing, those of the archbishop and the dean – government supporters who greatly favoured the advance of royal forces into the area, but in the expectation that this would mean the defence of Armagh, not its obliteration. It would be many years before the city recovered. When the archbishop, George Dowdall, wailed his outrage, Sussex shrugged off the protest, representing the ruin of the city as an instance, literally, of 'friendly fire'; by torching everything in sight, he suggested, the royal army had saved the prelate from the prospect of suffering future rebel intrusion.[69]

The effects of such unrestrained destructiveness, perpetrated by both government and rebel armies, were every bit as dire as might be expected. As early as 1558 large parts of the country were destroyed by war, whole areas depopulated. According to Archbishop Dowdall, it was possible to ride 30 miles across much of central and southern Ulster without seeing any sign of life. Famine stalked the province. Everywhere houses were burned out and uninhabited, all the cornfields were destroyed, and nowhere were there any cattle; all across the countryside between Armagh and Termonfeckin, since the

---

66 T. Ó Laidhin (ed.), *Sidney State Papers, 1565–70* (IMC, Dublin, 1962), no. 12 (10). 67 HMC, *Haliday MSS*, p. 282. 68 Richard Bagwell, *Ireland under the Tudors* (3 volumes, London, 1885–90), 2, pp 29–30. 69 HMC, *Haliday MSS*, p. 43.

outbreak of hostilities between Sussex and O'Neill in 1556, besides those slain by the sword, 'there [had] died many hundred[s] of men, women and children ... by famine and hunger'. And because, more than most Irish leaders, O'Neill had given as good as he got, the destruction was not confined to Gaelic areas. Throughout 'every quarter of the English marches', especially in the borders of Louth, the incidence of 'burning, preying, stealths, murders and robbery' had exploded, and everything, 'corn, cattle and houses', was spoiled. A Louth man by birth and a near-permanent resident of the north-east by virtue of his ecclesiastical office, Primate Dowdall was clearly best informed about the extent of desolation in northern Leinster and southern Ulster. However, the contents of his 'Book' of observations about the growing emergency in Ireland also reveal a lot about declining conditions in other areas. In Co. Meath, for instance, he notes that the lands of the Dillons and the Daltons had been ravaged by the O'Connors, O'Mores, O'Molloys and others, and that broad tracts of prime arable ground had been burnt almost to the gates of Trim; so too Co. Kildare, where it seems farmers and peasants were compelled to abandon the countryside, leaving their crops untended, such was the constant fear of attack.[70]

Dowdall's alarming picture is confirmed by other sources. By 1560, from Antrim to Athlone, and Dublin to Nenagh, much of Ireland was either on the brink, or else fully in the throes, of a gathering subsistence/mortality crisis. That food was scarce throughout the Midlands or large stretches of the north and north-east is hardly surprising, given the scale, frequency and sheer severity of the ongoing warfare, but the fact that people were beginning to starve even in the very heart of the Pale, the richest and most heavily defended part of the country, is testament to the extent of the deterioration. Hitherto for many years plague had represented the single biggest threat to the population levels of the Pale; besides the events of 1534–5, war had rarely constituted a major demographic factor, occurring as it did far away, or only peripherally, and usually without lasting very long. The constant dread of dearth that recent research has identified as characterising Dublin records between 1555 and 1560[71] suggests that the ground had shifted, and that the markedly more prolonged, intensive warfare of the mid-Tudor period had begun to affect the life-expectancy of people previously rarely exposed to its perils. Little wonder that Primate Dowdall opined that his 'poor native country' had never been 'in worse case'. An elderly man, he had lived through the growing native violence of the 1520s and seen at first hand the horrors of the Geraldine wars and the English response of the 1530s, yet he felt certain that the extent of death and devastation caused by the mid-Tudor conflicts was on another level entirely,

---

70 PRO, SP 62/2/44.   71 Colm Lennon, *The lords of Dublin in the age of Reformation* (Dublin, 1989), pp 95–6; British Library, Add. MS 4813, f. 68v; HMC, *Haliday MSS*, pp 44, 50.

something 'the like [of which] was never seen nor heard in Ireland', 'of any man's remembrance'.[72] Unless Irish historians take note of this they will continue to minimize the importance of the period 1546–67 and misinterpret the chronological and typological patterns that underpinned the escalation of violence in sixteenth-century Ireland.

V

According to the reform-centred orthodoxy, before 1580 the situation in Ireland worsened mainly because of the 'chronic' endemic violence of the native lords, and had little to do with the conduct of English government forces. Given the evidence outlined above, it is difficult to accept such a hypothesis. Equally hard to accept is the claim that the royal government did not have a policy of conquest. Although it is true that none of the mid-Tudor monarchs, Edward VI, Mary I or Elizabeth I, approved a programme of military expansion that envisaged the immediate subjugation of the whole country, they most definitely approved a programme that allowed successive governors to attempt to seize greater control of a very extensive area for the state (effectively doubling its territory), and to do so by extreme force. Seeing as the Oxford English Dictionary defines 'conquest' simply as subjugation by force, I would suggest that all Irish Tudor historians embrace the term (without the parentheses), and drop the pretence that the Tudor monarchy treated Ireland the same as England. That may well have been the crown's long-term ambition, its ideal, but between ideal and reality there was a very sizeable, and very bloody, divergence.

---

[72] PRO, SP 62/2/44.

Atrocity and history: Grey, Spenser and the slaughter at Smerwick (1580)

VINCENT P. CAREY

The brutal massacre of a Spanish and Italian force by the English army under the command of Arthur Grey, fourteenth baron of Wilton, on the wild western coast of Kerry in November 1580 was just one incident in what was an exceedingly bloody conquest of Ireland in the latter quarter of Elizabeth I's reign. Though relatively insignificant in terms of casualties in comparison with the scorched-earth tactics of Lord Deputy Mountjoy and Sir George Carew, the lord president of Munster, both before and after the battle of Kinsale (1602),[1] nonetheless the slaughter of this Papal garrison at Smerwick (or Dún an Óir) has resonated down the centuries because of its link to the career, poetry and prose of the renaissance English poet, 'the poets' poet', Edmund Spenser, author of the influential *Faerie Queene*. Whether warranted or not, this incident at Smerwick has received a recent prominence primarily because of its association with the poet and his administrative and literary career in Ireland (which lasted from 1580 to 1599). This essay aims to reexamine the atrocity at Smerwick and to suggest that while the ongoing emphasis on Spenser is understandable it unintentionally serves to diminish the real significance of the event. Smerwick is important not alone because England's leading renaissance poet may have been present – and certainly wrote about it as if he were – but because it marks an important stage in the development of an xenophobic and anti-Catholic rationale for brutal war in Ireland, and for war against Spain in England.

The literary and historical connections between Spenser, his poetry, and Ireland have been the focus of intense study over the last 25 or so years, a renewed international scholarly interest which can be dated to the seminal essay on Spenser's *Faerie Queene* by Stephen Greenblatt in *Renaissance Self-Fashioning* published in 1980.[2] Greenblatt did not mince his words when it came to asserting Spenser's role in the actual violence of the Elizabethan conquest:

---

[1] Vincent Carey, '"What pen can paint or tears atone?": Mountjoy's scorched earth campaign', in Hiram Morgan (ed.), *The battle of Kinsale* (Dublin, 2004), pp 205–16. [2] Stephen Greenblatt, *Renaissance self-fashioning: from More to Shakespeare* (Chicago, 1980). It should be noted, however, that the study of Spenser in Ireland was extensive prior to Greenblatt's intervention. For a review of this literature see Willy Maley, 'Spenser and Ireland: an

Here on the periphery, Spenser was an agent of and an apologist for massacre, the burning of mean hovels and of crops with the deliberate intention of starving the inhabitants, forced relocation of peoples ... the endless repetition of acts of military 'justice' calculated to intimidate and break the spirit.³

Furthermore, Greenblatt advanced the provocative argument that 'Ireland is not only in Book V of *The Faerie Queene*; it pervades the poem. Civility is won through the exercise of violence over what is deemed barbarous and evil, and the passages of love and leisure are not moments set apart from this process but its rewards.'⁴

This new historicist insight literally opened the floodgates to a torrent of publications on the subject ever since. Two examples of the pervasiveness of the Irish connection in studies of Spenser's work should suffice to illustrate my point: five of the seven essays in volume 12 of the *Spenser Studies* annual (1998) were directly related to Ireland;⁵ while the *Cambridge companion to Spenser* (2001) edited by Andrew Hadfield is awash in historicist readings and Irish content.⁶ For Hadfield, Spenser's interest in England's imperial expansion is crucial to understanding his poetic work. In his book *Spenser's Irish experience: wilde fruit and salvage soyl*, Hadfield argues that *The Faerie Queene* is not a work which deals incidentally with Ireland but one which is framed by its author's Irish experience, a fact registered both in the form and the content of its allegorical design. The poem and its author ceased to be 'mere English' when both left England in the late 1570s or 1580 and were 'corrupted' by their relationship with Ireland.⁷ Hadfield elsewhere alerts the readers of Spenser's epic poem that 'there can be no obvious escape to the peaceful idyll of fairyland' and demands that they 'face up to the reality that even the most apparently innocent and dream-like sections of the poem may be reflections on contemporary political problems.'⁸

While this might appear a contentious statement to some, none can deny the political ramifications of Spenser's prose works, in particular his humanist dialogue *A view of the present state of Ireland* which was entered into the Stationers' Register in 1598. No other single work of Spenser's, with the excep-

---

annotated bibliography', *Irish University Review*, 26:2 (1996), 342–53, and also his 'Spenser and Ireland: a select bibliography', *Spenser Studies*, 9 (1991), 227–42. Pauline Henley's *Spenser in Ireland* (Cork, 1928) remains an insightful introduction to the subject. 3 Greenblatt, *Renaissance self-fashioning*, p. 186. 4 Ibid.; see also David Edwards, 'Ideology and experience: Spenser's *View* and martial law in Ireland', in Hiram Morgan (ed.), *Political ideology in Ireland, 1541–1641* (Dublin, 1991), pp 127–57. 5 Patrick Cullen and Thomas P. Roche (eds), *Spenser studies: a Renaissance poetry annual*, 12 (New York, 1998). 6 Andrew Hadfield (ed.), *The Cambridge companion to Spenser* (Cambridge, 2001). 7 Andrew Hadfield, *Spenser's Irish experience: wilde fruit and salvage soyl* (Oxford, 1997), p. 202. 8 Hadfield,

tion of *The Faerie Queene*, has received more attention recently, and none has been as controversial in its interpretation.[9] At its simplest, the text is a debate in dialogue form between Eudoxus, an English man (good judgment, repute) and Irenius (man of peace, man of anger, man of Ireland), a New English settler in Ireland. The author's intent was apparently 'to persuade those in authority to take the bull by the horns, send over a huge army, and crush Irish resistance to the spread of English authority so that Ireland could be transformed into a land peopled by loyal subjects, profitable to the crown at long last.'[10] Irenius outlines the cultural inferiority of the Irish, the threat of their vulgar society to English civility, the process whereby such cultural 'degeneration' had already taken place with the Old English in Ireland, and the necessity of military force, 'the sword', to transform them into a 'civil' people. The tactics endorsed include brutal war, state-induced famine, dispossession, transplantation, and the elimination of the Gaelic learned and ruling elites.

Even today these sections of Spenser's *View* make for shocking reading and, needless to say, have occasioned much spilt ink in recent years. In debating Spenser's views on Irish cultural inferiority and drastic military measures, scholars have noted Spenser's experiences, his baptism of fire in the brutal wars in Munster, and his schooling in forced starvation at the side of Arthur Grey de Wilton, Lord Deputy of Ireland from July 1580 to August 1582. As Richard Rambuss makes clear, Spenser was no desk-bound secretary but an intimate of the deputy in the field, the keeper of his master's secrets, narrator of his exploits, and paymaster to his intelligence operatives.[11] Literary scholars have also constantly referred to his defense of Lord Grey's methods both in his prose work and in his poetry, arguing convincingly that Book V, especially Cantos xi-xii, of *The Faerie Queene* should be read as a strident defense of Grey and a glorification of his violent government.[12]

His gratitude to Grey in fact prefaces the *The Faerie Queene* in one of the dedicatory sonnets:

Cambridge companion to Spenser, p. 5.   **9** While there has been an extensive debate on this text since Greenblatt's intervention, the most recent and significant Irish contributions remain Nicholas Canny's 'Edmund Spenser and the development of Anglo-Irish identity', *Yearbook of English Studies*, 13 (1983), 1–19, and Ciaran Brady's, 'Spenser's Irish crisis: humanism and experience in the 1590s', *Past and Present*, 111 (1986), 17–49.   **10** Hadfield, *The Cambridge companion to Spenser*, p. 52.   **11** Richard Rambuss, 'Spenser's life and career', in Hadfield, *The Cambridge companion to Spenser*, p. 27. For more detail see the same author's *Spenser's secret career* (Cambridge, 1993).   **12** Hadfield, *Companion to Spenser*, p. 18. See also Willy Maley, *Salvaging Spenser: colonialism, culture and identity* (London, 1997); Edwards, 'Ideology and experience'.

> Most noble lord the pillor of my life
> And patrone of my Muses pupillage
> Through whose large bountie poured on me rife,
> In the first season of my feeble age
> I now doe liue, bound yours by vassalage.[13]

As will become apparent, this defense of Spenser's patron also extended in his writings to a justification for the deputy's actions against the defenseless Spanish and Italian soldiers at Dún an Óir. In fact, one stirring scene in Book V (viii.50, 7–8) of the *Faerie Queene*, where the poet recounts the slaughter of Souldan's men as if they were fleeing goats, is so evocative of contemporary accounts of the melee in the fort of Smerwick that one might speculate that Spenser was there and that the atrocity resonated with him years later:

> Then *Artegall* himselfe discovering plaine
> Did issue forth gainst all that warlike rout
> Of knights and armed men,
> ... and to the Souldan lout:
> All which he did assault with courage stout
> All were they nigh an hundred knights of name,
> And like wyld Goates them chased all about
> Flying from place to place with cowheard shame,
> So that with finall force them all he overcame.[14]

With one modern exception, to whom I will return later, most literary scholars and historians agree that Spenser was probably with Grey during the slaughter and that it did indeed have a profound psychological impact on him.[15] This is in contrast to most early twentieth-century commentators who found Spenser's political associations distasteful, and felt that they and their prose manifestations should best be ignored. Commentators like W.B. Yeats and C.S. Lewis concluded that the poetry should be studied separate from the prose. Yeats wanted readers to distinguish between when Spenser was speaking as a poet from when he was writing as a government official.[16] While W.L. Renwick, who

---

13 A.C. Judson, *The life of Edmund Spenser*, ed. C.G. Osgood, E. Greenlaw, F.M. Padleford, and R. Heffner, *The works of Edmund Spenser: a variorum edition* (10 vols, Baltimore, 1945), vol. 8. For Spenser's factional allegiances see also Clare Carroll and Vincent Carey, 'Factions and fictions: Spenser's reflections of and on Elizabethan politics', in Judith H. Anderson and David A. Richardson (eds), *Spenser's life and the subject of biography* (Amherst, 1996). 14 Edmund Spenser, *The faerie queene* ed. Thomas P. Roche (London, 1978), p. 823. 15 See especially Tom Herron, *Spenser's Irish work: plantation and Reformation in the Faerie Queene* (forthcoming), where he makes a direct association between the Souldan episode where the troops are butchered like goats and Smerwick in the context of Spenser's celebration of slaughter. 16 Andrew Hadfield, 'Introduction: the relevance of Edmund Spenser', in

edited *The view* in the early 1930s, acknowledged the poet's association with the brutality of English rule and even the atrocity at Smerwick, he wanted his readers to understand that it did not taint his mind or his poetry:

> If then we recall Spenser the poet, it is to praise him that amidst such influences ... he should have retained so human an ideal as he expressed in the *The Faerie Queene*, and indeed ... to be glad that his studious turn of mind forced him continually to seek the larger world he could find only in his books; and most of all, to rejoice that the poet in him was never killed, but remained to do his poet's office of testifying to those things which outlast all the schemes of the politicians.[17]

Andrew Hadfield wants us avoid such a bifurcation and demands that we read the poetry and prose together as contemporary political commentaries.[18] Yet even the recent commentators, who meticulously examine Spenser's poetry and prose for political associations, neglect to study the incident at Smerwick itself and few seem aware as to why exactly it exerted such an influence on the participants and their futures.[19]

It is necessary, therefore, that we turn our attention to the windswept western coast of Ireland in early September 1580 where a small force of European Catholics under the command of Colonel Sebastiano di San Giuseppi had been sent by Pope Gregory XIII to assist a rebellion of the Munster Geraldines, the Fitzgerald earls of Desmond, and their followers. After a brief period in the countryside, the continental unit had retreated to a fortification established in 1579 by James Fitzmaurice and an even smaller continental contingent.[20] The early September landing had in fact coincided with the appointment of Lord Arthur Grey de Wilton, whose job it was to crush the growing rebellion. The newly arrived Lord Deputy then set out in late September to destroy this invading force. After a very difficult trek south hampered by swollen rivers and limited food supplies, Grey camped for a few days in Dingle, near Smerwick, to allow reinforcements to catch up and to rendezvous with a naval contingent, before he moved towards the enemy positions.[21] In early November the long-awaited English flotilla arrived under the command of Admiral William Winter and a siege of the fort began. During the night of 7 November, trenches were

---

Hadfield, *The Cambridge companion to Spenser*, pp 3–5. 17 W.L. Renwick, 'Commentary', in *A view of the present state of Ireland* (London, 1934), p. 251. I am grateful to Tom Herron for this reference and for mutinously reading this paper and sharing his knowledge on Grey and Spenser with me. 18 Hadfield, *Cambridge companion to Spenser*, pp 3–5. 19 A notable exception is Ciaran Brady, 'Grey, Arthur, fourteenth baron of Wilton', in A.C. Hamilton (ed.), *The Spenser encyclopedia* (Toronto, 1990), pp 341–2. 20 Colm Lennon, *Sixteenth-century Ireland: the incomplete conquest* (Dublin, 1994), pp 225–6. 21 'Grey to Elizabeth', 12 November 1580 (PRO, SP 63/78/29).

dug and naval artillery was dragged up the rocky and steep shore by Richard Bingham, future President of Connacht, among others. The latter scene is recorded in a coloured sketch preserved in the Public Record Office and reproduced in two colour plates by Colin Martin and Geoffrey Parker in their 1988 book *The Spanish Armada*.[22] As described in Grey's letter of 12 November the English engaged the forward positions of the continental force with arquebus shot, while, as illustrated, the English sailors dragged the guns up the slope. Meanwhile the English ships, the origin of the artillery pieces, lay at anchor close to the shore and also pounded the fort. Drawing his inference from the detail depicted on the map and the formation of the naval flotilla in particular, Tom Glasgow concludes the fort sustained 'murderous fire,' a detail left out of most of the contemporary accounts.[23] The illustration also suggests to us the near-impossible position of the besieged Spanish and Italian force, hemmed in on a rocky peninsula with an English flotilla to their rear on the seaside and on the cliff-face to the right and left, and an English land force blocking their outer-works to the front.[24] It was hardly surprising, then, that after two days of steady bombardment negotiations began on the evening of the 9th, and on the 10th the garrison, at least according to the English sources, surrendered unconditionally.[25]

On the morning of 10 November, Grey and his officers, and presumably his secretary, watched as the continental officers marched forward to surrender 'trayling theyr ensigns rolled'.[26] The lord deputy then sent one of his officers and company into the fort to ensure that the rest of the garrison had laid down their arms. Having ascertained that the armour and weapons of the enemy were taken care of, by assigning officers of gentleman status to guard over both them and the booty, he ordered his bands drawn up, and sent them to execute the defenseless prisoners. There is little dispute as to the nature of the deed. In fact, the only really interesting nugget of information that emerges from at least one of the sources regarding the actual work of killing the 500 or more men, is that the slaughter was carried out by no less a figure than Sir Walter Raleigh, as he and the Midland servitor Captain Macworth were in charge of the executioners. According to Hooker, 'capteine Raleigh together with capteine macworth, who

22 Colin Martin and Geoffrey Parker, *The Spanish Armada* (New York, 1988), colour plates 22 and 23, between pp 112–13. It should be noted that the date attribution of the 5 November for the action is erroneous in that Grey did not engage the continental force until the 7th of the same month. 23 Tom Glasgow, 'Elizabethan ships pictured on Smerwick map, 1580. Background, authentication and evaluation', *Mariner's Mirror*, 52 (1966), 157–65. 24 Glasgow refers to PRO, M.P.F. 75, as his source. Brian Donovan and David Edwards located another version in the National Maritime Museum in London: see *British sources for Irish history, 1485–1641* (Dublin, 1997), p. 173. 25 'Grey to Elizabeth', 12 November 1580 (PRO, SP 63/78/29), also the vivid account in Sir John Pope Hennessy, *Sir Walter Raleigh in Ireland* (London, 1883), pp 207–11. 26 'Grey to Elizabeth', 12 November 1580 (PRO, SP 63/78/29).

had the ward of that daie, entered into the castell & made a great slaughter, manie or the most part of them being put to the sword.'[27] Despite the efforts of the officers, the soldiers, 'pumped up' as they would have to have been to kill up to 600 unarmed individuals, eventually ran amok and pillaged the fort and their victims. On the restoration of order the bodies were disposed of, mostly by being thrown over the cliff, although there is local folklore and emerging forensic evidence that some were interred in a cemetery nearby.[28]

As indefensible as these actions seem today, viewed in the context of the European wars of the age the killing itself and the numbers involved are unremarkable in terms of contemporary military engagements and religiously inspired outrages. Nor would the treatment of the Irish prisoners collected in the fort strike contemporary commentators as shocking: they and the women and children camp followers were simply hanged. The treatment of the Catholic priests who were captured in the fort would not seem remarkable in the Elizabethan Irish context either. As far as the English military were concerned, in the period from 1570 to 1603 there was an open season on 'massing priests'. At Smerwick the recusant prisoners were kept alive for a day, interrogated, allegedly tortured by having their bones broken by a blacksmith's hammer, and finally also hanged from the wall of the fort. The priest, Lawrence More, and the English gentleman, William Wollick, simply joined a long list of Catholic martyrs brutally killed in the line of their work battling what they considered to be a 'heretic' regime.[29]

---

[27] John Hooker, 'The supplie of this Irish chronicle continued from the death of King Henrie the Eight, 1546 untill this present yeare 1586', in Raphael Holinshed, *The second volume of chronicles: conteining the description, conquest, inhabitation, and troublesome estate of Ireland; first collected by Raphael Holinshed and now recognized, augmented and continued from the death of King Henrie the eight untill this present time of Sir John Perot knight, lord deputie: As appeareth in the supplie … by John Hooker alias Vowell gent.* (London, 1586). D.B. Quinn acknowledges that Raleigh's company was sent in to carry out the task, but is uncertain as to its commander's participation in the slaughter: 'It is not certain that Raleigh took a personal part in the massacre, but if he did it was as a soldier under orders, although there is no reason to suppose that he would have objected to his task', in *Raleigh and the British Empire* (London, 1947), pp 33–4.   [28] Anne Lucey, 'Ghosts ride in on a tide of death: coastal erosion dislodges skeletons from seaside medieval burial site', *Irish Independent*, 14 April 2004, p. 11. See also, Isabel Bennett, 'Archaeological investigations at Caherquin, near Ballyferriter, Co. Kerry', *Kerry Archaeological and Historical Society Journal*, 29 (1996), 5–30 I am extremely grateful to René Gapert of Forensic Anthropology Unit, Department of Human Anatomy, University College Dublin, who sent me copies of these two publications. I also want to acknowledge his generosity in sharing with me the results of his ongoing research on skeletal remains from the area, where he has uncovered evidence of sharp weapon trauma.   [29] John Copinger, *The theatre of Catolique and Protestant religion, diuided into twelue books* (Saint-Omer, 1620) pp 578–9. For the most recent and important study of the construct of martyrdom in this context see Clodagh Tait, 'Adored for saints: Catholic martyrdom in Ireland c.1560–1655', *Journal of Early Modern History*, 5:2 (2001), 128–59.

Given this contextual light of the age of religious wars, why should this event still resonate today? As recently as 1998, an American scholar attempted to exonerate both Grey and Spenser and rescue their reputation in the light of the events of the dark and dreary November days of 1580.[30] The simple answer is that, within less than month, the incident had become the focus of a diplomatic dispute in London, when the Spanish ambassador, Bernardino de Mendoza, in a formal complaint to Elizabeth accused her Lord Deputy of bad faith, in that he had promised the garrison their lives but then reneged on his commitment. The hanging of pregnant women was also seen as scandalous.[31] In Catholic international correspondence and news books, de Mendoza's opinion rapidly became enshrined as truth.[32] Spenser in the *View* would later passionately deny 'Grey's bad faith', adding weight to his denial by causing his mouthpiece, Irenius to assert, 'myself being as nar then as any'.[33] Yet this version of Grey's dishonesty became the standard Irish Catholic and protonationalist interpretation. In a 1600 tract, part of an emerging Irish literature of Catholic vindication published in Latin in order to ensure an international audience and support for the Irish cause, then at its height with the rebellion of Hugh O'Neill, earl of Tyrone, Peter Lombard cited Grey's bad faith as typical of English perfidious dealings.[34] Distinctively, the Jesuit, John Howling's, account of the sufferings of Catholic churchmen in Ireland raised Lawrence Moore's sufferings to the status of martyrdom.[35] Not surprisingly, the events at the fort and the issue of Grey's word would make their appearance in the subsequent Irish and English recusant martyrologies written in exile in the continent in the early seventeenth century. In John Copinger's *Theatre of the Catholic and Protestant religion* published in 1620, the slaughter of the garrison was noted, and the torture of the priest elaborated upon.[36] These accounts rapidly achieved the status of orthodoxy in the emerging Irish Catholic continental polemical literature, eventually becoming the staples of Irish nationalist propaganda in the nineteenth century. They also entered Irish folklore, with the expression 'Grey's faith'[37] coming to denote gross dishonesty.

30 Catherine G. Canino, 'Reconstructing Lord Grey's reputation: a new view of the *View*', *Sixteenth Century Journal*, 29 (1998), 3–18.   31 Bernardino de Mendoza to Philip II of Spain, 11 December 1580, *Cal. S.P. Spanish, 1580–86*, as summarized in Alfred O'Rahilly, 'The massacre at Smerwick (1580)', *Journal of the Cork Historical and Archaeological Society*, 42 (1937), 1–15, 65–83.   32 Though the numbers were exaggerated in the Fugger News-Letters, the notion of Grey's 'bad faith' was not present, 'Letter from Antwerp', 24 December 1580, as quoted in O'Rahilly, 'The massacre at Smerwick (1580)', 12–13. 33 Judson, *The life of Edmund Spenser*, p. 92.   34 O'Rahilly, 'The massacre at Smerwick (1580)', 66.   35 Ibid., 70.   36 Copinger, *The theatre of Catolique and Protestant religion*, pp 578–9. For a recent study of English martyrologies, see Sarah Covington, *The trail of martyrdom: persecution and resistance in sixteenth-century England* (Notre Dame, 2003). 37 The expression is first noted in Philip O'Sullivan Beare, *Historiae Catholicae Iberniae compendium* (Lisbon, 1621): see O'Rahilly, 'The massacre at Smerwick (1580)', 67.

In addition, in the Kerry Gaeltacht as late as the end of the nineteenth century, parents are reported to have substituted the traditional phrase of admonishment to children for bad behavior 'cughat and pucha' with the warning 'cughat an Rawley', or watch out for the Raleigh![38]

What the above-noted early modern polemical literature has in common with modern scholarship is the focus on Grey's word, and consequently on Spenser's defense of his reputation. This issue made commentators like W.B. Yeats and C.S. Lewis very uncomfortable, leading them to conclude that the poetry of the period should be studied separate from the prose and the political context that it emanated from.[39] Hadfield, as noted earlier, wants us avoid such a bifurcation and is eager that we read the poetry and prose together as contemporary political commentaries.[40] He has, of course, a good point, but even he, acknowledging the formative experience that this service with Grey was for the poet, and particularly the effect that the atrocity had on his imagination, seems unwilling (like most other literary and historical scholars) to examine the immediate documentation. The basic thrust of most of these literary scholars' efforts seems to concern itself with ascertaining Spenser's presence or absence or, like the Old Historicist biographers of Spenser, Rudolf Gottfried, Raymond Jenkins and Alexander Judson, Grey's guilt or innocence. What is missed in all of this is an opportunity to study in the immediate English sources an equally compelling contemporary reality and worldview. Because what we have in the contemporary English sources is a perpetrator's justification for what we would nowadays call a war crime. By exploring these sources in their immediate context we can come closer to understanding the world inhabited by these literary and historical figures – a more rewarding experience than trying to determine Grey's guilt or innocence. What we find is a rhetoric of participation and deliverance designed not alone to justify the events at Smerwick, but to make comprehensible to the world of contemporary English men and women just how vulnerable their society was to an outside threat, the threat of the 'Antichrist'. Surprisingly, or maybe not surprisingly at all in the European context, what we find is an alternative religious polemic that at first glance seems to be entirely opposite, yet is in fact in many ways similar, to the Catholic examples noted earlier.

This rhetoric of 'deliverance' is immediately evident in Queen Elizabeth's letter of congratulation to Grey written on 12 December 1580:

> As the most happie successe youe have latly had against certaine invad[e]rs sent by the Pope, contayned in yo[u]r l[ette]res brought unto us by our servant [Edward] Denny doth incomparably shew the greatnes

---

38 Sir John Pope Hennessy, *Raleigh in Ireland* (London, 1883). 39 Hadfield, 'Introduction', in *The Cambridge companion to Spenser*, pp 3–5. 40 Ibid.

of God's love and favor towards us; so your care and paine in following the same and courage in execucon thereof deserveth great thancks and commencions at our hands.[41]

This sense of divine intervention is much more evident in the field itself and much more important to us in understanding the motivations of the perpetrators. Writing days after the event on 28 November, Grey asserted that English success against the foreign force could not be attributed to their own efforts 'but of the providence and mighty power of god'.[42] This sense was especially prevalent in the emotive letter sent by Grey to the Queen, the one she refers to above, the day after the executions were completed.[43] The Lord Deputy's account opens with a description of the terrible weather conditions under which the English had marched to Dingle. As the days dragged on the situation worsened for his rain-sodden force, as they were in hostile territory without munitions, siege equipment or basic provisions. Luckily for Grey, Admiral Winter's flotilla arrived in the nick of time and the deputy could begin the siege on 7 November. The strain on the participants is evident as is the sense of release from an invidious threat, represented in providentialist terms.

This is particularly the case in the passages in Grey's letter where he reports on the death of John Cheke, who is noted, 'by God's grace', as the only English casualty of the entire incident. Grey sets the scene by describing the beseigers' efforts to trench their way closer to the fort on the nights of the 7th and 8th. Day and night the garrison poured shot on the trenchers while the forward English companies variously under Denny, Mackworth and Zouche returned fire.[44] Miraculously, the English suffered no casualties, 'as God would, for a good time without hurt', until at daybreak, presumably on the 9th, John Cheeke was shot after carelessly sticking his head over the trench. Grey's reconstruction of the scene for Elizabeth provides him with an opportunity for didactic reflections on God's engagement on the English side:

> [Cheeke] stricken on the head tumbled down at my feet. Dead I took him & for so I caused him to be carried away, yet yt pleaseth God to send him spright again & doth yet in speache & greatest memory that ever was seen wt such a wound ... so disposed to God & made so divine a confession of

---

[41] 'Elizabeth to Grey', 12 December 1580, as transcribed in Hennessy, *Sir Walter Raleigh*, pp 212–14. [42] 'Grey to the Lord Treasurer', 28 Nov. 1580 (BL, Add. MS 3392). On Grey's Puritanism and Smerwick, see Richard McCabe, *Spenser's monstrous regiment: Elizabethan Ireland and the poetics of difference* (Oxford, 2002), pp 83–9. [43] 'Grey to Elizabeth', 12 November 1580, (PRO SP 63/78/29). Geoffrey Fenton also attributed the English success to divine favour: see 'Fenton to Gerrarde', 11 November 1580 (PRO SP 63/78/25). [44] 'Grey to Elizabeth', 12 November 1580, (PRO SP 63/78/29).

his faith, as all divines in either of her maties realms could not have passed, if matched it, So wrought in him Gods spirit, plainly declaring him a child of his elected, to the no les comfort of his good and godly friends then great instruction & manifest motion of every other hearer that stood by, of whom there was a good troupe.[45]

Grey, though apologizing to Elizabeth for his lengthy digression, was eager to frame the events of the preceding hours in terms of divine providence. Cheeke, presumably like Grey, was one of the elect and was so loyal to his monarch that he prayed for her in his death throes. As in the Catholic polemic, here too we have a martyr, a model to be emulated of godly youth and loyal Protestantism, a construction eerily prescient of the death of Philip Sidney at Zutphen in the Netherlands in 1586. This is contrasted sharply with Grey's account of the snivelling and devious efforts of the Spanish and Italian officers to gain mercy after he had ascertained that they were not sent by the king of Spain but by the 'Pope for the defence of the Catholica fede' and so refused them another day to consider surrendering without conditions. In his disdain he describes how Colonel San Giuseppi 'then embraced my knees, simply putting himself to my mercy, onely he prayed yt for yt night hee might abyde in ye fort an yt in ye morning all should be putt into my handes'.[46] Grey prefaces his brief account of the slaughter with his version of the Spanish and Italian officers' justification for landing in Ireland in the first place, affording him an opportunity to suggest they were servants of the Antichrist, not sent by any king and therefore undeserving of mercy.

> [One of them] avouched yt they were all sent by ye Pope for ye defence of ye Catholic fede. My answere was yt I would not greatly haue merveyled yf men being commaunded by naturall & absolute princes did sometimes take in hande wrong actions: but yt men & yt of accoumpt, as some of them made showe of, should be carried unto uniust & wicked actions by one yt nether from God nor man could clayme any princely power or empire, but indeed a destable shaveling ye right Antichriste & generall ambitious tyrant over all right principalities & patrone of Diabolica fede, I could not but greatly reste to wonder.[47]

We of course must wonder if the lord deputy uttered these very words in his encounter with the representatives of the besieged. However, his letter to the queen is suggestive of the intensity of his views about the diabolical nature of his opponents' religion. Grey's laconic description of the slaughter itself unintentionally betrays the intensity of the moment after the surrender and

[45] Ibid. [46] Ibid. [47] Ibid.

securing of the fort when he describes how some of the booty was destroyed. He notes that the soldiers ran amok:

> I sent straight certin gentlemen in to see their weapons and armures layed downe & to gard ye munition & victaile there lefte for spoile. Then putt I in certeyn bandes who straight fell to execution. There were 600 slayne; munition & vittaile great store, though much wasted through the disorder of ye souldier, *w[hi]ch in yt furie could not bee helped* [my italics].⁴⁸

That the soldiers assigned to the task temporarily went berserk cannot be doubted. Nor can the fact that this was an unusual end to a negotiated lifting of a siege, yet for the advanced Protestant Grey, and maybe for some of his fellow officers, this day represented deliverance after a confrontation with the 'darkness' of their enemy, and the awful necessities that combating the Antichrist entailed.⁴⁹ Geoffrey Fenton opened his 11 November letter to Gerrarde with the assertion that 'god hath geven us the expugnation of the forte and the killing of the strangers.'⁵⁰ Grey, in recounting the toil, the weariness and the extremity of their situation, describeed the English common soldiers as virtually naked. He not only allowed for the deed but concluded that it was God's will: 'So hath yt pleased the Lord of hostes to deliver your enemies into [your] Highnes handes'.⁵¹

This sense of heavy responsibility of combating Antichrist is by and large absent from the immediate English reaction to the news of his 'victory'. Evidence that it was heralded in London is provided in a hitherto neglected pamphlet published in early 1581, as *The true reporte of the prosperous successe which God gave unto our English souldiours against the forraine bands of our Romaine enemies, lately ariued (but soon inough to theyr cost) in Ireland in the yeare 1580*.⁵² This pamphlet has rarely been noted in this context, but is important as a source for both the official and popular perception of the sense of deliverance from the threat of foreign invasion occasioned by the Papal landing. Here was Popery in all its 'foreignness, corruption and otherness.'⁵³ Associations with the beast of the Apocalypse are evident in the very poem that opens the work:

---

48 Ibid. **49** Bingham attests to the fury of the killing and the rampage of the common soldiers: '[they] fell to ryvelinge and spoylinge and wit all to kyllinge in wch they never seased whilest ther lyved one,' in 'Bingham to Walsingham', 12 November 1580 (PRO SP 63/78/32). **50** 'Fenton to Gerrarde', 11 November 1580 (PRO SP 63/78/25). **51** 'Grey to Elizabeth', 12 November 1580, (PRO SP 63/78/29). **52** A.M., *The true reporte of the prosperous successe which God gave unto our English souldiours against the forraine bands of our Romaine enemies, lately ariued (but soon inough to theyr cost) in Ireland in the yeare 1580* (London, 1581). **53** Peter Lake and Michael Questier, 'Puritans, papists, and the "public sphere" in early modern England: the Edmund Campion affair in context', *Journal of Modern History*, 72 (2000), 587–672, on 591.

> To rob all princes of their rule and right,
> God of the glory doe to him alone:
> man of soule and Sathan of his might,
> To boulster Rebelles gainst their Princes throne
> To seeke Gods truthe and Gospell to suppresse.
> Let all men judge if this be *Holynesse*
>
> O *Roome*, the roome, where all outrage is wrought,
> The sea of ... the beast with sevenfold head:
> The shop wherein all shame is sould and bought,
> The Cup whence poison through the world is spred,
> Well maist thou draw the simple with a Dreame,
> And ween to win, yet strive against the streame.[54]

The pamphlet's semiofficial status is evident from the fact that the author asserts that his 'sound discourse' was 'presented unto me (by the advertisements of men of good crediti) out of those letters which were sent unto her maiestie' with the express purpose of 'dismaying ... the supersticious disloyall recusant'.[55] The author, probably the controversial polemicist Anthony Munday, goes on to reinforce the providentialist interpretation of the event:

> the Lord Deputie, beeing (in so great disadvauntage) almost in dispayre of dooing any good, was soone recomforted with the happy arriuall of the Queenes Shippes, which it is to be thought that the verie great and woonderfull providence of God (quite beside their expectation) sent thither so luckely for their succour.[56]

And it is certainly clear that the interpretation of events was similar to those of the perpetrators in the camp, obviously emanating from that very source, Lord Grey's letter to the Queen, with editorial comments: 'some presented unto me in writing out of Ireland.'[57] Indeed a cursory examination of the passage quoted below is strongly suggestive of the syntactic resemblances to the passages already noted from Grey's letter.

> Then issued out a braue Italian who ... demaunded by my Lord Deputie who sent him there ... The holy father wyll you (sayd my lord) adventure in the service of a shaveling, an Antichrist, a murtherer both bothe of the soule and body against such a Prince as my mistress is: you shall have the just reward of your service. And requiring him to bring forth the cheefe

---

[54] A.M., *The true reporte of the prosperous successe*, p. A2.   [55] Ibid., p. A2v.   [56] Ibid., p. A3.
[57] Ibid., p. A2v.

of the Spaniardes, he asked the sayd Spaniarde, who sent him thether: he sayd he could not tell Whether the kinge of Spaine: He sayd no: Whether with the kinges knowledge: He answered no: For (sayd he) at Porto in Portugall, the Governor there comanded mee, to go to such a place, where I should receyve my chardge, which I dyd, but whether I should goe, or against whome I knew not, and so brought to this place as blindfold, and (as I see now) utterly betrayed. Then (quoth my Lord) if you be not sent by the king, you come as a runnagate, and will receyve the lyke byer.[58]

Munday, if he is the author, treats of the actual mass killing as an act of military necessity and, somewhat humorously, juxtaposes the wealth of the Continentals with the poverty of the English soldiers as a means of accounting for the 'meleey':

The rest to the number of five hundred and sixe were slaine, and seventeene hanged. The poore English Soldiers that lacked hose and shooes and were barely cloathed by means of this meeley, served to apparell them, *Al modo Italiano*. Wine and Bisket they met with good store, and other victuals for a good space: fowre thousand Armois, with many good peeces, (and as they say) some reasonable share of Ecclesiasticall Italian money.[59]

Though regretting Cheeke's unfortunate death, Munday marvels at the ease with which the fort was eventually won considering, as he relates (or fabricates), the terrible odds against the Elizabethan army. Estimating that it would have cost 10,000 English lives to take the fort, the author concludes that their victory was solely due to divine intervention: 'thus ... we see how God fighteth for us' and with his 'providence and assistaunce' they overcame their superior enemies. In the author's eyes, and in the view of both the ecclesiastical and secular authorities in London, the Spanish and Italians had been 'incited by a blasphemous Antichristian prelate, against a zealous Christian prince', and deserved their fate.[60] In the atmosphere of heightened anti-Catholicism occasioned by the hunt for Edmund Campion, the bishop of London had authorized a series of pamphlets against the Jesuit mission and clearly associated it with the Spanish and Italian landing in Ireland.[61] Munday's offering was more than likely a part of this same campaign – in fact, the title page alludes to another printed pamphlet on the subject, and the words 'Seene and allowed' indicates it had official backing.'[62]

Utilizing the vituperative rhetoric of the Papal Antichrist, Munday and, by extension, the authorities excused the massacre of their foes and the necessity

[58] Ibid., p. A3v. [59] Ibid. [60] Ibid. [61] Edward Arber (ed.), *A transcript of the registers of the Company of Stationers of London 1554–1640* (5 volumes, London, 1875), 2; Lake and Questier, 'Puritans, papists, and the "public sphere"'. [62] A.M., *The true reporte of the*

of eliminating all the rebellious enemies of the regime, those 'whose ensignes they spread on theyr fort, with [his] Crowne, miters, croskeyes and other lyke trumperie',[63] whether in England and Ireland. Munday's text, employing scatalogical word play, derisively attempted to excuse the slaughter of the papal-supported forces at Smerwick: 'which have beene ever sowers of sedition, raisers of rebellion, maineteyners of disobedience, authors of infinite bloudshedding, which is even growne to be the Badge of their Catholike (or rather acolike) profession, and the true segnificance of their holinesse.'[64] As greedy foreigners, supporters of rebellion and Catholic servants of 'an infamous foole', these 'gallants' had no legitimate excuse for being in Ireland, and brought by divine providence to the 'Shipwracke of theyr lyves' deserved no pity.[65]

> Who favours, feares, or followes with desire,
> Thy state, thy strength, thy vaine and wicked reed:
> Deserves dislikes, and iustly dooth acquire,
> The sword, thy swaye, destruction for his meed.
> Let Pope, let Turke, let Sathan rage their fill,
> God keepth us, if we doo keepe his will.[66]

It is of course possible to consider a variety of other more prosaic explanations for Grey's decision to slaughter the unarmed continental prisoners and their Irish allies and camp followers. Grey's military situation in rain-sodden hostile territory was problematic, and the unappealing prospect of moving and feeding 500–600 prisoners may have been a factor in the decision. He also may have deemed the therapeutic effects of a slaughter good for his troops who had had a mauling earlier at Glenmalure and who were clearly hungry and poorly shod and clothed. The boost to morale supplied not alone by the Italian clothing and money, but by the venting of their rage, might have been a factor in his deliberations. Whether field considerations were a factor or not, Grey clearly represented the event in terms of divine deliverance. Munday's pamphlet echoed his thanks to the divine for giving the 'good Captaines and Soldiers' the 'force and power' to overcome the enemy and 'to withstand the assaultes of the Deuill, and the tyranny of Antichrist his dearling (our spirituall enemy).'[67]

Grey's exploits against the Spaniards and Italians at Dún an Óir would join a long list of moments of deliverance, the most notable of which was another occasion when God intervened on the Protestant side at the crisis of the Spanish Armada in 1588. Even before the deliverance from the Armada, Grey's atrocity at Smerwick was celebrated in John Hooker's 1586 'Supplie of the Irish Chronicle', an updating of Holinshed's *Chronicles*. Hooker celebrated Smerwick as a victory, noted John Cheeke's death, and excused the mass killing on the

prosperous successse, title page.   63 Ibid., pp A4–A4v.   64 Ibid., p. A4   65 Ibid., p. A4.
66 Ibid., p. A2   67 Ibid., p. A4v.

basis that the victims were soldiers of the Pope intent on recovering the land of Ireland to 'the holie church of Rome'.[68] The only notable difference in this slightly later account was a greater emphasis on the role of Sir Walter Raleigh in the killing.[69] By 1615, Camden in his *Annales* would make the case that the slaughter was necessary on the grounds of numbers and as a terror to the Irish, but he suggested that his heroine Elizabeth detested the cruelty and that Grey shed tears on deciding to butcher the soldiers:

> But forasmuch as those which yeelded equalled the English in number, and some danger threatened from the Rebels, who were above fifteene hundred strong, and the English were so destitute of [victuals] and apparell, that they were ready to mutine, unless they were relieved out of the fort by the spoyles of the Enemy, and there lacked shipping to carry away the Enemies; it was concluded against the minde of the lord deputie who shed teares, that the captaines should be saved, and the rest promiscously put to the sword for a terrour, and that the Irish should be hanged; which was presently performed: Yet the Queene wished rather it had beene left undone detesting from her heart the cruelty though necessary against those that yeelded themselves, hardly did she allow of the reasons of the slaughter comitted.[70]

Camden's account, written in a time of exhausted peace in Ireland, and peace with Spain, is devoid of the virulent anti-Catholicism of those precarious days of November and December 1580 when Grey wrote to the queen, when the Campion-Jesuit scare was at its height, and when Munday's tract was entered on the Stationer's Register. That the Lord Deputy's and the London-based polemicist's respective texts provided a rationale for slaughter cannot be doubted, nor can the fact that this was a product of a moment of paranoiac crisis for the Protestant state. This pattern of Anti-Catholic polemic was to be nauseatingly repeated throughout the early modern period whenever the establishment felt threatened.[71]

---

68 Hooker, 'The supplie of this Irish chronicle', p. 436.   69 Ibid., p. 439.   70 The quote is from the 1635 English translation: William Camden, *Annales or, the history of the most renowed and victorious Princesse Elizabeth, late Queen of England containing all the important and remarkable passages of state, both at home and abroad during her long and prosperous reign* (London, 1635), p. 215.   71 Versions of this paper were presented to the Folger Shakespeare Library colloquium, the English department at the University of Maryland College Park, the British History Seminar at Princeton University, and to the Yale Genocide Studies Program Seminar. I am grateful for the critical comments of Anna Battigelli, Karl Bottigheimer, Sarah Covington, Tom Herron, Ben Kiernan, and Claude Rawson. I also want to thank the National Endowment for the Humanities and the staff of the Folger Shakespeare Library for the luxury of a Long-Term Fellowship for the 2001–2 academic year when the research for this essay was carried out.

'Slán Dé fút go hoíche':[1] Hugh O'Neill's murders

HIRAM MORGAN

As regards killing people, Hugh O'Neill (1550–1616) was a typical Irish dynast and warlord. His actions were undertaken on the grounds of expediency and political necessity rather than mere cruelty. Generally it is Shane O'Neill who has gained a reputation for violence but Hugh also was a past master of it. And like all great men, he never committed such acts himself – others committed them on his behalf. O'Neill lived in a violent place in violent times. Sixteenth-century Ireland was seeing unparallelled militarization – frequent and often large English troop movements, continuous Scots mercenary recruitment and increasing local mobilisation. Furthermore experience of Shane O'Neill had shown the young Hugh that violence was an integral part of the Irish political process – that it was either 'kill or be killed'. In 1558 Hugh's father Matthew, baron of Dungannon, having been driven out of Tyrone, was assassinated by Shane.[2] In 1562 Hugh's elder brother Brian, attempted to enter Tyrone during Shane's absence at court, and was murdered by Shane's deputy, Turlough Luineach O'Neill. In 1567 Shane himself met a sudden and violent death at the hands of the MacDonnells.[3] It was this event which provided the opportunity for the return of Hugh O'Neill to the North as a government counter-weight against Shane's tanaiste and successor, the Strabane-based Turlough Luineach O'Neill. As William Camden, the chronicler of Queen Elizabeth's reign, states 'Hugh, commonly called Baron of Dungannon, nephew to Shane by Matthew his base brother, a young man then little set by, who proved afterward the disturber, yea the plague of his Country, was received into grace of Queen Elizabeth, that she might have one to oppose against Turlough, if he should chance to fall away from his duty'.[4] In Hugh's subsequent pursuit of power the

---

1 'God's defiance to you till nightfall' – the earl's alleged farewell to Phelim McTurlough O'Neill just prior to his murder by the O'Hagans. The original deposition of Ever O'Neill (PRO SP 63/170, 1) reads 'Slean diu fuid go hie'; the title version has been supplied by Dr Kevin Murray of the Department of Irish, UCC. 2 *AFM*, s.a. 1558, pp 1562–5. 3 *AFM*, s.a. 1567, pp 1618–21. 4 William Camden, *History of the most renowned and victorious princess Elizabeth, late Queen of England* (London, 1675), p. 106.

only difference from the violent political activism of predecessors such as Shane O'Neill was his need to justify or have authorization for his actions.

In Giraldus Cambrensis's famous depiction of Irish barbarity, one particular nasty trait attributed to his subjects was a propensity for treachery coupled with a penchant for carrying axes and using them at the first opportunity. 'Their arts are therefore more to be feared than their arms, their friendship than their firebrands, their sweets more than their bitters, their malignity more than their martial spirit, their treachery than their open attacks, their specious friendship than their spiteful enmity'.[5] As a result, the frequency of political murder in Gaelic Ireland had been seized upon by Giraldus and the English colonial commentators who followed him as a means of portraying the natural order in Ireland as murderous and barbarous. This paper investigates a number of murders in which Hugh O'Neill was implicated to ascertain his level of responsibility and, where he did claim responsibility, to assess his justifications. Murder was a last resort and it is interesting that the most notorious cases date from the time of his revolt against the state. The more usual method of controlling opponents was to take hostages from them as pledges for good behaviour. Imprisonment involved a greater degree of force because it mandated compliance upon the opponent's followers to ensure their leader's safety. The ultimate exaction was murder, and there are plenty of earlier examples of this method being used against political opponents scattered throughout the Gaelic annals. However, it was not necessarily as effective as a compliant living opponent because the Gaelic system would invariably throw up another rival as head of a competing sept or as lord of a resisting lordship. Hugh O'Neill used all these traditional methods – the problem was he now had to justify himself in the new world being wrought by the centralising state in Europe. In this respect a better guide to his actions – since they were calculated rather than random – might be the Renaissance statecraft of Machiavelli rather than the bigoted musings of the medieval Welsh cleric.

As regards justification, O'Neill could claim for long periods of his career that he was an acknowledged agent of the crown with the task of opposing Turlough or withstanding the alleged trouble-making potential of the sons of Shane O'Neill. By 1580, Hugh's ambition was already clearly evident to the crown when he proposed to become Turlough Luineach's tanaiste by marrying his daughter. However, on the outbreak of the Desmond revolt in Munster a rapprochement was attempted, with the baron offering to defend the Pale in return for more troops in government pay. Lord Justice Pelham provided 25 horsemen but the proposed marriage was not finally called off until the arrival

---

5 Giraldus Cambrensis, *The topography of Ireland*, trans. Thomas Forrester (In Parenthesis Publications, Medieval Latin Series, Cambridge, Ontario, 2000), p. 76 (www.yorku.ca/inpar/topography_ireland.pdf, accessed 2 April 2007).

of Lord Grey.⁶ The baron struck a better deal with Grey than had been offered by Pelham but in the first instance he was forced under pressure from Turlough to withdraw from the province and spent six weeks campaigning in Munster – though he had returned North by the time of the Smerwick massacre. He made a good impression under Grey, who described him as 'the only Irish nobleman that hath done any service and drawn blood since my coming'.⁷ Now with an allowance for 100 footmen, 50 horsemen and sundry officers, the baron made an excellent job of defending the Pale (in his own interests, of course, because he was extending his influence over the Irish border lords as he did so).⁸ Early in Lord Deputy Perrot's government, the baron's area of responsibility was transformed into a lieutenancy covering that part of Ulster which had been shired as counties Armagh and Monaghan.⁹ It is not clear whether the commission for peacekeeping on the borders of the Pale or the subsequent lieutenancy included martial authority but certainly the baron was afforded considerable discretionary powers. However, when Hugh subsequently gained recognition as earl of Tyrone and then succeeded to his grandfather's lands, the government began to take measures to contain his growing power and shore up Turlough instead. It was in these circumstances that we must investigate the Inishowen massacre.

THE MASSACRE OF ARMADA SURVIVORS

It was standard practice in the early modern period to liquidate invading foreigners. For instance, Spanish forces executed the 250 males in the Huguenot colony at Port Royal in Florida in 1565. When the French ambassador complained to the Spanish king, Philip II defended the action as 'exemplary punishment', because 'to preserve kingdoms and states it is sometimes necessary to depart from the norm in order to repel aggression'.¹⁰ The same grounds – reasons of state – would have justified the actions taken by English officers at Smerwick in 1580 (discussed by Vincent Carey in this volume) and again against Armada survivors in 1588. In the latter case, however hapless the shipwrecked Spaniards seemed, there was always the possibility that they might unite into a bigger force succoured by the local Irish or that they might merely be the precursors of a better organized invasion force. Therefore from the standpoint of the English crown and its officers in Ireland there could be no half-measures. Ostensibly the Inishowen massacre looks similar to crown actions

6 PRO SP 63/70, 22; J. Hogan and N.M. Farrell (eds), *The Walsingham letter-book or register of Ireland, May 1578 to December 1579* (Dublin, 1959), pp 252–3.   7 PRO SP 63/79, 5.
8 PRO SP 63/80, 25(2); PRO SP 63/104, 28; *The Irish Fiants of the Tudor sovereigns* (Dublin, 1994), no. 4054.   9 PRO SP 63/105, 87–9.   10 Quoted in Henry Kamen, *Philip of Spain* (London, 1998), p. 110.

in Connacht against other groups of Armada survivors, but in Ulster it was intimately bound up with the succession crisis then taking place.

The earl's composition forces – soldiers flying the Queen's colours though in the pay of Ulster lords – committed the biggest single massacre of Armada survivors. The sick, bedraggled, hungry men who managed to disembark from *La Trinidad Valencera* foundering on the coast of Inishowen in early September 1588 were at first succoured by the local 'savage people' as they called them – the O'Dohertys. But when they marched inland, they were encountered in open, boggy ground by 150 troops led by Richard and Henry Hovenden and possibly an equal number of O'Donnell's men. The Spanish officers, Alonso de Luzon, Master of the Camp of the Tercio of Naples, and Baltaser del Árbol, Sergeant-Major of the Tercio, who were taken prisoner and later interviewed at Drogheda, gave their number as 450,[11] though the Hovendens thought that 'they were in number above 600 men'. The Hovendens sent to Dungannon and Dublin for assistance and sounded their drums as a signal for a parley with the Spaniards.[12] Juan de Nova, an escapee, told his debriefers in the Spanish embassy in Paris that negotiations were carried on with John Kelly, the Hovendens' lieutenant, but Sergeant-Major Árbol, imprisoned at Drogheda, said the negotiations were with O'Donnell and his wife, with Henry Hovenden interpreting in Latin and Richard in French. At first the Spaniards refused to surrender and eventually there was a night-time skirmish in which a number of Armada men were killed and wounded.

The Spanish commanders decided to surrender after another parley in which a number of promises were made to conduct them to the viceroy in Dublin. However, according to Nova's report, as soon as the Hovendens' men had taken charge of them, 'they fell upon the Spaniards in a body and despoiled them of everything they possessed, leaving them quite naked and killing those who offered the least resistance'. When the Spanish commander complained, Kelly replied that the soldiery had acted without orders and promised no further maltreatment, but according to Luzon and Arbol, Kelly was the chief despoiler of a large amount of money and valuables. On the following morning the Spanish officers and notables were separated and placed inside a square of armed men. 'The remaining soldiers were then made to go into an open field, and a line of the enemy's harquebussiers approached them on one side and a body of his cavalry on the other, killing over 300 of them with lance and bullet'. One hundred and fifty of the Spaniards managed to escape across a bog and sought refuge in a castle held by Bishop Redmond O'Gallagher who arranged for the conveyance of many of them, including Juan de Nova, to Scotland. In Scotland Nova was told by 'a savage who spoke Latin' that 'the man who had ordered all the soldiers to be murdered was an Irish Earl named O'Neill'.[13]

11 PRO SP 63/137, 15 & 16.   12 PRO SP 63/136, 36(2) & 43(12).   13 *Cal. of Spanish State Papers, Eliz., 1587–1603*, pp 506–10.

The only other account of this incident is a letter from Dungannon written by the Hovendens to Lord Deputy Fitzwilliam. They related the skirmish and surrender but not the massacre:

> the same night about midnight we did skirmish with them for the space of ii hours and in that skirmish did slay their lieutenant of the field and above twenty more besides the hurting of a great number of their men. So as the next day they were forced to yield themselves and we lost but one man.

This may not have been an attempt to conceal the fact – the reader should easily have inferred as much since the Hovendens said they had originally encountered 600 Spaniards and that O'Donnell was now on his way to Dublin with a small number of them as prisoners. 'The best of them seemeth to carry some kind of majesty and hath been governor of thirty thousand of men this xxiiii years past; the rest of the prisoners are men of great calling and, such as (in our opinions) are not amiss to be questioned withal.'[14]

Who had ordered the massacre? The information Nova received in Scotland probably came from a McLean source hostile to the earl. The Hovendens would have had time to send for further instructions from the earl in Dungannon. But Henry Hovenden, the earl's secretary and right-hand man, was on the spot and so this may have not been deemed necessary. We know from a later instance when Art McBaron, his half-brother, took the Blackwater fort in 1595 (discussed below) that the earl was unabashed when it came to recommending the killing of common soldiers.[15] In this case it would have been militarily stupid to repatriate trained soldiers to an enemy country, and equally would have involved huge expense to feed, clothe and imprison these men in the long term. Therefore it was more expedient to kill them there and then. That would be the case if they were killed in the interests of the English crown. However, it is far more likely that they were instead killed to prevent them being recruited by Turlough Luineach to fight against the earl.

In the event, the actions of the earl's men served as a demonstration of his loyalty at a moment of crisis for the Tudor state. Furthermore, the earl sought to benefit from the situation because the prisoners were surrendered in the hope – vain as it transpired – that his son-in-law Red Hugh O'Donnell might be released as a result. In 1594, when airing his grievances to the state, the earl effectively claimed responsibility for the massacre. He said the troops were led by his foster-brothers and complained that he did not receive some 'part of the ransom of those prisoners which was great' as recompense for a service done by soldiers fitted out at his own charges.[16] The earl may indeed have had cause

14 PRO SP 63/136, 43(12).   15 PRO SP 63/178, 53(5).   16 Lambeth Palace Library (Carew Papers) MS 617, f. 206.

to feel aggrieved because at the time of the Armada crisis the state did not believe him. At that stage the Dublin government, with only a small number of troops under their own command, were very jittery as large numbers of shipwrecked Spaniards began to come ashore in Ireland. The reports were confusing, escalating in scale, and coming at them from all quarters. In September, when the Inishowen landing was first reported, the Irish Council was sending Sir Henry Bagenal to help the earl and his foster-brothers, who were already in O'Doherty's country dealing with the Spaniards, but by October they were increasingly worried about their loyalty.[17] The Irish Council informed London that 'for just causes we have conceived in this time, we have an especial distrust in the earl of Tyrone', and these fears are manifest in the annotations to the letters they enclosed in which the earl and his commanders had asked for extra munition, men and authority. They wanted more gun-powder sent from Dublin, another company established under John Kelly, and martial law to stop men deserting.[18]

The problem was that the Irish Council was not sure – initially at least – whether the bulk of the Spaniards in Inishowen had in fact been massacred. The Lord Deputy thought the Hovendens' 'report in their first letters was so untrue for the killing of Spaniards as maketh me now both loath and afraid to send them powder, match or shot'. Furthermore, the earl was reporting that another 1,500 Spaniards had landed in north-west Donegal. On the earl's request for 'a commission to my self to serve not only against the Spaniards but also against all those that taketh their parts and to take victuals where I can during the time of my abode at that service', Lord Deputy Fitzwilliam postilled with this suspicious note: 'If I should grant the earl this commission and liberty, no doubt he would use it against T O'Neill and such other as be his enemies. And that under colour of feeding and relieving the Spaniards.'[19] The examinations of Luzon and Árbol were full of questions which evidenced mistrust of the earl about how much money he may have acquired from the Spaniards and how many prisoners remained with him.[20] Fitzwilliam's doubts would have been fuelled further by the fact that Luzon had not witnessed the actual massacre of the common soldiers and that Árbol's report about 100 surviving the slaughter was secondhand.[21] The major cause of these fears was probably the reports reaching Dublin from Governor Bingham in Connacht who was deeply distrustful of the earl and his fosterbrothers in their dealing with the Spaniards. His intelligencers were intimating that O'Donnell was discontented – presumably because he had returned empty-handed from Dublin – and that the earl had bitterly reproved him 'for doing service upon the Spaniards saying that he and his posterity may go seek a dwelling in another country, for that they

17 PRO SP 63/136, 36 & 36(1–6). 18 PRO SP 63/137, 10 & 10(1–3, 9). 19 PRO SP 63/137, 10(8). 20 PRO SP 63/137, 14. 21 PRO SP 63/137, 15 & 16.

had betrayed the Spaniards, who were their best friends and their only refuge in all extremities'.[22] This alleged criticism of O'Donnell is unlikely, given the Hovendens' involvement in summary dispatch of the Inishowen survivors. The earl certainly did not join up with the remaining Spaniards as the state had feared but he did assist individual Spaniards. The deponents in Drogheda reported that on their way from Inishowen Don Alvero Mendoza, Don Antonio Manrique and Don Rodrigo Ponce de León had been left behind at Dungannon as they were too sick to travel further, along with, according to Luzon and Árbol, one or more common soldiers who were in a similarly bad condition. When the earl informed Fitzwilliam 'Your lordship wrote unto me for executing such Spaniards as are remaining in the country, but vi or vii who were very sick, whereof there be but three alive and are not like to recover', the Lord Deputy added this note for Burghley 'These three that remain alive are still with him and shalbe if they die not, and whether the other four be dead or not it is to be doubted, as after in some other letters, by report of a friar shall appear to your lordship.'[23] This was a reference to the earl's reproof to O'Donnell, news of which had been carried by a friar.

It appears that the earl tried to have it all ways – to prove his loyalty to the English, to deny trained troops to Turlough Luineach, and also to get into the good books of the Spaniards. Fitzwilliam, despite his fears at the time, visited Dungannon soon afterwards and accepted the earl's *bona fides* and entertainment, and probably a large bribe as well.[24] We do know for certain that the earl at this time acquired a faithful manservant in Pedro Blanco who had survived the wreck of the *Juliana* on Streedagh strand, Co. Sligo. When, years later, Blanco asked the earl, then exiled in Rome, to provide a testimonial on his behalf to the Spanish king, he wrote somewhat disingenuously that whereas the English had beheaded any Spanish survivors who were wandering and lost, he had on the contrary 'received all of those who reached my lands and kept them with me until some died fighting valiantly in my wars and others returned to Spain'.[25] More critically at the time, the McShanes alleged that the earl had succoured and forwarded to Scotland at least one Spanish nobleman and that a messenger of his being sent to Spain was captured in Scotland.

HUGH GAVELACH McSHANE

These allegations had begun when Hugh Gavelach McShane O'Neill had returned to Ireland after 18 months' exile with his cousin Lachlan McLean of

---

22 PRO SP 63/137, 10(4–6).   23 PRO SP 63/137, 10(1).   24 *Cal. S.P. Ire., 1588–92*, pp 94–5.   25 M. Kerney-Walsh, *Destruction by peace: Hugh O'Neill after Kinsale* (Armagh, 1986), pp 369–70.

Duart in Scotland at the beginning of February 1589. He took refuge under Turlough Luineach who in turn had released Gavelach's brother, Conn McShane, from captivity and given them both free range against the earl. There were at least eight, possibly ten sons of Shane O'Neill with whom the earl had to contend: Shane Óg and Henry were sons of Catherine McDonnell; Hugh Gavelach and Art were sons of Catherine McLean; while Conn was his son by the daughter of Shane Óg Maguire. The other sons, Brian, Edmond and Turlough, along with Niall and Cormac who were recorded only in the Carew geneaology, were less important and were presumably the offspring of less prominent women. Including many other fosterers both within and without the lordship of Tyrone, all the McShanes had a strong connection with the O'Donnellys who were the hereditary marshals of Tyrone and leaders of the O'Neill cavalry.[26] Miler Magrath, the government's chief informant on the background to Ulster politics and an old partisan of Shane's, noted 'the said sons of Shane O'Neill are taken amongst the Irishry to have more right than any other to the principality in that country, for that they have descended by the right line from the O'Neill's principal house by many descents, and so they think no right against themselves'.[27]

It was Turlough Luineach's plans to make Shane Óg tanaiste in 1578/9 that had prompted Hugh O'Neill to make overtures to his long-standing rival. Turlough's slackening grip on the reins of power and the growing threat of the McShanes backed by their Scottish allies, the McLeans, had enabled Hugh to occupy central Tyrone in 1584–5, and the Dublin government had acquiesced in this partly out of impotence and partly out of fear that the McShanes were a much worse alternative than the earl. At this time the state had Art McShane in the jail of Dublin Castle and Turlough Luineach now handed Henry over to them as well. The state could now hold these men as counters against the earl. When Henry Hovenden petitioned London for the earldom's lands for his master, he also requested on his behalf 'that the Traitor Shane O'Neill his two sons that are in the castle of Dublin may reap the due reward of their father and their own defects and that there may be direction sent unto Lord Deputy to end them'. He adverted to the disturbances the McShanes caused when they were free and claimed that whilst they still lived their followers always lived in expectation of their liberty and, as such, their very existence was a brake on the earl's civilizing mission in Ulster.[28] Of course, Hovenden also wanted rid of these men because the state was in fact holding them as counters against the earl himself. As Turlough's power continued to wane in the later 1580s, the only way he could fight back was increasingly to let the McShanes and their followers off the leash. In 1589 there was turmoil as the Hovendens and the McShanes, both

---

26 H. Morgan, *Tyrone's rebellion: the outbreak of the Nine Years War in Tudor Ireland* (Woodbridge, 1993), pp 92–4.   27 *Cal. S.P. Ire, 1588–92*, p. 497.   28 PRO SP 63/117, 53.

backed by composition bands and Scots mercenary forces, battled it out for supremacy in West Tyrone.[29]

Almost immediately on his return, Hugh Gavelach wrote to Fitzwilliam for a safe-conduct to Dublin; the deliverer of his letter claiming that the earl had practised with Spain and that Gavelach had apprehended in Scotland and brought over with him the messenger the earl had sent to Spain.[30] As a result, Gavelach travelled to Dublin in April:

> Hugh Gavelach hath upon protection been before me and the council, who with myself having perused such letters as he brought with him and further heard his own speeches, we cannot find but all this is a mere practice proceeding from the great and inveterate malice which Sir Turlough and the sons of Shane O'Neill and their race have ever borne against the honour and well-doing of the Earl.[31]

Though the Lord Deputy did not entirely dismiss the allegations, he and his colleagues were very unwilling to act because they feared that the McShanes, who allegedly had a strong popular constituency in Tyrone, might overthrow Turlough completely, cause troubles, bring in Scots mercenaries and return Ulster to Irish government.[32] Hugh Gavelach had another opportunity when he travelled with Turlough to Drogheda in May 1589 and made his allegations directly against the earl, this time bringing with him as a witness 'a man of this country birth who was with him in Scotland'. 'They have both been heard at large in council, where the matter not appearing so full as was expected, Hugh hath desired that another man might be examined, by whom it seemeth he pretendeth to fortify the information further, which is granted to him'.[33]

At the beginning of 1590 the earl executed Hugh Gavelach. Owen Wood reported to the former Lord Deputy, Sir John Perrot, that: 'The earl of Tyrone has hanged Hugh Gavelach, first taken by Maguire and purchased there hence to be executed on a thorn tree and some say with the earl's own hands, the deputy storms at it but your honour knoweth his counsels will be swallowed'.[34] Gavelach had been captured by one of the Maguires around the Catholic Christmastime and was handed over to the earl in exchange for a number of horses and cows.[35] The Lord Deputy and Council demanded a stay of execution and his handing over in Dublin. Meanwhile, the O'Donnellys, Gavalach's foster-brothers and hereditary marshals of Tyrone, reportedly made great offers (300 horses and all their creaghts amounting to 5000 cows) to have him

29 PRO SP 63/158, 47; 161, 46; Lambeth (Carew) MS 605, f.178. 30 PRO SP 63/142, 12 & 12 (1–4). 31 PRO SP 63/143, 46. 32 PRO SP 63/142, 12; PRO SP 63/144, 38. 33 PRO SP 63/144, 38. 34 PRO SP 63/150, 21. 35 PRO SP 63/150, 71. On the use of the Gregorian calendar by Catholics in the ecclesiastical province of Armagh, see H. Morgan, 'Calendars in conflict: dating the battle of Kinsale', *History Ireland*, 10:2 (2002), 16–20.

released.³⁶ However, the earl went ahead and executed him. Later in Dublin when he was forced to answer for his behaviour, the Lord Deputy and Council were remarkably lenient in allowing Tyrone to enter into a recognisance of £2000 and giving him license to travel to England to explain himself.³⁷ There is considerable evidence to suggest that the earl was bribing these top officials. Thomas Lee states that Lord Deputy Fitzwilliam 'most unconscionably in respect of a great bribe hath pardoned the heinous offence'.³⁸ Fitzwilliam and Lord Chancellor Loftus even wrote the earl letters of introduction for him to give Lord Burghley when he reached court.³⁹

The earl gave a more detailed explanation at court. Whereas his critics held the killing of Gavelach up as an atrocious act of murder perpetrated against a political opponent, the earl here had the opportunity to represent his action as that of a servitor of the state forwarding the task of reforming Ulster by removing a mass murderer. Tyrone claimed that a first communication from Loftus acknowledging Hugh Gavelach's apprehension had merely advised against executing the captive, and that the Lord Deputy's letter forbidding an execution only arrived eight or nine days after the event. He said that the execution was carried out because:

> Hugh Gavelach had many ways provoked me to do my uttermost for his apprehension and execution by committing many notable murders and spoils upon the poor followers of my country of which I complained by my letters to the Lord Deputy and after that to my honourable good friend Sir Thomas Cecil at his being at Dungannon where testimony was produced that many women and infants were by him murdered, besides others that with great wounds had escaped his fury. For which respects I had an eye unto him, as to the chief disturber of the country and the peace thereof, and therefore procured his apprehension by all the means I could.

When he did finally lay hands upon him, the execution was delayed for a fortnight – the earl claimed that he made this decision on receipt of the letter from Loftus. What is apparent is that the earl was considering an offer from Brian McShane, who had already submitted to his government, that if Hugh Gavalach was spared, Gavalach and Conn, like Brian, would also submit to the earl with each of them taking turns to stand hostage for the other two. Hugh Gavelach swore an oath to undertake this and agreed to the deadline for its ratification. Conn met the earl to discuss the deal but then refused to comply after failing to get Turlough Luineach's approval. As a result Hugh Gavelach, after the expiration of the fourteen days' grace, was executed by Melaughlin and Cormac McMurrehy before the earl and 100 chief men of the country.

36 PRO SP 63/150, 27 & 28.   37 PRO SP 63/150, 75; BL Add. MS 19,837, f. 876.   38 BL, Harleian MS 35 ff 258–65.   39 PRO SP 63/150, 78 & 80.

In justification, the earl claimed that, in absence of the common law, he had a right to do what he had either by Gaelic custom or as the queen's lieutenant:

> I am not altogether ignorant but that in the strict course of her majesty's laws I might be reprehensible for this execution. Nevertheless I humbly desire that consideration may be had to the place where this fact was done, and to the person – a notable murderer – and to the ancient form of government amongst us in Ulster where there is neither magistrate, judge, sheriff nor course of the laws of this Realm, but certain customs by which both O'Neill, and I and others of our sort do govern our followers. Neither have we at any time been restrained from executing evil doers nor of such as be invaders of our country or professed enemies of the same ... And I hope also that her majesty will consider that as her highness lieutenant under her deputy (as I take myself within mine own territory) I am bound to do justice upon thieves and murderers, otherwise if I be restrained from such like executions and liberty left to O'Neill, O'Donnell and others to use their ancient customs, then should not I be able to defend my country from their violence and wrongs. But whensoever a general order shall be taken for that province to be governed by law, as other the reformed parts of that Realm now is, I will be more forward than any other of my sort to accomplish all her majesty's directions.[40]

To get out of his predicament at court, the earl was forced by the Privy Council to agree to a number of articles to abolish Gaelic customs and to speed up the introduction of English law. This included his agreement not to interfere with the uirríthe and:

> that he forbear to execute any person taken for murder or felony within his country, but by due course of law, except he have from the Lord Deputy under the broad seal, commission of martial laws and that to be qualified by instructions and limitations as the state shall think good, and in that manner the Lord Deputy is to grant it unto him'.[41]

Captain Thomas Lee in his 1594 'Brief Declaration of the Government of Ireland' claimed that the earl had had the power of martial law taken away from him as a result of his using it to execute Gavelach.[42] However the Privy Council article quoted here, and the earl's own exculpation above, would seem to

---

40 PRO SP 63/151, 20.   41 Cambridge University Library, Kk 1.15.5 ff 15–6.   42 Lee, 'A brief declaration of the government of Ireland ... 1594', in J. Lodge (ed.), *Desiderata curiosa Hibernica* (2 vols, Dublin, 1772), 1, pp 107–8. For more on Thomas Lee see H. Morgan, 'Tom Lee: the posing peacemaker', in B. Bradshaw, A. Hadfield and W. Maley (eds), *Representing Ireland* (Cambridge, 1993), pp 132–65.

indicate that he did not in fact have the explicit right to exercise martial law at the time of the execution. Two years' later Sir Henry Bagenal, who could see precious little progress towards the implementation of the articled agreement with the Privy Council, made a statement in terms similar to the earl's own exculpation in London. However, he plainly regarded the earl's local authority not as a temporary expedient pending the establishment of crown government, but rather as the major impediment to reform in Ulster. He noted that the greatness of the O'Neills had over a long time won 'an opinion of sovereignty' among the Irish and that whilst 'the earl of Tyrone is suffered at his pleasure to rule and impose by way of fine, loss of limb or life (the very marks and signs of sovereignty), it were a great vanity to expect any sound or settled reformation in other places'.[43]

Just as the earl was about to take his leave of the court he was prevented from doing so by the arrival of Conn McShane who presented further allegations against him. From the list of crimes presented by Conn it appeared that, far from promoting crown government and English law in Ulster, the earl was actually strengthening his own authority and actively undermining reform. Besides hanging Hugh Gavelach, Conn also claimed that the earl had earlier hanged another McShane – Edmond – and had encouraged Maguire to kill Conn himself. In another article he asserted that 'the earl of mere malice did hang with his own hands and partly upon his own back, one Patrick O'Hanlon without any kind of authority', in revenge for O'Hanlon's killing of a friend of his whom McShane described as 'a common disturber of the English Pale'. There is no independent corroboration of these last two events. Furthermore Conn gave more details of the earl's assistance to a Spanish nobleman, Don Antonio Manicio, about whom Hugh Gavelach had presented evidence to the Lord Deputy.[44] Conn, on earlier seeking permission from Fitzwilliam to travel to England, had claimed that it was Hugh Gavelach's knowledge of the earl's treacherous dealings with the Spaniards that had led to his execution by 'usurpative tyranny'.[45] According to Sir James Perrot, the earl at court denied some of charges made by Conn and subtly excused and evaded the rest. He claimed that the McShanes mortally hated him because he was keeping them from the usurped title of O'Neill. As a result:

> the Queen and her council through the persuation of Tyrone's power and the protestation of his innocency – who still avowed his great desire to do service unto the state and to keep that country – were induced to pass over this accusation and to accept of his submission, offered in the humblest manner.[46]

43 *Cal. S.P. Ire., 1588–92*, p. 459.   **44** Sir James Perrot, *The chronicle of Ireland, 1584–1608*, ed. H. Wood, (Dublin, 1933), pp 65–7.   **45** PRO SP 63/155, 20 & 20(1).   **46** Perrot, *Chronicle of Ireland*, p. 67.

In retrospect, the negotiations which the earl had with two other McShanes with regard to the fate of their brother seem quite plausible since imprisonment was the earl's preferred method of dealing with the McShanes during the Nine Years War. During negotiations, the crown's representatives frequently demanded their handing over as token of good faith. The earl was never likely to do this in case they would be used as leverage against him. By the same token, there was never any likelihood that he would have complied with the state's demand in this regard when it first heard of Hugh Gavelach's apprehension. Indeed the long-term imprisonment of the McShanes, like the execution of their brother, was simply another example of the earl's exercise of sovereignty. When the earl and Red Hugh O'Donnell complained to government commissioners in 1596 about the apprehension and detention of the latter in Dublin Castle, they were reminded that it was a matter of policy and power which they themselves exercised: 'all princes in policy may and do use to take their subjects in pledge for the good peace of their countries and you both do use the like and therefore should less dislike that course'.[47]

KILLING COLLABORATORS

In 1593 the earl had, with the help of Red Hugh, whose escape from Dublin Castle he had aided and abetted, finally ousted Turlough Luineach to gain control in Ulster. However, he now had to turn his attentions to the development of a strategy to prevent the government's reform project from diminishing his new-found power. The government plan was the piecemeal reform of Ulster along the lines of the transformation of the Oriel lordship of the McMahons into the county of Monaghan, achieved in 1589–90 by executing the ruling lord and breaking up the lordship. A major beneficiary of this developing process was Sir Henry Bagenal, nominal chief commissioner of Ulster and would-be provincial president, with the sort of powers which the earl had been denied or deprived of in London.[48] He was building on his father, Nicholas's, power base in the Newry area and had succeeded to his job as Marshal of the Queen's army in Ireland. In the process, Bagenal used as his tools many minor lords, often former dependents of the O'Neills, to advance government reform. In the new settlement of Monaghan the earl was himself a loser – he lost the traditional dues of one of the uirríthe and some lands held by the O'Neills in mortgage from the McMahons that had been deemed to be inside the new county and were granted instead to Bagenal. As in many cases before and after, the earl operated through proxies whose actions he would then deny. In the case of Monaghan, his bastard son, Conn Mac an Íarla, was accused in the July 1592 of

47 CUL, Kk 1.15.63, f.140.   48 Morgan, *Tyrone's rebellion*, pp 61–81.

taking a great prey from the lands of Patrick McKenna in the barony of Trough while the freeholders were at the court sessions then meeting in Monaghan town.[49] The court broke up in panic – Fitzwilliam denounced it as a satanic attempt 'to subvert the young and weak planted good estate of Monaghan'.[50] The earl excused the action as merely a hot pursuit of 'a notorious thief' by Conn and two other horsemen into the neighbouring county. Earlier, at the time of the Monaghan settlement, as a sign of his dissatisfaction, the earl had claimed that he should been given a large parcel of lands in lieu of the dowry of his daughter when she had married its former patentee, Sir Ross McMahon, and interestingly this is reiterated in the same letter as this weak excuse.[51] When the government sent Captain Humphrey Willis as sheriff into Fermanagh at Easter 1593, the earl was in danger of losing the services of another urrí, his cousin, Hugh Maguire, who had recently married another daughter of the earl's. Disclaiming responsibility, O'Neill sent his brother, Cormac McBaron, and his foster brethren, the O'Hagans, to assist Maguire in the eviction of Willis.[52] The O'Hagans were later involved in a big raid which Maguire made into Co. Sligo.[53] The latter was planned at a meeting at Toome on the banks of the Bann at a time when the Ulstermen were establishing an oath-bound confederacy to oppose further government intrusion. Phelim McTurlough O'Neill, lord of Killetra, was murdered after the meeting broke up.[54]

Phelim was from Killetra at the strategic north-east entrance into Tyrone where the river Bann joined Lough Neagh, and his murder took place on 17 May 1593 at a crannog he had formerly occupied. All the details about the murder come from Marshal Bagenal and from associates of Phelim who witnessed the event. Nevertheless, the wealth of detail smacks of authenticity. Bagenal, whom the witnesses first approached, described Phelim as being:

> of good regard among that people and a personage of the best sept of Tyrone, holding a very fast piece of ground by descent from his ancestors, according the manner of that country and like enough to carry great sway in any action there to what part he were inclined.

Bagenal may have been exaggerating, and was certainly incorrect in referring to Phelim as a Tyrone O'Neill when in fact he was of a Clandeboye lineage.[55] According to Bagenal, the earl, apparently jealous of Phelim's popularity, had used his royal patent which had included Killetra within the bounds of Tyrone

---

[49] HMC, *Calendars of the manuscripts of the Marquis of Salisbury (or Cecil MSS)* (14 vols, 1883–1923), 4, p. 219. [50] PRO SP 63/166, 4. [51] *Cal. S.P. Ire., 1588–92*, pp 566–7. [52] PRO SP 63/170, 23(13). [53] *Cal. S.P. Ire., 1592–96*, p. 105. [54] There is an earlier more romanticized account of this murder in S. O'Grady, *Bog of Stairs and other stories and sketches of Elizabethan Ireland* (London, 1893), pp 46–64. [55] Genealogical information from K.W. Nicholls.

to evict Phelim from his lands in favour of one of the O'Hagans. Phelim had killed this O'Hagan and entered into hostilities against the earl. Subsequently Bagenal had arranged for Phelim's safe-conduct out of Tyrone and had obtained a pardon for him and his adherents. He returned to Tyrone after the earl had promised before the Lord Deputy and Council to guarantee his safety. Basically Phelim was, or had become, a client of Bagenal's and his killing was damaging to the latter's reputation. As he informed his patron Lord Burghley:

> So have I great cause in private (learning the indignity done to Her Majesty most of all to be regarded therein) to bemoan me to your honourable lordship in that hereby my poor credit is greatly touched and myself much disabled upon any like occasion hereafter to do Her Majesty service.[56]

On 1 June 1593, Ever O'Neill made a declaration before Bagenal with Phelim O'Hanlon acting as interpreter, and then on 21 June at Dundalk he and Collo McFerdoragh O'Neill, both described as being of Killetra and kinsmen of the deceased, made a petition to the Lord Deputy and Council. Both statements coincide though the second is more detailed. Phelim had arrived in the earl's camp near the crannog where he was coshering with the O'Hagans to ask him about a fosterage arrangement for his son. The earl was having secret meetings with Hugh Maguire and with Owen Óg O'Hagan, Henry O'Hagan and Hugh Óg O'Hagan, and when Phelim finally gained access to the earl he was put off until the next morning. However the earl departed early, taking a boat up the Bann. Phelim and the suppliants saw him off, Phelim bading him farewell, 'God be with you, my Lord' to which the earl aloud replied 'God be at defiance with you 'til night'. Phelim took this in jest but his kinsmen were terrified. Once the earl's boat left, the O'Hagans gladhanded Phelim and Owen, with his arm round Phelim's shoulder, marched him towards the camp. Just inside, and in full view of the earl's people, Owen drew his sword and lopped off one of Phelim's arms and then the other two O'Hagans fell upon him, mortally wounding and then hacking him to pieces. His servant, Donal Óg McEvagh, tried to escape across the river but was caught and drowned; the two suppliants managed to make it to the woods and hide there. Meanwhile the O'Hagans preyed Phelim's creaghts, killing his younger brother, another gentleman and two others. What happened next the deponents had second-hand. The earl had stopped at Portglenone further up the river. Hugh O'Gallagher, coming along in a boat with victuals, reported that he had witnessed an ill deed – the killing of Phelim McTurlough. 'Aye and is Donal Óg killed too? Aye both killed and drowned. What became of my shot that went over the river?, saith the earl'. Plainly the

56 PRO SP 63/170, 1.

earl had placed marksmen across the river in case any of the targets escaped. The Countess Mabel was at his side and clapped her hands in sorrow at what had taken place 'to whom the earl in English spake with vehemency, which most of the company did not understand and so could not come to your supplicant's knowledge'. Three days after the murder the earl ordered another prey from Phelim's creaghts in destraint of unpaid rents and issued a proclamation 'for the banishing of your suppliants and their kinsmen out of the said lands and for the cutting off of their heads if they should come upon the same'.[57]

At Dundalk in late June the earl was confronted by the Lord Deputy and Council with a number of charges – foreign conspiracy, aiding Maguire and killing Phelim. His refutation was a litany of excuses. He claimed, similar to the flimsy excuse for the Monaghan raid, that Cormac and Conn Mac an Íarla had only gone into Fermanagh to see what the commotion was there. As regards the killing of Phelim, he claimed that the victim was a bad man and a great murderer who had spoiled and killed his tenants. About two years previously, Phelim had killed a brother of the O'Hagans who, when they encountered him in the earl's camp, killed him in revenge. The earl swore by Her Majesty's hand that he was not privy to the murder, claiming that the witness statements had been finessed to incriminate him.[58] Despite these protestations, it is plain that this had been a political assassination to dispose of a potential government collaborator who controlled a strategic area – the crossing point from Clandeboye into Tyrone at the top of Lough Neagh. It was also the silencing of a man who may have known too much, the open destruction of a client of Marshal Bagenal and, above all, a salutary warning to any other would-be local dissidents as the earl manoeuvred Ulster into revolt. It was a clear signal to waverers to get in line or face the consequences. At Dundalk the Irish Council, fearful of a large force gathered in the vicinity by Cormac MacBaron (and some of their number possibly in the earl's pocket), was divided about proceeding against the earl. Fitzwilliam would have liked to have charged him with Phelim's murder but he gave in to majority opinion on the matter.[59]

To get out of the predicament he found himself in at Dundalk, the earl had to agree to make war on his dependent, Hugh Maguire. However, by early 1594 he had the McShanes, whom he earlier had disarmed for taking preys from the defeated Maguires, imprisoned in separate locations and he was once again using his relatives and followers as proxies to undermine government authority on the borders and to bring the uirríthe back to their traditional allegiance.[60] A section of the government believed or wished to believe that the earl was unable to control these individuals who were in fact working energetically on his behalf. First, in February, Hugh Maguire, Brian McHugh Óg and other McMahons

57 PRO SP 63/170, 1(5); *Cal. S.P. Ire., 1592–96*, pp 107–9.   58 PRO SP 63/170, 53.
59 *Cal. S.P. Ire., 1592–96*, p. 148.   60 PRO SP 63/173, 64(1); CUL, Kk 1.15.25, ff 75–8.

(who were camped near Dungannon), aided by the earl's brother and half-brother, Cormac McBaron and Turlough McHenry, began plaguing Monaghan.[61] Conn Mac An Íarla gave special treatment to Owen O'Duffy, Bagenal's tenant in next-door Muckno. He was 'the first that brought in the new establishment in Monaghan and so that country was drawn from the earl', and as a result Conn now spoiled him to the point of destitution.[62] At the start of March, the McMahons raided the counties of Louth and Meath, putting the Palesmen into great fear and placing the preys they took in Turlough McHenry's country of the Fews for safe-keeping.[63] Even though the earl had agreed to control such activities and to restore preys when he aired his grievances to government commissioners at Dundalk, the preys continued.[64] Four days later Bagenal was reporting the invasion and destruction of his lordships of Newry and Cooley by the earl's followers in an orgy of burning, murder and theft.[65] If anything, the raids intensified after the so-called 'conclusion' with the government commissioners. The earl's brother and half-brother (Cormac McBaron and Turlough McHenry), bastard son (Conn Mac An Íarla), son-in-law (Henry Óg), the O'Hagans, O'Quinns and McMahons descended on Connor Roe, the government collaborator in Fermanagh. They spoiled him of his herds, of which the earl got a share from each captain. Connor Roe had to flee to Dublin and by the end of the summer, because of continued pressure, he was forced to come to Dungannon to submit to Hugh Maguire's lordship with the earl standing slanty.[66]

Next, Sir Henry Duke, sheriff of Cavan, reported Henry Óg's attack and spoil of the tenants he had settled at Clones, and Conn Mac An Íarla and the McMahon's attack on the Monaghan loyalists. Duke was fed up with the earl's feeble excuses:

> in my simple judgement the daily outrages and traiterous actions committed and done by the earl's brother and his brother's sons, his bastard son and his son-in-law, with their men and followers do manifestly prove who doth maintain and uphold this last rebellion begun by the traitors the McMahons and that so apparently their accustomed Irish Sheanames shall no longer prevail in cloaking their rebellious attempts, seeing their manifest actions do foreshow their greater intention of further mischief.[67]

It is plain from this statement of growing exasperation that there was an established term in the official lexicon of the English establishment in Ireland – derived from the Irish *séanaim* meaning 'I deny' – for actions from which the

---

61 PRO SP 63/173, 26; PRO SP 63/173, 64(4).   62 PRO SP 63/173, 64(11).   63 PRO SP 63/173, 81.   64 PRO SP 63/173, 89(3).   65 PRO SP 63/173, 98(1).   66 *Cal. S.P. Ire., 1592–96*, p. 233; PRO SP 63/176, 40   67 *Cal. S.P. Ire., 1592–96*, pp 235, 240.

Irish lords wanted to excuse themselves. Secretary Fenton opined that, although the earl claimed that the raids were being executed by actors he could not rule, the same were in fact 'robin hoods whom he may order and pacify if he will'.[68]

There was a similar pattern in east Ulster where the earl's nephew, Brian McArt McBaron, was the chief actor on the earl's behalf. When he presented his grievances to the government commissioners at Dundalk in March 1594, the earl had stated:

> Whereas (with the countenance and furtherance of the Queen's most excellent majesty) the earl brought into subjection the Upper Clandeboyes in the time of Con McNeill Óg, Killutagh, Kilwarlyn, McCartan's country, O'Hanlon's country and all McMahon's country, the same was no sooner done but such as appertained to the Earl (bearing rule in any of those places) were presently removed and those base and servile fellows whom the Marshall thought fittest to be of his faction against him were placed in their rooms, where through their inability the earl can have no satisfaction of them.[69]

As in south Ulster, the O'Neills had always tried to exercise overlordship over the Clandeboyes and other lordships east of the Bann. After his first bid for the O'Neill title in 1583, Hugh O'Neill had demanded not only letters patent to the lands of Tyrone but also to the territories in the Lagan Valley as far as Belfast.[70] In the mid-1580s, 'The Treatise of Ireland', a government gazetteer, stated that Magennis's country (Sir Hugh McGennis) and Killutagh (Cormac McNeill) had been drawn away from being forced to pay tribute to the O'Neill by Marshal Sir Nicholas Bagenal, and that Magennis's country, Killultagh and Kilwarlin (Ever McRory) now held patents from the Queen.[71] Bagenal had been assisted in this by Perrot's grant of east Ulster to him as a lieutenancy and by the same Lord Deputy's renewal of the surrender and regrant scheme. However, when Bagenal was away in England in 1586 and in the interviceregnum at the end of Perrot's government, the earl openly flouted these arrangements demanding his traditional rights from the uirríthe.[72] Now in 1594 he was rapidly making up for lost time.

In March, Brian McArt, with the local support of James McSorley McDonnell and Neil McHugh O'Neill, began operations in North Clandeboye and then entered South Clandeboye. Backed by 300 foot and 50 horse, they took away Marshal Bagenal's stud from the vicinity of Carrickfergus and transferred it across the Bann. Then they killed one Rory Magee to force the rest of that clan into submission. Next they demanded the submission of Neill McBrian O'Neill

---

68 PRO SP 63/174, 43.   69 Lambeth (Carew) MS 617, f. 205.   70 PRO SP 63/102, 72.
71 NLI MS 669, ff 45–6.   72 *Cal. S.P. Ire., 1586–88*, pp 97–100, 396–7.

the lord of South Clandeboye based at Castlereagh. First they preyed his cattle and then the following month returned assisted by Shane McBrian at Belfast and with a letter from the earl.[73] Afterwards they attacked Randal Brerton's lands of the Dufferin, who reported that they had 'preyed, spoiled and burned the whole country to the number of ten or XII towns and killed some of Her Majesty's poor subjects there and assaulted by two houses which is called Killough and Ringaheddy.[74] Dufferin was eventually given to Eoin McHugh who had had temporary charge in South Clandeboye until Neill McBrian finally submitted.[75]

Ever McRory Magennis was another lord who refused to submit and was eventually murdered. Ever was captain of the small wooded lordship of Kilwarlin which controlled one of the routes to Carrickfergus. At the end of April 1594 he wrote to the Lord Deputy having fled into Co. Louth. 'At the beginning of March last', he reported:

> the earl of Tyrone sent one unto me to require me to be his man and to serve none but himself and I returned him this answer that I was the Queen's subject and that her Majesty had most graciously given me my lands and country by patent[76] and therefore I would neither depend upon nor serve any but Her Majesty.

As a result, the earl sent his nephew, Brian McArt McBaron O'Neill, with some of his own forces into Kilwarlin where the took 500 cows and other goods worth £500 and 'killed and murdered a great number of my people'. At the beginning of April, Brian McArt's forces were back again. When Ever again refused to serve the earl, they entered Kilwarlin and 'set it all on fire, killed men, women and children and took with them all the cows and other spoils they could get which was far greater than the former'. McRory retreated to a crannog where he was soon besieged. When he came out to negotiate 'a buying' under which they had promised to restore his goods 'they contrary to their oaths took me presently in hand and tied me most cruelly with withes and threatened to hang me presently unless I would yield them up my island which for safeguard of his life he was forced to do'. Since, unlike his neighbours, he as a loyal subject had been unwilling to submit to the earl and give pledges, he had since been forced to flee his own country with a small company. He was now destitute and using Bagenal to intercede with the state on his behalf.[77] Six months later, Marshal Bagenal reported Ever's death. He had been in Dublin ready to put matters against the earl face to face while the latter was being carpetted by the new Lord

---

73 PRO SP 63/173, 79; PRO SP 63/174, 37 (1 & 2); *Cal. S.P. Ire.*, *1592–96*, p. 220.   74 PRO SP 63/174, 37(3).   75 PRO SP 63/175, 5(19); PRO SP 63/177, 30(7).   76 *Irish fiants of the Tudor sovereigns*, nos. 4649–50.   77 PRO SP 63/174, 37(4).

Deputy, Sir William Russell. Obviously he had been brought there by Bagenal or perhaps summoned by the state to witness against the earl but it seems unlikely that any such confrontation had taken place. Returning home, 'the first night he approached the frontiers of his own country [he was] most cruelly murdered by the earl's nephews'.[78]

Clearly those who opposed Hugh O'Neill or collaborated with the government against him were in danger of their lives. Bagenal, writing to court at the end of September 1594, said the earl feared such powerful individuals being used by the government against him. He claimed that failing to succour Turlough Luineach and allowing the earl 'the absolute estate of the country' had been 'the very prime cause, foundation and root of all those garboils, which ever since have ensued'. Other opportunities to counterpoise the earl's power such as supporting Phelim McTurlough had been passed over, and now by murder, imprisonment and forced submission the earl had no internal rivals (such as Hugh Maguire had had in Fermanagh in the person of Conor Roe) from whom the state could get support.[79] One commentator insisted that a consistent policy of surrender and regrant pursued towards minor lordlings would have overthrown O'Neill: 'For he hath feared this course and hath therefore suppressed all them who attempted the same. He murdered for this matter the Lord of Killultagh [*sic*],[80] to whose mind I was privy, with much more that may be proved'.[81]

Having dealt ruthlessly with his internal opponents, the earl became very gung-ho and anxious that no mercy be shown to crown forces as matters drifted towards open war. When in the summer of 1594 Conn Mac An Íarla and Henry Óg botched an attack, he was reportedly angry that the English churls had not been wiped out and told Conn that he was not fit to be called his son.[82] 'Many incursions', Secretary Fenton reported in December 1594, 'are made into the county of Louth, notwithstanding the garrison laid upon the borders for defence'.[83] In February 1595, the Blackwater Fort surrendered to an assault by Art McBaron after some resistance:

> Presently after the yielding of the Castle, the earl of Tyrone, only accompanied with Henry Hovenden and his man John Bath came in all post haste to his brother Art McBaron, and after long conference had with him seeing so many of his men slain, especially those Hagans, willed Art to kill all the churls that were of the ward, which Art refused to do, for that he had past his oath and promise for the safe-sending of them to the Newry.

78 PRO SP 63/176, 40. 79 Ibid. 80 *Recte* Kilwarlin. This is surely a transposition of 'Killultagh' for 'Kilwarlin'. There is no evidence that O'Neill meted out similar treatment to the captain of the loughside lordship as he had to the neighbouring Ever McRory of Kilwarlin. 81 *Cal. S.P. Ire., 1596–97*, pp 346–8 82 PRO SP 63/175, 13(5). 83 PRO SP 63/177, 43.

In the same letter, Sir Henry Duke also reported another disagreement where the earl had advocated the burning of Dundalk to prevent it being garrisoned but Art objected on the grounds 'that their ancestors and especially themselves for the most part had been here bred and brought up'.[84] With Lord Deputy Russell deciding to attack Feagh McHugh in Wicklow, Cormac McBaron was soon afterwards able to invade the Pale, plundering the country and burning down the town of Cavan and the abbey there which acted as an army storage facility in that county. Simultaneously, Art McBaron and the new-won allies of east Ulster attacked Bagenal's tenants in Mourne 'burning, wasting and defacing all show that it was ever inhabited'. Fenton reported the slowness of the Palesmen in hosting whilst meanwhile the Ulstermen burned even in daytime within seven miles of Drogheda and threatened to cross the Boyne 'which is now made a border'.[85] At about this time the Annals of the Four Masters record big O'Neill raids which devastated the lands of the baron of Slane and the country around Kells.[86] In May the state received news of the loss of Enniskillen 'the ward by sickness being reduced to 14 and they being promised by Maguire their lives were all put to the sword by Cormac McBaron'.[87] This was, no doubt, revenge for the fact that no quarter was shown to its original Irish keepers when it had been taken by crown forces fifteen months previously.[88] Soon afterwards the earl was himself in action against Bagenal at Clontibret. In June the state proclaimed him a traitor, denouncing him as the rebellion's chief author whose ambition was to be 'a prince of Ulster'.[89] In the autumn of 1595 the earl was inaugurated as O'Neill on the demise of Turlough Luineach O'Neill. The Church of Ireland bishop of Limerick reported that 'the priests and bishops confess that Tyrone was a traitor, but lawful for him to rebel: both they and the whole Irishry are now taught a new lesson: O'Neill is no traitor. Tyrone was one, but O'Neill none'.[90] Although Tyrone later renounced this Gaelic title in negotiations with the crown, as Philip O'Reilly pointed out some time afterwards, 'howsoever he denied it to you, he retained it amongst us'.[91]

In 1981, Brendan Bradshaw discussed models for Ireland's development in this period in one of his many important review articles:

> we need to remind ourselves that the process of state-building that characterizes the political history of Renaissance Europe provides not one but two designs for the consolidated Renaissance State: that of national monarchy, the pattern that developed in England, France and Spain and

---

84 PRO SP 63/178, 53(5).   85 PRO SP 63/178, 68 & 70.   86 *AFM*, s.a. 1595, pp 1958–9.
87 PRO SP 63/179, 93.   88 BL, Harleian MS 35 ff 258–65.   89 CUL, Kk 1.15.39, ff 98–9; PRO SP 63/179, 82; PRO SP 63/180, 48, 48(2).   90 *Cal. S.P. Ire., 1592–96*, pp 435–6.
91 PRO SP 63/190, 44(9).

that of the regional principality, the pattern that established itself in fifteenth-century Italy and sixteenth-century Germany. The relevance of the latter pattern of development to the Irish situation needs to be considered.

In this regard he referred the reader to James Lydon, *Ireland in the later Middle Ages* (Dublin 1973).

The history of the development of the great dynastic lordships in Ireland in the late middle ages, as depicted by Lydon, provides some striking parallels with the reorganization of political space in Italy at the same time. If Lydon is correct, then it would seem that the appropriate model of the conflict in sixteenth-century Ireland is not that of a modernizing Renaissance State coming to grips with an archaic political culture. It is rather the case of a conflict between two political systems in the process of modernisation: a centralizing monarchy and consolidating regional principalities.[92]

Thinking of the number of political murders in Machiavelli's *Prince* or, indeed, in Shakespeare's Italian plays, it might be useful to extend Bradshaw's comparison between Gaelic and Gaelicized Ireland and Renaissance Italy to the question of political violence. Burckhardt's famous essay on Renaissance Italy shows a level of violence, often of the most illegitimate, vicious and mercenary nature, in the competition for power within the Italian state system not unlike that of the Irish lordships.[93] Subsequently this violence escalated when the peninsula was competed over by foreign powers during the Italian Wars in the same way as the Tudor conquest of Ireland ratcheted up its scale in Ireland.

Indeed, it seems to me that Camden's Tacitean verdict on O'Neill, entered in his *Annales* at the point where he had Gavelach murdered, could only have been written in the world of state-building and statecraft shaped by Machiavelli's *Prince*.

He had a strong body, able to endure labour, watching and hunger: his industry was great, his soul large and fit for the weightiest business; much knowledge he had in military affairs and a profound dissembling heart: in so much as some did prognosticate of him, that he was born for the very great good or the great hurt of Ireland.[94]

---

92 B. Bradshaw, 'The Elizabethans and the Irish: a muddled model', *Studies* (Summer/Autumn, 1981), p. 239. This was a review of Richard Berleth, *The twilight lords* (London, 1978) which broadened out into a larger historiographical essay.   93 J. Burckhardt, *The civilisation of the Renaissance in Italy* (London, 1990), especially part 1.   94 Camden, *History*, pp 446–7.

Certainly the murders committed by O'Neill would not have been out of place in Machiavelli's representation of the acquisition of new princedoms. However, it may also be that the amorality depicted in *The Prince* actually helped force a change in the way political violence could be represented. It now had to be legitimate or authorized by a higher power. Many of O'Neill's medieval predecessors killed their rivals as well. However, secrecy now had be used not just to commit murder in the first place but also to cover it up from the growing power of the state. It was no longer a case of getting some sort of absolution from the church; it was about getting a pardon from the state. As a result, O'Neill went to extraordinary and often ridiculous lengths to cover up his pursuit of power – claiming that acts from which he was plainly the main beneficiary were the acts of uncontrollable followers or alternatively asserting authority as a crown officer using martial law or a Gaelic lord exercising ancient custom or later as a patriotic Catholic backed by the Pope. Similarly the involvement of O'Neill – or, to be exact, the involvement of his agents the Hovendens – in the execution of Armada survivors could be comprehended within contemporary European raisons d'état, although in the case of Inishowen the circumstances plainly differ from Florida or Smerwick and suggest an even more Machiavellian aspect, if not indeed a Machiavellian moment.

The murders investigated here can, I believe, be comprehended within the Renaissance mind-set; however the widespread killing of non-combatants in wartime raiding was a different matter. The distinguishing factor in the Irish wars was the widespread use of pillage and arson to weaken the resource base and killing of 'churls' to destroy the labour force of one's opponents. The Spanish Armada survivor, Francisco de Cuellar, noted the prevalence of borderages: 'The chief inclination of these people is to be robbers, and to plunder each other; so that no day passes without a call to arms among them'.[95] In wartime, however, raiding changed qualitatively and quantitatively. Continentals themselves got a taste of this when Irish kerne served in Henry VIII's Boulogne campaign in the early 1540s where their deployment as auxiliaries in search and destroy missions gained the Irish a reputation for savagery.[96] Their methods must have deviated from the Western European norm. The big raid was an important feature of the Nine Years War – indeed it is an element in the strategy and tactics of the war which G.A. Hayes-McCoy surprising pays little attention to.[97] Hugh O'Neill was a major exponent of the raid.[98] His prowess in this, especially evident during his tour of the Midlands

---

95 P. Gallagher and D.W. Cruickshank, *God's obvious design: papers for the Spanish Armada Symposium, Sligo, 1988; with an edition and translation of the account of Francisco de Cuéllar* (London, 1990), p. 238.   **96** D.G. White, 'Henry VIII's kerne in France and Scotland', *Irish Sword*, 3 (1957–8), 213–25.   **97** G.A. Hayes-McCoy, 'Strategy and tactics in Irish warfare, 1593–1601', *IHS*, 2 (1941), 255–79.   **98** O'Neill's use of Gaelic marauding as part of his

and Munster in 1600, was praised in the Annals of the Four Masters.[99] His confederates, especially Red Hugh O'Donnell, were masters as well and were similarly praised.[1] To win in Ireland, the English had to employ similar tactics to the Irish themselves – only more systematically. They switched from the big raid to continuous raiding, from economic war to total war. That is what Mountjoy and his lieutenants did after Kinsale.

military strategy is obviously a subject of some importance and merits a detailed separate paper.   **99** *AFM*, s.a. 1600, pp 2146–63.   **1** See H. Morgan, 'The real Red Hugh', in P. Ó Riain (ed.), *Beatha Aodha Ruaidh: the Life of Red Hugh O'Donnell, historical and literary contexts* (London, 2002), esp. pp 27–9.

The pacification of Ulster, 1600–3

JOHN MCGURK

On grass and shamrocks now they make their feasts
O England, never better news can be,
Than this to hear, how God doth fight for thee.[1]

The many treatises and tracts on how to govern Ireland in the sixteenth century were informed by a sense of moral and cultural superiority over natives who needed first to be chastised before they could be 'reformed'. That so-called barbarians must be subdued by the sword before they can be civilized is reiterated, from Giraldus Cambrensis's *Topography and history of Ireland and his Conquest of Ireland*, down to Thomas More's *Utopia* (1516), and on to Spenser's *View of the present state of Ireland*, Richard Beacon's *Solon his folly*, along with Barnaby Rich and other choleric captains in military service in late Elizabethan Ireland. Sir John Davies, when justifying the severity of the war in the north, succinctly put the classical argument: 'a barbarous countrie must be first broke by a war'. The literate Elizabethan military caste had much to say about Ireland and the Irish people, displaying in their writings that they had learned much from commentators on the Spanish conquistadores like Oviedio and Las Casas. The debt is traced in the works of the late D.B. Quinn and, more recently, in the widely ranging works of Nicholas Canny and Brendan Bradshaw which have opened the eyes of their readers to the wider perspectives and contexts of the Elizabethan conquest.[2]

Many English sixteenth-century writers, and Palesmen too, anticipated Darwin in seeing the Irish in evolutionary terms as being in a state of arrested

---

[1] R.V., *England's joy* (London, 1601). [2] D.B. Quinn, 'Renaissance influences in English colonization', *Transactions of the Royal Historical Society*, 5th ser, 25 (1976), 73–93; N. Canny, *Making Ireland British, 1580–1650* (Oxford, 2001). For revisionist case studies see the respective essays of Canny and Bradshaw in N. Canny, J. Andrews, and P. Hair (eds), *The westward enterprise* (Liverpool, 1978), and C. Brady in Brady and R. Gillespie (eds), *Natives and newcomers* (Dublin, 1986). See also V.P. Carey and C.L. Carroll, 'Factions and fictions: Spenser's reflections of and on Elizabethan politics', in J.H. Anderson, D.A. Richardson, and D. Cheney (eds), *Spenser's life and the subject of biography* (Amherst, MA, 1996). See Carroll's comparison of O'Sullivan Beare's *Compendium* (1619) with Las Casas in H. Morgan (ed.), *Political Ideology in Ireland, 1541–1641* (Dublin 1999), pp 238–44.

development. Some of these commentators then deployed the by now wellworn anthropological argument: since such native peoples were on a low rung of humanity they could be eliminated by fire, famine and sword. During more formal hostilities the pretensions and procedures of martial law, common law, or both, were brought to bear in individual cases: where land and property was at stake, common law was preferred over martial. Common law procedures in cases of high treason and other pleas of the crown prepared the way for the taking over or forfeiture to the crown of such lands and property as victims possessed. The Tudors introduced commissions of martial law and the legal processes and procedures of the common law courts slowly and patchily across Ireland and latterly Ulster. It would be naïve to overlook the motives behind such outward shows of legality; the greed for gold, plunder, and the everprevalent land covetousness of the conquistador, especially younger sons.[3] A younger son was often an angry young man embittered because he was cut out of inheritance at home by primogeniture as normally practised throughout England.

The other old colonial justification was religion. If Indians were heathens the Irish were at least acknowledged to be Christians, albeit corrupt, deluded and superstitious Christians. Their spiritual welfare therefore shouted out for a godly Protestant reformation that would wean them from allegiance to the papacy and inordinate attachment to Spain. Many in high military and official positions in Ireland during the Elizabethan conquest were Puritan in their preferences and therefore inclined towards strong anti-Catholic Calvinistic teachings. The Calvinistic argument that military severity was nothing more than the just judgment of Almighty God and condign punishment at his merciful hands for unruly disobedience against his lawful and anointed sovereign, stressed the Old Testament view of God's justice rather than the New Testament one of his mercy. Historians such as Nicholas Canny argue convincingly that the behaviour of the English soldiery in Ireland can be best understood in this context of their Calvinistic religious and racial ideology. And yet, instances of murder and massacre of un-armed Christian civilians and of man's inhumanity to man are found in every historical epoch with or without religious or philosophical justifications.

In the context of the last phase of the Nine Years War, it is not always easy to see or pronounce on the religious proclivities of the more notable military commanders. Certainly, Sir Arthur Chichester and Sir George Carew did little to hide their deep anti-Catholicism. Mountjoy, while supporting the official

---

[3] See also J. Ohlmeyer, 'Civilizing of those rude parts', in N. Canny (ed.), *The origins of empire* (Oxford, 1998), pp 124–47. David Edwards has made detailed studies of martial law commissions in the period: see 'Legacy of defeat: the reduction of Gaelic Ireland after Kinsale', in H. Morgan (ed.), *The battle of Kinsale* (Bray, 2004).

Protestantism of the reformed Church, may well indeed have been a crypto-papist. He was of the opinion that all religions grow under persecution and pointed out how the Inquisition 'did lose the King of Spain the Low Countries'.[4] Sir Henry Docwra appears to have been one of the more tolerant commanders in respect of religion; he kept one of the ecclesiastical buildings on the Derry site for the Catholic worship of his many Irish troops. He allowed Aodh Buidh Mac Daebhéid (Hugh Boy McDavitt), a quondam ally but distrusted as a double-agent by others, his own chaplain. On the other hand, Docwra did not lift a finger to prevent his soldiers slaying McDavitt's brother, Ruadh. Furthermore, when his deputy, Sir John Bolles', soldiers murdered Réamonn Ó Gallchobhair (Raymond O'Gallagher), the last pre-reformation bishop of Derry, Docwra neither condemned nor condoned the killing when he heard the news. Docwra's critics and enemies in Dublin and London (among their many complaints of his governance of the Derry garrisons) pointed out how he employed but one preacher for something like 3,000 soldiers, and then only engaged his services whenever his men were to face the enemy on a 'journey' on which it was almost certain there would be fatalities.[5] Barnaby Rich, an especially violent Puritan, was scathing about the quality of the preachers sent to Ireland to undertake the work of conversion among the native Irish, 'their prattle more suited to the tavern than the temple'. Most of them had not a word of either Latin or Irish, he claimed, and were good only for 'the tippling of ale and aqua vitae, the getting of bastards and never giving themselves up to study or preaching'.[6]

It must be added that such anti-clerical outbursts castigate English, Irish, Catholic and Protestant clergy alike. Spenser too pitched in with his pen and in no less strident terms in the *View* claimed that even if England sent her best ministers they would do no good in Ireland for the Irish would not listen to them even if they could understand them.[7]

A quick end to a war of attrition after Kinsale seems to have been the first concern of the majority of the military commanders. The civilizing missions of colonization and Protestant evangelization could then follow all the more quickly: such was the rationalization. The Council in London now listened to them. The days when Queen and Council agreed that 'no extirpation [was] intended' in the 1570s and 1580s had gone. The Queen's proclamation of 31 March 1599 reminds rebels of 'the extreme misery whereunto they shall throw themselves' but finds 'the very name of Conquest absurd'. She is sending over Essex's huge army 'to minister our justice and mercy', and it is only

[4] PRO SP 63/212, f.118 [5] John McCavitt's *Sir Arthur Chichester: Lord Deputy of Ireland 1605–16* (Belfast, 1998), brings out the fierce anti-Catholicism and brutality of Chichester and his men in the final phase of the war. [6] PRO SP 63/205/no.72, ff 1–10: Barnaby Rich, 'A looking-glass for Her Majesty wherein to view Ireland'. [7] Edmund Spenser, *A view of the present state of Ireland* ed. W.L. Renwick (Oxford, 1970), pp 88, 89.

'wicked and barbarous rebels' who allege 'that we intend an utter extirpation and rooting out of that nation and Conquest of the country'. Despite the Queen's disclaimer, it was becoming evident to her Privy Council that Ireland could no longer pay for its own conquest, hence the massive military efforts from 1600 to just before the Queen's death in March 1603.[8]

By 1602 the previously much talked-of strategy of ringing Ulster with garrisoned castles, forts and blockhouses was a reality to the extent that barely six square miles of Ulster lay beyond the range of cavalry raiders from a military outpost. No fort or garrison was more than a day's march from one another. For example, Docwra's men under Captain Leigh in Omagh were but ten miles from the halting post at Termonmagurk (Carrickmore) and another ten miles from Ó Neill's headquarters at Dungannon. Commanders had learned the lessons of Clontibret and the Yellow Ford wherein long marches to relieve beleaguered garrisons led to military defeats unprecedented in sixteenth-century Irish warfare. Such proximity and co-ordination between forts became essential in searching for and destroying the rebels' forces and those who fed them.

Scorched earth tactics of causing famine by burning barns of corn, destroying cattle, and sheep, and ripping up growing crops, proved the most effective means of bringing war to an end. In a frequently cited dispatch from Sir Arthur Chichester when he raided across Lough Neagh into east Co. Tyrone in 1601 he claimed:

> We have burned and destroyed along the Lough even within four miles of Dungannon where we killed man, woman, child, horse, beast and whatever we found. The last service from which we returned yesterday was upon Patrick O'Quinn, one of the chief men of Tyrone, dwelling within four miles of Dungannon, fearing nothing, but we lighted upon him and killed him, his wife, sons and daughters, servants and followers being many, and burned all to the ground.[9]

A week later in a further note he added that 'we killed in that journey about 100, besides such as were burned, how many I know not'. Nor did he care, presumably. Docwra carried out a similar massacre on Inch Island in Lough Swilly, reporting 150 killed when he attacked the fertile lands of MacSweeney Fanad, Red Hugh O'Donnell's gallowglass clan. His report speaks of his troops torching 400–500 houses and barns, destroying about £3000 worth of corn, and driving off 2,000 sheep, 250 cattle, and 200 garrons or small Irish horses. When MacSweeney was brought to his knees, Docwra returned some of the stock to

---

8 The Queen's proclamation of 31 March 1599, as cited and paraphrased in D.B. Quinn, *The Elizabethans and the Irish* (Ithaca, NY, 1966), p. 137.   9 PRO SP 63/208/ii, 68, Sir Arthur Chichester to Sir Robert Cecil.

him.¹⁰ Sir John Bolles, Docwra's second-in-command in Derry, attacked Cumber in O'Cahan's country and reported killing nearly 100 people. These included Réamonn Ó Gallochbhair:

> God gave unto my hand upon Ash Wednesday at night ... the Bishop of Derry who is said to be the first and chief contriver of this general defection and combination with the Spaniards and has himself been thrice at Rome and oft in Spain ... before I could come unto him my soldiers had slain him.

Mountjoy reported the incident, or an incident, to Cecil from Drogheda on 12 March 1601: when the soldiers captured a church they put to the sword 'the Prior of Derry and twenty of the principal priests in all Ulster'. It is possible that this was a separate slaughter, as Mountjoy and his secretary, Fynes Moryson, would hardly confuse a prior with a bishop.¹¹

Mountjoy led the way in scorched earth tactics, as he seemed to have few qualms of conscience about the killing of civilian non-combatants claiming that 'even the very best of the Irish people were in their nature little better than devils'. He noted that if fish live in water as rebels do among the people of the countryside, then you dry up the water, repeating Julius Caesar's commentaries on the Gallic wars and anticipating Chairman Mao in the twentieth century. Mountjoy wrote as follows to his fellow Devonian, Sir George Carew, in Munster, who was using the same tactics against the remnants of resistance among the O'Sullivans and O'Driscolls after Kinsale: 'Here in Ulster we do continually hunt all their woods, spoil their corn, burn their houses, and kill as many churls as it grieveth me to think it is necessary to do so'. His secretary and companion in the field, Fynes Moryson, wrote of these last days of the war in Ulster: 'No spectacle was more frequent than to see multitudes of these poor people dead with their mouths all coloured green by eating nettles, shamrocks and docks and all things they could rend up above ground'.¹²

Famine became a tool of warfare as provisions were denied all who resisted; those submitting were left unmolested to rear their own cattle. Moryson spares no horrific detail of that terrifying campaign of 1602, not even the gruesome and macabre scenes of cannibalism which he claims took place near Newry. William Farmer, Mountjoy's field army surgeon and later chronicler of these

---

10 PRO SP 63/207/pvi 85, and see the more accessible edition of Docwra's *Narration* re-edited from J. O'Donovan's 1849 edition by W. Kelly as *Docwra's Derry* (Belfast, 2003), pp 54–5. See also J. McGurk, *Sir Henry Docwra, 1564–1631: Derry's second founder* (Dublin, 2005). 11 For both reports of Bishop O'Gallaher's murder see *Cal. S.P. Ire* (1601), pp 205–7, Bolles to Cecil, 7 March 1601, and pp 247–8, Mountjoy to Cecil, 31 March 1601. 12 F. Moryson, *An Itinerary ... and a Description of Ireland*, ed. J. MacLehose (Glasgow, 1907), 3, p. 283

events, is even more explicit than Moryson in his account of children roasting and broiling the flesh of their dead mother and eating it. When questioned by soldiers who came across them, the children said their cattle were taken away by Englishmen. When asked if they would rather have meat or money for relief, 'they answered both meat and money'. Moved to compassion the commander 'ordered a collection of victuals from among the soldiers' knapsacks and left it with them and so departed'.[13]

Contemporaneously with these awful incidents, Mountjoy marched from Armagh to Dungannon and then smashed, in a symbolic gesture, the O'Neill inauguration chair at Tullyhogue. He followed up his triumphal march by the further destruction of crops and the infrastructure of O'Neill's own mensal lands around Dungannon, Donaghmore, and up the Glenshane pass towards Dungiven. South of these lands he allowed the MacShane O'Neills, Henry Óg and Conn, with their submissive followers, to relocate south of the Blackwater into north Co. Armagh and re-establish their farms there. But, as Fynes Moryson relates of the general area of east Co. Tyrone, they had: 'daily seen the lamentable state of that country wherein we found everywhere men dead of famine'. The O'Hagan chief related how in his own homeland between Tullyhogue and Toome, just 20 miles, 'there lay unburied a thousand dead, and that since our first drawing unto the Blackwater there were above three thousand starved in Tyrone'.[14] Moryson collated many of the original dispatches of the campaign; it may be argued that some are exaggerated to convince the government that Kinsale did not end the war and to have it continue its support in men, money and arms. Atrocities are reported in an offhand manner to the Privy Council as if they were dispatches of military victories. In July 1602 Mountjoy seems to have taken the credit from Docwra of the latter's incursions into O'Cahan's country around Coleraine when he reported to the Privy Council about how they were closing in on O'Neill:

> we can assure your lordships, that from O'Cane's country, where he now liveth, which is to the northward of his own country of Tirone we have left none to give us opposition, nor of late have seen any but dead carcases, merely starved for want of meat of which we found many in divers places as we passed.[15]

13 W. Farmer, 'Chronicles of Ireland, 1594–1613', ed. C. Litton Falkiner, *English Historical Review*, 85 (1907), 129–30. Farmer's account of Carew's severity after the siege of Dunboy in September 1602 is not well known. No timber could be found to make a gallows to hang the prisoners and 'a carpenter brought a piece of timber out of the castle –he bored many holes a slope-wise and drove strong pins of wood into them; the same being set fast into the ground, four score Spaniards and rebels were hanged thereon, 2, 3, or 4 upon it, until all were hanged, as well women and boys as men of service where they hung all that night.' Ibid., p. 128.   14 Moryson, *Itinerary*, 2, p. 208.   15 *Calendar of Carew MSS 4 (1601–1603)*, pp 282–4. Mountjoy to the Privy Council, 29 July 1602.

In a moment of unusual optimism, Mountjoy reckoned that Ulster could be made 'one of the quietest countries in all Ireland', but not 'until it is reduced and the name of O'Neale utterly suppressed, never look for a sound peace in Ireland'.[16] It is also symptomatic of the brutality of the harrying of the north that a distinguished captain of the old school of chivalry, Calisthenes Brooke, applied for a transfer to the Netherlands, asserting that he was not fulfilling his proper calling as a commissioned officer of the queen of England in the Irish war which, he said, required huntsmen and not professional soldiers.[17] Indeed, head-hunting could almost be a dominant motif of Elizabeth's Irish wars: John Derricke in the celebrated woodcuts of his *Image of Irelande* depicts soldiers hacking off heads and carrying them by the hair to be stuck on spikes on the turrets of Dublin Castle and Newgate prison (figure 4, p. 73).

The impact of the Irish war on the shires of England and Wales also helps explain its bitterness. In Sir Robert Cecil's telling pun, 'that Land of Ire hath exhausted this land of promise'.[18] As the numbers of men between the ages of 16 and 60 dwindled by the end years of the war, the government emptied the gaols, pressed vagabonds, and 'lifted' men in their seventies in Wales for the Irish stations hoping, no doubt, that the vagabonds would never return to England to be a burden on the parish poor law rates.[19] Retaliation and personal revenge also played their part in embittering Irish warfare. Sir Arthur Chichester, for example, was likely enraged against the Irish for the killing and beheading of his brother, Sir John Chichester, earlier on in the war. Moreover, the harsh practice of pledgecraft or hostage-taking perpetuated revenge killings on both sides. It is needless here to give examples, for the records of the Irish State Papers are blood-stained by the hangings of hostages, many of them innocent children of the Gaelic chiefs in rebellion. James Anthony Froude, the eminent Victorian and no lover of Irish Catholics wrote of Tudor Ireland in his now little-read multi-volume history of England: 'The English nation was shuddering over the atrocities of the duke of Alva, yet Alva's bloody sword never touched the young, the defenceless, or those whose sex even dogs can recognize and respect'.[20]

Many garrison commanders got the rewards of their labours and wounds in lands around their forts in the massive land confiscations that would follow the Flight of the Earls and O'Doherty's rebellion of 1607 and 1608.[21] Some, like Toby Caulfield, John Sidney, Chichester, and Docwra, would live to regret the impact of scorched earth tactics and post-war deportations which left a reduced native work force. In their later rôle as servitors, many of these military men

16 Moryson, *Itinerary*, 2, 208   17 Cited in my *Elizabethan conquest of Ireland* (Manchester, 1997), p. 226.   18 HMC, *Calendar of the manuscripts of the Marquess of Salisbury* (24 vols, London, 1883–1976), 10, p. 345.   19 McGurk, *Elizabethan conquest of Ireland*, chapters 3 and 5.   20 J.A. Froude, *History of England, Elizabeth I* (London, 1930), 4, p. 23.   21 John McCavitt, *The Flight of the Earls* (Dublin, 2002), chapter 1.

regarded themselves as frontiersmen, caught up in local Gaelic politics, some marrying into local families (contrary to the conditions under which they had accepted land from the crown), learning Irish, and acquiring estates and large debts around the places they had defended during the war. The names of Captains Brooke, Leigh, Cole, Blaney, Caulfield, and Brett come to mind. 'Ulster', wrote the servitor, Thomas Blenerhasset, in 1610: 'presents herself, as it were, in a ragged, sad, sabled robe, ragged indeed, for there is nothing but ruins and desolation with a very little show of humanity'. His picture of a depopulated Ulster is confirmed by modern demographers and plantation historians.[22]

The wider historical perspective of the conduct of the Spanish against the Aztecs and Incas is often cited in mitigation of the ruthlessness of early modern warfare in the late Elizabethan conquest of England's oldest colony. The wider world view does not diminish the realities of the Ulster experiences of atrocity and catastrophe in the first years of the seventeenth century. Neither does it clarify this reality to argue that that what an ill-disciplined, hungry and armed soldiery did to civilians surrounding their garrisons was 'normal' in the conduct of war at the time. The slaughter of clergy, women, children, and other defenceless non-combatants who did not carry arms, was perpetrated on a scale hardly paralleled elsewhere in Europe at that time. The medieval church had promulgated the *Lex Innocentium* or Law of the Innocents ever since the seventh century; this was particularly focussed on women, who were not to be killed, assaulted or abused, and urged all rulers to protect them from such dangers. The law that women should have no part in warfare, attributed to the work of Adamnán at the Synod of Tara 697, was absorbed into Gaelic legal traditons through the Brehon laws.[23] This code was generally ignored and deemed barbaric by the new English adventurers, and yet was used by some lawyers like Sir John Davies, one of the architects of the Ulster plantation when it suited his schemes of land

---

22 In his promotional pamphlet to attract tenants to his Fermanagh lands at Castlehasset, Blenerhasset likely underestimated the native population. 'Direction for the plantation in Ulster, 1610', J.T. Gilbert (ed.), *A contemporary history of affairs in Ireland* (Dublin, 1879), 1:1, pp 323–4. However, in a magnificent rhetorical flourish he tells prospective settlers that they cannot enjoy 'the happy Elizian fields ... until they pass over the black river Stix ... [but then] they can do God and the Prince excellent service. Use there [in Ulster] thy talent, it will be quickly a million'. Population figures for Ireland as a whole, and Ulster in particular, in the pre-plantation years of the seventeenth century are speculative. Cullen suggests that Irish population grew from about 1.4 million in 1600 to 2.1 million by 1641, others, notably Clarkson and Canny, suggest the population in 1600 was nearer one million. L.M. Cullen, 'Population trends in seventeenth-century Ireland', *Economic and Social Review*, 6:2 (1974/5), 149–65; M. Perceval-Maxwell, *The Scottish migration to Ulster in the reign of James I* (London, 1973), p. 17. For detailed researched figures on one county, see W. Macafee, 'The population of county Tyrone, 1600–1991', in C. Dillon and H. Jeffries (eds), *Tyrone: history and society* (Dublin, 2002), p. 433.   23 See 'Law' in S.J. Connolly (ed.), *The Oxford companion to Irish history* (Oxford, 1998) and 'Adamnán' in M. Walsh (ed.), *Dictionary of Christian biography*

reform.²⁴ The brutality of Humphrey Gilbert (d.1583) is well known but his justification for murdering women is less so:

> the men of war could not be maintained without their churls and *Calliackes* [*cailleacha*], old women and those women who milked their Creaghts [*creacha*, herds] and provided their victuals and other necessaries. So that the killing of them by the sword was the way to kill the men of war by famine.²⁵

A more sophisticated version of this argument was the Machiavellian prescription of *necessitas* to rationalize killing civilians acting, even if unwittingly or unwillingly, as accessories to rebellion. Mountjoy likely had read Machiavelli's *Il Principe* and, according to Fynes Moryson, Caesar's *Gallic Wars*, became his *vade mecum* on campaign.²⁶ In writing to Carew of his harrying of Ulster he said that 'it grieveth me to think that it is *necessary* to do this', that is, spoil their corn, burn their houses and kill their churls.²⁷ Unrestricted violence against non-combatant civilians then appeared to be justified by a rather perverted sense of natural law, justice and necessity. Needless to say, such scholastic and rationalistic posturings were not usually indulged in by young bloods far away from the restrictions of Mother England.²⁸ Many times in excusing the harshness of his men from the Derry/Foyle garrisons, Sir Henry Docwra stressed to the Privy Council that if the government of England would not feed them he could not be responsible for their killing of civilians when they went foraging and plundering. Here was another variant of the argument that necessity knew no law.

Other, more sophisticated, rationalizations include a recurrent Elizabethan emphasis on due processes of law, mainly because Gaelic Ireland was not regarded as a separate polity but as a subject realm of the English Crown. Ideally, in the reformers' prescriptions, the benefits of English common law and manorial custom were to be the basis of civil society, not military controls. David Edwards, an authority on martial law, has stressed that martial law was not confined to the barracks and garrison in the interests of military discipline, but also extended to civilians to facilitate social control in lieu of any local policing. Likewise, in England the mayors of ports were given martial law powers to discipline unruly recruits awaiting favourable winds for embarkation.

(London, 2001). **24** See S. Kelsey, 'Sir John Davies', *New dictionary of national biography* (Oxford, 2004). **25** Cited from T. Churchyard, *A generall rehearsall of warres*, in Quinn, *The Elizabethans and the Irish*, p. 127 **26** For modern biographies of Mountjoy see F.M. Jones, *Mountjoy, the last Elizabethan deputy* (Dublin, 1958), the entry in the *New dictionary of national biography* by C. Maginn, and V. Carey, 'The Irish face of Machiavelli: Richard Beacon's *Solon his Follie* (1594)', in Morgan, *Political ideology in Ireland*, pp 83–109. **27** *Cal. S.P. Ire. 1601–1603*, pp 263–4, Mountjoy to Carew, 2 July 1602. **28** N. Canny, 'The permissive frontier: the problem of social control in English settlements in Ireland and Virginia', in Canny et al., *The westward enterprise*.

Intended as temporary solutions limited in time and place, martial law commissions became widespread and common in Ireland in the 1590s.[29]

Any historian of this period has to be even-handed and admit, from the abundant evidence of feuding among and within Gaelic clans or septs, that ravaging enemy land was a well-worn tactic before the Nine Years War. Hugh O'Neill, in his own aggressive climb to power and control over other rival branches of that princely family, burnt out the MacShane O'Neills of the Sliocht Airt territory between Omagh and Strabane. If he did not exactly hang Hugh Gavelach McShane with his own hands he had his executioners, the O'Quinns, carry out that murder. Red Hugh O'Donnell reputedly dashed out the brains of his nephew, an infant son of his sister Nuala who married his rival, Niall Garbh O'Donnell. Family feuds and greed for power and lands caused most of the dreadful atrocities besmirching the annals of the Gaelic nobility. Naturally, it was this feature of the tyranny of the Gaelic lords which was given much propaganda value by the new English military caste when it posed as the liberator of the common people. 'Tartarian' was so frequently used as an adjective of Gaelic society that it became an Elizabethan cliché. Hugh O'Neill, second earl of Tyrone, was likened to the Grand Turk. Whenever captains and commanders from Ireland wrote to the Privy Council or to Sir Robert Cecil in the 1590s (as they frequently did), they emphasized their role in Ireland as the deliverers of the common people to justify a 'forward' policy; an enduring Elizabethan euphemism. As discussed, such forward policies usually concluded in the seizure of lands and goods, thereby betraying the ulterior motivation for the measures taken in bringing a long-drawn-out war to an end.

To do so, Mountjoy and his commanders launched an exceptionally harsh campaign to create famine and decimate the civilian population. It was not the original intention of the Queen or Privy Council in the 1590s to clear Ulster of its native people, thereby creating a desert and calling it peace. As the war gained momentum with clear advantage to the Gaelic confederacy under Hugh O'Neill, especially after his notable victories at Clontibret in Monaghan and on the Blackwater at the Yellow Ford, extreme advocates of complete conquest and a *tabula rasa* of the entire island of Ireland made their voices heard in court and council in London. In Dublin, their voices were much more hushed.

In Ulster, Sir Henry Docwra, Sir Arthur Chichester and Mountjoy himself acknowledged the exceptional character of the Nine Years War in their many references to the deliberate slaughter of non-combatants. 'Ethnic cleansing' and 'genocide' had not then been invented as catch-all phrases but they come near to marrying rhetoric and the reality of what Ulster suffered from 1600 to 1603. From Dungannon in 1602, Mountjoy chillingly remarked about the rumours

---

29 D. Edwards, 'Ideology and experience: Spenser's *View* and martial law in Ireland', in H. Morgan (ed.), *Political ideology in Ireland, 1541–1641* (Dublin, 1999).

of a further Spanish landing in Ireland that 'if they do not come this year they would be too late as no foreign succours are able to raise the dead'.[30]

To conclude: the echoes of arguments about 'revisionism' have not yet died out. Some historians stood accused of de-traumatizing the history of the Tudors in Ireland by omitting the blood and gore in order to give more prominence to constitutional reform programmes, many of which emanated more from the theorists in the Pale than from England itself. They advanced rationalizations, 'easy speeches that comfort cruel men': the Irish were barbaric and this was a savage and brutal age when human life was cheap; man's inhumanity to man could be found in every colonial society; and English military men and would-be colonizers in Ireland were learning from the conduct of the Spaniards in South America. More recent accounts have faced up to the exceptional severity of the Nine Years War. Sometimes comparisons are drawn here with the later and atrocious behaviour of soldiers in the Thirty Years War which was more of a religious conflict than the Nine Years War had been. All wars of religion appear to have been particularly vicious. How far the Nine Years War was a religious conflict remains problematical.

It may very well be concluded that the post-Kinsale period in Ulster, in the putting down of the fifteen-month resistance movement, was carried out with unprecedented violence against non-combatants, clergy, women and children, who traditionally were immune in warfare. The main perpetrators were Sir Arthur Chichester's soldiers, then Mountjoy's, and lastly Sir Henry Docwra's. These officers had codes of military discipline (these were not 'rules of war', a medieval concept which had faded into oblivion by the late sixteenth century) for the conduct of their men both in field and garrison. Mountjoy's code was almost a replica of the one operated by Leicester in the Netherlands; his set of instructions re-iterated by the Privy Council to Docwra and Chichester are also based on his own code. Medieval chivalric modes of conducting hostilities had virtually disappeared and did not constrain those bringing the higher benefits of Renaissance civility to a putatively barbarous and barely Christian people on a permissive frontier.

---

30 *Cal. S.P. Ire. 1601–1603*, cited in McGurk, 'Kinsale to Rathmullan, O'Neill *contra mundum*', *Dúiche Néill*, 14 (2003), 8.

'The just vengeance of God': reporting the violent deaths of persecutors in early modern Ireland

CLODAGH TAIT

In mid-August 1579 Bishop Patrick O'Healy of Mayo and Conn O'Rourke, both Franciscans, were executed in Kilmallock by martial law on the orders of Lord Justice William Drury.[1] The Annals of Lough Cé reported that:

> The Bishop O'hElidhe, i.e. the paragon of learning and piety of the whole world, and the son of O'Ruairce, i.e. Conbrather, the son of Brian, son of Eoghan O'Ruairc, came from the east, after their education and tour. The Justiciary of Erinn apprehended them; and they were both hanged, to the profanation of God and men. And that was a pitiful deed, i.e. to put an honourable, most pious bishop, and a friar minor of noble blood, to death in an unbecoming manner. But God performed a plain, manifest miracle on the Justiciary; i.e. a burning attacked his head the day those two were hanged, and this burning did not leave him until he died of it in the course of a short time.[2]

The attribution of Drury's death to divine vengeance was being circulated as early as 1580 by Nicholas Sanders, the English cleric who was the papal envoy to the Irish rebels: 'God is not mocked ... Mark ... Sir William Drurie's end who was the General against the Pope's Armies; and think not our part too weake, seeing God fighteth for us.'[3] Other Catholic sources supplied further twists to this saga of divine retribution. Before he died, the bishop had addressed the crowd from the gallows:

---

[1] B. Millett, 'The beatified martyrs of Ireland (1): Bishop Patrick O'Healy, O.F.M. and Conn O'Rourke, O.F.M.', *Irish Theological Quarterly*, 64 (1999), 55–78. [2] W.M. Hennessy (ed.), *The Annals of Lough Cé* (2 vols, London, 1871), 2, pp 427–8. [3] J. Strype, *The life and acts of Matthew Parker, the first archbishop of Canterbury in the reign of Queen Elizabeth* (London, 1711), p. 378; R. Bagwell, *Ireland under the Tudors* (3 vols, London, 1963 [1885–90]), 3, p. 28.

and then he named the day of reckoning for the viceroy to render an account of his unjust sentence of him, an anointed bishop, and for his extensive cruelties against friars, bidding him in the name of God to stand before the divine tribunal before the fifteenth day.

The same report claims that Drury subsequently 'fell into a horrible disease, and suffering great pain rotted daily from an incurable corruption, accompanied by a most repulsive stench, and on the fourteenth day from the martyrs' death he died at Waterford perpetually tormented by wicked devils.'[4] According to a 1606 account:

> William Drury, an Englishman, Viceroy of Ireland, was summoned by the Most Rev. Patrick Hely ... (whom with his brother in religion he had condemned to death solely on account of his faith), before the judgement-seat of God to give an account of his deed. He was seized with a very violent disease, and died soon after mad and uttering blasphemies. On the day he was buried, there was such darkness, thunder and lightening as Ireland never saw before or since.[5]

In 1620, Copinger added some further touches. He claimed that the two clerics had been hanged from trees, that their bodies had been mistreated and that: 'Immediately after their execution the said Lord Justice sickened in the camp, and ended his life at Waterford, crying out upon those blessed martyrs whom he had put to death but one month before.'[6]

AN AGE OF WONDERS

It is increasingly apparent from recent discussions of belief in the early modern period that Christians of all denominations considered that God was actively at work in the world, and that all sorts of wonders might be read as signs of his favour or displeasure. Raymond Gillespie has underlined the extent to which such understandings were fundamental to the worldviews of the inhabitants of sixteenth- and seventeenth-century Ireland.[7] Alexandra Walsham, in her book

---

4 P. O'Sullivan Beare, *Ireland under Elizabeth: chapters towards a history of Ireland in the reign of Elizabeth, being a portion of the history of Catholic Ireland by Don Philip O'Sullivan Bear*, ed. and trans. M.J. Byrne (New York and London, 1970), p. 16.   5 'On the punishment of some of the persecutors of the faith in Ireland', in P. Moran (ed.), *Spicilegium Ossoriense* (3 vols, Dublin, 1884), 3, p. 25, translated in D. Murphy, *Our martyrs: a record of those who suffered for the Catholic faith under the penal laws in Ireland* (Dublin, 1896), p. 105.   6 John Copinger, 'Irish martyrs and confessors under Elizabeth and James I', in Moran, *Spicilegium Ossoriense* 3, p. 37. 7 R. Gillespie, *Devoted people: belief and religion in early modern Ireland* (Manchester, 1997),

Providence in Early Modern England, provides a variety of tales of gruesome deaths that were ascribed to divine vengeance, drawn from sources like contemporary catalogues of wonders such as Thomas Beard's, *The theatre of Gods judgments* and examples contained in Foxe's *Book of martyrs*. A bad death was the sign of a bad life: it was very tempting, therefore, to credit God for the dramatic demise of an enemy or one whose behaviour marked him out as an enemy of God. The tropes used were fairly formulaic, often with parallels in tales of the deaths of biblical persecutors and universal folkloric 'types' of the deaths of the iniquitous. Such tales were disseminated to entertain and astonish but also to edify, by indicating God's antipathy towards wrongdoers and the enemies of his chosen people, and to convince that group that their cause was righteous.[8] These are the other side of the coin of the martyrological collections that were circulated at this time.[9] As Brad Gregory has pointed out, God's miraculous judgement on persecutors went hand in hand with the patient suffering of adversity on the part of the martyrs and even underlined some of their reputations for sanctity.[10] Stories of providential vengeance were thus eagerly collected by martyrologists of all creeds during the early modern period. Given our clear comprehension of these issues, what can evidence from Ireland add to our understanding of such phenomena in a general sense, or what can they reveal about the political and cultural situation prevailing in Ireland in the sixteenth and seventeenth centuries and subsequently?

This article deals with the deaths of four prominent government officials in Ireland which were ascribed to divine vengeance in late sixteenth- and seventeenth-century Ireland – those of Drury, Henry Ireton, Charles Coote and Henry Brouncker. Since these deaths were widely documented by both sides as well as going down in folklore it is possible to compare to some degree how the 'facts' of their deaths compared to the 'facts' circulated by the Catholic side and,

---

especially chapter 3. 8 A. Walsham, *Providence in early modern England* (Oxford, 1999); 'Reformed folklore? Cautionary tales and oral tradition in early modern England', in A. Fox and D. Woolf (eds), *The spoken word: oral culture in Britain 1500–1850* (Manchester, 2002), pp 173–95; T.S. Freeman, 'Fate, faction and fiction in Foxe's *Book of Martyrs*', *Historical Journal*, 43 (2000), 601–23; P.C. Maddern, *Violence and social order: East Anglia, 1422–1442* (Oxford, 1992), pp 79–84. 9 See C. Tait, 'Adored for saints: Catholic martyrdom in Ireland c.1560–1655', *Journal of Early Modern History*, 5 (2001), 128–59; 'The making of a nation-saint: the beatification and canonisation of Oliver Plunkett' (forthcoming); A. Ford, 'Martyrdom, history and memory in early modern Ireland', in I. McBride (ed.), *History and memory in Modern Ireland* (Cambridge, 2001), pp 43–66; C. Lennon, 'Taking sides: the emergence of Irish Catholic ideology', in V. Carey and U. Lotz-Heumann (eds), *Taking sides: colonial and confessional mentalités in early modern Ireland* (Dublin, 2003), pp 78–93; 'Religious wars in Ireland: plantations and martyrs of the Catholic Church', in B. Bradshaw and D. Keogh, *Christianity in Ireland: revisiting the story* (Dublin, 2002), pp 86–95. 10 B.S. Gregory, *Salvation at stake: Christian martyrdom in early modern Europe* (Cambridge, MA, 1999), pp 325–6.

in Ireton's case, amongst his other opponents, the royalists. Tales of divine vengeance were not always clear-cut, therefore. These men's colleagues sometimes sought to diminish the propaganda potential of their deaths by what might be called 'antidemonology' (efforts to put forward more positive opinions about the manner of these deaths), alongside the process of conventional antimartyrology (the process of denigrating those viewed as martyrs by indicating the flaws in their credentials). Furthermore, within Ireland in this period, the cheap pamphlets that were the usual vehicles of this type of providential tale elsewhere were far less available. The necessity of using alternative documents to investigate ideas about divine vengeance makes us far more aware of the patterns of oral dissemination of such stories.[11] Interrogation of a wider range of sources than are usually considered by historians of this subject is thus essential. The letters by Protestant witnesses to deaths such as Drury's, and to the rumours that surrounded them, demonstrate that the reality could be rather more mundane and that allegations of providential intervention might be contested by the victim's coreligionists. Letters by the Catholic clergy to their brethren on the Continent demonstrate the official church's reaction to phenomena that might be seen to have been 'popular' in origin. Meanwhile, poets and playwrights might offer their own conflicting reactions. Accounts also appear in the compendia of sufferings of Ireland's Catholics largely produced in Latin for a European audience that were often composed at a distance from the events they describe, thereby chronicling the long-term impact and uses of such accounts. There is also some evidence that allows us to follow the journeys of the deaths of our four subjects through later folklore, demonstrating how such deaths might long continue to be a resource for the Catholic community.

DRURY

Despite the aforementioned dramatic accounts of the deaths of O'Healy and O'Rourke which portrayed them as martyrs for the Catholic faith, killed for no reason other than their Catholicism by a man subsequently convincingly the victim of divine vengeance, there is evidence for an alternative version of the story of their executions and Lord Justice Drury's death and funeral. Drury and the other commanders of the queen's troops in Ireland were under tremendous pressure by that time. James Fitzmaurice, after a decade on the continent drumming up support for a religious war in Ireland, had just landed in the country. His associate, Sanders, had long been active in schemes to dethrone Elizabeth I. A number of former Desmond clients had joined Fitzmaurice's

---

[11] The state of the Irish printing industry is dealt with in M. Ó Siochrú's article in this volume.

revolt. Though Fitzmaurice was killed soon after in a skirmish, the loyalty of the earl of Desmond also hung in the balance – it was feared that he too was on the verge of rebellion. It was known that in the past O'Healy had been an associate of Fitzmaurice's. Even if, as various Catholic historians have argued, he and his travelling companion had no involvement in the rebellion, the timing and location of his arrival in Ireland (in Smerwick, just ahead of Fitzmaurice's own landing there) led Drury to an obvious conclusions that did not need to be proved in any kind of a court since he had held a commission to exercise martial law since 1576.[12] O'Healy's visit to Desmond's castle in Askeaton was also unfortunate – the earl's wife, seemingly in an attempt to avert trouble, notified the authorities of the identity of her guests and they were arrested. In an age when religious rhetoric and temporal concerns were increasingly becoming intertwined, the executions of O'Healy and O'Rourke cannot be seen as merely stemming from religious discrimination. However summarily ordered, they also had a logical political rationale in removing any immediate chance of the clerics aiding or encouraging rebellion, and as a warning to the Irish rebels and their increasingly influential clerical supporters, who 'have been the instruments to seduce [the Queen's] subjectes from their dueties and loyalties.'[13]

The State Papers make little reference to the nature and progress of Drury's illness, though he and others had referred to his poor health in letters shortly before his death. They do, however, give a more extended timescale between the deaths of the Franciscans and that of the Lord Justice, dating the latter event to the beginning of October.[14] In regard to the storms that allegedly accompanied Drury's funeral, the official correspondence of the time certainly reveals that the weather around that time was inclement. Chancellor Gerrard, who travelled to Drury's deathbed in Waterford, refers to it as 'extreme', while Henry Wallop later reported damages caused by high winds to the ship *The Handmaid* and to a number of churches.

But while adverse meterological events may have occurred at around the time of his death (it seems to have been a bad winter in general), it is difficult to reconstruct what happened on the day of Drury's burial. As a series of unusual letters demonstrate, the actual date cannot be pinpointed. He seems to have been interred in St Patrick's cathedral, Dublin, in or around late February or

---

12 D. Edwards, 'Ideology and experience: Spenser's *View* and martial law in Ireland', in H. Morgan (ed.), *Political ideology in Ireland, 1541–1641* (Dublin, 1999), pp 133–4. 13 J. Hogan and N. McNeill O'Farrell (eds), *The Walsingham letter-book or register of Ireland* (Dublin, 1959), p. 142. See C. Brady, 'Faction and the origins of the Desmond rebellion of 1579', *Irish Historical Studies*, 22 (1981), 289–313; S.G. Ellis, *Ireland in the age of the Tudors, 1447–1603* (London, 1998); S. Kelsey, 'Drury, Sir William', http://www.oxforddnb.com/view/article/8101, accessed 3 February 2005. 14 Hogan and O'Farrell, *Walsingham letter-book*, p. 199; W. Camden, *The history of the most renowned and victorious princess Elizabeth late Queen of England* (fourth edition, London, 1688), pp 238–9.

early March 1580 – nearly five months after his death. The corpse had at some point been 'honourably conveyed' from Waterford to Dublin, but the subsequent gap seems to have resulted from the poverty of Drury's estate and the reluctance of his widow Margery Williams, Lady Thame, to consent to a funeral that was less honourable than his status demanded. She herself wrote to Francis Walsingham on 18 November, bemoaning the situation she and her children found themselves in, claiming that without relief from the queen 'I am neither hable to enterr him, n[or] yet to paie his Debtes made in her maties service.'[15] Despite Wallop's earlier suggestion that Drury 'be honourably buried at the princes charge', the money does not seem to have been forthcoming.[16] A letter of 16 February from William Pelham, Drury's replacement as Lord Justice, to the Queen's secretary, Thomas Wilson, is worth quoting at length:

> For the burial of Sir William Drurie, which you prescribe to be done with the ordinary garrison, and without further expense to he[r] Majesty, if my lady of thame might have been so persuaded or that in her judgment it had been fit for his place to have had such funerals, that [would have] been long since performed, but it may be she will alter her opinion. Nevertheless, your Honour's direction coming now when we are drawn to the field with the soldiers, cannot possibly be performed until their return. In the mean time I have advised my Lady to be as secretly buried as may be, and to leave a coffin for form sake, to be attended with three or four of her servants and to give forth that her Majesty will bury him according to his place and office, and so she to depart and leave me to perform the obsequy.[17]

A letter dispatched from Pelham to the English Privy Council indicated that Lady Thame had agreed to allow him to bury the body when he returned with the soldiers. He does not mention the elaborate subterfuge involving an empty coffin: maybe that plan was abandoned, maybe it was already in operation. In any case it is doubtful that any military funeral was eventually performed.

In this context the extant 'Epitaph upon the death of syr William Drury' written by the controversialist Barnaby Rich, himself a soldier by trade, becomes especially interesting. Rich's poem painted a picture of a martial funeral procession led by the mythical figure of 'Report' and addressed by 'Lady Fame'. Indeed, his first stanza suggests that he had written the piece (perhaps on the commission of Drury's family?) in response to a perceived neglect of Drury, who, as he pointed out, had achieved considerable military

---

15 Margery Wylliams to Walsingham, PRO, SP 63/70, 9. A comparable model for the type of military funeral that Drury's family might have expected may be found in the account of the burial of Sir Peter Carew in Waterford in 1575 – J. Hooker, *The life and times of Sir Peter Carew, Kt.* ed. J. MacLean (London, 1857), pp 107–9. 16 PRO, SP 63/69, 10. 17 *Cal. S.P. Carew 1575–88*, pp 222–3.

success in France, Scotland, and elsewhere prior to his campaigns and death in Ireland:

> In place where wantes Apollo with his Lute,
> There peevish Pan may p[l]ease to pipe a daunce,
> Where men of skill and learned Clarkes are mute,
> There Fooles may prate, and hit the truth perchaunce,
> Why spare I then to speake, when all are mumme,
> And vertue left forgot in time to come.[18]

Rich was speaking out when everyone else was silent. Perhaps the poetic funeral was a replacement for the real thing. The effigial monument seemingly eventually erected to Drury's memory in St Patrick's, possibly by his widow, may also have been a means of compensating for this neglect of an appropriate funeral, though it unfortunately has not survived.[19]

So here we are presented with contrasting versions of what might be termed the 'memorable' aspects of the same story, told from the providential, personal and poetical perspectives. There is the story of the persecutor who had wrongfully condemned two martyrs to death, and who had paid the price, divine vengeance being expressed in the manner of Drury's death and the events of his funeral, not to mention the reports circulating of the miraculous preservation of the remains of his victims. Conversely, there is the far more prosaic story of the man charged with putting down a local rebellion who had made so little profit from his talents in military matters and his energetic work in the queen's cause in Ireland and elsewhere that his widow alleged she could not afford to bury him – to the embarrassment of both herself and the Irish administration. This shabby treatment may even have bolstered the story of divine intervention. It certainly was a lost opportunity to present an alternative meaning in regard to Drury's death.

IRETON

Drury's is far from being the only case in which conflicting versions of the deaths of individuals and groups, incorporating a suggestion of divine intervention, exist. The 1640s and 50s provided two notorious victims of providential vengeance: Charles Coote and Lord Deputy Henry Ireton. Ireton, Cromwell's son-in-law, had been left in command of the army in Ireland on Cromwell's return to England.[20] As in the case of Lord Justice Drury, the occasion of the

18 H.E. Collins, *The paradise of dainty devices (1576–1606)* (Cambridge, MA, 1927), pp 121–3. Though the poem mentions the date of Drury's death, it could have been written slightly later.
19 W.M. Mason, *History of the Collegiate Church of St. Patrick near Dublin* (Dublin, 1819), p. 173.
20 I.J. Gentles, 'Ireton, Henry', http:/www.oxforddnb.com/view/article/14452, accessed 10

alleged divine intervention that ended Ireton's life was the death of a bishop-martyr, this time Terence Albert O'Brien, Catholic Bishop of Emly. As part of the terms of the surrender of Limerick in October 1651, O'Brien was one of the small number of its defenders excluded from quarter and was arrested, court-martialled and hanged, his head being displayed on the gates of the city.[21] In the eyes of the Parliamentarians, O'Brien's execution was entirely just, since he was counted as one of the 'three Persons of principal Activity and Influence' in extending the siege, as well as, with Major-General Purcell, one of the 'original Incendiaries of the Rebellion and Mischiefs in it, or prime Engagers therein'. O'Brien was guilty of many of these charges, and even as the siege was coming to an end he, along with Bishop O'Dwyer of Limerick, attempted unsuccessfully to prolong it by excommunicating those who advocated surrender (self-preservation may have been a strong motivation, since the terms of surrender excluded the bishops and other clerics from quarter: O'Dwyer eventually managed to escape the city by disguising himself and marching out with the soldiers).[22] Edmund Ludlow, one of Ireton's close associates and a witness to the end of the siege, recorded that O'Brien was condemned to death along with Major-General Purcell, one of the other leaders of the defending forces. 'The Bishop said, that having many Sins to confess, he desired time to prepare himself to that purpose, which was granted.' Purcell begged for his life, and allegedly had to be supported by two soldiers at his execution, but 'The Bishop died with more Resolution.' This may be a reference to O'Brien's speech from the gallows, a masterpiece of the genre, which would have helped consolidate the impression amongst his flock that he was a martyr for Catholicism.[23]

Dominic O'Daly, who claimed to have received his information from an alternative eyewitness, gave a more elaborate account of the proceedings:

> when brought before Ireton ... [the bishop] replied, as it were, prophetically, and told the canting Puritan to his face that he would soon have to answer before the tribunal of God; and it eventually came to pass, for heaven so disposed, that, eight days after the bishop's death, Ireton was seized with the plague and died, exclaiming that the prelate's blood hastened his death.

November 2004. **21** See A. Valkenburg, 'The beatified martyrs of Ireland (10) Terence Albert O'Brien, O.P., Bishop of Emly', *Irish Theological Quarterly*, 66 (2001), 165–72. **22** *A letter from the Lord Deputy-General of Ireland unto the Honorable William Lenthal Esq; Speaker of the Parliament of England; concerning the rendition of the city of Limerick* (London, 1651), pp 8, 23; E. Borlase, *The history of the Irish rebellion* (Dublin, 1743), pp 357–8. **23** *Memoirs of Edmund Ludlow Esq; Lieutenant General of the Horse, Commander in Chief of the forces in Ireland, one of the Council of State, and a Member of the Parliament which began on November 3, 1640* (2 vols, Vivay, 1698), I, pp 373–4; H. Fenning, 'The last speech and prayer of Blessed Terence Albert O'Brien, Bishop of Emly, 1651', *Collectanea Hibernica*, 38 (1996), 52–8.

Meanwhile the bishop's head, displayed on a spike, allegedly remained incorrupt.[24] O'Heyne later added that Ireton became very agitated following the prophecy and

> confessed openly to his military captains standing around him, that the execution of the innocent bishop would prove fatal to him, and he often repeated these words: 'I never counselled the death of that bishop; never! Never! The council of war did it' ... He also exclaimed 'Would that I had not seen that Papist bishop even from a distance.' While uttering these and similar words he breathed his last.[25]

John Lynch gave a similar account, drawn from other eyewitnesses. One writer alleged that for some time thereafter the Protestant citizens of Limerick kept Thursdays as a festival 'lest the Catholics should point to his untimely end as a visible mark of divine vengeance.'[26] Given that Ireton died on a Wednesday, this would seem an exaggeration. Rumours of the manner of Ireton's death were celebrated in England as well as Ireland both at the time and long afterwards. In the 1670s Philip Warwick, a vocally royalist chronicler of the reign of Charles I and restoration of Charles II, alleged that Ireton:

> who, as he was a man of blood, (for he had deeply dyed himselfe in the Kings) expired with the word in his mouth (for in his raving, as I was told by one that was then there, he cryed out) *I will have more blood, blood, blood.*'[27]

It is interesting that the royalist version (note again the allegation of eyewitness authority) was adapted to link Ireton's raving end with the death of the King rather than with any other incident. The idea of Ireton as a 'man of blood' is a reference to the vividly articulated contemporary notion of blood guilt. The shedding of innocent blood 'would not be left unavenged' by God.[28]

The issue of the exact cause of Ireton's death seems also to have been of significance to commentators. O'Daly explicitly claimed plague to be the cause. Likewise James Heath, who published *A chronicle of the late intestine war* in 1675, declared that 'he fell sick on the 15 of November and after Purging and Bleeding, and other means used, died of the Plague ... on the 27 of the same month'.[29]

24 D. O'Daly, *The rise, increase and exit of the Geraldines*, ed. C.P. Meehan (Dublin, 1878), p. 205.   25 J. O'Heyne, *The Irish Dominicans of the seventeenth century*, ed. and trans. A. Coleman (Dundalk, 1902), p. 85.   26 R. Walsh, 'Some of our martyrs', *Irish Ecclesiastical Record*, 3rd series, 15 (1894), p. 110.   27 P. Warwick, *Memoires of the reigne of King Charles I with a continuation to the happy restauration of King Charles II* (London, 1701), p. 354.   28 P. Crawford, 'Charles Stuart: that man of blood', *Journal of British Studies*, 16 (1977), 41–61.   29 J. Heath, *A chronicle of the late intestine war in the three kingdoms of England, Scotland and Ireland* (London, 1675), p. 305. See also J. Ferrar, *An history of the city of*

However, soon after hearing of Ireton's death, one of his close associates, John Cook, Chief Justice of Munster, had been quick to assert that a fever occasioned by Ireton's 'last tedious and wet march into Connaught' was the cause, adding that 'his heavenly Father would not suffer him to dye by the hand of the enemy, nor of the Pestilence, whereby many of his deere servants have been called home.'[30] Plague was often seen as an expression of God's wrath – a pamphlet published by Ireton's orders in Cork in 1650 called for 'fasting and prayer' in response to the threat[31] – so Cook may have had a serious purpose in denying it was instrumental in the loss of such an 'able, painfull, provident and industrious servant' of the Commonwealth.[32] Ludlow is our main direct witness to the progress of the Lord Deputy's last illness. Ireton's demise actually occurred on 26 November, almost a month after O'Brien's execution (and at a time of year when levels of plague deaths would usually have declined). Like Cook, Ludlow attributed it to a cold caught the week before while out scouting for suitable garrisons in Co. Clare, which was exacerbated by the fact that Ireton had not taken very good care of his health during the siege of Limerick. Ludlow highlighted Ireton's dedication to duty during his sickness – he continued to work, despite sweats and a 'burning Fever' (incidentally, the symptoms as well as the timescale of the illness suggest plague was not the cause) – and stressed what he saw as his commander's unfailing humanity in his dealings with his men and with the Irish. Unfortunately, however, Ludlow had been dispatched to Dublin by the time the Lord Deputy actually expired 'which was universally lamented by all good Men'.[33]

Ireton's corpse was transported to London, where it was honourably buried in Westminster Abbey on 6 February 1652, amidst a flurry of elegies. Though the sermon preached on this occasion conspicuously avoided the topic of his death, it must be assumed that the trouble taken to bring the corpse to England and the fact that it was allowed to lie in state in Somerset House indicate that none of Ireton's colleagues believed him to have died of plague.[34] The attendant ceremonial was condemned by Ludlow, who felt that the Deputy would have preferred 'that his Body might have found a Grave where his Soul left it, so much did his despise those pompous and expensive Vanities.'[35]

Limerick (Limerick, 1767), p. 34.   30 J. Cook, *Monarchy no creature of Gods making, &c. Wherein is proved by scripture and reason that monarchical government is against the mind of God* (Waterford, 1652), verso of p.g; Borlase, *The history of the Irish rebellion*, p. 363.   31 *A declaration and prolcamation [sic] of the Deputy-General of Ireland concerning the present hand of God in the visitation of the plague* (Cork, 1650).   32 Cook, *Monarchy*, p.g.   33 *Memoirs of Edmund Ludlow*, pp 380–3. Gentles, 'Ireton, Henry', also attributes the death to a cold that became a fever, and was exacerbated by the treatment offered.   34 J. Owen, *The labouring saints dismission to rest. A sermon preached at the funeral of the right honourable Henry Ireton Lord Deputy of Ireland* (London, 1652); *An elegy [sacred] to the immortal memory of … Henry Ireton* (London, 1652); T. M., *Veni; vidi; vici. The triumphs of the most excellent & illustrious Oliver Cromwell … Whereunto is added an elegy upon … Henry Ireton* (London, 1652).   35 *Memoirs of Edmund Ludlow*, p. 384.

Ireton did not rest in peace. Along with Cromwell and Bradshaw, he was disinterred on the anniversary of King Charles I's death in January 1661 and symbolically hanged, beheaded and buried under the gallows at Tyburn as a posthumous punishment for regicide: Ireton's head was still on display 26 years later. His effigial monument in Westminster Abbey was also destroyed by supporters of the Restoration. Later folklore suggested that the bodies of Ireton, Cromwell and Bradshaw had been recovered from Tyburn and buried in Derbyshire or another location: numerous sites were suggested as the burial place of Cromwell's body in particular, and a skull supposed to be his was later immured in Sidney Sussex College, Cambridge, his alma mater. Other traditions even claimed that when Ireton's and Cromwell's graves were opened they were found to be empty, and that other bodies had to be substituted for them during the symbolic hangings. The ghosts of the regicides were also alleged to appear regularly at Basing House in Hampshire, and at other sites.[36] Such tales are a sign of the contradictions in perceptions of Cromwell and his generals that lingered following the Wars of the Three Kingdoms in England in particular. Those who had formerly sympathized with their cause may have found comfort in the idea of the escape of their bodies and meaning in the actions of their restless ghosts. These were men who haunted Irish as well as English politics long after their deaths. For example, when in 1896 James G. Barry of the Royal Society of Antiquaries in Ireland lamented the demolition in Limerick of an Elizabethan building called Ireton's House, he noted that part of the reason given by the 'iconoclastic' city corporation for their decision was that 'it was undesirable that it should be preserved as a memorial of a man of infamous memory'. Ireton was supposed to have stayed in the house, and local legend (which Barry viewed as being of late origin) claimed that Bishop O'Brien had even been hanged from one of its windows. The destruction of part of the city's heritage was thus justified by reference to its symbolic erasure of the memory of past traumas.[37]

---

36 A. Smith, 'Images of Cromwell in folklore and tradition', *Folklore*, 79 (1968), 37–8. See also A. Miles, *The last farewell of three bould traytors* (London, [1661]); M. Noble, *Memoirs of ... the protectorate-house of Cromwell* (2 vols, Birmingham, 1784), 2, pp 297–8. H.F. McMains and others have suggested that Ireton was buried in Ireland, and that his funeral occurred around an empty coffin: *The death of Oliver Cromwell* (Lexington, 2000); S.K. Roberts, 'Review of H.F. McMains, *The death of Oliver Cromwell*', H-Albion, H-Net Reviews, February, 2000, http://www.h-net.org/reviews/showrev.cgi?path+31644950218888, accessed 3 March 2007; The Cromwell Association, 'Cromwell's body', http://www.olivercromwell.org/faqs2.htm, accessed 3 March 2007; Gentles, 'Ireton, Henry'. The repeated references in the State Papers to the transport of Ireton's 'body' and 'corpse' suggest the conspiracy theorists to be incorrect. *Cal. S.P. (Domestic) 1651–1652*, especially pp 56, 66, 546.   37 J.G. Barry, 'Report from the Hon. Local Secretary for Limerick', *Journal of the Royal Society of Antiquaries in Ireland*, 24 (1894), 385–9. A fort at Limerick called 'Ireton's Fort' was renamed after 1691: Ferrar, *History of the city of Limerick*, p. 48.

COOTE

Nearly ten years before Ireton's demise, Sir Charles Coote, a military commander and privy councillor, was similarly presented in the Irish sources as both a tyrant and a victim of God's judgement.[38] He died at Trim in May 1642, apparently accidentally shot by one of his own troops, though triumphant rumours circulating amongst Catholics claimed that he had been defeated by Lord Fingal's forces and hanged ignominiously.[39] Coote, 'the Pearl of the World', had previously been lauded by the English press for his victories against the Irish – including a number of brutal massacres. Several contemporary news pamphlets printed in London lamented his death, one of them describing how on the Sunday after his demise 'every pulpit was fill'd with funerall Sermons, and teares ... for he is not to us like other dead men, which dying are soon forgot, but he is still daily remembered, and that justly, our want of him calls for it.'[40] The same pamphleteer bemoaned the fact that 'we have lost him ... whose name was their terror'. Another agreed 'he was the man who did so amaze the enemies, and damp their resolutions, that the Rebels doe more triumph, and confidently insult in his fall, and expiration, than if they had demolished (Dublin excepted) any City in that Kingdom, or given chase to our Army.'[41] Yet another described how Coote's death had so emboldened the rebels that they had begun to trouble his garrison at Naas, something they dared not do during his lifetime.[42]

The hatred and awe in which Coote was held by the Irish is confirmed by other sources. The Irish rebels in Wicklow were reported as stating that they would 'Hange as many of the English as they colde lay handes on for Sr Charles Coote his sake.'[43] The deposition of Hannagh Ffarrell of 29 January 1642 described how the house of Samuell Jefferies of Maynooth, Co. Kildare, had been ransacked by the sons of Mr Welsh of Mooretowne for arms 'to fight wth Sr Charles Coote who (as they said) was in battle with them of their religion.' The Welshes had allegedly urged the people of the town to fight against Coote, saying that he 'Was the Divell, or the sonne of a Divill, and that they would

---

38 P. Lenihan, 'Coote, Sir Charles, first baronet (*d*. 1642)', http://www.oxforddnb.com/view/article/6239, accessed 3 February 2005.   39 *Report on Franciscan manuscripts preserved at the convent, Merchant's Quay, Dublin* (Dublin, 1906), pp 149, 150, 157, 162.   40 Anon., *The best and happiest tydings from Ireland* (London, 1642); Anon., *True intelligence from Ireland relating many passages of consequence betweene the Protestants and the rebells* (London, 1642), pp 2–3; Anon., *A perfect relation of the proceedings of the English army against the rebels in Ireland* (London, 1642); W. Bias, *Good newes from Ireland* (London, 1642); M.S., *A discourse concerning the rebellion in Ireland* (London, 1642), pp 1–4; Anon., *A remonstrance of divers remarkable passages and proceedings of our army in the kingdom of Ireland* (London, 1642), n/p.   41 Anon., *True intelligence*, p. 6; S., *A discourse concerning the rebellion*, p. 4.   42 Anon., *A true relation*, p. A2.   43 1641 Depositions, Trinity College Dublin MS 811, f. 47.

have his head.'[44] In letters to Luke Wadding reporting news from Ireland, two Irish clerics based in France described the deceased commander as 'the devilish Coote' and 'that enemy to mankind' (the devil too was described as the enemy of mankind).[45] Lord Castlehaven claimed that even the Protestant side considered him 'a hot-headed and bloody man'.[46]

Overtones of just religious war against Coote also pervade an important contemporary Catholic account of the 1640s. *The aphorismical discovery of treasonable faction* which described Coote as a 'humaine-bloudsucker', a 'tiranicall minister, contemner of all lawes', and which incorporated several accounts of his actions against Catholics, was unsurprisingly keen to attribute his death to the workings of providence. As the final straw, on the day of his death Coote's son, Rice, had supposedly had an ancient statue of the Virgin Mary[47] chopped up to provide firewood, as his father had complained of the cold:

> Butt God Allmight[y], the righteous judge, did not prolong the punishment of this impietie, for as soone as Sir Charles thought to enioy the benefitt of that transformed-divine fire, worde came to him that the Irish alreadie intred the towne.

During the alarm, Coote was killed, though the author claimed he had never been able to ascertain by whom: a marginal note suggests that his fate may have been miraculous. He continues:

> A generall joy was conceauded in all loyall and royallist brest for the death of this tirant, as beinge generally hated of all well or humanly affected; see how he payed for his firinge ... sure he gave an account in hell of it, for thither he receaued his tickett that night.[48]

About three years later, we get an indication of the enduring nature of antipathy to Coote: Patricia Coughlan has recently demonstrated that the eponymous leading character of Henry Burkhead's play, *Cola's furie*, represents him. Cola is portrayed 'as in the grip of a dementia, the "fury" if the title, which causes him to commit senseless cruelties.' Cola, like Coote himself, is killed by a shot from the wings, and this death is likewise presented as an instance of divine intervention.[49] Some thirty years later, in his *Cambrensis*

---

44 1641 Depositions, Trinity College Dublin MS 813, f. 248. See also N. Canny, *Making Ireland British, 1580–1650* (Oxford, 2001), pp 526–7.   **45** *Report on Franciscan manuscripts*, pp 157, 162.   **46** Walsh, 'Some of our martyrs', p. 563.   **47** Gillespie, *Devoted people*, pp 1, 88; M. Potterton, *The history and archaeology of medieval Trim* (Dublin, 2005).   **48** Anon., *Aphorismical discovery of treasonable faction*, in J.T. Gilbert (ed.), *A contemporary history of affairs in Ireland from 1641 to 1652* (6 vols, Dublin, 1879), 1(1), pp 31–2.   **49** P. Coughlan, '"The modell of its sad afflictions": Henry Burkhead's *Tragedy of Cola's Furie*', in M. Ó

Eversus, Lynch too presented Coote as 'a most bloodthirsty monster' and a perpetrator of massacres on 'old men, women and children' and of other instances if casual cruelty against the Irish, including the case of a noblewoman who had given him hospitality and who he allegedly had 'hanged before her own front door', before cutting her unborn child from her womb and hanging it with her hair. However, he 'suffered the just punishment of his most atrocious cruelty; he was mortally wounded by some unknown hand, and thus, like another Julianus the apostate appears to have fallen under a judgment sent down on him by God himself.'[50]

As Kevin Forkan's article in this volume shows, an alternative view of Coote was strongly pushed by certain Protestant groups in Ireland in the early 1640s. Indeed, Faithfull Teate, who preached the sermon at the funeral of 'our deceased champion', 'a true mirror of Piety, Prowess & Prudence', and sought therein to legitimize the prosecution of just war, presented the manner of Coote's demise as an 'eligible, beautiful, honourable death' in the arms of his son.[51] However, neither Teate's panegyric, nor the complimentary pamplets mentioned above, nor even Coote's presentation as a martyr in the cause of God and as 'England's honour, Scotland's wonder, Ireland's terror' in an elegy that pictured him scaling the walls of heaven on Jacob's Ladder, went far in the long term as a vindication of his reputation.[52] He (or, perhaps, an amalgam of him and his son, another Charles)[53] went down in the folklore of Cootehall, Co. Roscommon, and Cootehill, Co. Cavan, as a cruel despot. In Cootehill an oak tree on which Coote had allegedly hanged one of the O'Reillys who had previously owned the lands and which had withered immediately as a result was pointed out by locals into the nineteenth century.[54] As late as the 1930s, Padraic Golden of Cootehall told that 'There are many stories current in this locality of the terrible deeds done by Coote in his day.' Castle Coote was allegedly haunted by his ghost:

> This Coote when alive was a planter of Cromwells and was a terrible tyrant ... it is told that at his bidding a young girl was tied to the tail of a young horse and he was turned loose and the girls head came off ... His end came at the ford over the river Boyle where the present Cootehall

---

Siochrú (ed.), *Kingdoms in crisis: Ireland in the 1640s* (Dublin, 2001), pp 192–211, especially pp 205–9. **50** J. Lynch, *Cambrensis eversus* ed. and trans. M. Kelly (3 vols, Dublin, 1848–51), 3, pp 93–4, 96, 101. **51** F. Teate, *The souldiers commission, charge & reward* (London, 1658), n.p. **52** 'An elegie upon the much lamented death of that famous & late Renowned knt & Colonell Sir Charles Coote', in A. Carpenter, *Verse in English from Tudor and Stuart Ireland* (Cork, 2003). **53** P. Little, 'Coote, Charles, first earl of Mountrath', http://www.oxforddnb.com/view/article,/6240, accessed 3 February 2005. **54** R. McCollum, *Sketches of the highlands of Cavan and of Shirley Castle in Farney* (Belfast, 1856), p. 236. Patrick Cassidy identifies the victim as Mulmorie O'Reilly who lost the estates after the Nine Years War: 'The Cootes of Cootehill', *Breifne*, 9 (37) (2001), 345.

bridge stands. He was crossing the river to capture a priest that was living on the Hill of Usnagh, and as the horse stooped to drink he fell from the saddle and broke his neck. We are told that the garrison of the castle then fled, after setting fire to the castle. It is said that molten silver ran down the castle courtyard and on to the road below.[55]

Other informants to the Folklore Commission elaborated on these legends. William Maxwell explained that the reason Coote killed the young woman – in his version, by tying her plaits to two young horses which were then released – was because she allegedly refused him his traditional 'ius primae noctis' (the right of the lord to spend a bride's first night of marriage with her). Coote had also hanged a young man whose father had complained of his wild ways with the comment 'Now ... you'll have aise [ease] from him', and other informants, as in Cootehill, were also clear on Coote's reputation for summary executions, something that may reflect the real Coote's possession of a commission of martial law. Maxwell and his brother, James, also attributed a prophecy of Coote's death to the 'little friar' he was hunting. Watching their pursuers from a hill, the friar's companion suggested they move on but the friar said: '"He won't go much further." And with that, the horse reared up on his hind legs, up straight an' fell back. An' killed Coote.'[56]

BROUNCKER

A final case of alleged divine vengeance also concerns a man considered a particularly vigorous persecutor of Catholics, Sir Henry Brouncker. He too had helped make a martyr, John Burke of Brittas.[57] Once again, Lynch provides an entertaining version of the events leading to Brouncker's death:

> Within the recollection of our fathers, Bruncard, President of Munster, was as ferocious in his hatred of the Catholics as Antiochus was against the Jews; but he met the fate of Antiochus. Worms swarmed out from his whole body; he was devoured piecemeal by vermin, and expired emitting a most horrid stench.[58]

That 'in the recollection of our fathers' is important: clearly Brouncker's death was long remembered in oral tradition as a significant event. What is most intriguing about this case is that though Lynch wrote many years afterwards,

---

[55] Irish Folklore Commission [IFC], Schools Folklore Collection [S] MS 232, ff 191–2, also f. 109. [56] IFC MS 1781, ff 46–9, 4–7, 168–71. [57] *Cal. S.P. Ire. 1603–1610*, pp 33–5, 101–4. [58] Lynch, *Cambrensis eversus*, 3, p. 101.

we can again trace the contemporary rumours circulating about it. For example, on 20 August 1607, Fr Bryan O'Kearney wrote to the Secretary of the Society of Jesus:

> Ireland has never seen a more cruel man than Brouncker ... When the President was at Waterford, he uttered many calumnies against the Jesuits and the priests, boasted that he never enjoyed better health than since he began to 'persecute the papists and their superstitious priests.' He, as was his wont, blurted out many blasphemies against the Head of the Church, the Jesuits and pupils of the seminaries; then, turning to a priest recently captured, he said: 'Curse me now.' The priest said his duty was to bless them that curse him, and pray for those that persecute and calumniate him. The President waxed furious, heaped curses on curses, and loaded the priest with insult. God did not long delay punishing the blasphemous mouth of the shameless monster, for that very night he was stricken with a frightful disease; he soon became insane, his neck swelled, his tongue protruded to a great length, his eyes rolled about in despair, and he appeared before the judgment seat of God. There was joy all over Ireland.

Two day later, Fr Wise of Waterford wrote.

> We hope for more toleration through the death of the President, who was the greatest persecutor we ever had. Walter ... has written to you the details of that death, except this, he took an Office and Rosary of the Blessed Virgin, and, having flung them into the fire, and once felt sick and never recovered.[59]

Brouncker's 'impiety and tyranny' still rankled in 1609, when Dr Kearney, archbishop of Cashel, added another facet to the story of the man he termed 'another emissary of the Antichrist':

> it was his boast that his health improved the more the maledictions of the Catholics were heaped upon him; but lo! God is ever with his beloved in their afflictions: this wretch, struck with insanity, in a frenetical fit, departed this life.[60]

On 3 June 1607, Parr Lane, Brouncker's Master of Horse, who was later to write an extensive poem suggesting reforms in Ireland and defending Brouncker's reputation, took it upon himself to write to the earl of Salisbury in order to

---

59 H. Fitzsimon, *Words of comfort to persecuted Catholics written in exile, anno 1607*, ed. E. Hogan (Dublin, 1881), pp 175–6.   60 P.F. Moran, *History of the Catholic archbishops of Dublin since the Reformation* (2 vols, Dublin, 1864), 1, pp 235, 432.

acquaint him with the events of the Lord President's deathbed. He had been present throughout Brouncker's illness 'and hearing the strange reports that are invented against him by the malice and envy that this country bears to the most sincere and worthiest governors, fearing they may fly overseas' had resolved to '[oppose] truth to the base and barbarous calumniations which are and were, a fortnight at least before his departure, given out in the country.' For six weeks Brouncker had endured a series of afflictions: gallstones, pain in his side and head, and swelling of his face,

> in the end whereof he wrestled in conscience towards God (which he often most seriously avowed to his preacher), and settled upon an assurance of his Lordship's favour for matters of the work, which he likewise protested. He died without any show of the least impatience, contrary to that which this country hath bred and spread against him, that he died raving and eating his flesh from his arms, lamenting his rigour against recusants.[61]

Unfortunately for Lane, and for Brouncker, the administrations in London and Dublin were unlikely to have worried very much about what had happened on his deathbed, or how this had been perceived, since his death removed the problem of dealing with him. Edmund Sexton, a Limerick Protestant, perhaps encapsulated the reasons for this when he recorded in his diary: 'Sir Henry Brouncker lo: president a religious honest gent dyed at Corke which was much rejoyced at for that he strove much to bring all men to church.'[62] Brouncker had been forced repeatedly to defend his hard-line and coercive methods of enforcing religious conformity, particularly amongst the townspeople of Munster, who had complained vocally at their treatment. On his death the English authorities were presented with a chance to sideline such policies, which they saw as mainly serving to stir up Irish dissent. This reversal doubtless reinforced the ruin of Brouncker's reputation: the protests of his wife, who felt that Brouncker had not been adequately rewarded for his zealous and lengthy service, and Parr Lane's later poetic vindication ('Death could not kill thee whose vertue fame and honnor livinge bee'), largely fell on deaf ears.[63]

---

[61] *Cal. S.P. Ire. 1606–8*, p. 188. See A. Ford, 'Parr Lane, "Newes from the Holy Ile"', *Proceedings of the Royal Irish Academy*, 99 (1999), 115–56; Ford, 'Reforming the Holy Isle: Parr Lane and the conversion of the Irish', in T. Barnard, D. Ó Cróinín, and K. Simms (eds), *A miracle of learning: studies in manuscript and Irish learning* (Aldershot, 1998), pp 137–63. [62] Diary of Edmund Sexton, National Library of Ireland MS 16,085, f. 59. [63] For Brouncker's energetic prosecution of the 'Mandates' policy, see J. McCavitt, *Sir Arthur Chichester Lord Deputy of Ireland 1605–16* (Belfast, 1998), especially chapter 7. Also Ford, 'Reforming the Holy Isle'; Ford, 'Parr Lane', 149; Anne Brouncker to James I, PRO, SPI 221/69.

UNDERSTANDING PROVIDENCE

All of these men were not only well known as persecutors of the Catholic community in Ireland, but had reputations as killers of Catholics: Drury during his time as Lord President of Munster and Lord Justice, Brouncker during the time of the controversial 'mandates' policy, and Coote and Ireton in the 1640s and 50s. To continue the connection with martyrology it is also worth pointing out that three of them were associated, to a greater or lesser degree, with specific Catholic martyrs from religious orders – Drury with O'Healy and O'Rourke, Ireton with O'Brien, and Coote with Peter Higgins or O'Higgins, a Dominican who he had summarily hanged in Dublin in March 1642 and whose death seems to have caused a large degree of controversy, not least since the earl of Ormond had guaranteed the Dominican his protection.[64] Brouncker had killed John Burke of Brittas, and harassed and ordered the exile of various priests. These associations perhaps in part explain the preservation of the stories of their deaths. Each of the religious orders was keen to preserve accounts of their martyrs and the associated downfalls of their persecutors.

However, it should be noted that divine vengeance was not merely reserved for the powerful. Lesser individuals, mostly anonymous English soldiers who had injured righteous people or holy objects, suffered the anger of God as expressed in stray bullets, horrible diseases, flashes of lightening, falling masonry and even, in one case, spontaneous combustion.[65] Copinger's account of *The theater of Catholick and Protestant religion* included accounts of various instances of divine vengeance, including the fate of three soldiers who, in an echo of Coote's destruction of a statue of the Virgin Mary, 'did caste downe and burne the holye roode' in the Dominican priory in Youghal, Co. Cork. All died within a week, one mad, one eaten by lice, and one killed in a skirmish 'all which many of that towne now livinge can witnesse.'[66] The deaths of certain of the Irish who were seen to have colluded with the English forces were also presented in providential terms. One example was Calvagh O'Donnell, accused by O'Sullivan Beare of introducing iconoclastic 'heretics' to Derry, who allegedly fell dead from his horse 'in the heyday of his health and vigour' while leading an army against Shane O'Neill in 1566.[67] Nor did God merely express his support on the Catholic side in the conflict. Protestant accounts also described the more extraordinary deaths of persecutors, particularly during the 1640s, a time when, as in England, providential propaganda became entirely

---

64 On O'Higgins see A. Valkenburg, 'The beatified martyrs of Ireland (9) Peter Higgins, O.P.', *Irish Theological Quarterly*, 66 (2001), 67–74; Walsh, 'Some of our martyrs', pp 558–65, 637–48.   65 C. Tait, *Death, burial and commemoration in Ireland, c.1550–1650* (Basingstoke, 2002), pp 24–5.   66 J. Copinger, *The theatre of Catholique and Protestant religion* (Saint-Omer, 1620), p. 435.   67 O'Sullivan Beare, *Ireland under Elizabeth*, pp 4–5; S. Ellis, *Tudor Ireland* (London and New York, 1985), pp 254–5.

ubiquitous. The Revd William Fitzgerald of Armagh told of how Brian McHugh Boy O'Neill who had carried out Sir Phelim O'Neill's order to burn the cathedral of Armagh: 'within short time after fell sick of an ague, grew frantick, and in this raving manner cried out allwaies to kill the English churles and Scottes in which woful case he shortly ended his miserable life.'[68] In his book detailing the sufferings of Irish Protestants, James Cranford described how: 'An Irish Rebell (as a credible friend reports) snatched an innocent babe out of the arms of the mother, and cast it into the fire before her face, but God met with this bloudy wretch: for before he went from that place, hee brake his neck.'[69]

Tales of divine vengeance had both immediate and long-term implications. It is clear from work by Adam Fox and Ethan Shagan on early modern England that remarkable news might travel very quickly and have a direct effect on public opinion and actions.[70] It might provide an impression of immediate practical relief from persecution: hence reports of the increased boldness of the Irish following Coote's demise and the joy and relief expressed on the death of Brouncker. The tales were seized on to justify particular political causes. Neither their fantastic elements, nor our glimpses of their exaggeration in transit, should blind us to the fact that they 'were anything but casual in their inception, composition or dissemination.'[71] They presented Catholics and Protestants with powerful and convincing visible and aural evidence of the infernal destination of the leaders of their opponents, whose raving, miserable ends were believed to hold a divine message. The frisson of horror made them all the more interesting – it is easy to imagine them being told and elaborated on with relish – and, ultimately, more enduring. The fact that, in some of the cases cited, the authorities or concerned bystanders moved to present alternative interpretations of events, indicates how an element of antidemonology paralleled and complemented the process of antimartyrology. But cases such as Brouncker's also demonstrate that it was not always considered expedient to counter such rumours. Parr Lane was keenly aware that Brouncker had become a convenient scapegoat for an unsuccessful policy. He argued that the strict enforcement of religious conformity was the only way forward and that 'had but Bruncker lived Mounster had seene/the monster Errour had confounded beene', but his poem rehabilitating Brouncker's memory and suggesting reforms for Ireland along the lines of his former master's policies seems to have been little heeded.

---

68 T. Fitzpatrick, *The bloody bridge and other papers relating to the insurrection of 1641* (Dublin, 1903), p. 101. See Tait, *Death, burial and commemoration*, pp 24–5, for further examples. 69 I. Cranford, *The teares of Ireland* (London, 1642), p. 59. 70 A. Fox, *Oral and literate culture in England, 1500–1700* (Oxford, 2000); E.H. Shagan, 'Rumours and popular politics in the reign of Henry VIII', in T. Harris (ed.), *The politics of the excluded, c.1500–1850* (Basingstoke, 2001), pp 30–66. For an Irish example of the rapidity of oral transmission of information see S.J. Connolly, 'The "blessed turf": cholera and popular panic in Ireland, June 1832', *Irish Historical Studies*, 23 (1983), 214–32. 71 Freeman, 'Fate, faction, and fiction', p. 622.

Stories of divine vengeance might also have far-reaching effects. Some of them continued to be harnessed as vindications of the Irish cause, and as cautionary tales, suiting many literary genres. They were especially useful to authors like Lynch who aimed to promote Ireland on the continent and raise awareness of the sufferings of Catholics there in the hopes of attracting financial and practical support. Clearly, Irish Counter-Reformation clerics, like their English counterparts, were willing to make use of tales of the miraculous that they might in other circumstances have distanced themselves from in 'the service of casuistical instruction and confessional propaganda'.[72] Furthermore, contemporary accounts of the deaths of the four persecutors considered here were still accepted during the renewed phase of Irish Catholic martyrology in the late nineteenth century, at a time when the project of beatification of the Irish martyrs was as much a matter of national pride as of religious devotion. They continue to appear, with interpretation left more open, in modern biographies of those amongst the Irish martyrs who have recently been beatified or are still being considered for beatification.

In stories of divine vengeance literary models, biblical forerunners and folkloric paradigms met and merged. As already mentioned, providential literature was a staple part of the output of sixteenth-and seventeenth-century presses. Although prior to the late 1600s, few Irish presses were in operation, some elements of Irish audiences would have been familiar with English and continental examples. The fact that Copinger chose *The theater of Catholick and Protestant religion* as the title for a work that included a significant section on the providential punishment of persecutors of Catholics strongly indicates the influence of books such as Thomas Beard's regularly reprinted *The theatre of Gods judgments*.[73] Ancient Irish literature itself provided myriad instances of various types of mysterious providential punishments of wrongdoers.[74]

Other influences were present. The Bible and Apocrypha were, of course, the ultimate universal literary model. Lynch, for example, was especially fond of drawing direct links between ancient and recent examples, equating the suffering of Irish Catholics with those of the chosen people of the Bible. His vivid portrayal of Brouncker's death – 'Worms swarmed out from his whole body; he was devoured piecemeal by vermin, and expired emitting a most horrid stench' – closely parallels the 'fate of Antiochus', a persecutor of the Jews, in 2 Maccabees 9:9–11 – 'Worms swarmed from the whole body of this godless man and, while he was still alive and in agony, his flesh rotted off, and the whole army was overwhelmed by the stench of decay.' Like Antiochus, not to mention

---

72 A. Walsham, 'Miracles and the Counter-Reformation mission to England', *Historical Journal*, 46 (2003), 790.   73 T. Beard, *Theatre of God's judgements* (London, 1597).   74 T.P. Cross, *Motif-index of early Irish literature* (Bloomington, 1952), section Q: 'Rewards and punishments', pp 436–63.

Drury, Coote and Ireton, specific incidents of persecution had allegedly preceded his death, and Antiochus too was alleged to have begun to regret his actions and 'to moderate his monstrous arrogance' prior to his demise. The account of the death of Herod the Great by Eusebius, based on the authority of Flavius Josephus's *War of the Jews* and *Antiquities of the Jews*, with their details of abdominal pain, worms, stench, and rage, may also have been influential. Eusebius presented Herod's fate as the direct result of the Massacre of the Innocents.[75] Jacobus de Voragine's *The golden legend*, a hugely popular medieval compendium of the exploits of the saints, held a similar version of Herod's death (this time alleging that his disease had led him to suicide), and illustrated the nasty ends of a variety of other persecutors.[76] According to Acts 12:23, Herod Agrippa had died similarly after persecuting Christ's apostles: 'immediately the angel of the Lord smote him, because he gave not God the glory, and he was eaten of worms, and gave up the ghost.' Further famous classical examples could be similarly useful. David Rothe, author of the celebrated *Analecta Sacra*, compared Brouncker's persecution policy 'to the efforts of Julian the Apostate to replace Christianity with paganism', while Lynch likewise described Coote as 'another Julianus the Apostate'. Compare also the folklore relating to celebrated medieval martyrdoms, such as that of Thomas Beckett, whose murderers allegedly all had bad ends.[77]

But people did not even have to be familiar with pamphlets and the Bible to be aware of the trope of the violent death of the persecutor. It is clear that oral accounts of such deaths fitted themselves to universal folkloric 'types' of the

[75] 'But the disease of Herod grew more severe, God inflicting punishment for his crimes. For a slow fire burned in him which was not so apparent to those who touched him, but augmented his internal distress; for he had a terrible desire for food which it was not possible to resist. He was affected also with ulceration of the intestines, and with especially severe pains in the colon, while a watery and transparent humor settled about his feet. He suffered also from a similar trouble in his abdomen. Nay more, his privy member was putrefied and produced worms. He found also excessive difficulty in breathing, and it was particularly disagreeable because of the offensiveness of the odor and the rapidity of respiration. He had convulsions also in every limb, which gave him uncontrollable strength. It was said, indeed, by those who possessed the power of divination and wisdom to explain such events, that God had inflicted this punishment upon the King on account of his great impiety.' Eusebius, *Church history*, Book 1, Chapter 8: http://www.newadvent.org/fathers/250101.htm; Flavius Josephus, *Antiquities of the Jews*, Book 17, Chapters 6, 8: http://www.ccel.org/j/josephus/works/ant-17.htm; *War of the Jews*, Book 1, Chapter 33: http://www.ccel.org/j/josephus/works/war-1.htm, all accessed 3 March 2007. Herod's afflictions have recently been attributed to chronic kidney disease: B.P. Trivedi, 'What disease killed King Herod?', http://news.nationalgeographic.com/news/2002/01/0128_020128_KingHerod.html, accessed 3 March 2007. [76] J. de Voraigne, *The golden legend* ed. and trans. G. Ryan and H. Ripperger (New York, 1969), pp 67–8. [77] Ford, 'Reforming the Holy Isle', p. 144; P.F. Moran (ed.), *The analecta of David Rothe, bishop of Ossory* (Dublin, 1884), p. 177; Lynch, *Cambrensis eversus*, 3, p. 101; T. Borenius, 'The murderers of St. Thomas Becket in popular

deaths of the iniquitous. Furthermore, as highlighted by English historians such as Fox, Walsham and Freeman, the writing down of such tales usually followed significant oral dissemination.[78] It seems from their text versions that several variants of the story of Brouncker's and Drury's deaths in particular were in circulation, presumably the result of their oral transmission before being written down. As they were passed on, the tales of the deaths of Drury, Ireton, Coote, and Brouncker were subtly transformed for ease of recall and for maximum drama, according to many of the hallmarks of oral transmission. Formulaic patterns (persecutor kills martyr/destroys holy object, dies badly) aided recall, timescales and people were telescoped so that the 'significant' events were presented as following directly one from the other, and particular notorious people drew to themselves the deeds of others.[79]

Furthermore, the formal recording of these stories did not codify them or stop their further oral dissemination. For example, in 1937, a Kilmallock informant described how 'Behind the catholic church at Kilmallock is a field … The field is known as Crocta [hanged]. Bishop O'Healy and Father O'Rourke were hanged at Crocta in the year 1651 by the Cromwellian soldiers.' The alleged location of their deaths is still pointed out, and in 1988 a monument in the shape of a standing stone was erected to them.[80] In Irish tradition, the 'penal times' were a vaguely defined era of random suffering and death, often connected with specific points on the landscape, full of wondrous events (some clearly connected with historical occurances, others seemingly fictional), and in which Cromwell was the star performer.[81] Oral tradition tended towards rationalizing memories for easy remembrance so that Cromwell was blamed for O'Healy and O'Rourke's deaths and so that their timing could be absorbed into the elastic timescale of the penal era. In English as well as Irish tradition, Oliver Cromwell became a universal bogeyman and church- and castle-wrecker.[82] Likewise, in

---

tradition', *Folklore*, 43 (1932), 175–92. 78 Fox, *Oral and literate culture*; Freeman, 'Fate, faction, and fiction'; Walsham, *Providence*. 79 On oral tradition and its transmission see J. Fentress and C. Wickham, *Social memory* (Oxford, 1992); E. Tonkin, *Narrating our pasts: the social construction of oral history* (Cambridge, 1992); W. J. Ong, *Orality and literacy: the technologizing of the word* (London, 1982); J. Vansina, *Oral tradition: a study in historical methodology* trans. H.M. Wright (London, 1961). On the early modern period, see Fox, *Oral and literate culture*. A good account of how the 1798 was presented in folklore is G. Beiner, 'Negotiations of memory: rethinking 1798 commemoration', *The Irish Review*, 26 (2000), 60–70. 80 IFC S MS 528, f. 500. See my 'Relics and the past: the material culture of Catholic martyrdom', in J. Lyttleton and C. Rynne (eds), *Settlement and material culture in plantation Ireland* (forthcoming). 81 For a French example of a similar sense of past religious persecution, see Fentress and Wickham, *Social memory*, pp 92–114. 82 See Smith, 'Images of Cromwell', pp 17–38; Fox, *Oral and literate culture*, pp 255–7; S. Ó Súilleabháin, 'Oliver Cromwell in Irish oral tradition', in L. Dégh, H. Glassie, F. Joinas (eds), *Folklore today: essays in honour of Richard Dorson* (Bloomington, 1976), pp 473–83; R.C. Richardson (ed.), *Images of Oliver Cromwell* (Manchester, 1993).

the folklore of Co. Cavan and Co. Roscommon, the picture of Charles Coote as 'an awful aul' tyrant' survived quite vividly and may have attracted other deeds by other persecutors. After all 'Colorless personalities cannot survive oral mnemonics ... heroic [and wicked] figures tend to be type figures.'[83]

What is also striking is the role in the stories of Drury and Ireton, and the later folklore of Coote, of clerics, especially bishops, as heroic figures. They endure their own deaths with fortitude, as per the universal model of martyrdom, but with an added twist. O'Healy and O'Brien are given the gift of prophecy, and not a little magic: their curses were seemingly as effective as those of the medieval Irish poets who were believed to have the power to call down misfortune on those who had slighted them. Collections of later Irish folklore provide myriad examples of the supernatural power of the priest, a power that was something internal to himself, not entirely dependant on the fact of his consecration. Priests were strong and weak at the same time. Their sufferings in the 'penal times', in which divine intervention often thwarted or brought revenge on their persecutors, also became a staple feature. For example, an informant in the 1930s in Cootehall mentioned that 'Priest[s] suffered great hardship at the hands of Coote and other English army officials.'[84] But yet, they were also the repositories of great power, power that in later tradition was frequently presented as being used to confound Protestants (especially Protestant landlords) and wrongdoers.[85]

When we look at stories of persecutors, priestly martyrs and providential intervention, therefore, we should consider sources other than pamphlets and literary accounts, and be aware of the wider context of their oral as well as written transmission. We also need to weigh up the uses of such tales to the historian, despite their more fantastic elements, as indicators of popular attitudes and of the ongoing process of interpretation of past events that served as the origin myth of what was increasingly defined as a Catholic nation. Cautionary tales of persecution and triumph over persecution continued to be a staple in Irish tradition because they continued to have a role in justifying antipathy to Protestantism and Protestants, and confirming Catholic views of their own moral superiority. As Ong points out: 'oral traditions reflect a society's present cultural values rather than idle curiosity about the past.' As long as such stories remain relevant they are retold.[86] On the other hand, tales of God's intervention in the Protestant cause had little long-term resonance for that group, the evidence of the 1641 depositions being instead seized on in written accounts to illustrate the suffering of the Protestant population of early modern Ireland and the untrustworthiness of their Catholic neighbours.[87]

83 Ong, *Orality and literacy*, p. 70.   84 IFC S MS 232, f.109.   85 P. Ó Héalaí, 'Cumacht an tsagairt sa béaloideas', *Léachtaí Cholm Cille VIII: ár ndúchas creidimh* (Maynooth, 1977), pp 109–31; D. Ó hÓgáin, *The hero in Irish folk history* (Dublin, 1985), pp 204–15, 273–6.   86 Ong, *Orality and literacy*, p. 40.   87 T. Barnard, '"Parlour entertainment of an evening"?

Tales of violent death by divine vengeance were long relevant in Irish oral tradition and in written accounts of the sixteenth and seventeenth centuries. As Parr Lane found out, it was never the specific truth of the deaths of persecutors that was important: what counted was the meaning applied by those who reported and elaborated on them. Interpretations of the manner of the deaths of William Drury, Henry Ireton, Charles Coote and Henry Brouncker in large measure negated the effects of their actions during life for their Catholic audiences, and went hand-in-hand with the impulse to hail the Catholic casualties of this period as martyrs. In the case of Ireton in particular, their deaths might hold resonances for Protestant opponents as well. In the course of their transmission accounts were subtly influenced by conventions of structuring of folk narratives as well as by literary, especially biblical precedents, to form other types of 'truth' that were relevant to the society in which they were told, helping to confirm peoples' ideas about the workings of the world and of God, and their own place within that scheme. The raving words of Drury and Ireton, the sudden, shocking demise of Coote, and the image of Brouncker crawling with worms and 'eating his flesh from his arms', illustrate that it is at the interchange between the prosaic and the fantastic that some of the most revealing insights about early modern Irish society are to be found.[88]

Histories of the 1640s', in Ó Siochrú (ed.), *Kingdoms in crisis*, pp 20–43. [88] Some of the initial research for this article was carried out under the auspices of a postdoctoral fellowship from the Irish Research Council for the Humanities and Social Sciences held at NUI Maynooth. I wish to thank Bill Frazer, Andrew Carpenter, John Walter, my co-editors, and audiences at the early modern seminar in the University of Warwick and the 'Early Modern Terrorism' conference at the University of Manchester for their comments and assistance.

Religious violence against settlers in south Ulster, 1641-2

BRIAN MAC CUARTA

Referring to an episode where settlers were killed by the Ulster Irish in the winter of 1641-2, one survivor alluded to 'those poor martyred Protestants'[1]. Modern historians have not, by and large, shared this contemporary focus on the religious dimension to this aggression.[2] Widespread, largely spontaneous attacks by the Irish on the British in their midst characterized the early days of the 1641 revolt in Ulster. Native resentment against their new neighbours was varied in origin. Many of the Irish were in debt to the British, or had mortgaged lands to the newcomers, reflected in the targeting of the papers which documented these arrangements, and the extent and frequency with which refugees noted debts owing to them. Some Irish were bitterly resentful at their families' land losses a generation earlier, and wished to reverse the Plantation by expelling the settlers, alleging 'that the land was theirs and lost by their fathers'.[3] A general revulsion against all things English animated the Irish populace – in Cavan, it was advocated that English be no longer spoken, and that the former place names should replace the English versions.[4] Within this

---

1 Ellen Matchett, 3 Sept 1642, TCD MS 836, f. 59r. This essay draws chiefly on the following volumes of the 1641 Depositions: Armagh, TCD MS 836; Cavan, MSS 832-3; Fermanagh, MS 835; Louth and Monaghan, MS 834; Tyrone, Londonderry, and Donegal, MS 839; henceforth, the number refers to the relevant volume of the depositions (date of deposition is given with first citation). 2 However, Nicholas Canny has explored the religious dimension to the revolt in the case of Leinster, 'Religion, politics and the Irish rising of 1641', in J. Devlin and R Fanning (eds), *Historical studies XX: religion and rebellion* (Dublin, 1997), pp 40-70; the role of Catholic clergy in the revolt in Ulster is considered in Canny, *Making Ireland British, 1580-1650* (Oxford, 2003), pp 488-91; the broader contemporary religious *mentalité* is explored in R. Gillespie, *Devoted people: belief and religion in early modern Ireland* (Manchester, 1997). 3 William Thorpe, 10 Jan 1641-2, 833, f. 72r; on the rising in Ulster, see Canny, *Making Ireland British*, pp 469-91; A. Clarke, 'The genesis of the Ulster rising of 1641', in P. Roebuck (ed.), *Plantation to partition* (Belfast, 1981), pp 29-45; M. Perceval-Maxwell, *The outbreak of the Irish Rebellion of 1641* (Dublin, 1994), pp 213-33; R. Gillespie, 'The end of an era: Ulster and the outbreak of the 1641 rising', in C. Brady and R. Gillespie (eds), *Natives and newcomers: the making of Irish colonial society, 1534-1641* (Dublin, 1986), pp 191-213. 4 George Creichton, 15 Apr. 1643, 832, f. 150v.

context of a general outburst against colonial society, native animosity against the religion of the settlers may be located. The settlers were attacked, not only because they were British, but also because they were Protestant. That the Irish were prepared to offer violence on strictly denominational, as distinct from ethnic grounds, was illustrated in their treatment of the farm stock of Lord Robert Dillon in Co. Cavan. Dillon, who had conformed to the established church by 1619, belonged to an Old English family settled in Ireland for several centuries.[5] In the winter of 1641, the 'common sort' destroyed 2500 sheep and 140 cattle belonging to him. On being asked to desist, the perpetrators said 'they would not forbear, though he [Dillon] was an Irishman, yet he was a Protestant, and they would take his goods again'.[6]

Irish attitudes to the Protestantism of the settlers may be explored through the 1641 depositions. Those for the south Ulster counties of Armagh, Monaghan, Cavan, and Fermanagh are especially valuable. These are particularly numerous, representing 90 per cent of all Ulster depositions with most sworn within a year of the events recounted and, indeed, some were taken in the first days of January 1641–2, about ten weeks after the outbreak of the revolt.[7] As a result, the words and deeds of the insurgents were reported independently by many British survivors, shortly after the events described. Many deponents were witnesses of the happenings and conversations related; while differing in detail, the depositions tend to corroborate trends illustrative of the conduct and motivation of the Irish. Their behaviour towards Protestantism may be examined in the light of several themes: the impact of the broader confessional landscape of 1641 in the Ulster localities, antipathy towards the state clergy, and the implications of the settlers' status as heretics.

In considering the confessional dimension to attacks on the Ulster settlers in 1641–2, it is helpful to distinguish the proximate cause from more long-term trends. Arising from the heightened religious tension in England and Scotland in the years before 1641, the Ulster Irish feared that their religion was threatened by the growing puritan ascendancy in England. In the months before the rising, this climate of fear, fed by rumours of anti-Catholic developments in England, sharpened Catholic sensibilities in Ulster. It played a considerable role in inspiring the gentry who initiated the revolt; the Irish sought to follow the Scottish example of the use of force to protect their religion.[8] Once the revolt

5 J. Lodge, *The peerage of Ireland* (Dublin, 1789), 4, p. 157; Robert Dillon, styled Lord Dillon of Kilkenny-West, succeeded as 2nd earl of Roscommon on the death of his father in Mar. 1641–2, G.E.C., *Complete Peerage*, sub Roscommon.   6 Thomas Crant, n.d., 832, f. 77r; Lodge, *Peerage*, sub Dillon.   7 The 572 depositions made in 1642–3 by residents of Ulster counties include 54 from Armagh, 249 from Cavan, 143 from Fermanagh, and 62 from Monaghan: Canny, *Making Ireland British*, p. 347.   8 The Irish in Cavan were reported as saying, 'their main reason of rising was to enjoy all their lands again, and have their conscience. And that they had a precedent for the same out of Scotland', Thomas Tailor, 3

began, however, it emerged that such concerns had been widely disseminated throughout the Catholic community. These concerns contributed significantly to the sectarian dimension inherent in the emerging anti-settler animosity. In the autumn, the Ulster localities were rife with rumours of a puritan campaign against Catholicism in London; there was a fear that similar measures were about to be introduced in Ireland. In Co. Cavan and Co. Monaghan, the belief was current that the Irish Catholics were about to be deprived of their religion, by being forced to attend the services of the state church.[9] Thus in Cavan, a priest was reported as saying that 'there was a statute made in England that all papists should go to church before a certain time or be banished'.[10] A related motif was the alleged execution of the queen's chaplain. These rumours focused on the queen, the Catholic Henrietta Maria, and it was alleged that one of her chaplains had been executed.[11] The link between Ulster revolt and Irish perception of Catholic persecution in London was epitomized in the words of insurgents in Cavan: 'We rise for our religion. They hang our priests in England'.[12] Arising from these reported threats against Catholicism, the queen became a focus of Ulster Irish loyalty; Irish insurgents were justifying their attacks on the settlers by reference to what they believed had happened to the queen's chaplain.[13]

As a result of the fears engendered by these rumours, the rhetoric of a Catholic crusade, ostensibly defensive in nature, was present in the justifications offered for attacks on the British. In claiming that theirs was a religious struggle, the Irish were consciously following the Scottish example of armed revolt in defence of their faith. It was in this context of Catholicism under threat from the puritans that priests in the north Armagh area were preaching spiritual privileges for those who died in the Catholic cause. A papal bull was in circulation, allegedly granted to Sir Phelim O'Neill and his followers, promising full remission of sins to those who fasted once a week, should they die on the Catholic side.[14] This comforted the rebels, who told their Protestant neighbours and victims 'that

---

Jan. 1641–2, 832, f. 98v; similarly, 'The Scots have taught us our ABC', George Creichton, 832, f. 146v. 9 Richard Parsons, vicar of Dronge and Lerrah, Kilmore diocese, 24 Feb. 1644–5, 832, f. 89r. 10 Henry Reynolds, 4 Jan. 1641–2, 833, f. 57r; similarly, William Racye, 8 Jan. 1641–2, 834, f. 77v; Mulmore O'Reilly, high sheriff of Cavan, explained the disarming of the settlers by the need 'to bring into subjection the puritan faction of the parliament of England', Arthur Culme, 9 May 1642, 833, f. 133r-v. 11 Charles McGowan told a deponent that the London Protestants had killed some of the queen's friars, John McKewne, 12 Nov 1642, 833, f. 165v; similarly, John Montgomery of Clones, 26 Jan 1641–2, 834, f. 71v; Elizabeth Goughe, 8 Feb. 1641–2, 832, f. 119v. 12 Faithfull Teate, 10 Mar. 1641–2, 832, f. 79v. 13 Reply of Cahil O'Reilly, c.25 Nov 1641, in Elizabeth Gough, 8 Feb. 1641–2, 833, f. 2r; a variation of this theme was articulated by Brian Boy McCabe, who said that the king was dead, that the young king went to mass, that the Irish were the queen's soldiers, and that the settlers were traitors, John Perkins, 8 Jan. 1641–2, 833, f. 47r. 14 A deponent asserted he saw the bull in the hands of the priest Pelomy O Cunigan; William O Doolin related that a priest at mass in Benburb said, 'that the bodies of such men as died in that quarrel should

they knew that if they themselves [Irish] should die, the next morning their souls should go to God'.[15] Part of the self-understanding of those in revolt was that they were engaged in pre-emptive strikes against the puritans: thus one insurgent held that, by expelling the English, the Irish would have liberty of conscience.[16] In attacking the settlers, the Irish alleged that they were anticipating the action of the puritans against themselves.

In the diffusion of these rumours, and in the development of the rhetoric of Catholic defence which formed part of the insurgents' vocabulary of revolt, the Franciscans played a pivotal role. By the late 1620s, the Franciscan convent network had been re-established across Ulster, and travel to and from the continent, often via London, was habitual among them.[17] Thus their preachers played a leading part in spreading news of anti-Catholic developments in England among the Ulster populace. The friars' role in promoting the denominational aspect of the rising was epitomized in a report of preaching in the Franciscan friary in Brantry, near Dungannon, about 1 November 1641. A friar displayed a picture purporting to show the execution of Father Phillips, the queen's chaplain, in London; the preacher's message was an exhortation to the Irish to fight for their faith.[18] Similarly, in Co. Monaghan, the Irish said they attacked the settlers 'only to secure themselves against an order made at the council table of Ireland to hang all them that should refuse to come to church on the All Saints Day after, which order divers friars affirmed in this deponent's hearing that they had seen'.[19] Already in the summer preceding the rising, this climate added a further element of anxiety and panic to existing animosity against the state church. With the rapid collapse of law and order in the localities, these recent confessional anxieties contributed to the channelling of popular anger against the Protestantism of the settlers. With the revolt underway, the friars drew on exemplars from the Jewish struggle for religious and national liberation from foreign domination, as recounted in the Old Testament, to encourage the insurgents. Thus at the beginning of Lent 1642, George Burne was one a group of English settlers who were forced to attend a sermon delivered by a friar in the sessions house in Dungannon. Addressing the English

---

not be cold, before the souls should ascend up into heaven. And that they should be free from the pains of purgatory', John Parrie, ult May 1642, 836, f. 62v. **15** Margret Bromley, 22 Aug. 1642, 836, f. 40v. **16** Henry Hocklefish, 5 Jan. 1641–2, 833, f. 9v. **17** Cavan, Dundalk, Lisgaul (Co. Fermanagh), Armagh, Carrickfergus, Down, Donegal, Monaghan, Creeveleagh (Co. Leitrim), list of guardians, 15 Aug. 1629, C. Giblin (ed.), *Liber Lovaniensis* (Dublin, 1956), pp 4–7; on Irish clerics passing through London in the 1630s, see papal envoys' correspondence (1634–9), E. Mac Fhinn (ed.), 'Scribhinni i gCartlann an Vatican: Tuarscbhail' [MSS in Vatican Archive: Report], *Analecta Hibernica*, 16 (1946), 15–24. **18** John Parrie, 836, f. 62v; on the Franciscan presence in this area, see C. Mooney, 'The Franciscan First Order Friary at Dungannon', *Seanchas Ard Mhacha*, 1:2 (1955), 72–93. **19** Nicholas Simpson, 6 Apr. 1643, 834, f. 182r.

captives, and a 'multitude of Irish rebels', his theme was the story of Judith (recounted in the Book of Judith), who went to the camp of the Assyrian general Holofernes, charmed him, and then cut off his head, thereby ensuring victory for the Jews.[20] By emphasizing the victory of the weak over the strong, the choice of text was designed to hearten the Irish in what was portrayed as a religious struggle, and to demoralize the Protestant settlers.

The perceived puritan threat to Roman Catholicism in 1641 heightened existing resentments against the state clergy. Contemporaries noted that ministers in Ulster were an especial focus of native attack in the early months of the rising.[21] This perception was current among clergy themselves: in Cavan, Dr Teate and Mr Aldrich assured their fellow-minister George Creichton 'that the whole north was risen, and that of all men the ministers were like to be in greatest danger'.[22] The evidence of the depositions supports this assessment. The Irish were particularly violent towards men on realizing that they were ecclesiastics.[23] In Co. Monaghan, targetting of churchmen was also exemplified in that three clergy featured among the British kept prisoner in the Carrickmacross area.[24] In the same county, Mr Lindfoote, a minister, was stripped and killed.[25] Similarly, Archibald Deneston, curate, was evicted from his house by Patrick Groome O Murphy, proctor to the archdeacon, and was immediately 'stripped mother naked [and] beaten black and blue', so that he was considered dead.[26] However, while attacks on ministers were widespread, this trend was particularly strong in the British settlements of north Armagh and east Tyrone. Here, more than in other areas, the Irish were seeking to kill the ministers. For this area, we have the names of fifteen clergy who, deponents stated, were killed by rebels in the early months of the revolt; there may have been more.[27] At one level, these

---

20 George Burne, 12 Jan. 1643–4, 839, f. 7r-v. 21 In Co. Cavan, it was held that most ministers across Ulster (except Cavan) were attacked and pillaged ('destroyed'), Richard Parsons, 832, f. 91r; although particularly virulent in Ulster, attacks on clergy took place elsewhere in Ireland, 'The humble petition of Henry Jones DD on behalf of the distressed servants of Jesus Christ the ministers of the Gospel in Ireland', TCD MS 840, f. 29r-v; H. Jones, *A remonstrance of divers remarkable passages concerning the church and kingdome of Ireland* (London, 1642), p. 10; for a continental example of the targetting of clergy in a popular revolt, see H. Cohn, 'Anticlericalism in the German Peasants' War, 1525', *Past and Present*, 83 (1979), 3–31. 22 George Creichton, 832, f. 145r; ministers, followed by royal officers, were the chief targets of the Irish, G.S., *A briefe declaration of the barbarous and inhumane dealings of the northerne Irish rebels* (London, 1641), p. 5. 23 At Kells, Co. Meath, insurgents murdered Mr Sharpe, '(perceiving [him] to be a Protestant minister)', George Cooke, 22 Jan. 1641–2, 832, f. 104v. 24 Sir Henry Spotswood, 15 Jan. 1641–2, 834, f. 73v. 25 Jane Feild, 1 Mar. 1642–3, 834, f. 62v. 26 Henry Steele, 10 Jan. 1641–2, 834, f. 84r; Mr Dunbarr, minister of Donoghenry, Tyrone, together with his family, were stripped: the minister was driven 'to tie some straw about his thighs', as one deponent was informed, John Kerdiff, ult Feb. 1641–2, 839, f. 3v. 27 Mr New, curate, Ardtra, Tyrone (839, f. 3v); John Griffith, Armagh (836, ff 44v, 62r, 107v); Robinson, Kilmore, Armagh (836, ff 44v, 62r, 107v); Hudson (836, ff 44v, 62r); Berige, Killyman, Tyrone (836, ff 62r, 107v); William

killings merely reflected the density of British settlement, and the intensity of native violence towards settlers in general, in this area.[28] Moreover, at times of especial stress, killings of settlers increased. Thus just before the Irish under Sir Phelim O'Neill vacated and burned Armagh, about three or four ministers were among those killed there.[29]

Longstanding animosities against the clergy were based on the impositions of the state church since its inception thirty years previously. Ulster Irish ferocity against everything Protestant was fuelled by resentment at the wealth of the church in Ulster, exceptional in contemporary Ireland. Under the Plantation, the Church of Ireland was generously endowed.[30] In the mid-1630s, the church's revenues in Ulster increased dramatically under Wentworth's government, thanks in part to the unusual diligence of Bishop Bramhall.[31] By 1641, rectors and prelates were a notably wealthy grouping within colonial Ulster – there were clergy across south Ulster who reported losses of over £1000.[32] In addition to a substantial income as incumbents, many were actively

Fullerton, Loughgall, Armagh (836, ff 44v, 60v, 71v, 107v; 839, f. 3v); James Blith, Dungannon, Tyrone (836, ff 44v, 107v, 115r; 839, 3v); Starcky, near Armagh (836, f. 107v); Mr Darragh (836, f. 107v, 115r); James Fiffie, Drumcree, Armagh (836, f. 107v); John Maddre, Donoghmore, Tyrone (836, f. 115r; 839, ff 1r, 3v); Hastings, (836, f. 115r); Smith (836, f. 115r), Fleming (836, f. 117r); one deponent, after naming six clergy, stated that a further eight were killed, whose names he had forgotten, Anthony Stratford, [2] Mar. 1643–4, 836, f. 115r; allegedly, Master Madder, near Dungannon, and Nicholas Drayton, of Tandragee, were hacked to death, G.S., *A briefe declaration*, p. 11.   28 P. Robinson, *The Plantation of Ulster* (Belfast, 1994), chapter four; H. Simms, 'Violence in County Armagh, 1641', in B. Mac Cuarta (ed.), *Ulster 1641: aspects of the Rising* (Belfast, 1993), pp 123–38.   29 Nicholas Simpson, 834, f. 185r.   30 In the Plantation scheme, ecclesiastical lands amounted to some 75,000 acres, Robinson, *The Plantation of Ulster*, pp 69–72; the link between native alienation and state church exactions in south Ulster is discussed in Alan Ford, 'The reformation in Kilmore before 1641', in R. Gillespie (ed.), *Cavan: essays on the history of an Irish county* (Dublin, 1995), pp 85, 94–6.   31 On the increasing revenues of the church in Ulster, see H. Kearney, *Strafford in Ireland* (Manchester, 1959), pp 122–5. In the province of Armagh, by 1640 there was an increase of £14,600 p.a. over 1629, of which half went to the lower clergy, ibid. Even allowing for self-assessment as the basis of the 1641–2 figures, an indication of the increase between 1634 and 1641 is provided by the annual value of the following livings in each year.

Disertragh, Tyrone	£60	£100	(839, f. 3r-v)
Termonmagurk, Tyrone	£80	£300	(Co. Down, 837, f. 21r)
Mullabrack, Armagh	£80	£200	(837, f. 21r)
Maghereculmonie, Fermanagh	£100	£200	(835, f. 26)
Enismcshane, Fermanagh	£120	£160	(835, f. 27r-v)
Cleenish, Fermanagh	£100	£200	(835, f. 28v–29r)
Killeshandra, Cavan	£80	£200	(833, f. 201r)
Kilran and Knockbride, Cavan	£50	£140	(832, f. 205r)
Drumgoone, Cavan	£120	£200	(832, f. 54r)

1634 figures: lists of patrons and values of livings, and ministers [1634], TCD MS 1040, ff 1r–38r.   32 In Cavan: Henry Jones, dean of Kilmore, £3019, 840, f. 32v; William Aldrich, £1010, Faithful Teate, £3930, 832, ff 54r, 79v; Bishop Bedell, £4060, Adam Watson, £1340,

involved in farming, acquiring lands by purchase and lease, presumably, at least initially, from the profits of their livings. The range of the clergy's farming interests may be illustrated in the case of Henry Boine, in Dungannon barony. He owned two townlands worth £400, and leased a further two-and-half townlands, worth £200. In addition to corn, hay and cattle to the value of £300, he had timber and barrel staves worth £200; farming tools, together with plate and household goods came to £100, while the clergy's money-lending role was reflected in debts owed him of about £100.[33] The extensive farming interests of the clergy were further indicated by the fact that one Tyrone minister had at least 80 cattle.[34] The substantial increase in clerical income in mid-Ulster in the years immediately preceding the rising heightened native animosity towards the established church, and contributed to the virulence of attacks on state clergy in this area.

Arising from their access to tithes and other charges imposed by the church, clergy were ideally placed to accumulate the cash necessary for giving loans. The large sums noted in ministers' depositions indicated that senior clergy (parish incumbents, and higher) were in fact lending money, an impression strengthened by references to debts owing them. The role of diocesan officials in gathering ecclesiastical impositions, and as money-lenders, was illustrated by Simon Crane, registrar of Clogher diocese, to whom £450 was due in debts.[35] Given the relative poverty of the Irish, it is safe to presume that many of the clergy's debtors were natives. As beneficiaries of church monies, and as money-lenders, the state clergy were doubly detested; popular resentment was accentuated by the growing numbers of Catholic clergy, themselves seeking maintenance from their people, adding economic competition to the Roman clergy's fulminations against the representatives of a heretical church. The case of William Fullerton illustrates how their riches and money-lending made the clergy an especial target of the impoverished Irish. Fullerton was rector of the two parishes of Loughgall and Derrylonan, in north Co. Armagh. He was involved in extensive money-lending in the area, for by 1641 debts owing to him amounted to £1200.[36] The rector was among those English imprisoned by Manas O'Cane in

---

plus living worth £200, 833, ff 105r, 201r; in Fermanagh: Richard Bourk, £900, plus income of £290 p.a.; Richard Morse, £1280, George Fercher, £980 plus church living, 835, ff 20r, 28r, 30v; in Armagh: William Fullerton, £2200, 836, f. 50r; in Monaghan: Robert Boyle, £1520 plus lands worth £200 p.a., 834, f. 98r; in Tyrone: Mr Bradley, £1000, Henry Boine, £1400, 839, ff 2r-3v; the lower clergy were of more modest means, as Jonathan White's losses of £249 testify, 5 Jan. 1641–2, 833, f. 84r. **33** Henry Boine, 16 Feb. 1641–2, 839, f. 2r. About 1641, a Cavan minister was able to pay £2000 for a manor house and 1000 acres in Co. Fermanagh, William Baxter, 22 Sept. 1642, 835, f. 48v. **34** Henry Boine, 839, f. 2v. **35** Simon Crane, 9 Aug. 164[2], 835, f. 14r. On moneylending and the marked social advance of clergy in Co. Fermanagh, see Canny, *Making Ireland British*, pp 356–7. **36** He had a library (allegedly worth £80), and plate (£30), Ellenor Fullerton (minister's widow), 16 Sept. 1642, 836, f. 50r.

Loughgall church, shortly after the outbreak of the rising. Indicative of his wealth, he acquired a pass from the Irish captain for £35. In November 1641, a convoy of settlers set off, and they understood they were being sent to England. However, on the road between Loughgall eastwards to Portadown, Fullerton was among those killed by the local Irish who were escorting the convoy.[37] Hence the minister was slain by people who knew him, and who may have been among those who owed him money. A particularly egregious example of clerical wealth was Dr Faithful Teate, of Kilmore diocese. On hearing of the outbreak of the revolt, Teate was able to take £300 sterling in gold and some silver, and ride off to inform the Dublin authorities. His estimated losses amounted to almost £4000, a huge sum relative to other settlers, placing this ecclesiastic among the richest of the British in Ulster. His wealth included farm stock, rents, a mortgage, tithes, about £230 in debts, freehold lands, gold and silver to the value of £340 (indicative of the scale of church impositions under his stewardship), and an annual income of over £260 from his livings.[38]

Another indication of the socially-explosive nature of clerical wealth was the enrichment of the clergy's proctors in the 1620s and 1630s. Many of these were Irish. Hugh Brady had been the proctor of the aforementioned Faithful Teate for many years, and in the course of his duties had risen 'from poverty to a rich estate'.[39] In similar vein, native anger was vented against these collectors: already in November 1641, the Irish killed the proctor to the minister of Clones, Co. Monaghan, having first persuaded the tithe-gatherer to go to mass with them.[40] The wealth and high social standing of the parish incumbents was further illustrated in an episode in Co. Cavan. In the parish of Kilkan, Joan Betagh, wife to Hugh McMulmore Relie, a local Irish leader, took possession of the minister's dwelling, carried away the furnishings, and made an inventory of the contents of the premises; she installed the local parish priest in the house.[41] More generally, Irish anger at the tithes of the state church over the previous 30 years was reflected in the demand that, if any Protestants remained, their clergy should be henceforth maintained as the priests had been, namely, by the contributions of their congregation.[42]

The case of James Montgomery, parson of Dunamain, Co. Monaghan, throws light on Irish motivation in attacking the clergy. His widow's self-assessment of his losses (£703) places the minister among the wealthier of the British, though, as noted above, there were Protestant clergy who were wealthier again. Significantly, he was lending money to local people. However, it was only in the wake of military failure that the insurgents decided to kill the churchman.

---

37 Richard Newberrie, 27 June 1642, 836, f. 60v; Edward Saltenstall, 1 June 1642, 836, f. 71v.
38 Faithful Teate, 833, f. 61v. 39 Ibid., f. 61r. 40 James Grear, 6 Apr. 1642, 834, f. 59r.
41 The minister's losses totalled £770, Alexander Comine, vicar, 2 Mar. 1641–2, 832, f. 205r.
42 Matthew Browne, Clones, 24 Mar. 1641–2, 834, f. 88v.

About May Day, 1642, the Irish who had been defeated by the English army at Ardee, Co. Louth, returned to Carrickmacross, Co. Monaghan. There they put Montgomery to death, saying 'they would not leave a minister alive in Ireland because (as they said) the English army killed all their priests at Ardee. And the chief captains and colonels in the Carrick said, they did God good service in killing the ministers'.[43] This episode brings together recurrent motives for violence against ministers: resentment of their wealth and their usury, and anger at real or rumoured violence against Catholic clergy.

Economic and social resentment at the rapaciousness of church personnel in the plantation decades contributed to the eruption of violence against Church of Ireland clergy. In the febrile political and confessional climate of 1641, these tensions, together with the collapse of order, led to anti-Protestant aggression in the Ulster localities. More narrowly confessional animosities, already gestating in native society over many decades, also emerged. The breakdown of 1641 provided a catalyst which enabled long-held abhorrence of Protestantism to be aired, and to be acted upon. In the course of attacks on the settlers, the negative view of the reformed faith widely held by the Irish was regularly expressed in word and deed, and contributed to shaping Irish conduct towards the settlers. Underlying this attitude lay the belief that Protestantism was heresy, and its adherents were heretics. This view was deeply embedded in the consciousness of the Irish by 1641, thanks to preaching in earlier generations. The Franciscans were the main preachers in Gaelic Ulster in the early modern period, a role strengthened by their revival in the north with the return of continentally-trained friars from the early 1610s.[44] The anti-Protestant thrust of their sermons was exemplified in friar Eugene Duffy, based in the Cavan convent in the later sixteenth century; a renowned preacher, he was accustomed to express his fulminations against the new denomination both in Gaelic verses, and in ordinary speech.[45]

In 1641–2, Catholic clergy were articulating the implications of the settlers' ecclesial status. A priest in Cavan allegedly told his parishioners, that the Protestants were not Christians, 'and that [the Protestants] were no better than dogs'.[46] Heretics were not to be tolerated within the community. Accordingly, the settlers were to be given the option of conversion to Catholicism, and

---

[43] Denny Montgomery, 17 Nov. 1642, 834, ff 64r–v. [44] Accounts of the 1613 Franciscan mission in Ulster are given in 'Deposition of Teag Modder M'Glone ... 21 Oct 1613', PRO SP 63/232/21–2, and 'The examination of Shane McPhelomy O Donnelly taken ... 22 Oct 1613', BL Cott MSS, Tit.B. X, f. 236r-v (*Cal. S.P. Ire., 1611–4*, pp 429–31). [45] On friar Duffy, see B. Jennings (ed.), 'Brussels MS 3947: Donatus Moneyus, De provincia Hiberniae S. Francisci', *Analecta Hibernica*, 6 (1934), 49–50. On the pastoral, spiritual and cultural role of the Franciscans, see M. Elliott, *The Catholics of Ulster: a history* (London, 2000), pp 57–80. [46] George Creichton, 832, f. 154v. Similarly, it was reported that the friars preached, 'it was as lawful to kill an Englishman as a dog', Nicholas Simpson, 834, f. 184r.

pressure by Catholic clergy on Protestants to convert was common. Following this clerical lead, laity too placed great emphasis on getting the Protestants 'to turn', in circumstances where the settlers were under considerable pressure from the Irish.[47] The early months of the rising were characterized by the lack of centralized leadership among the insurgents. Yet widespread attempts to secure conversions were in some places underpinned by edicts of the Irish leaders, inspired in this regard by the prompting of senior Catholic clergy.[48] Bishop Eugene MacSweeney of Kilmore illustrates the role of Catholic prelates in 1641–2; he was particularly active in promoting conversions, and having those who refused imprisoned.[49] MacSweeney attended the meeting of bishops and diocesan vicars of the northern church province held at Kells, Co. Meath, on 22 March 1642. On his return to Virginia, Co. Cavan, alighting at an alehouse, the prelate informed the local minister that '[t]he council of their common weale had made a law, that all that went not to mass should be sent out of the county'. On his refusal to convert, the bishop ordered that the churchman be imprisoned.[50]

The insurgents were particularly keen to secure the conversion of settlers of high social standing. Thus Turlogh Oge O'Neill, Sir Phelim's brother, regularly

---

[47] When disarming a settler, Mulmore O Rely, high sheriff, said, 'That if [he] would deny the king, and go to mass, he should speed as well as they did', T. Tailor, 12 Jan 1641–2, 832, f. 60r. Owen McDonnell, a rebel captain, 'did hang up [William Jameson] to confess money and to go to mass two several times', W. Jameson, 7 July 1642, 832, f. 62v. '[A] priest laboured to have him [Alexander Lord, yeoman] go to mass, and then his goods should be restored, or otherwise the residue should be all taken from him, which (upon the deponent's refusal) fell out accordingly', A. Lord, 7 Mar. 1641–2, 832, f. 94v. In an encounter which ended with two brothers giving 17 shillings to their attackers, Owen McDonell Rely threatened to hang them, 'and desired them to send for the priest'; on refusing, McDonell said, 'It were fit to hang them all seeing they would not send for a priest before their death', James Mardoghe, 12 Nov. 1642, 832, f. 110v. A Cavan settler family, sheltering with their Irish in-laws (all Protestant) were threatened with death 'unless they would go to mass', John Hickman, 6 Feb. 1642–3, 832, f. 142r. [48] A Cavan deponent reported seeing 'articles agreed on by Sir Phelim O Neile and his captains, that whosoever would not go to mass within a fortnight should be imprisoned and lose all their goods. Shortly after they published another edict that whosoever would not go to mass by Easter should be hanged, this was some ten days before Easter', Arthur Culme, 832, f. 117r. [49] The bishop claimed to have converted 3000 Protestants, George Creichton, 832, f. 151v; these efforts lay behind one deponent's claim that MacSweeney 'a frequent and shameless drunkard ... was a bloody persecutor of the Protestants', William Reinoldes, 12 July 1643, 832, f. 129r; Thomas Crant, 15 Feb. 1641–2, 832, f. 213r. Eugene MacSweeney (c1590–1669), consecrated bishop of Kilmore in 1630, had studied in Rouen, and gained a doctorate in divinity in Paris, D. Cregan, 'The social and cultural background of a counter-reformation episcopate, 1618–60', in A. Cosgrove and D. McCartney (eds), *Studies in Irish history presented to R. Dudley Edwards* (Dublin, 1979), pp 87, 112; for an outline of his career, see J. Lynch, *De praesulibus Hiberniae*, ed. J. O'Doherty (Dublin, 1944), i, pp 254–6. [50] G. Creichton, 832, f. 151r; after leaving the alehouse in Virginia on horseback, the bishop was chased by a dog, nearly unsaddling him, and the prelate allegedly

pleaded with Nicholas Simpson, MP for Monaghan, to attend mass 'for [Turlogh said] he loved me, and for my soul's health'; Turlough Oge even sought to soften this step by suggesting that Simpson attend mass in the more private location of O'Neill's house. The MP refused. At this, O'Neill explained he could no longer protect Simpson.[51] Similarly, referring to the incarceration of ministers and gentry in Monaghan gaol, the conversion efforts of the priests were noted: 'And their mass-priests, those sowers of tares, working upon the extremities of forlorn men, do by all means possible, seek to turn weak christians, to their superstitions, both by threats and promises, and prevaile with too many'.[52] The situation in Clones throws light on the atmosphere in which some Protestants converted. About five weeks after the outbreak, the Irish issued a proclamation, summoning all British – men, women, and children – to assemble at the high cross of Clones within two hours, or face death. There, the gathered settlers were robbed and stripped of their clothes, and sent off naked. In this setting, a local priest allegedly said, 'that the law was so in their [Irish] hands that they might put all those to death that would not be of their religion'.[53] It happened that settlers were compelled to attend mass, before being stripped and expelled.[54] In this instance, forced attendance at mass may have been part of the process of expulsion.

In early modern Europe, uniformity of religion lay at the heart of contemporary notions of society. Any deviation represented a rent in the fabric of community. Thus the rebels in Monaghan articulated the prevalent Irish view, 'that all should go to mass'.[55] The real presence of Christ in the Eucharist, together with the pope as head of the church, were two articles of Roman Catholic faith which featured in the examination of Protestant converts as part of their new adherence to the Catholic community. These issues featured in conversations led by both laity and clergy among the Irish. In north Armagh, Captain Art O'Neale told John Greg that unless Greg would 'take up arms and go to mass there was no hope of his life'.[56] These were no idle threats. In Co. Cavan, a deponent was told his goods would be spared, 'if he would go to mass but one Sunday'. He refused. At this, some Irish determined to kill him, but he got notice of their intention, and fled to Dublin with his wife and children.[57] A

---

opined that 'the very dogs here are not yet converted', ibid., f. 152r; for Kells meeting, *N.H.I.*, iii, pp 297–8. **51** Nicholas Simpson, 834, f. 185r; similarly, John Whitman, late sovereign of Cavan town, while held a prisoner, 'was greatly solicited, attempted and offered to be seduced by divers priests and friars, and by a rebellious monk ... to turn from the Protestant religion, and to become a papist', J. Whitman, 14 July 1643, 832, f. 58v. The monk Fitzsimon saw to it that a merchant was kept in prison for refusing to attend mass, John Anderson, 11 July 1642, 832, f. 69r. **52** G.S., *A briefe declaration*, p. 11. **53** James Grear, 834, f. 59r; in similar vein, one deponent heard the priest McClery of Tehollan say, 'That all the English in Monaghan must be hanged', Hugh Culme, 25 Jan. 1641–2, 834, f. 58r. **54** John Martin, 4 Jan. 1641–2, 834, f. 126r. **55** John Montgomery, 834, f. 71v. **56** John Greg, 5 Jan. 1641–2, 836, f. 4r. **57** William Thomas, 9 Mar. 1641–2, 832, f. 65v.

rebel band asked the settlers under their control, 'whether they would turn to mass[,] change their religion and acknowledge the pope to be supreme head of the church'.[58] According to a report circulating among the Irish in Monaghan, the priest Hugh Mac O Degan Maguire in neighbouring Co. Fermanagh allegedly converted up to 50 English and Scottish settlers to the Church of Rome:

> after giving them the sacrament [he] demanded whether Christ's body was now really in that sacrament or no, and they said yea. And that he demanded of them further whether they held the pope to be supreme head of the church they likewise acknowledged he was. And that thereupon he presently told them they were in a good faith, and for fear they should fall from it and turn heretics, he and the rest that were with him cut all their throats.[59]

The account of the alleged killing may not be accurate. However, the fact that the cleric was mentioned by name, and that other deponents noted his leading role in the killing of Protestants in Fermanagh (noted below), suggest some basis in reality. The conversation reported in this deposition may illustrate the question and response sequence typical of a rushed mass conversion.

Under these pressures, a portion of the Protestant community did in fact convert to Roman Catholicism.[60] In Co. Cavan, those Irish who had joined the Church of Ireland, largely as a result of Bishop Bedell's interest in engaging with the native community, reverted en masse to the denomination of their kin. There were converts, too, among the settlers. Contrary to the teaching of the Roman church, in their desire to demonize and so marginalize the settlers, the insurgents invariably refused to recognize Church of Ireland baptisms, doubtless reflecting sermons given in the localities. Indicative of Catholic preaching on the importance of the mass, the Irish in north Armagh held that 'the Protestants were worse than dogs, and were no christians, but those that were christened at mass were christians'.[61] In the chaotic anti-colonial atmosphere, conversion did not always serve to spare the settlers. In Co. Monaghan, after the outbreak of the rising the Irish persuaded James Netterfield, proctor to the

---

58 Christian Stanhawe, 23 July 1642, 836, f. 76r. **59** Alexander Creichtoune, ult. Feb. 1641–2, 834, f. 85v. **60** Several Protestants in Carrickmacross, Co. Monaghan, converted, and attended mass, Jane Houghes, 28 Apr. 1642, 834, f. 91v.m. It was reported that four English, and their wives, recanted their Protestantism, and were received into the Roman church by Bishop MacSweeney, Thomas Crant, 832, f. 74r. **61** Margaret Bromley, 836, f. 40v; similarly, the Irish in Cavan held that the Protestants 'were no christians unless [they] were christened again by [the] priests', William Watte, 12 Nov. 1642, 832, f. 114r. Patrick O Gowen held that the Protestants were 'unchristened people', William Jameson, 832, f. 63v. On rebaptism at mass as indicative of popular appreciation of the power of the mass, and of priests, see Gillespie, *Devoted people*, pp 66–7.

minister of Clones, to attend mass. Nevertheless, during the expulsion of the British from the Clones area, at the end of November, Netterfield was killed. His stabbing arose in part from Irish resentment at the heavy exactions collected by the proctors of the state church. Around the same time, also in Monaghan, a 'lowly' Scotsman and his wife were hanged, even though he had converted by going to mass.[62] Similarly, in the ethnic violence that engulfed north Armagh in the winter of 1641–2, conversion was no protection against native resentment: 'some English carried young children to the church to be christened at mass but the priest refused to baptize them and when they were out of the churchyard the Irish killed the children and the people that brought them also they killed the English people that had gone to mass with them above a month saying they were heretics and they would not leave a heretic in Ireland.'[63] Thus at times native antagonism towards the colonists was so great that it could not be contained by the conversion of the British.

Forced conversions were one means whereby the Irish desire to purify the community of Protestantism was realized. Concern for the religious purity of the community also contributed, in part, to the widespread expulsion and killing of settlers.[64] That this policy may have received some backing from the Irish leadership, as distinct from being purely the spontaneous reaction of the populace, is suggested by a reference to Sir Phelim O'Neill's commission to his officers. This commission allegedly included 'the banishment of all damned puritans' among the goals of the Irish, though the word 'puritan' may have been used as a term of political abuse, and not in a strict denominational sense, and the deponent may not have been a reliable guide to the activities of Sir Phelim.[65] The broad principle that no Protestants (also referred to as 'heretics') were to remain in Ireland was derived from the Irish Catholic religious *mentalité*. The options facing the settlers were conversion, expulsion or, indeed, death.[66] This hard-line stance was shaped by the immediate circumstances of 1641–2 but it also derived in part from Catholic preaching over the previous half century.

In attacks on settlers, most of the priests noted by deponents played a subordinate role, as part of their kin-group.[67] However, their widespread

---

62 James Grear, 834, f. 59r. Similarly, in Co. Cavan, John Baly was killed while plowing for the Irish, even though 'he had turned to mass', Jane Cuthbertson, 3 Feb. 1643–4, 832, f. 141r. 63 Francis Sacheverell, 21 July 1643, 836, f. 108v. 64 The Irish spoke of their desire to 'kill all the Protestants', Elizabeth Croftes, 8 Mar. 1642–3, 832, f. 55v. While robbing a deponent, Torlogh Brady said, 'that the Protestants must be banished out of the kingdom, and the papists would have the same themselves', George Cooke, 832, f. 104v. 65 John Parrie, 836, f. 62r. 66 Friar Malone was reported as saying in December 1641, 'all puritans and Protestants they should all suffer but such as shall turn to mass', Roger Holland, 4 Mar. 1641–2, 834, f. 119v. In Co. Monaghan, at the start of the revolt, Art O'Neill and Patrick Cardow said, 'they would not leave one alive neither rich nor poor who went to church', Richard Grave, 25 Oct 1641, 834, f. 92r; similarly, in north Armagh, Art O'Neale said 'that it was intended by them [Irish] not to leave an English Protestant alive in this kingdom', John Greg, 836, f. 4r. 67 The priest Shane

involvement probably lent some legitimacy to the robbing and expulsion of the settlers, in addition to what the clergy were saying in sermons. One minister in Cavan asserted 'that the friars had preached in his parish that the Irish should not leave with any English Protestant the worth of 2d of any goods'; similarly the Irish there claimed 'they had direction from the priests and friars to kill' the British.[68] However, while priests encouraged the expulsion and robbing of the settlers, it appears that they exercised a moderating influence in some situations. An Irishman from Cavan was reported as saying, 'that the priest had commanded them to take all the English Protestants' clothes and goods, and let them go, and not meddle to take away their lives'.[69] Some deponents noted the clergy's restraining influence, reporting that these castigated the perpetrators of atrocities; and some even related how they were helped by individual clerics.[70]

Several of the lower clergy were particularly virulent in deploying religious sanctions to reinforce antipathy against the settlers. Hugh McAdegane (or Mac O Degan) Maguire was involved as commander in the hanging of Protestants at various times in Co. Fermanagh; he used tell those involved that he would pardon them for killing heretics, calling them 'English dogs'.[71] James O'Hallagan was active in a group which was attacking the English in north Armagh. O'Hallagan

> did read a command in the church which as he alleged came from the Irish primate terrifying his parishioners therewith and told them that from that day forth whosoever did harbour or relieve any English Scots or Welsh or give them any alms at all at their houses should be excommunicated and not be permitted to come to the mass until he were absolved.[72]

Preaching such as that of O'Hallagan gave rise to a report from the same area that priests threatened excommunication against those relieving Protestants or burying them; the Irish there were persuaded that 'it was a mortal and unpardonable sin to protect heretics'.[73] Reinforcing the perception of priestly

---

Donoghoe, of Ellistafery parish, Co. Monaghan, joined with his neighbours in stripping a couple 'stark naked' in a search for money, Dorothy Warde, Jan. 1641–2, 834, f. 76v. 68 George Creichton, 832, ff 149v, 151r. 69 William Raicye, 834, f. 137r. 70 A Cavan minister attributed his safety to the friars and priests, G. Creichton, 832, f. 156r. Other examples include a parish priest lodging in a household which was threatened by a drunken rebel band, who 'threatened them [Irish] with curses till they promised not to hurt them [household]', Ellenor Reynolds, n.d., 832, f. 167r–v; and a friar who 'kindly entertained' Protestant refugees from the north who arrived in north Co. Dublin, John Wisdome, 8 Feb. 1641–2, 836, f. 15r. Turlough O'Connolly, priest in Clones, rescued a deponent several times, Francis Wyne, 1 Nov. 1643, 835, f. 22r. 71 Elizabeth Fletcher, 16 Aug. 1643, 835, f. 26v; (quote), Simon Crane, 835, f. 15r. 72 Francis Sacheverell, 836, f. 109v. 'Mr O Hallagan, the popish parish priest' was among the Irish who robbed Brigett Drewrie and her husband in north Armagh, B.Drewrie, ult June 1642, 836, f. 46v. 73 Nicholas Simpson, 834, ff 184r,

intransigence in north Armagh, the Irish were reported as saying 'it was no more pity to kill the English than to kill dogs calling the English heretics and saying they were God's enemies and therefore ought not to be relieved'; such assertions, couched in religious terms, reflected the influence of Catholic preaching on popular attitudes and conduct.[74] It is difficult to judge how representative these quotes were of Catholic preaching, even in the maelstrom of north Armagh. However, the naming of these two clerics by deponents suggests that their utterances and behaviour were viewed as exceptional.

Irish concern to purify the community of Protestants extended to the dead. The prohibition on burying Protestants in the normal grounds, namely, churches or churchyards, was a further consequence of their status as heretics. This ban was expounded by the clergy in their sermons in 1641–2, was widely observed, and frequently mentioned in reports of what the Irish said.[75] The role of the priests in instigating this policy was illustrated in the case of a Cavan cleric, after seven British Protestants were killed in one episode: 'Cormuck McClery priest would not suffer any of the said people that was murdered by the rebels to be buried in the church yard. But they were buried or laid in the open field. For he said they were heretics and no christians, and were not worthy to be buried in any church or churchyard'.[76] It is possible that this teaching had already formed part of the preaching against Protestantism current in the preceding decades. However, in the wave of anti-settler violence which swept Ulster in 1641, Catholic teaching on burial merely offered a veneer of religious sanction to the native urge to purify the community by getting rid of the colonists, whether dead or alive. While in theory the prohibition was restricted to interment in church premises, in practice the exclusion was more extensive. At the level of the Irish populace, the injunction was often understood to entail a complete prohibition on the burial of those who were not adherents of the Roman church. Hence reports were frequent of corpses lying on highways and

---

185r.   **74** Bridgett Drewrie, 836, f. 46v.   **75** After the killings of about twelve Scots in Clankee barony, Co. Cavan, the Irish 'would not suffer them to be buried in church or churchyard, alleging they were no christians', William Mardoghe, 12 Nov. 1642, 832, f. 72r. In Cavan, a deponent explained why those killed by the Irish were buried in fields: 'the Irish natives there would not suffer any of the British nation to be buried in church or churchyard', Jane Cuthbertson, 832, f. 141v. This conduct was common throughout Ireland, C. Tait, *Death, burial and commemoration in Ireland, 1550–1650* (Basingstoke, 2002), pp 82–3. **76** John Stevinson, 29 Oct. 1642, 832, f. 86v; a similar report from this incident was given by Simon Greame, 12 Nov 1642, 832, f. 106r, and John Sharpe, 9 Nov 1642, 832, f. 114v. The general point that 'Protestants were no christians but heretics' was made by Patrick Brady, as related by John McSkemeine, 12 Nov 1642, 832, f. 110r. On the role of priests in prohibiting Christian burial, Richard Bourk, 12 July 1643, 835, f. 21v, and Nathaniel Higginson, 7 Jan 1641–2, 835, f. 7r; priests and friars 'denied [dead Protestants] burial in the churchyard, but made them bury those that died in gardens and flung them they killed into ditches, or left them for the dogs to devour their carcases', N. Simpson, 834, f. 184r.

fields, sometimes for many months, with dogs and crows feeding on the bodies.[77] As part of this ban, the insurgents used to threaten those who attempted to bury dead Protestants. This attitude clearly derived from the basic insight that members of the established church, as heretics, were a pollution on the body of society; not only society, but also the land, had to be purified of their presence, otherwise both society and land were defiled. In this regard, the contemporary confessional rhetoric of extirpating heresy may have overlain deeper atavistic notions of the sacredness of the land inhabited by the Irish. Thus, the process of ritual purification of the territory extended to proscribing the burial of Protestants. With the collapse of structures of authority and control in winter 1641–2, these trends within the popular *mentalité* were given full rein. The violence, expulsion, and disrespect towards the dead shown by the Irish to the British were partly construed, within the Irish *mentalité*, as rites of purification of the territory.

That Protestants were intrinsically linked to the devil was a position explicitly articulated and widely held by those engaged in the attacks. In making this link, the insurgents were drawing on a strand of European counter-reformation preaching well-established in Gaelic Ireland. It arose from the motif alleging that Luther was the son of Lucifer; as part of a broader concern with personal spiritual renewal, this theme featured in the catechetical material produced by the Franciscans for Irish Catholics in the early seventeenth century.[78] The Franciscans, almost exclusively, were the preachers in Ulster in the late sixteenth and early seventeenth centuries, and, as noted in the case of friar Duffy, they were strident in combating Protestantism. In their missionary tour of the north in 1613, for example, the friars warned against any involvement with the new church order; among their arguments, they linked the newly-emerging state church with the devil, and worship within the Church of Ireland was 'the devil's service'.[79] Thus the association between the devil and

77 Thomas Crant, 832, f. 74v. Many infants died, as a Cavan deponent related, and 'some of the rebels vowed, that if any digged graves wherein to bury the dead children they should be buried therein themselves. So as the poor people left the most of them unburied, exposed to ravenous beasts and fowl and some few the poor parents carried a great way to bury them after they were dead', Adam Glover, 4 Jan. 1641–2, 832, f. 99r. Similarly, Coll McBrian McMaghan and his men, having killed 28 of Lord Moore's servants at Mellifont, Co. Louth, 'would not suffer the greatest part of them to be buried, but to lie upon the ground and be devoured by dogs, crows and ravenous creatures', a fate the deponent saw befall other Protestants killed in Co. Monaghan, John Montgomery, 834, f. 72v. 78 On the treatment of Protestantism within Aodh Mac Aingeal, *Scathan shacramuinte na h-aithridhe* [The mirror of the sacrament of penance] (Louvain, 1618), see M. Mac Craith, 'The Gaelic reaction to the Reformation', in S. Ellis and S. Barber (eds), *Conquest and union: fashioning a British state, 1485–1725* (London and New York, 1995), pp 139–61, especially pp 151–3; also M. O Riordan, 'The native Ulster mentalite as revealed in Gaelic sources, 1600–1650', in Mac Cuarta, *Ulster 1641*, pp 84–5. On the vilification of Protestantism within Gaelic devotional writing, see Canny, *Making Ireland British*, pp 424–5. 79 Reports of the friars' preaching are contained

the established church, which featured so prominently in the rhetoric of the insurgents in 1641–2, was imbued in the popular Irish consciousness in the course of the preceding decades; its prevalence was indicative of the wide impact of Catholic preaching against Protestantism on the popular *mentalité*.

By the 1630s, and probably several decades earlier, belief in the association of Protestantism and the devil determined the Irish view of the religion professed by the great majority of the settlers. Consequently, while allowing for the full range of native resentment, this confessional perspective significantly shaped Irish violence against the newcomers. On surprising a group of Protestants at worship in a settler's house in Co. Cavan, the Irish said, 'they were at the devil's service', and 'it was a good deed to burn the house over their heads'.[80] In north Armagh, 'it was commonly reported amongst the Irish … that the Protestants were devils and served the devil'.[81] Demonization of the Protestants made it easier to kill them. One deponent reported that the Irish often said to those they were about to kill, 'Cuir do anim in dioull, which in English is, Give or bequeath thy soul to the Divell'. In a similarly dismissive way, attackers would say to their victims, 'why should you pray[,] for your soul is with the devil already', before proceeding to slay them.[82] Similarly, the Irish view of the link between Protestantism and the devil was illustrated in the conversation reported at the hanging of Richard Blaney in Monaghan town. Having refused the priests' invitation to be reconciled with the Roman church, Blaney was asked if he wished to see the minister, to which he gladly assented. Thereat Art McBrian Lavagh McMaghan allegedly interjected, 'Truss him up and he goes deep enough into hell; he needs no minister to plunge him deeper'.[83] The prevalence of this negative view of Protestantism among the rebels in south Ulster in 1641 is striking testimony to the effectiveness of Catholic preaching over the previous generations. Insurgents in Fermanagh articulated a widely held belief that 'all that went to the church went to the devil …': as allies of the devil, Protestants were displeasing to God and posed a danger to the community.[84] In Cavan, it was claimed that Protestants even polluted the ground they trod on: the Irish 'sinned in looking upon [the settlers], going on the ground by them'.[85]

If Protestantism was widely seen as a pollution of the community, the various forms of violence directed against the reformed faith were, in effect, purification rites.[86] The destruction of Protestant books was widespread and

---

in the two accounts of the 1613 Franciscan mission to Ulster cited in footnote 44. 80 William Mardoghe, 832, f. 72r; James Mardoghe (brother of William), both depositions taken 12 Nov. 1642, 832, f. 110v. For Ireland in the 1640s, this theme is developed in Tait, *Death, burial and commemoration in Ireland*, pp 137–8.   81 William Duffield, 9 Aug. 1642, 836, f. 49r.   82 Elizabeth Price, 26 June 1643, 836, f. 104v.   83 Henry Steele, 834, f. 83v. 84 Katherin Maddison, 17 Nov. 1642, 835, f. 16r.   85 William Watte, 12 Nov. 1642, 832, f. 114r.   86 On religious violence as rites of purification within the French context of the

systematic. As in other early-modern revolts with a religious dimension, the bible, as the central artefact of Protestantism, was particularly execrated. This would suggest that Catholic criticism of the wide diffusion of the bible among laity featured in preaching against Protestantism in the 1620s and 1630s, and indeed earlier; this had predisposed the Irish to target bibles, once the breakdown was underway. On throwing bibles and prayer books into the fire, one friar, reflecting Catholic belief, alluded to the risk of mis-instruction (arising from unsupervised bible reading).[87] The central role of the bible in inter-confessional strife was reflected in the treatment of a minister's bible in Fermanagh. The insurgents threw it in a puddle of water, jumped and stamped on it, saying 'a plague on it. This book had bred all the quarrel. And they hoped that within three weeks all the bibles in Ireland should be used as that was or worse and that none should be left in the kingdom'.[88] The Irish gentry leaders led by example: on coming to the church in Newtownbutler, in Fermanagh, Captain Rory Maguire and Captain Newgent tore up the church bible, and scattered the pages.[89]

Church bibles and service books were particularly targeted for destruction.[90] Bibles and other Protestant books may have been destroyed in a ritual manner; it was reported that these 'were burned in great heaps at the high cross of Belturbet'.[91] At times of acute tension, desecration of bibles took unusual forms. During the burning of Armagh city on the orders of Sir Phelim O'Neill, one deponent reported an eyewitness account to the effect that the rebels killed and stripped the Protestants there, and then 'laid the sacred bible on their privy parts in contempt of the same'. In similar vein, it was reported that one Patrick Carragh O Cullan 'opening the sacred bible, pissed upon the same, saying if I could do worse with it I would'.[92] While burning a church bible Patrick O Gowen of Cavan articulated a prevalent Irish view disseminated by Catholic preachers: 'It was the word of the devil'.[93] As in other revolutionary situations in early modern Europe, the insurgents in 1641–2 used parody and mockery to

---

1560s and 1570s, see Natalie Zemon Davis, 'The rites of violence', in *Society and culture in early modern France: eight essays* (Stanford, 1975), pp 152–88. **87** In the English Northern Revolt (1569), bibles and prayer books were ritually burnt, E. Duffy, *The stripping of the altars* (New Haven, 1992), p. 583. See Roger Holland, 4 Mar. 1641–2, 834, f. 119r. On strictures against personal interpretation of the scriptures, and other misuses of the bible, see Council of Trent, session four (8 Apr. 1546), 2nd decree, in N. Tanner (ed.), *Decrees of the Ecumenical Councils* (London and Washington, 1990), 2, pp 664–5. **88** Edward Slack, 4 Jan. 1641–2, 835, ff 30r–31v. **89** Robert French, 12 Mar. 1641–2, 835, f. 45v. **90** At Glaslough, Co. Monaghan, the Irish burnt two or three bibles and service books, A. Creichtowne, 834, f. 85v. **91** Richard Parsons, minister, Kilmore diocese, 24 Feb. 1644–5, 832, f. 91r. Significantly, however, an earlier deposition was less dramatic: this deponent merely noted that as part of the destruction of the church at Belturbet, the bible and service books were burnt, John Anderson, 11 July 1642, 832, f. 68r. **92** John Parrie, 836, ff 63v–64r. **93** William Jameson, 832, f. 63v.

express their resentment and contempt for various forms of authority.[94] Rites of religious violence, too, were interspersed with comedy, for the Irish sometimes parodied the worship of the established church. In one Cavan parish, named Irishmen 'did then often take into their hands the Protestant bibles, and then wetting them in the dirty water, did five or six several times dash the same on the face of this deponent and other Protestants saying Come I know you love a good lesson, here is a most excellent one for you, and come tomorrow, and you shall have as good a sermon as this'.[95]

Apart from bibles, ministers' libraries were burnt or otherwise destroyed.[96] Some of their books were ledgers, recording debts, loans and mortgages, which attackers were keen to destroy; yet the venom with which the rebels treated the clergy's books was noteworthy, reflecting in part the depth of native animosity to the Protestantism of the settlers. In Cavan, Rose Ny Rylie, wife of the local leader Philip McHugh McShane O'Reilly, despoiled the home of Dr Faithful Teate; during that episode, she 'burned his books in the fire, [and] threw some in the dirt'.[97] In north Armagh, one deponent reported that some rebels 'took from this deponent's wife a bible and a sermon book, tore them in pieces, and threw them away'.[98] Local Irish commanders may have given specific instructions to have ministers' books and papers destroyed – those attacking a minister in Cavan alleged that the high sheriff of the county, Mulmore O'Reilly, had ordered them to destroy the cleric's books and papers.[99]

The insurgents were keen to repossess the parish churches in their localities. From the 1610s, some new churches were being built in areas of British settlement. In that decade, however, the majority of existing churches were appropriated to the use of the established church. These sites, often associated with the cult of local saints, were a prominent part of the sacred landscape of Gaelic Ulster. Their loss, with the emergence of the new ecclesiastical dispen-

---

[94] At the hanging of a poor woman in Clones, it was reported that she 'was guarded to the place of execution by Margret McMaghan wife of the said Rory McGillapatrick McMaghan who went before her with a white rod in her hand and a skine by her side saying she would be sheriff for that turne, and so stood by, till the poor woman was hanged accordingly', Robert Aldrich, 10 Feb. 1643–4, 834, f. 62r. On parody in religious riots in France, see Zemon Davis, 'The rites of violence', p. 180. [95] Adam Glover, 832, f. 99v; another exercise in parody occurred in the same area, when rebels took 'divers Protestants ... to the church by the hair of the heads, and in other cruel manner, and dragging them into the church, there stripped, robbed, whipped and most cruelly used them. Saying, if you come tomorrow, you shall hear the like sermon', ibid. [96] The rebels burnt and spoiled all the Protestant books they could find in Co. Fermanagh, Robert Flack, 12 Aug. 164[2], 835, f. 16v. Individual ministers usually mentioned books among their losses, e.g. Joseph Bury, clerk, Castleblayney, declared he lost books to the value of £100, J. Bury, 5 Mar. 1641–2, 834, f. 102r. [97] Faithful Teate, 833, f. 61r; it is possible that these books included records of mortgages and loans. [98] William Duffield, 836, f. 49r. The Irish also burnt two of Ellen Matchett's bibles 'with the rest of the books they found there', E. Matchett, 836, f. 58v. [99] Jonathan White, 833, f. 84r.

sation, was keenly felt by the indigenous population. Irish refusal of burial to Protestants in 1641 reflected, in part, native concern to purify these premises, thus restoring their sacred character. In the course of the revolt, Protestant churches were normally reconsecrated for Catholic use, after royal insignia in them had been defaced, and used thereafter by the community for the regular celebration of mass.[1] The Irish sense of *revanche* was expressed by a priest in Cavan, who demanded the key of the church of Larah. On receiving it, the priest said, 'That the papists would have their churches lands and kingdom to themselves from the English, and be no more slaves to the English (as they had been).'[2] However, some churches were desecrated, others turned into slaughter-houses, and some set on fire by retreating Irish forces while burning the towns and villages they were evacuating.

Sectarian impulses featured only as part of a more general rage against the colonists in 1641–2. Massive resentment at native marginalization in Ulster society had emerged by 1641 and underlay the animosity which exploded in that winter of discontent. Yet the northern depositions indicate that hostility was frequently expressed in religious terms. In the months preceding the rising, rumours of impending persecution of Catholicism were rife in the Ulster localities. The Franciscans had reports of puritan pressure on the old faith from their international contacts. In these reports Queen Henrietta Maria and her chaplain were the focus of Catholic worries. The prominent role of the friars in preaching to northern Catholics may have amplified this unease by comparison with other regions. The political and confessional fears thus unleashed in native society heightened anxieties over the exercise of their faith, and channelled popular fury against the Protestantism of the settlers, once the breakdown in colonial society got underway.

However, the language and conduct of the Irish in 1641 suggest that anti-Protestantism was already widespread in native society, articulated and reinforced by Catholic preaching in the preceding decades. As Protestants, the settlers were considered heretics, to be deprived of inclusion in the community, should they persist in their heresy. Accordingly, insurgents could draw on the

---

1 The condition of church buildings was noted in the 1622 diocesan visitations, TCD MS 550. For the names of saints who were patrons of parish churches and chapels in one Ulster diocese, see H. Jefferies, 'Bishop George Montgomery's survey of the parishes of Derry diocese: a complete text from *c*.1609', *Seanchas Ard Mhacha*, 17:1 (1996–7), 44–76; G.S., *A briefe declaration*, p. 6. It was reported that in December 1641, the Catholic bishop of Kilmore took over the cathedral, 'and there did consecrate it anew and set up an altar there, and said mass', T. Crant, 832, f. 77v. I am grateful to Edel Bhreatnach and Elva Johnston for a discussion on sacred sites. 2 George Cooke, 832, f. 104v. The Irish concern to redress the position of the Roman Church under the Plantation was quoted by a Monaghan deponent: 'they would never lay down arms till their church were put into its due place', Alexander Creichtowne, 834, f. 85v.

rhetoric of religious purification to explain to themselves and to their victims what was happening in the expulsions, and in the refusal of Christian burial. Sectarian attitudes of lengthy gestation within Irish society contributed to the vocabulary of revolt, once the structures of law and order collapsed. There was a widespread tendency to demonize Protestantism, perhaps indicative of popular responsiveness to this aspect of the friars' preaching. This confessional outlook had major implications for the Irish treatment of the British at that time, for it contributed to animating, shaping, and legitimizing popular violence against the settlers. The Catholic ecclesiastics who feature individually in the settlers' depositions were few, and overwhelmingly of the lower clergy. It would appear that many of these identified with the responses of their parishioners to the breakdown of 1641, though they exercised a largely restraining influence; only one or two were named as being actively involved in promoting the killing of settlers. The Ulster depositions are for the most part silent on the doings of the higher clergy; evidence from Connacht suggests that these reflected the disdain for the unruly rural populace which featured among the Irish gentry; Malachy O'Queely, archbishop of Tuam, organized a militia to combat the Irish mob; it was probable that in the breakdown of law and order the Ulster hierarchy, too, sided with their kinsfolk in the native gentry.[3] In addition to articulating the confessional mentalité underpinning native relations with the settlers, Catholic clergy played various roles: they assumed the role of the state church in the localities by taking over the churches; they were keen to secure conversions to Catholicism; many of the parochial clergy participated with their neighbours in robberies of the British; some few actively incited the Irish to violence against the planters; while others exercised a restraining and protective influence in favour of the beleaguered colonists.

In addition to popular anxieties about the broader political and confessional situation in 1641, and clerical fulminations against heresy, antipathy to Protestantism had more concrete grounds. The ministers in the north were the especial targets of the populace's fury in the early weeks of the revolt, especially in mid-Ulster. Animosity against the established church arose from resentment at the avarice of church personnel over the previous decades, reflected in the elevated social and economic position of the clergy within planter society, and their considerable enrichment especially in the years just preceding the revolt. The especially severe violence against the clergy of the Church of Ireland in Ulster in 1641–2 was related to their relatively recent arrival in that province, and their rapid enrichment, particularly under Wentworth in the 1630s.

Attention to the confessional dimension throws light on significant facets of Irish behaviour, at the popular level, towards the settlers in Ulster in 1641–2,

---

3 John Lynch, *The portrait of a pious bishop: or, the life and death of ... Francis Kirwan, bishop of Killala*, trans. C.P. Meehan (Dublin, 1884), p. 109.

and it alerts us more generally to the power of religious animosity latent within early seventeenth-century Irish society, and to the role of confessional strife in the early months of the rising in the other provinces. South Ulster in 1641–2 affords a well-documented case-study of the motivation and forms of sectarian violence in early modern Ireland. Religiously-inspired animosity took broadly similar forms in Leinster, suggesting that sectarianism in Ulster differed merely in degree, and not in kind, from the rest of the country; only exploration of these themes in the case of the other provinces can lead to a proper evaluation of the role of confessional strife in Ulster in the breakdown of 1641.[4]

4 Canny, 'Religion, politics and the Irish rising of 1641', pp 40–70.

The other massacre: English killings of Irish, 1641–2

KENNETH NICHOLLS

The pseudonymous author of *A collection of some of the murthers and massacres committed on the Irish since the 23rd of October 1641* declares in his introduction that 'it is undeniable that the first Massacre committed in the time of the said rebellion was as done upon the Irish, and the several Murthers perpetrated in cold blood upon them did twenty fould exceed these which were committed on the English'.[1] It is unlikely that it would ever be possible to make even an approximate tally of the deaths on either side in the period of war between 1641 and 1653, or indeed to distinguish between those killed in combat and those – including non-combatants, women and children – slaughtered in cold blood, or even, in certain cases, to draw a clear line between these two categories. My own impression, from admittedly incomplete and anecdotal evidence, is that deaths in both these categories on the Irish side probably far exceeded those on the other. Though I would hesitate to affirm that they exceeded them 'twenty-fold', yet, if one adds in (as 'R.S.' probably intended to) the deaths during the Cromwellian war of conquest, by famine and hardship as well as by the sword, and given the relative size of the two communities, it may not be very far from the truth. R.S.'s other contention, that the first massacres – using this term to denote the killing of non-combatants or of combatants who had surrendered on promise of quarter – were committed upon the Irish, is a more debatable one. My own impression is that, while it is certainly untrue for Ulster, accepting that the massacre of the Irish inhabitants of Islandmagee (Co. Antrim) which R.S. placed at the beginning of November 1641, with the comment that 'this was to be the first massacre committed in Ireland of either side', in fact occurred 'about the 8th of January'[2] – it is with equal certainty true for Leinster and Munster. If in mid-Ulster the killing was almost certainly

---

1 R.S., *A collection of some of the murthers and massacres committed on the Irish in Ireland since the 23rd of October 1641* (London, 1662). For this tract, which the Dublin government sought (with considerable success) to suppress, see Toby Barnard, '1641: a bibliographical essay', in Brian MacCuarta (ed.), *Ulster 1641: aspects of the rising* (Belfast, 1993), pp 177–8. It was reprinted (without the author's introduction) as an appendix to Edward Hyde, earl of Clarendon, *The history of the rebellion and the civil wars in Ireland* (London, 1720), pp 329–69. 2 TCD MS 838, ff 198–200.

commenced by the Irish,[3] in the southern provinces the evidence suggests that the killings of Protestant[4] settlers were in most cases reprisals provoked by the indiscriminate and bloody repression carried out by the government forces, but falling, as almost invariably happens in such cycles of violence, upon the innocent.

Confirmation of both these conclusions depends on the achievement of a reliable chronology of confirmed killings, something which, with the notable exception of Hilary Simms' work on Armagh,[5] has not taken place. There is no doubt that in Munster from the time the Lord President, Sir William St Leger, moved into Tipperary in November 1641, and in Leinster a few months later, when the forces of the Dublin administration regained the initiative with their expedition into Kildare at the end of January 1642, the Protestant forces (as they are usually styled in the English pamphlet literature, whose producers had no doubt that this was a War of Religion) indulged not only in the devastation of the countryside through which they passed, destroying the houses and property of nobility, gentry and the people at large, but also in wholesale killings of men, women and children, involving again members of the gentry as well as the mass of the people.[6] In speaking of massacres, I have not included the routine killing or hanging of the Irish taken in arms, or even (as was thought) on their way to join the Irish forces.[7] As rebels and, in twenty-first-century terminology, 'unlawful combatants', they were devoid of rights. Such executions of prisoners took place even when they could have been, or even were expected to be, exchanged for Protestants held prisoner by the Irish.[8] But such executions had been a norm of medieval European warfare and were only, with the professionalization of war brought in by the military revolution, giving way to a system of mutual respect for prisoners, based on hard practical considerations. Only when the prisoners so put to death had, as too often happened in

---

[3] Hilary Simms, 'Violence in county Armagh, 1641', in MacCuarta, *Ulster 1641*, pp 123–38.
[4] I have emphasized this adjective deliberately. English Catholic settlers – of whom there were many in Ireland – seem for the most part to have joined the Irish in the revolt: D. Edwards, 'A haven of Popery: English Catholic migration to Ireland in the age of plantations', in A. Ford and J. McCafferty (eds), *The origins of sectarianism in early modern Ireland* (Cambridge, 2005), pp 95–126. An example of an English Catholic convert who joined the Irish is Samuel East of Ballymanus, Co. Wicklow: TCD MS 815, f. 106; N. Canny, *Making Ireland British, 1580–1850* (Oxford, 2001), p. 522.   [5] Simms, 'Violence in county Armagh'.   [6] See for example 'The protestation of the Catholics', issued 8 February 1642/3, in J.T. Gilbert (ed.), *History of the Irish Confederation and the war in Ireland, 1641–1643* (3 vols, Dublin, 1882), 2, p. 26; Preston's letter to Clanricarde, 18 January 1642/3, in T. Carte, *A collection of original letters* (London, 1735) = *The history of the life of James, Duke of Ormonde*, 3 (henceforth Carte, *Ormonde*), no. 120.   [7] P.D. Vigors (ed.), 'Rebellion 1641–2, described in a letter of Rev. Urban Vigors to Rev. Henry Jones', *Journal of the Cork Historical and Archaeological Society*, 2nd series, 2 (1896), 299.   [8] T. Fitzpatrick, *The bloody bridge, and other papers relating to the insurrection of 1641* (Dublin, 1903), pp 16–17.

Ireland, been promised quarter, that is, security for their lives, should such executions fall within the definition of massacres, however brutal and repellent they may seem, and however they might have provoked Irish reprisals. An exception to this routine execution of Irish prisoners might sometimes be made in the case of landowners – where this fact could be ascertained – since (the clean sweep of the Cromwellian confiscation not yet being visualized) condemnation by a formal legal process was felt to be necessary to secure the confiscation of their estates.[9]

In late seventeenth-century England, John Nalson, who had no doubt regarding the atrocities committed by the Irish during the Rising, criticized Temple, Borlase and other writers who had 'not the least mention of any cruelty exercised upon the Irish ... they take no notice of the severities of the Provost Martials, nor of the barbarism of the soldiers to the Irish'. He instanced how a relation of his own, a former officer in Ireland, told him that it was usual to kill the children along with the rest.[10] What is perhaps surprising is that while the atrocities against Protestant settlers have continued to command attention, those committed against the native Irish population, although rehearsed in detail by John Curry in the eighteenth century and researched by Thomas Fitzpatrick at the beginning of the twentieth,[11] would seem to be completely passed over in the recent historiography of the 1640s. Professor Nicholas Canny, in his two most recent studies of the 1641 insurrection,[12] dwells in detail on atrocities committed – or alleged to have been committed – against the settlers but, unlike Nalson, makes no reference whatever to any committed against the Irish. The same is true of Dr Mary O'Dowd's article on 'Women and war in Ireland in the 1640s', published in 1991.[13]

My own intrusion into a field very remote from those which I have hitherto cultivated has arisen indirectly from my observation many years since of the fact that in the wars of the 1640s the Irish in general – or perhaps always – respected

---

9 *Calendar of the manuscripts of the Marquess of Ormonde* [*Ormonde MSS*] (11 vols, London, 1895–1920), new series, 2, p. 72; Gilbert, *History of the Irish Confederation*, 2, p. 178. The former Irish precedents to the contrary (T. Carte, *An history of the life of James, Duke of Ormonde* (3 vols, London, 1736), 1, p. 276) may not have been felt to be legal, perhaps as contrary to English practice. This issue of summary execution imperilling the confiscation of rebels' estates had arisen in England in the aftermath of the 1569 rebellion, the only occasion when martial law had been deployed in England on an 'Irish' scale: R.J. Kesselring, 'Mercy and liberality: the aftermath of the 1569 Northern Rebellion', *History*, 90:2 (2005), 218, 222.   **10** J. Nalson, *An impartial collection of the great affairs of state* (London, 1682), introduction, pp vi, vii, quoted in Fitzpatrick, *Bloody bridge*, pp 160–1.   **11** John Curry, *An historical and critical review of the Civil Wars in Ireland* (Dublin, various editions from 1775); Fitzpatrick, *Bloody bridge*.   **12** N. Canny, 'What really happened in Ireland in 1641?', in J.H. Ohlmeyer (ed.), *Ireland: from independence to occupation, 1641–1660* (Cambridge, 1995); Canny, *Making Ireland British*, pp 61–578.   **13** In M. MacCurtain and M. O'Dowd (eds), *Women in early modern Ireland* (Edinburgh, 1991), pp 91–111.

high social status in their opponents. Settlers of high social status or birth did not experience personal violence or violent death, though their property might be looted. The murder of Lord Charlemont, an apparent exception, was punished by Sir Phelim O Neill: we have no idea of the precise circumstances, and it could have conceivably have arisen from drunken violence by his warders, perhaps provoked by his threats of future revenge. I have not been able to discover any instance of an upper-class English or Protestant woman suffering actual physical violence (including the stripping of clothes for the purposes of robbery) at the hands of the Irish insurgents. The English (Protestant) forces, on the other hand, appear to have deliberately targeted the Irish (*scilicet*, Roman Catholic) gentry, including, or perhaps especially, their womenfolk.[14] A distinguished historian of this period, to whom I commented on this difference at a conference in 1992, suggested that it was because 'the English were fighting an ideological war: the Irish were fighting an old-fashioned one'. I would interpret it along slightly different, but nevertheless similar lines; the Irish attitude to rank was a manifestation of the essentially conservative, indeed reactionary, nature of Irish political culture, based on traditional power structures in which birth was still the dominant element, over-riding political and even religious considerations. The fact that native Irish Protestants of elite status seem to have experienced only verbal violence and attempts at conversion points in the same direction, to the still overwhelming influence of kinship in Irish social culture; all had Roman Catholic kindred and some had Catholic wives and children. Although lethal violence within the elites arising from disputes over power and property had been a norm of Gaelic society in Ireland and Highland Scotland, this must be seen as an extreme form of the right of private war, normal among aristocratic elites over most of Europe, and the killing of a member of the elite by a social inferior was regarded with horror.[15] Much of this slaughter occurred between close kinsmen, and parallels what is recorded of lineage-based societies elsewhere. Women were apparently exempt, at least in the later medieval period, and the unintentional death of a girl of the elite in the attack on a castle in 1495 was regarded by the Ulster annalist as worthy of note.[16] It is almost unique in this period. In short, the existence of frequent lethal violence among the Irish elites does not invalidate the notion that Irish society adhered to the hierarchical social model found elsewhere in Europe and, indeed, outside it.

14 For examples of atrocities against upper-class Irishwomen ('gentlewomen') see below, passim. Cf also the hanging by martial law of Evelyn MacMahon, daughter of one MacMahon chieftain and widow of another, at Carrickmacross on 3 October 1642 (T. Ó Donnchadha (ed.), 'Cín Lae Ó Meallàin', *Analecta Hibernica*, 3 (1931), 17. The extreme example of the targeting of an upper-class woman – in this case belonging to the high nobility – is the execution at Cork in 1654 of Ellen Power, the elderly wife of Viscount Fermoy, on what appears to have been the trumped-up charge of murdering an unnamed man. 15 See *AC*, 1452.5, 1478.13 (cf. *AFM*, 4, p. 982); *AU*, 3, pp 350, 368–70, 596. 16 *AU*, 3, p. 392.

English and Scots settlers, on the other hand, new men in an Irish context whatever might be their social origins at home, can be seen as social revolutionaries to whom the traditional local hierarchies of respect were irrelevant.[17] A previous generation of settlers had intermarried with the native elites, with the result that in 1641 many of their descendants can be found making common cause with the native Irish.[18] But by 1641 the religious polarization which had developed over the previous fifty years meant that this no longer occurred, and only among native Protestants does one still find occasional mixed families and cross-confessional marriages. Brian Óg (Barnaby) O Dunne of Brittas was an ardent Protestant ('a rank Puritan', as a prejudiced Irish contemporary called him); he had married as his second wife a New English woman and is found fighting alongside her brother on the English side. But his son and heir (by his first marriage), Charles, was an active Confederate.[19] There are a few similar examples among families of Elizabethan settler descent, such as the Bowens and the Hetheringtons. In general it would probably be true to say that by 1641 religious polarization was almost complete, but that among the native elites it could be over-ridden by considerations of kinship or class. Many native Protestants seem to have taken an almost neutral stance in the wars of the 1640s. In this the influence of wives may have been decisive in determining political allegiance: it is noteworthy that one native Irishman who was totally committed to the English Protestant cause, Murrough O Brien, Lord Inchiquin, had married Sir William St Leger's daughter, and the earls of Kildare and Barrymore, both strongly committed to the settler cause, were married to daughters of Richard Boyle.

Our major problem in dealing with atrocities committed against the Irish during the 1640s is the absence of reliable contemporary evidence from the Irish side. For the atrocities committed by the Irish, we have the great body of the Depositions.[20] Unreliable though the information in many, or perhaps most, of these may be, they still constitute an easily accessible body of evidence which can be sifted and analyzed. For those committed against the Irish, on the other hand, with a few exceptions, such as the confirmation of the Clongoeswood massacre in the deposition of Richard Greames, whose wife and children perished in it,[21] and the evidence collected under the Commonwealth regarding the Ulster massacres at Islandmagee and Ballydavy,[22] the Depositions provide

---

17 Is this why some present-day historians, of Irish nationalist background, seem to prefer them?   18 Edwards, 'A haven of Popery'.   19 K.W. Nicholls (ed.), *The O Doyne (Ó Duinn) Manuscript* (Dublin, 1983), p. 133. For Brian Óg's position see J.T. Gilbert (ed.), *A contemporary history of affairs in Ireland* (3 vols, Dublin, 1879), 1, p. 129. He seems subsequently to have adopted a more neutralist stance (ibid., 2, p. 130).   20 For a brief survey of the Depositions, and the classes into which they fall, see Aidan Clarke, 'The 1641 depositions', in P. Fox (ed.), *Treasures of the library, Trinity College Dublin* (Dublin, 1986), pp 111–22.   21 TCD MS 813, f. 71.   22 The Ballydavy evidence (or part of it) is printed (from TCD MS 837) by Fitzpatrick, *Bloody bridge*, pp 106–9.

little help. (Was it the fact that the perpetrators of these atrocities against innocent Irish were Scots, a community regarded with almost as much disfavour as the Irish by the Commonwealth authorities, that led the latter to investigate them?) The accounts written from the Irish side[23] are of much later date, anecdotal, sometimes confused, and often, when we are able to check, exaggerated. In his tract, R.S. dates the Islandmagee massacre in the beginning of November 1641 and gives the number of victims as 3,000, 'men, women and children': the evidence of the Depositions dates it in early January and makes the number of victims far lower, below a hundred.[24] R.S. also misdates in 1641 the massacres at Rathcoffey and Clongoeswood, which occurred in July 1642. John Lynch, writing in the same year as R.S., 1662, repeats twice over the account of the massacre at Timolin, Co. Kildare, when men, women and children were killed after the castle was surrendered on promise of quarter (an event confirmed by an English account); once with the place-name, and again as 'the house of a gentleman called Ashboll' (Archbold).[25] Presumably he had misinterpreted the account found in *Commentarius Rinuccinianus*. Sometimes the atrocity stories give no indication of time or place; as in those provided by the English Catholic Royalist William Blundell (who does, however, name his informants, some of them eye-witnesses). One would like to know who was the clergyman 'born in Wirral in Cheshire, and beneficed in Ireland', who 'killed with his own hands' one Sunday morning 53 of his parishioners, 'most or all of them women and children', or who was the gentlewoman who was hanged by Major [John] Morice 'only because she looked (as he was pleased to phrase it) like an Irish lady'.[26] A further difficulty is that the Irish recounters of atrocities, writing in

---

[23] R.S., *A collection*; [Peter Talbot?], *The polititian's cathechisme* (Antwerp, 1658); J. Lynch, *Cambrensis Eversus*, ed. and trans. Mathew Kelly (Dublin, 1848), 3, pp 90–5, 188–91; R. O'Ferrall and R. O'Connell, *Commentarius Rinuccinianus* (5 vols, Dublin, 1932–49), 5, pp 185–6.   [24] R.S., *A collection*, p. 1. The depositions regarding it are in TCD MS 838, ff 198–223. Even if the number of non-combatants killed was far lower than was alleged it is difficult to see why Dr Ray Gillespie should, in referring to it, put the word 'massacre' in inverted commas: R. Gillespie, *Colonial Ulster* (Cork, 1985), p. 155.   [25] *Cambrensis Eversus*, 3, pp 190–1. For the Timolin massacre, carried out in violation of quarter, see Gilbert, *History of the Irish Confederation*, 2, pp 250, 259n (the full title of the source quoted there can be found at ibid., p. xvi); *Commentarius Rinuccinianus*, 5, p. 186. The siege was conducted by George Monck, who had been left to continue it while Ormonde went ahead with the main body of the army.   [26] T. Elliott Gibson, *Crosby records: a Cavalier's notebook* (London, 1880), pp 230–2, reproduced by Philip Caraman, *The years of siege* (London, 1966), pp 91–2. Here, as in his source, *The polititian's cathechisme*, the name *Comain* is a misprint for *Coniam* (as correctly in *Cambrensis Eversus*, 3, p. 90. The person meant is Denis Coniam of Glenealy). For John Morrice, who began his career as a page to Strafford in Ireland, and subsequently went to England where, having deserted the Royal service for the Parliamentarian, he turned Royalist again in the Second Civil War and was eventually executed at York by the Parliamentarians, see the *Dictionary of National Biography* and Robert Ashton, *Counter-revolution: the Second Civil War and its origins* (New Haven and London, 1994), pp 261–2, 405–6, 416.

the Restoration period and seeking to identify their cause with that of the English Royalists then in the ascendant, tended to concentrate more heavily on those committed in the Commonwealth period. Yet a further consideration was the need to avoid criticism that might reflect on Ormond, the commander (at least nominally) of many of the forces responsible for them.

Much more precise information on atrocities committed on the Irish can be found in the pamphlet literature published in London after February 1642. While the English pamphlet literature during the first three months of the rising is, in its accounts of alleged events in Ireland, almost entirely fiction, naming imaginary persons[27] and places and recounting impossible happenings,[28] from the time when the Protestant forces seized the initiative against the Irish, a new generation of pamphlets emerged embodying the information which was flowing back to England from those in the forces in Ireland and those who had heard their stories, which frequently involved candid accounts of atrocities against the Irish. The argument that the writers of these narratives were unlikely to invent material discreditable to their own side (such, as at Timolin, the violation of promises of quarter) is not an infallible one, but can I think be taken as a general rule. I have no doubt that an exhaustive trawl of the pamphlet literature, and of similar narratives remaining in manuscript,[29] would be highly productive of relevant and credible material. Such however is the bulk of the material that such a search would be a lengthy, indeed a Herculean, task, and I have for the purposes of this paper been forced to confine myself to a small sample.

As an example of the problems of reliability, as well as the detail which the pamphlets provide, I will comment here on one pamphlet in particular. This is *Exceeding happy news from Ireland, declaring the proceedings of the Protestant army in Kildare, sent from Captain Stephens to his brother William Stephens*,[30] which contains the accounts of the very strange happenings at the taking of the Castle of Blackwood, Co. Kildare.[31] Two problematical points may be noted. First, a

---

[27] Such as 'Lord Osmond', 'Chief Commander to the Rebels' (E.H. Shagan, 'Constructing discord: ideology, propaganda and English responses to the Irish Rebellion of 1641', *Journal of British Studies*, 36 (1997), 12–3), apparently based on Lord Esmonde who, however, was fighting on the other side (although his son Sir Thomas was a Confederate!). Cf. also Gilbert, *History of the Irish Confederation*, 2, p. cxviii n. [28] Such as the cavern excavated by friars under the main road at Rathcoole ('Rockoll'), Co. Dublin, and filled with gunpowder to blow up the English army as it passed over! (Fitzpatrick, *Bloody bridge*, pp 25–8). Such echoes of the Gunpowder Plot were also to be found in contemporary propaganda in England (Shagan, 'Constructing discord', 24–5). [29] Such as in the Carte Manuscripts in the Bodleian Library, but there are others scattered elsewhere. [30] Stephens, *Exceeding happy news from Ireland, declaring the proceedings of the Protestant army in Kildare, sent from Captain Stephens to his brother William Stephens* (London, 1642). A copy is in the Royal Irish Academy, Halliday Pamphlets, vol. 30. [31] The Civil Survey strangely gives the proprietor of Blackwood as Edward Dungan (see R.C. Simington (ed.), *The Civil Survey, AD 1654–56* (10 vols, Dublin, 1931–61), 8, p. 161). In fact he was only occupying it in right of his wife Cicely Fitzgerald,

further title[32] states that it was a letter 'from Steven Stephens' at Dublin, 30 August, 1642. But Captain Stephens' Christian name, according to the only army list which gives it, was John.[33] It may be that Steven was another brother, who forwarded the Captain's account to London. More disturbing is a reference to 'Viscount Musgrave' as a rebel commander.[34] Musgrave would be an easy blunder for Muskerry, but the context suggests rather Mountgarret. The narrative relates how the women in the castle threw down stones on the besiegers from the top of the castle, one of which slightly wounded the commander, Colonel George Monck, on the chin. 'But these creatures desiring quarter, the soldiers told them that they should have quarter, and thereupon they came forth; the soldiers being enraged against them, because they did the greatest mischiefe, by flinging of stones, quartered both women and children, excepting some five that are brought to town'. The men, 68 in number, were given quarter by Monck, insofar as to be brought to Dublin along with the 5 women who survived 'and there left to the [Lord] Justice's pleasure'.[35] I have not found this siege of Blackwood, or the expedition of Monck in August 1642 on which it occurred, mentioned in any other source. The sparing of the male prisoners on this occasion may not have benefited them very much if, like those from Rathcoffey and Clongoeswood a month earlier, they were hanged by martial law on arriving at Dublin! Fulfilling the promise of 'quarter' to the women by cutting them and their children into quarters was a particularly gruesome jest: quartering of the body was part of the formal ritual for the execution of male traitors, but not for female ones.[36] *Exceeding happy news* also provides an account of the siege of the castle of Knock (or Lynch's Knock, now Summerhill in Laracor Parish, Co. Meath) where Monck also commanded, but which occurred in late June previously.[37] Here 'our army gave quarter to all the gentlewomen, excepting two or three which the soldiers laid hold on' and killed or hanged all the men.[38] Were the non-gentry women also killed?

the widowed mother of the noted Irish commander Piers FitzGerald ('MacThomas'), who held it as her jointure. Blackwood and the adjacent townlands were restored to Cicely (widowed for a second time) after the Restoration, and descended to her son Garret Fitzgerald and his descendants.   32 Stephens, *Exceeding happy news*, 2.   33 *Ormonde MSS*, old series, 1, p. 177. 34 Stephens, *Exceeding happy news*, 7.   35 Ibid., pp 2–3.   36 S.L. Jansen, *Dangerous talk and strange behaviour: women and popular resistance to the reforms of Henry VIII* (New York, 1996), pp 25, 101, 161, gives two alleged examples of women being hanged, drawn and quartered in England under Henry VIII, but I am not convinced that they actually occurred. Women convicted of treason under the Statute of 26 Henry VIII (1537) for denying the legitimacy of Prince Edward could, as occurred in a case at Lincoln, be drawn to the gallows on a hurdle and then simply hanged (without disembowelling or quartering) as an alternative to being burned alive (the regular punishment of women for treason); see Dalyson's Reports, British Library Harleian MSS 5141, ff 20–20 v.   37 *Ormonde MSS*, new series, 2, pp 160–1. Can the absence of any reference to Rathcoffey or Clongoeswood in *Exceeding happy news* be credibly explained by Captain Stephens not being present there?   38 Stephens, *Exceeding happy news*, p. 3.

Knock would seem to have been an exception to the general practice of the Protestant forces in their campaigns of 'giving no quarter to women and children'. This had been partially defended by the Lords Justices in their report to the English Parliament of 7 June 1642 and complained of in a Confederate pamphlet issued at Kilkenny in the following December.[39] It can be seen practised after Monck's capture of the castles of Rathcoffey and Clongoeswood, Co. Kildare, in the early days of July 1642. Here, although the occupants had been promised quarter, the women and children were killed out of hand and the male prisoners taken to Dublin where, after being interrogated, they were executed by martial law.[40] We are fortunate that among the Depositions are preserved those taken from the 30 prisoners from Clongoeswood, who ranged from a New English Catholic gentleman, Richard Greames (his wife, a sister of William Sarsfield of Lucan, and their two children had been among those killed) to a 'beggar-boy', and included two priests.[41] Twelve of the 30 were monoglots who were questioned through interpreters. The purpose of this interrogation – there is no record of a similar interrogation of the Rathcoffey prisoners – seems to have been to establish the responsibility for the murder of an unfortunate English couple, Francis Cardinall and his wife. The Cardinalls had been living at Donadea (presumably as tenants of its Catholic landlord, Sir Andrew Aylmer) but after being robbed, hearing of the presence of an English army, sought to join it. They were however intercepted and killed, although their six-year-old son was spared and sent back to Donadea. The culprits were apparently the three Barnewall brothers, minor gentry and refugees who had fled before the English armies, first from Fingall to the Navan area, and then to Kildare; it is quite possible that they had lost family members to the soldiers in Meath, and that the Cardinalls were victims of a reprisal killing. The two survivors, George and Roger, sought to throw the blame on their brother James, killed in conflict a short time before.[42]

An analysis of the movements of the government forces in the Pale and adjacent counties during 1642, operations which were accompanied by widespread atrocities against the local population, has yet to be attempted. These came after the administration had recovered its confidence through the failure of the insurgents to capture Drogheda, and, probably, their realization of the military weakness of the Irish, almost devoid of leaders with military

---

39 *Ormonde MSS*, new series, 2, pp 130–1; A. Clarke (ed.), 'A discourse between two Councillors of State', *Analecta Hibernica*, 26 (1970), 173–4. 40 *Ormonde MSS*, new series, 2, pp 130–1; R.S., *A collection*, p. 11. R.S.'s statement that they had been promised quarter is confirmed by the evidence of Richard Greames (TCD MS 813, f. 71). 41 TCD MS 813, ff 71–84. I intend to publish these Depositions in a coming number of *Archivium Hibernicum*. 42 Relations of the Barnewalls sought to have them freed in exchange for some of the Protestants held prisoner at Virginia, Co. Cavan: Gilbert, *A contemporary history of affairs in Ireland*, 1, pp 538, 541.

experience and starved of the basic ammunitions of war, especially gunpowder.⁴³ The first military expedition by the forces of the Dublin administration into Kildare, which – apart from the English garrison of Athy – had been in the unchallenged control of the insurgents since December 1641, seems to have been that, led by Ormond, which set out on 31 January 1642. After burning the little town of Newcastle, Co. Dublin, and the castles and villages in its vicinity, they went on to occupy Naas, which was plundered but spared burning in order to be garrisoned. From Naas they sent out parties which penetrated as far as Kilcullen and Castlemartin, burning the villages and the houses of the gentry.⁴⁴ It was at this time, or shortly afterwards, that the aged Mrs Eustace of Cradockstown (near Naas) was murdered in her own house along with another old gentlewoman and a girl of eight by a group of English officers whom she had entertained.⁴⁵ After the destruction and killing carried out by this army, it is little wonder that in the following April a convoy of Protestant settlers who had been sheltered by the earl of Castlehaven (an English Catholic) in his house at Maddenstown and were making their way to Dublin along with a consignment of the earl's wool sent for sale and escorted by his Protestant brother, Mervyn Touchet, were attacked at Rathcoole by the sons of Patrick Scurlock of Rathcredan (whose castle had been among those burned on 31 January) and other local gentry and others. Four Englishmen, along with the wife and child of one of them and an Irishman who accompanied the party were killed, and the others with the four wagonloads of wool carried off to Celbridge, where they were providentially rescued by Sir John Dungan of Castletown.⁴⁶ A few days later an avenging party set out from Dublin, but it had already been anticipated by the governor of Naas, Sir Arthur Loftus, who had come with a troop of cavalry, killing everyone whom they met on their way. Finding that several hundred of the local inhabitants, men, women and children, had taken refuge on a hill densely covered with furze, they set the furze on fire, burning them all to death.⁴⁷ We do not know if Sir Simon Harcourt's troops, in their

43 P. Lenihan, *Confederate Catholics at war, 1641–49* (Cork, 2001), pp 53–8.   44 *Ormonde MSS*, new series, 2, pp 70–1; Anon., *The particular relation of the present estate and condition of Ireland, as now it stands* (London, 1642) (RIA, Halliday Pamphlets, vol. 30), pp 3–4.   45 Talbot?, *The polititian's pathechisme*, p. 158, which dates it 'in or about February 1641' (old style). Peter Talbot (if he was the author) was Mrs Eustace's nephew, so likely to be well informed. R.S., *A collection*, p. 2, ascribes this outrage (and another one) to a Captain Thomas Hues, but I can find no one of this or a similar name in the army lists for 1641–43.   46 Deposition of Richard Paget, taken 29 April 1642, printed in Fitzpatrick, *The bloody bridge*, p. 156. Paget dates the attack as 'Tuesday last', presumably 21 rather than the 28 April. Mervyn Touchet's account, *Castlehaven memoirs* (Dublin, 1815), pp 37–8, was written long afterwards in 1683, and is much less informative.   47 Touchet, who had escaped on horseback from the attack and subsequently accompanied the party sent from Dublin saw 'the bodies and the furze still burning'. If this is the event related in *The polititians cathechisme*, p. 158, the latter is wrong in saying that 'no murder or pillage had previously

campaign in Co. Dublin in March 1642 were guilty of indiscriminate killing, but we know that when they captured Carrickmines Castle on 27 March, after a siege in which Sir Simon himself and a number of others were killed, all those in the castle, 18 men and many times that number of women and children, were slaughtered.[48]

The instructions by the Lords Justices to Ormond for his expedition to Meath, issued on 23 February and 4 March, 1641/2, commanded him to kill and destroy all the rebels, to burn, destroy and demolish 'all the places, towns and houses' where they or their adherents had been relieved or harboured, with all the corn and hay, and to kill all the men living there capable of bearing arms. A further instruction of 9 March laid down, in case of doubt, that the houses and goods of the nobility ('the Lords of the Pale') were to be included in the destruction, with further clauses highly insulting to Ormond.[49] The latter was told to forward copies of these instructions to Sir Henry Tichborne who commanded at Drogheda. The burnings were accordingly carried out, and the English armies 'fired all the whole Pale', as recorded in a triumphalist pamphlet of April (figure 5).[50] The evidence of the Irish sources[51] makes clear that killing by the armies in Meath, and by Tichborne and his companion, Lord Moore, in Louth, was not confined to men of military age, but extended also to women, children and the aged. As an example which can be dated precisely, a raid to Dunshaughlin by the Bective garrison on 11 May resulted in the killing of 40 civilians, women, children and old men, including the aged mother of Father Peter Reade, SJ, who was set up as a target and shot to death.[52] Had they discovered she was the mother of a Jesuit domiciled in Spain?

The terror inspired by the English forces in the counties around Dublin in 1642 led the local inhabitants to seek refuge in the many castles and fortified houses, whose subsequent defence was of course interpreted as an act of open rebellion. Such had probably been the case at Baldongan Castle in Fingal where, after it had been taken by government forces at the beginning of June 1642, the occupants, 120 men, women and children, were killed (allegedly in violation of promised quarter), except for a priest who was taken to Dublin and hanged.[53] Many of the Clongoeswood prisoners testified that they had taken refuge there for fear of being killed or hanged by the army. Richard Greames declared that

---

taken place', although it is certain that most, if not all, of those burned to death were innocent of any part in the attack on the refugees. The *Cathechisme* report may, however, refer to a similar but different incident.   48 See below.   49 Carte, *Ormonde*, 3, no. 60, 62, 64. By the last Ormond was expressly forbidden not only to negotiate surrenders with the rebels, but to have any personal contact with any who might surrender.   50 A.N., *Aprill the first, 1642. A continuation of the triumphant and courageous proceedings of the Protestant army in Ireland* (London, 1642).   51 R.S., *A collection*, pp 14–15.   52 Petrus Redanus (Peter Reade), *Commentarius in libros machabaeorum canonicos* (Lyons, 1651), p. 257; R.S., *A collection*, p. 12.   53 *Commentarius Rinuccinianus*, 5, pp 185–6; *Ormonde MSS*, new series, 2, p. 144.

5 Anon., *Aprill the first, 1642* (London, 1642), title page.

it was concern for the safety of his wife and children that led him, on discovering the presence of English troops in the vicinity, to turn out of his way to Clongoeswood.[54] But the same wholesale killing of the Irish, and the laying waste of the countryside, led to the killings in reprisal of isolated English Protestants, no doubt confident in the protection of their Irish landlords or their good relations with their Irish neighbours. Such was Ralph Howard of Cloniff, Co. Kildare, who is said to have actually fostered a child of his neighbour, the insurgent leader Rory O'Moore, but was murdered by the soldiers of the latter's

54 TCD MS 813, f. 71.

brother Lewis at the end of April 1642, along with his wife and two children.[55] Such also were the Cardinall family whose murder I have mentioned in connection with Clongoeswood. David Edwards has shown how, apart from some isolated cases, the killing of English Protestants in Kilkenny only began after the activities of the English army in Leinster in the spring of 1642.[56] The execution out of hand of the prisoners taken at the battle of Kilrush (15 April), many or most of whom would have been from the Kilkenny region, must have aroused a thirst for vengeance among their kinsfolk, who would have taken it out on the nearest available target.[57] In the very beginning of the Rising, the hanging of three Englishmen in Co. Wicklow around Christmas 1641 was alleged to be a reprisal for the killings by Coote's expedition to that county, although the victims – who should have been protected by the agreement made for the surrender of Knockrath Castle on 14 November – themselves thought they were targeted because of an 'old quarrel' with the sons of the insurgent commander Luke O Toole.[58] Here we have two alternative explanations for the killing of Protestant settlers: reprisals for killings by the English forces and the working out of private feuds and grudges.[59] Both would have been common motivations. In regard to the latter, it is generally overlooked that, little more than a generation before, Ireland, like Scotland, had been a feuding society in which lethal violence resulting from private disputes had been a commonplace.[60] How far could attacks on settlers in 1641, like the rustling of their cattle, be seen as a reversion to traditional patterns of behaviour, as much as expressing ethnic and religious hatred and political grievance?

As we have seen in our own time, in Bosnia and elsewhere in situations of ethno/religious conflict – and this, I think, is the accurate description for the

---

55 Ibid., f. 161. 56 D. Edwards, *The Ormond lordship in county Kilkenny, 1515–1642: the rise and fall of Butler feudal power* (Dublin, 2003), pp 322–3. 57 For the hanging of the prisoners taken at Kilrush see Anon., *A new declaration of the last affairs in Ireland, showing the great overthrow given to the Irish rebels* (London, 1642), (RIA, Halliday Pamphlets, vol. 30). 58 TCD MS 811, f. 190; for the terms of the surrender of Knockrath see 815, f. 99. 59 The killing of Arthur Champion and other English settlers (two of them local police officials) by Donn *Carrach* Maguire and others on 23 October 1641 (R. Gillespie, 'The murder of Arthur Champion and the 1641 Rising in Fermanagh', *Clogher Record* (1993), 52–66) probably fell into this latter category. Although Donn *Carrach*'s father Toirdhealbhach is not given the epithet *Maol* in the genealogies (as his grandfather is; such nicknames tend to be repeated in lineages), he is almost certainly the Turlough Moyle Maguire attainted of high treason (and presumably executed) for his part in the 1615 Ulster Conspiracy and the large grant which he had received in the plantation (as the former chieftain of Clankelly) confiscated (*Irish Patent Rolls of James I*, p. 407). 60 An example is to be found in the arbitration award made (17 June 1591) by the Palesman lawyer, Christopher Flattesbury, two other Palesmen, and a local, between John or Shane Oge MacCoghlan (afterwards Sir John) and the two leaders of a rival MacCoghlan sept: it provided that 'if any of the said parties shall seeke and procure to kill thother that the survivor shall have no benefit of this order after the death of the person so killed' (National Archives of Ireland, D.12263).

war in Ireland – killing led to reprisal killing, and atrocities, or rumours of atrocities, to counter-atrocities. The story of pregnant women being cut open and the unborn babies taken out and speared was a commonplace of the atrocity literature directed against the Irish;[61] it however first surfaces with a definite context in a letter from Lord Upper-Ossory (desperately trying to preserve his neutrality) to Ormond on 23 December 1641, as an atrocity by St Leger's forces in Tipperary.[62] John Lynch, writing in 1662, records two instances committed by English troops; in each case the victims were members of the higher gentry.[63] In one instance, described in more detail by the authors of *Commentarius Rinuccinianus*, she is actually named – Catherine Fleming 'wife of Hadsor of Cappoge', Co. Louth (presumably John Hadsor, the Catholic nephew and heir of the Protestant lawyer and government official Richard Hadsor).[64] Did the English forces do this to Irish ladies because they believed the Irish had done it to Protestant women, or did the Irish commit such horrors, when they took to reprisals, because they believed the English had done it too? Or did they ever happen at all? Given the proclivity of human beings to inhuman acts, one fears that they did.

In this essay I have confined myself almost entirely to the happenings in Leinster, but events in Munster seem to have followed the same pattern. There, a number of minor robberies committed against settlers in Tipperary and a major rustling raid against the livestock of William Kingsmill of Ballyowen, the brother-in-law of Sir Philip Percivall (Clerk of the hated Court of Wards and a large-scale land speculator in Cork and Tipperary), provoked a bloody and indiscriminate response by Sir William St Leger, Lord President of Munster. This in turn led to reprisals against local Protestant settlers, while St Leger's brutal threats against the principal local gentry, when they protested at his actions, forced the latter into a confrontational position.[65] Nor have I dwelt in detail on the killings committed on the native population by the Scots armies in Ulster. The massacres of non-combatants by Robert Monroe's Scottish army seem to be better documented than those perpetrated by the English forces, perhaps because they were less squeamish about admitting them. On 15 July 1642 Monroe's forces slaughtered 40 men and over 500 women and children

---

61 It appears in the Deposition of Maria Daniell from Co. Wicklow, dated 20 February, 1642 (*sic*: for 1641?), along with a fantastic story of a network of underground tunnels constructed by the Irish 'between Croneroe and Glenealy': TCD MS 811, f. 135.   62 Carte, *Ormonde*, 3, no. 50; also in Gilbert, *History of the Irish Confederation*, 1, p. 244. The original is in Bodleian Library, MS Carte 2, no. 111.   63 *Cambrensis Eversus*, 3, pp 92–5, 190–1.   64 *Commentarius Rinuccinianus*, 5, p. 186.   65 Carte, *Ormonde*, 1, pp 265–7; Mary Hickson (ed.), *Ireland in the seventeenth century; or, The Irish massacres of 1641–2* (London, 1884), 3, pp 240 ff. For a critique of Hickson's interpretation, see Fitzpatrick, *The bloody bridge*, p. 158n. The account of events in Tipperary in Canny, *Making Ireland British*, pp 524–8, is surprisingly one-sided: for a different picture see David Edwards, *The Ormond lordship*, p. 309.

who were fleeing southwards with their cattle over the mountains between Newry and Dundalk: the Irish, who were out of gunpowder, were unable to make any effective resistance, although they did manage to kill a few irregulars attached to the army.[66] In his campaign into the North Midlands in June 1644, Monroe's scouting parties in Westmeath and Longford not only burned everything before them, but killed all the country people whom they encountered.[67]

The preparation of this paper has impressed on me the need for a proper, chronologically accurate, study of what actually happened in the south of Ireland in the years immediately following the 1641 rebellion. Such a study, as I have observed, would be laborious and time-consuming. It would, however, be equally rewarding, and not only for the recording of atrocities. One of the more surprising discoveries that emerged from my brief excursus into the contemporary testimonies was the involvement of George Monck, later to rise so high as king-maker and duke of Albemarle, in repeated instances of violation of promised quarter. But while many, perhaps most, of the English atrocities against the Irish proceeded, as Richard Bellings put it, 'from command',[68] others arose from the uncontrolled, probably uncontrollable, rage of the soldiers and junior officers. The men, women and children slaughtered at Carrickmines fell victim to the fury of the soldiers, enraged by their losses (including that of their commander) so that they 'left not one to say who they were'.[69] Proof of the uncontrolled nature of the killing at Carrickmines is that the soldiers seem to have overlooked money hidden in the bloodstained and torn clothing of the victims.[70] Carrickmines, because of the commander's death, may have been a special case, but it is clear that many of the Protestant commanders had as little control over their troops as the Irish leaders had over their followers, such as those of Sir Phelim O Neill, who to Sir Phelim's distress murdered his English tenants at Kinard and killed the imprisoned Lord Charlemont.[71] Borlase claims that Sir Charles Vavasour was so angry at the killing (in his absence) of the prisoners (women and children as well as men) who had surrendered on promise of quarter at Cloghlea Castle in Co. Cork, that he intended to hang the officer who should have prevented it, an intention frustrated by his need to fight on the following day, when he was defeated and taken prisoner by the Confederate commander, the earl of Castlehaven.[72] The story may well be true.

---

66 Fitzpatrick, *The bloody bridge*, p. xiii (from TCD MS 840, f. 23); Carte, *Ormonde*, 1, p. 311.
67 Carte, *Ormonde*, 1, pp 495–6. 68 Gilbert, *History of the Irish Confederation*, 1, p. 110.
69 Anon., *The last true intelligence from Ireland, being a letter sent from Chester, dated the 2 of April 1642 from Mr William Owen* (London, 1642) (RIA, Halliday Pamphlets, vol. 30).
70 See chapter 9 in this volume. 71 Simms, 'Violence in county Armagh', pp 130–1.
72 E. Borlase, *The history of the execrable Irish rebellion* (Dublin, 1680), p. 117, quoted in Fitzpatrick, *The bloody bridge*, p. 57. For the violation of quarter on this occasion see also Castlehaven, *Memoirs*, p. 57.

I have described the Irish troubles of the 1640s as an ethno-religious conflict, and this seems to be the correct description. Nowhere else in Western Europe did the two elements of 'otherness', religious and ethnic (not racial) difference, coincide on each side in a single identity. Scots Catholics, for instance, must have been seen by their Calvinist fellow countrymen as backsliding members of Israel to be coerced back into the fold, not as members of a foreign nation of idolators to be extirpated. And the same would have been true of England. In Ireland, the Commonwealth administration knew only two categories, 'English Protestant' and 'Irish Papist', into which everyone had to fit. Only at the other end of Europe, in the Ukraine, does one find the same merging of ethnic and religious identity, in this case into Polish/Catholic and Russian/Orthodox. And only in the Ukraine, I think, does one find the same horrors routinely occurring as happened routinely in Ireland. Irish historians, perhaps from motives of national pride, have been too reluctant to admit that analogies to the Irish situation in the medieval and early modern periods have to be sought outside the Western Europe of that day, in other frontier areas of European Christendom.

Archaeology of massacre: the Carrickmines mass grave and the siege of March 1642

MARK CLINTON, LINDA FIBIGER
& DAMIAN SHIELS

THE DISCOVERY

Archaeological investigations took place at Carrickmines Castle between August 2000 and August 2002 (figure 6). In April of 2001, excavations at the site exposed two multiple burials containing the remains of 15 articulated individuals, including women, children and a number of adults too poorly preserved to sex (figure 7). They were aged between 3 and 45 years and lay in two tight clusters, orientated southwest to northeast and northeast to southwest within both burials. In addition, a single burial, located between the two multiple burials, containing the remains of a juvenile individual aged between 9 and 12 years, was excavated, as was another adult individual, a young male, buried face down 7.45m northeast of the two mass graves. Also present were 40 disarticulated human bones and bone fragments from various contexts across the site, most notably the fill of the moat fronting the western flank of the castle complex. These represented the remains of at least 6 individuals, including 5 adults and one juvenile. Most of the disarticulated remains, especially those from the moat, generally appeared to be larger and more robust than those retrieved from the mass graves. The majority probably belonged to adult and adolescent males.

The large number of individuals in the two main burials is striking, as is the general positioning of all the bodies, which partly overlie each other. They include an individual buried face down and generally do not conform to the standard east-west orientation for Christian burials. By itself, this mode of burial might be interpreted as the result of a fast-spreading, infectious and often fatal disease present within the population, followed by an unusually high number of dead to be buried fast and possibly less ceremoniously than under normal circumstances. Parallels for this are to be found in some of the plague-pits discovered throughout Europe. The individuals buried at Carrickmines, however, did not die a natural death.

The Carrickmines mass grave and the siege of March 1642 193

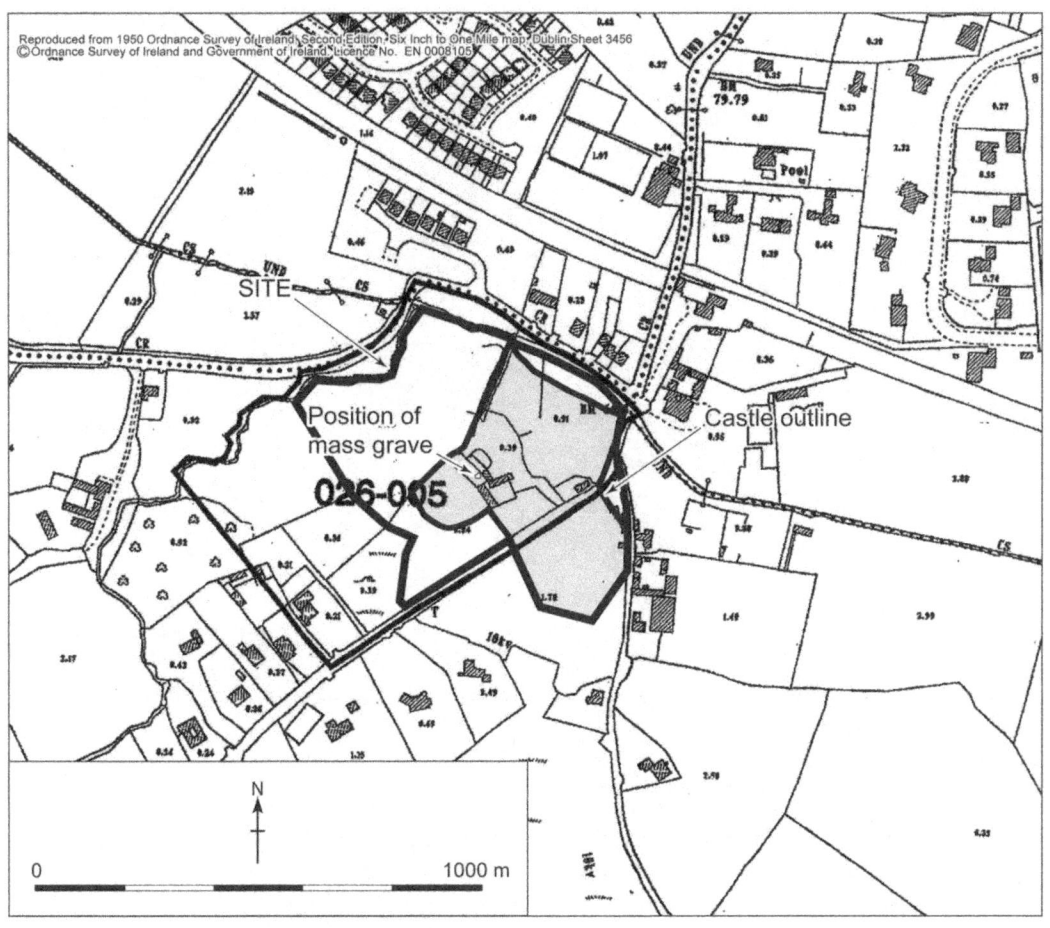

6 Excavation map of Carrickmines Castle, Co. Dublin.

A number of objects were recovered from the burial pit, of critical importance not just as an insight into the possessions carried by these doomed individuals, but also in providing dating evidence for the deposition of the bodies. The principal discoveries in this regard were 13 silver coins, 9 of which were discovered together, with the others in close proximity. All were of English mint, and in a remarkable state of preservation. At first glance, the hoard of 10 sixpences and 3 shillings appeared to be Elizabethan in date. This led to the conjecture that the remains may have related to the known 1599 attack on the site which is referred to by John Clifford in a letter to Sir Robert Cecil on 13 June 1599:

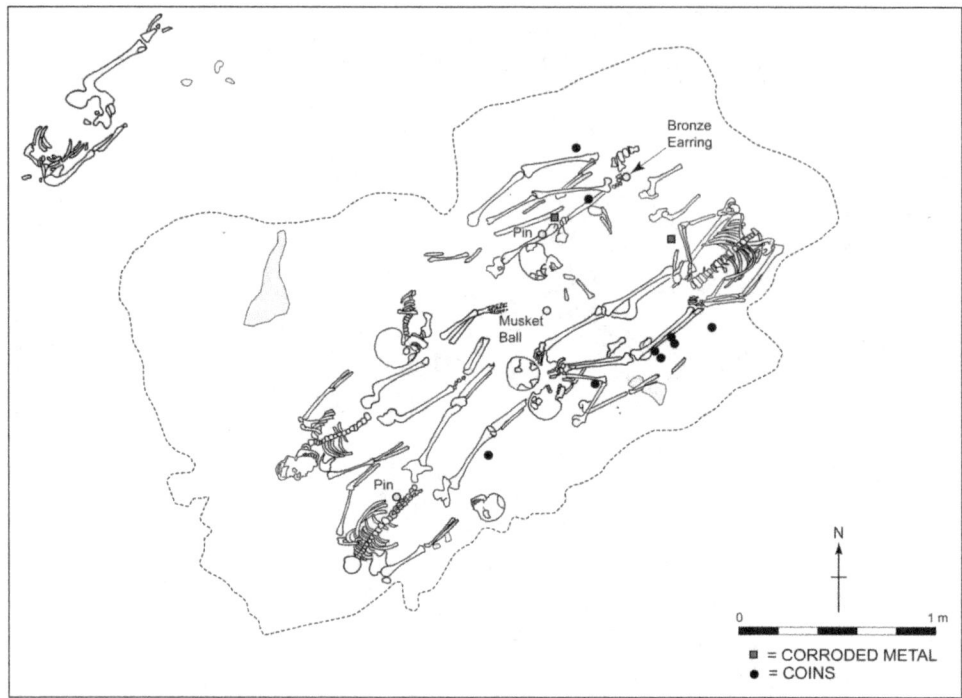

7 Mass graves at Carrickmines.

> Threescore horse and upwards of the Earl of Southampton's troop were placed at Carrickmayne, within five miles of Dublin. Last night the enemy cam thither, and took away the prey of the town, and burned it, and went away without harm, the horsemen being all in town.[1]

It was subsequently discovered following conservation that one of the shillings dated to the reign of James I, thus discounting a 1599 event. The years between 1603 and 1641 represented a period where mass deaths as a result of violence were less usual than in either the 1590s or 1640s, and there were no known episodes in the vicinity of Carrickmines. This leaves the well-recorded massacre in March 1642 as the only remaining event that could account for the disposal of such a substantial number of bodies.

As regards the large amount of Elizabethan coinage, it is estimated that half of the coinage in circulation when Charles I was executed was Elizabethan. Incredibly, of a hoard of 5,267 coins deposited in Welsh Back, Bristol in or around 1688, 36 per cent were of Elizabethan date.[2] The fact that the absence

1 *Cal. S.P. Ire., 1599–1600*, p. 63.   2 C.E. Challis, *The Tudor coinage* (Manchester, 1978), p. 231.

of the James I coin could have led to a completely different interpretation of the remains is a sobering thought, and serves as a cautionary tale when attempting to date archaeological levels in a historical context. It would appear strange that the coins were not stripped from the remains by their attackers, especially in light of the acrimony between the two parties. As the pay for a private soldier in the king's army at the time was eight pence per day,[3] a windfall of twelve days' pay would certainly be worth collecting. One possibility for the survival of the coins is that they were sewn into the victims' clothing to conceal them from their assailants. As they met a particularly savage end, there may have been copious quantities of blood and internal organs, dissuading the troops from adopting the usual practice of completely stripping the bodies.[4]

BACKGROUND EVENTS

As the 1641 Rebellion escalated into all-out war, reinforcements for the State were slow in arriving from England. Indeed the first shipments of soldiers did not arrive until the last day of December 1641 and these were not augmented until 21 and 22 February 1642. The Lords Justices, Sir William Parsons and Sir John Borlase, had remained in a virtual torpor since the outbreak of the insurgency. They had abandoned most of the new settlers to their fate and desperately gathered as many elements of the widely dispersed army as possible about them in the city of Dublin. The attempts of the earl of Ormond, the Lieutenant General of the army, to kick-start the war effort were thwarted at every turn by Parsons and Borlase. The slow arrival of the reinforcements from England was largely due to the inexorable passage of that kingdom towards open conflict between king and parliament. The regiment that finally landed on New Year's Eve consisted of 1,100 armed men under the command of Sir Simon Harcourt, a scion of an old Oxfordshire family.[5] He was an experienced and highly respected officer who had seen prolonged service in the Low Countries and had also fought in the recent war in Scotland.

After the rout suffered at the hands of the Old Irish Ulster army at Julianstown on the 29 November, and a contemporaneous successful foray into Co. Wicklow led by Sir Charles Coote, the government forces had restricted themselves to localized minor clashes to the immediate north of Dublin in the remaining weeks of 1641.[6] The arrival of Harcourt's regiment at the end of December did not radically alter the pattern of military activity in the

---

3 K. Roberts, *Matchlock musketeer, 1588–1688* (Oxford, 2002).   4 Kenneth Nicholls, pers. comm.   5 B. Burke, *A genealogical and heraldic history of the landed gentry of Great Britain* (12th ed, London, 1914), pp 883–5.   6 R. Bellings, 'History of the Irish Confederation', in J.T. Gilbert (ed.), *History of the Confederation and the war in Ireland, 1641–1653* (3 vols, Dublin, 1882), i, pp 32–4.

hinterland of the city. The only serious engagement there in the month of January 1642 was at Swords, where Sir Charles Coote heavily defeated and dislodged an insurgent force led by Luke Netterville.[7] On 31 January, James Butler, the earl of Ormond, embarked on a campaign with 2000 foot and 300 horse (together with five small field pieces) and dispelled insurgents from Newcastle and Lyons on the Dublin/Kildare border, before taking Naas without a fight.[8] He returned to Dublin on 3 February.

12 February marked the first serious encounter in the south Co. Dublin theatre. Lord Charles Lambart led a surprise attack on a party of insurgents drawn from Wicklow and Wexford and assembled at Deansgrange. He routed them without sustaining any casualties.[9] On 20 and 21 February, Lieutenant Colonel George Monck, Sir Richard Grenville, and the Lord Lieutenant-General's regiment disembarked at Dublin. A successful clearance of the insurgent army entrenched about Kilsallaghan Castle[10] in north Co. Dublin (commanded by Colonel Hugh Byrne) was followed through with a major campaign towards the river Boyne.[11] The dispatch of this expeditionary force on 5 March under the command of the earl of Ormond (attended by Harcourt, Sir Thomas Lucas and Sir Robert Farrer) proved to be the straw that broke the three-month siege around the town of Drogheda.[12] Without pressing home their advantage further, the army returned to Dublin on 17 March.

THE SIEGE OF CARRICKMINES

Early on Saturday 26 March, Sir Simon Harcourt and a detachment of horse left Dublin city and headed south. Within an hour or two they had arrived at the gates of Carrickmines Castle. Carrickmines was home to a leading branch of the Walsh family. Their ancestors had been in possession of the property since the twelfth century. By the seventeenth century the 'Walshes of Carrickmain' were at the height of their wealth and influence. They were enjoying the fruits of a countryside that a contemporary writer described as being 'very plentifull ... in corne and cattell [and] abounding also with game for pleasure.'[13] The environs of the castle and bawn contained 'an orchard and garden-plot', according to a survey made in 1654. The surrounding estate consisted of 446 acres in Carrickmines and 100 acres in the adjoining townland of 'Glanamuck'.[14]

---

7 Bellings, 'History', p. 44; *HMC, Ormonde*, n.s. 2, pp 62–3. 8 HMC, *Ormonde*, n.s. 2, pp 70–1 9 HMC, *Ormonde*, n.s. 2, p. 82. 10 A. Clarke, *The Old English in Ireland, 1625–1642* (London, 1966), p. 201; M. Clinton, *The history and archaeology of the parish of Kilsallaghan* (Swords, 2005), p. 58. 11 HMC, *Ormonde*, n.s. 2, p. 86. 12 T. Carte, *The life of James Duke of Ormond; containing an account of the most remarkable affairs of his time* (Oxford, 1851), 2, pp 190–1 13 G. Emerson, *A geographical description of the kingdom of Ireland* (London, 1642). 14 J. Lodge (ed.), 'A survey of the Half-Barony of Rathdown, in the County of Dublin – by order of

Theobald Walsh inherited the estate on the death of his father Richard. The precise year of Richard's death is unclear as there are contradictions in the available evidence.[15] What is certain is that Theobald had pursued a military career abroad in the service of Ferdinand II of the Holy Roman Empire, before settling down to the life of a member of the landed gentry. Theobald was involved on the rebel side at the battle of Deansgrange on 15 December 1641, but succeeded in escaping following the defeat.[16] He was not present at the siege itself, but he was marked as a rebel and his lands were later confiscated by the crown.

It is difficult to understand why a seasoned soldier of Harcourt's calibre would embark upon the siege of a castle with only a detachment of horse at his disposal. Although the full scale of the defences at this period remains unclear, he would have been well aware that artillery was required to effect a breach. The key probably lies in Edmund Borlase's description of the defenders of the castle not only openly defying, but graphically insulting Harcourt. As Borlase put it: 'This his spirit was not well able to brook'.[17] Sir Simon thereupon climbed down from his horse to watch and wait while a dispatch rider rode post haste to Dublin.

The most structured account of the subsequent supply and deployment of detachments was written by William Owen on 2 April 1642.[18] He maintains that 800 foot arrived at 'Careggmayne Castle' on Saturday afternoon. Approximately half of this complement would have consisted of Serjeant Major John Berry's firelocks. These, it seems, had only arrived in Dublin from England in the very recent past.[19] That these troops were armed with the newer 'firelocks' (flintlocks), as opposed to the older matchlock, marks them out as being well equipped with the most modern of firearms.[20]

As the requested ordnance had not yet arrived, both sides would have settled down for the night. Harcourt 'took special care for the surrounding of the Castle' to prevent any break-outs. He employed 200 firelocks in this task.[21] The use of firelocks in this role would have avoided troops armed with the matchlock from giving away their positions in the dark, as they required a lit 'match' to be

---

Charles Fleetwood, Lord Deputy, October 4th, 1654' in *Desiderata Curiosa Hibernica: or, A select collection of state papers* (Dublin, 1772), 2, pp 551–2.   **15** V. Hussey Walsh, 'The Austrian branches of the family of Walsh', in *The Genealogist*, 17 (1900–1), 219.   **16** Co. Dublin Depositions, TCD, MS 809, f. 259.   **17** E. Borlase, *The history of the execrable Irish Rebellion trac'd from many preceding Acts, to the grand eruption the 23 of October 1641 and thence pursued to the Act of Settlement* (London, 1680), p. 72   **18** W. Owen, *The last true intelligence from Ireland. Being a letter sent from Chester: dated the second of April 1642, from Mr. William Owen, to a friend of his in London* (London, 1642).   **19** W. Guy, *Good newes for England: or, Comfortable tidings from Ireland, to all true hearted Protestants. Being a real relation how Sir Simon Harcourt, Sergeant Major Berry, and Captain Paramore, with the joint assistance of divers other Protestants, obtained a famous victory over the rebels at Kildare* (London, 1642); Carte, *Life*, p. 246.   **20** J. Barratt, *Cavaliers: the Royalist army at war, 1642–1646* (Gloucestershire 2000), p. 54.   **21** Borlase, *The history of the execrable Irish Rebellion*, p. 72.

permanently ready for action.[22] While the matchlock used by the majority of the army needed this lit cord to ignite the powder, the firelocks used a flint spark which only became visible when the weapon was fired. The firelocks were augmented by a deployment of horse. According to William Owen the tactic he employed was to place a 'musketeer between each horse, and in that posture, stood all night'.[23] The brightest fire burning that late March night may not have been in Harcourt's camp, for it is further reported by Owen that the insurgents 'made a fire upon the battlements of the castle', which (alarmingly for the besiegers), was 'answered by another fire from the Mountaine'. A rider was consequently dispatched during the night to Dublin with a request for an additional 400 foot.

Daybreak proved to be the signal for an attempted breakout from the castle. The combination of the deployed firelocks and cavalry proved, however, to be too robust and the attempt failed. Despite this, the cost to the besiegers was a heavy one, with the death of Lieutenant Richard Cooke and the mortal wounding of Serjeant Major Berry.

At noon on Sunday the ordnance finally arrived and with the deployment of the additional 400 foot the battle could now commence in earnest. The cannon were demi-culverin, cumbersome to move. Preston's Leinster Army prior to the battle of Dungan's Hill (1647) had four such pieces, requiring 64 draught oxen to move them.[24] Despite this, they were only really capable of knocking in gates and windows or felling battlements – they could not create a significant breach in a stone wall.[25] Harcourt was well aware of the limitations of his guns, and realized that it was necessary to place them within 200 paces of the castle if they were to have any effect.[26] This would bring the ordnance into range of the defenders' weapons, so Harcourt took the responsibility of placing them himself. To the shock and utter dismay of his soldiers he was suddenly hit in the right chest 'with a shanker-bullet out of a long peece',[27] and slumped to the ground. The badly wounded Harcourt, unable to walk unaided, was assisted from the field by two fellow officers. Hearing that the ordnance was making little impact on the walls Sir Simon issued his last order, instructing his men to storm the gates instead. This was quickly achieved.

Surrender followed the forced entry into the main building of the castle. Unfortunately, the attackers were not in any frame of mind to accept a non-violent closure to hostilities. A number of sources indicate that a general killing-spree ensued; Borlase noted that, enraged by Harcourt's death, the troops

---

[22] K. Roberts, *Soldiers of the English Civil War (1) Infantry* (Oxford, 2002), p. 21.   [23] Owen, *The last true intelligence.*   [24] P. Lenihan, 'Leinster army and the battle of Dungan's Hill, 1647', in *The Irish Sword*, 18:72 (1991), 145.   [25] R. Hutton and W. Reeves, 'Sieges and fortifications', in J. Kenyon and J. Ohlmeyer (eds), *The Civil Wars: a military history of England, Scotland and Ireland, 1638–1660* (Oxford, 1998), p. 205.   [26] Ibid., p. 206.   [27] Owen, *The last true intelligence.*

'entered with great fury putting all to the sword, sparing neither man, woman or child',[28] while on 11 April 1642, John Berners reported that the crown forces had 'resolutely revenged' his killing, putting all there 'to the death'. Henry King, also writing in 1642, commented that the soldiers 'brake in desperately into the castle and they slew 250 men, women and children'.[29]

There are two pro-insurgent versions of what transpired on that weekend in late March 1642. The first is a fantastical account of the engagement at Carrickmines entitled 'An aphorismical discovery of treasonable faction', apparently written between 1652 and 1660.[30] The other is the deposition of John Joyce, vice-constable of the Black Castle of Wicklow, which was made on 8 April 1642, 12 days after the fall of Carrickmines. This recites a letter written to Joyce by the rebel, Walter O'Byrne of Newrath, which says that at Carrickmines 'the English army tooke the Castle ... on Sunday last, and killed 14 men that were warded there [i.e. soldiers], and many women and children'.[31]

There is a notable consistency on the subject in the records of the opposing side. Indeed, all available sources quantify the fatalities as being in the region of 200–350. It should be noted that, according to the 'Aphorismical discovery' tract, the number of castle defenders killed was two which is patently ridiculous.[32] Losses on the government side were listed in an official internal document. There is no reason, nor alternative evidence available, to doubt the general accuracy of the tally which lists seven dead and nine wounded.[33] It should be noted that at the time of its compilation Serjeant Major Berry was still lingering on, and so the final number of fatalities was set to rise. It already included Sir Simon Harcourt, who had passed away on Monday 28 March at Lord Fitzwilliam's castle at Merrion. He had been unable to endure the journey back to Dublin. His last concerns were that his wife Anne and his children should be looked after. Like the other fallen officers and soldiers who had fallen in action at Carrickmines, he was later interred in Dublin city.

A possible explanation for the high number of officer fatalities at the siege is that the defenders at Carrickmines had at least one marksman among their number. Armed with what were known as 'fowling peeces' or 'long peeces', they were able to achieve a higher degree of accuracy. Officers were the prime targets, and shooting them was a method advocated by George Monck himself, who stated that men so armed should 'shoot not at any, but at officers of that Division'. There are also a number of references to these marksmen targeting gun crews and officers at sieges during the English Civil War.[34] It would seem

---

28 Borlase, *The history of the execrable Irish Rebellion*, p. 73.   29 Charles McNeill (ed.), *The Tanner letters* (IMC, Dublin, 1943), pp 147, 155.   30 J.T. Gilbert (ed.), *A contemporary history of affairs in Ireland, from A.D. 1641 to 1652* (3 vols, Dublin, 1879), 1:1, pp vii, 24–5.   31 Wicklow Depositions, TCD, MS 811, f. 157.   32 Gilbert, *A contemporary history*, p. 25.   33 HMC, *Ormonde*, 1, p. 131.   34 Roberts, *Soldiers of the English Civil War (1)*, pp 21–2.

likely that with the castle surrounded by an overwhelming force, the defenders inside felt their only chance of reprieve was to undermine the morale and command structure of the besiegers by targeting the officers. As Harcourt and his officers led from the front, the task of picking them off was made easier, and there may have been real prospects of forcing the crown troops to retire. The other side of the coin is that the targeting of individuals within any body of troops can provoke outrage and frustration among the men, especially when it results in the loss of a commander such as Harcourt who appears to have been well liked. When the castle fell, the use of this tactic was undoubtedly a major reason for the resulting massacre. When a siege ended with an assault, garrisons were entirely at the mercy of the attackers.[35]

The final act in the fall of Carrickmines Castle was the destruction of the principal building. The extent of the destruction is unknown. Various accounts record that the castle was 'blown up with powder' or simply 'blown up'.[36] The evidence would seem to suggest that the shell of the building remained standing for a considerable time afterwards. The Civil Survey of 1654–6 described the premises as containing 'the walles of a Castle, an orchard, and garden plotte [and] a Bawne'.[37] The cartographical evidence corroborates the suggestion that there were standing remains, given that the Down Survey map indicates a fanciful winged structure at Carrickmines while a bracket-shaped building was denoted on John Rocque's map of 1760.

IDENTIFYING THE VICTIMS' REMAINS

Given that the area surrounding Carrickmines Castle would have been clear of government forces within a day or two of its destruction, it is inconceivable that its ruins were not visited by concerned parties, not to mention the curious. It is highly unlikely that the remains of the deceased members of the Walsh family were left to decay amongst the debris given the number of kith and kin that they had in the general area. What of Theobald Walsh himself, who had been absent during the siege? Surely he made the pilgrimage to his now destroyed home. It is almost certain that the slain Walshes were later interred in the ancestral family plot in Tully Church.

A number of the household staff and workers on the estate would probably have been from local families and thus it is likely that their remains would also have been removed for formal burial. It seems possible, however, that many of the insurgents that had fought in the castle were strangers to the place. Given the scale of casualties many of these may have been given very perfunctory

---

35 P. Lenihan, *Confederate Catholics at War, 1641–49* (Cork, 2001), p. 169.   36 HMC, *Ormonde*, n.s., 2, 100; Owen, *The last true intelligence*.   37 R.C. Simington (ed.), *The Civil Survey, AD 1654–1656, vol. 7: County of Dublin* (Dublin, 1945), p. 270.

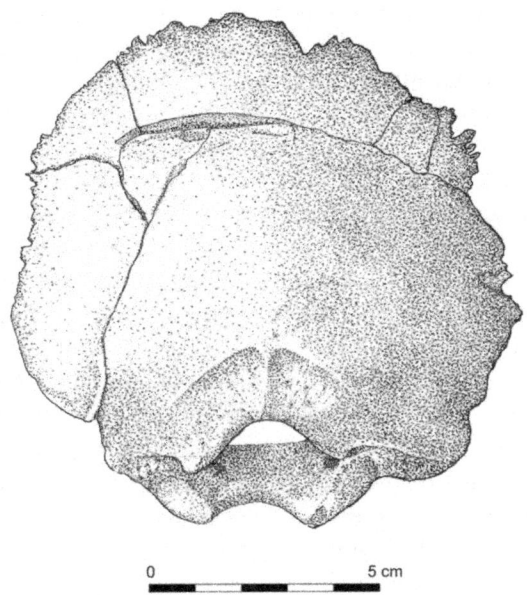

8 Skull fragment showing injuries (Alva McGowan).

burial, and these may be the individuals whose remains were uncovered during the excavations at Carrickmines. Alternatively, given that all of the remains found at Carrickmines had been deposited in crude shallow pits, disregarding normal Christian burial practices (it might be expected that even perfunctory interment would see bodies placed on an east-west orientation, and face up), it may also be the case that these represent burials of Walshes, retainers and strangers, all carried out carelessly and quickly by the besieging forces before their departure.

Seven of the articulated individuals present, and one disarticulated cranial fragment from the two mass graves, as well as three of the disarticulated bones showed evidence for unhealed blade injuries, and one individual presented with unhealed blunt force trauma to the head (figure 8). One of the finds closely associated with one of the multiple burials was a musket ball, indicating that at least one individual had also suffered a projectile injury. None of the injuries showed signs of healing, an indication that they were all inflicted around the time of death. Three individuals had suffered multiple injuries, and the majority of injuries affected the back or side of the head. The number of injuries delivered from a posterior position is an important indicator of the type of fighting that seems to have occurred at Carrickmines. It is generally assumed that a right-handed assailant facing his opponent will deliver blows that predominantly affect the anterior or left side of the victim's cranium. Injuries affecting the posterior part of the cranium, delivered from a posterior position, might indicate that the opponent was turning away, fleeing, or on the ground when the blow was delivered.[38] One of the injuries visible on the cranium of Skeleton 12 appears to have been inflicted from a superior position. Again, this might indicate that the victim was not standing at the time of the attack. Alternatively, the assailant could have been in an elevated position, for example on horseback, when the blow was delivered. It is undisputable that all of the injuries were the result of inter-personal conflict. In addition, the demographic profile of the remains clearly indicates that this conflict did involve all of those present at Carrickmines, not only those customarily involved in battle (that is, adult males). Consequently, the burials are better termed mass graves. It should also be noted that the uncovered human remains do not necessarily represent the total number still interred at the Carrickmines site. The last burial excavated was running under the limit of excavation near the Mooney farmhouse in the centre of the complex. As this is part of the site preserved as an island in the M50 motorway, there is a distinct possibility that further victims of the massacre await discovery there.

The identifiable methods of attack as mentioned above include at least three different weapon types. The ball present in the grave (based on pre- and post-conservation dimensions) had a calibre of between .732 inches and .645 inches. It is clear from this calibre that the ball was fired from a longarm. The blade injuries were most likely inflicted by sword cuts, perhaps some from dismounted cavalrymen, who we know were present at Carrickmines. The cause of the blunt injury is more difficult to determine and could have been inflicted by a number of objects, such as the butt end of a musket, the hilt of a sword or the handle of a hatchet. It has been recorded that in close quarter fighting, musketeers discharged their weapon and then used it as a heavy club to bludgeon opponents. The different methods of killing would seem to support the contemporary accounts describing the 'fury' of Harcourt's men. If a controlled decision had been taken to execute the occupants of the castle, one would expect them to have been rounded up and dispatched in a similar way, perhaps by hanging, or throat-cutting. It would certainly not have been deemed prudent to waste ammunition by using firearms, especially if there was a threat of attack from a nearby force in the mountains. The whole event would seem to indicate a general free-for-all, with the enraged besiegers falling upon their prisoners, who then desperately sought means of escape.

A number of other objects were recovered from the burial pit apart from the coins discussed above. More personal finds included what may have been the remains of a pin, and a small copper alloy ring, perhaps an earring. A

---

38 S.A. Novak, 'Battle-related trauma', in V. Fiorato, A. Boylston, and C. Knüsel (eds), *Blood red roses. The archaeology of a mass grave from the battle of Towton* (Oxford, 2000), p. 93; J. Wakely, 'Identification and analysis of violent and non-violent head injuries in osteo-archaeological material', in J. Corman (ed.), *Material harm: archaeological studies of war and violence* (Glasgow, 1997), pp 27f.

particularly poignant object was a key discovered directly under the right elbow of one of the individuals. It is unknown if this was to gain access to a room or chest, but it would indicate that the person in question was either of importance or held a place of trust.

Further evidence relating to the siege did become clear during the course of the excavations at Carrickmines. In the region of 28 musket balls were recovered from the different sections of the complex. Although it is impossible to determine how many of these directly relate to the siege (one must assume there were a number of casual losses of musket balls at the site, as well as the probable discharge of firearms at events such as the 1599 attack) it is reasonable to assert that a number are connected to 1642. Ten of the musket balls were impacted, indicating that they had been fired and had struck an obstacle of some kind (a musket ball that does not show signs of impaction may still have been fired – for example the ball found within the mass grave did not display impaction marks, perhaps as a result of striking only soft tissue). The highest concentration of musket balls (12) occurred between the castle and the Glenamuck stream, which lies on the Dublin side of the site near what may have been one of the principal entrances. It seems likely that this is the direction from which the crown troops advanced, and the concentration would suggest that, at the very least, there may have been concerted fire from this location (of the 12 balls recovered here, 8 were impacted). Another projectile recovered here was a highly impacted cannonball, which was from a demi-culverin. This may have been fired from the higher ground on the Dublin side of the Glenamuck stream. The number of impacted projectiles in this area does not necessarily mean that the main efforts against the castle came from this direction, but it does indicate that there were at least some exchanges there. Further analysis of the projectile distribution from the rest of the site may reveal clues as to the sequence of events.

The skirmishes and violent conflicts taking place at Carrickmines Castle as a result of its strategic position on the border of the Pale culminated in the siege of March 1642 and consequent destruction of the castle. It is most probable that the human remains excavated at Carrickmines are some of the victims of this event, therefore presenting a unique assemblage within Irish archaeology. Not only can they be dated to a well documented period within Irish history and that of Carrickmines Castle in particular, but they also demonstrate the violent nature and indiscriminate brutality prevailing during that time, which, true to Borlase's account, affected 'man, woman and child' alike.[39]

[39] Thanks to VJK Ltd for the invitation and opportunity to excavate the site; to Brian Ó'Donnchadha and the 370th for their work on the mass burial pits, and to Åsa Carlsson and the 837th for rounding up the stragglers. Special thanks to David Edwards and Kenneth Nicholls for references, and to P. David Sweetman, Nessa O'Connor, Dr Andrew Halpin, Chris Corlett, Eamonn P. Kelly and Professor Barry Raftery for their ongoing support, advice and encouragement.

Inventing a Protestant icon: the strange death of Sir Charles Coote, 1642[1]

KEVIN FORKAN

The 1640s saw, if not the birth, certainly the vigorous childhood of print propaganda in Britain and Ireland.[2] Although the Scottish Covenanters and the king had produced propagandistic declarations from 1639 onwards, during the early part of the 1640s the largest single stream in a flood of ideologically loaded publications flowed from the Irish rebellion of late 1641 and the resultant war between Catholic and Protestant in that kingdom.[3] English pamphlet writers already had experience of sensationalist reporting of the Thirty Years War in Germany, presenting that conflict as between the antichristian Catholic forces of the Hapsburgs, and the godly prince Fredrick V of the Palatinate and his wife Elizabeth of Bohemia, daughter of James VI and I.[4] The entry of the king of Sweden, Gustavus Adolphus, into the war in 1630 as the self-proclaimed

---

[1] My thanks to Pádraig Lenihan, John Gibney and Jane Ohlmeyer for their many valuable comments on this and a previous version of this essay, delivered at the conference, 'Icons and iconoclasts in the long seventeenth century, 1603 to 1714', at the Centre for Early Modern Studies, University of Aberdeen, in July 2006. My thanks also to the Irish Research Council for the Humanities and Social Sciences for providing me with the wherewithal, through a Government of Ireland Postdoctoral Fellowship, to complete the research for this essay.
[2] The most recent study of such material is in Jason Peacey, *Politicians and pamphleteers. Propaganda during the English Civil Wars and Interregnum* (Aldershot, 2004).   [3] Studies of this pamphlet literature include K. Lindley, 'The impact of the 1641 rebellion on England and Wales, 1641–5', *IHS*, 18 (1972), 145–7, 162–5; E. Shagan, 'Constructing discord: ideology, propaganda, and English responses to the Irish rebellion of 1641', *Journal of British Studies*, 36 (1997), 4–34; J. Raymond, *Pamphlets and pamphleteering in early modern Britain* (Cambridge, 2003), pp 173–81, 197–9; D. O'Hara, *English newsbooks and the Irish Rebellion, 1641–1649* (Dublin, 2006), pp 27–54. The abolition of the courts of Star Chamber and High Commission in 1641 led to a virtual end of censorship in England.   [4] Examples include *A short relation of the departure of the high and mightie Prince Frederick King Elect of Bohemia: with his royall & vertuous Ladie Elizabeth ... towards Prague, to receiue the crowne of that kingdome* (Dort, 1619); *The declaration and information of the high and puissant King of Bohemia, against the vniust mandates published in the name of the Emperour as also against those that are further threatned to be decreed and executed, touching the ... Crowne of Bohemia* (London, 1620); *Votiuae Angliae: or, the desires and vvishes of England ... to perswade his Majestie to drawe his royall sword, for the restoring of the Pallatynat, and Electorat, to his sonne*

saviour of the German Protestants allowed the English press to create a Protestant superman, the 'new starr of the north', celebrate his martial exploits against the Hapsburgs, and mourn his death in battle; an early death that let his legend flourish without blemish.⁵ As the three Stuart kingdoms slid into war in the early 1640s, therefore, English pamphleteers were familiar with the language of celestial conflict between Catholic and Protestant, now inflamed by the antipapist scaremongering of several prominent members of the successive English parliaments of 1640.⁶ Moreover, with the outbreak of the rising in Ireland, pamphleteers had a war that would increase the demand for their products and allow them to contextualize the affairs of the three kingdoms within the familiar parameters of the European conflict. What they now needed was appropriately edifying news from the equivalent of the German Protestants in Ireland and a new hero who would relieve these oppressed Protestants from destruction by the Irish Catholics. This article intends to examine how a grouping of Protestants from a settler background in Ireland provided and manipulated such source material, and built up a military commander, Sir Charles Coote, as the iconic Protestant hero so craved by the London pamphleteers and their readers. Such an image of Sir Charles Coote, embellished and burnished by Protestants writing from and about Ireland during the 1640s, will be juxtaposed against the portrayal that has survived up to the present, which is largely a construct of Catholic commentators writing in the immediate aftermath of the mid-seventeenth-century conflicts. The aim is to illustrate how a grouping of Protestants, mainly pre-1641 settlers of English origin, used propaganda in order to prioritize its aspirations over those of competing factions within Ireland, to create alliances with powerful elements elsewhere in the Stuart archipelago, and ultimately to achieve its goals.

In October 1641 several Irish Catholic nobles, based in Ulster, launched what was intended to be a limited rising, to seek redress of their grievances from a position of strength. While a number of government strongholds in central Ulster were seized, their planned *coup d'etat*, the seizure of Dublin Castle, failed. In subsequent weeks, the Ulster leaders lost control of their followers among the lower social orders. Outbreaks of looting quickly degenerated into

in law Prince Fredericke, to his onely daughter the Lady Elizabeth (London, 1624). 5 *The new starr of the north, shining vpon the victorious King of Sweden* (London, 1631); *A relation of the King of Svveden, his happie and incomparable successe and victories, against the forces of the Emperour* (London, 1631); *An elegie upon the death of the most illustrious and victorious Prince Gustavus Adolphus King of Swethland* (London, 1633); *The tvvo famous pitcht battels of Lypsich, and Lutzen wherein the ever-renowned Prince Gustavus the Great lived and died a conquerour* (London, 1634). 6 England's own position as an outpost of godly Protestantism threatened by powerful European Catholicism, and its Irish offshoot, was also a well developed theme of English print culture in the late Tudor and early Stuart period, see D. Cressy, *Bonfires and bells: national memory and the Protestant calendar in Elizabethan and early Stuart England* (London, 1989); Shagan, 'Constructing discord', 9–11.

an orgy of sectarian violence.[7] Protestant refugees fleeing the affected areas to centres of safety within Ireland, and to England and Scotland, carried with them gruesome tales of wholesale massacre; the figures for Protestants killed were quickly inflated to fantastic proportions. Disorder broke out across Leinster, and the local elite, the Old English Catholic gentry, were increasingly caught in a vice between their own rebellious tenantry, bands of Ulster and north Leinster Gaelic Irish rebels, and the apocalyptic reaction given to the rising by the Dublin administration.

The Lords Justices in Dublin Castle, William Parsons and John Borlase, had greeted the Ulster insurgency by blaming a universal conspiracy of 'evil affected Irish papists'.[8] In their panic this was understandable; the government was practically defenceless, and had only by chance foiled the plot to seize the Castle.[9] Their inept choice of words, however, raised deep concerns among the Old English gentry of the Pale, who had traditionally supported the government against rebellions. But by now almost a century of official religious discrimination against Catholics, and threats to their landed wealth by an influx of Protestant New English settlers, had gradually alienated the Old English from the government of Ireland.[10] They were not yet ready to throw their lot in with either side, but instead sought to end the rising through negotiation, and by using the Irish parliament, then sitting, to make contact with those they termed 'discontented gentlemen'. The Lords Justices, however, would tolerate no dealings with those whom they deemed 'rebels'. Parliament was prorogued, thus putting paid to this proposal to end the rising by peaceful means.[11] The end of their prospective political initiative was certainly discouraging to the Old English, but of more immediate concern was the military threat to their lands and persons. Disorder was now widespread in the Pale counties of Dublin, Kildare and Meath, with insurgent armies operating around Drogheda and Wicklow. A request that defensive arms be sent them from Dublin drew a meagre response, thereby reminding the Old English of government mistrust.[12] Furthermore, the actions of several government army commanders around Dublin had raised the suspicion that elements within Protestantism in Ireland

---

[7] N. Canny, *Making Ireland British* (Oxford, 2001), pp 461–534; M. Perceval-Maxwell, *The outbreak of the Irish Rebellion of 1641* (Dublin, 1994), pp 213–39.   [8] J.T. Gilbert (ed.), *History of the Irish Confederation and the war in Ireland* (7 vols, Dublin, 1882–91), 1, pp 226–7. An explanatory proclamation was published a few days later after complaints were made by the Old English leaders, explaining that 'by the words, Irish Papist, we intended only such of the old meer Irish of the province of Ulster, as have plotted, contrived and been actors in this treason', *A declaration by the Lords Justices and Council* (Dublin, 1641).   [9] R. Armstrong, *Protestant War: the 'British' of Ireland and the wars of the three kingdoms* (Manchester, 2005), pp 15–18.   [10] A. Clarke, *The Old English in Ireland, 1625–1642* (Dublin, 2000).   [11] Ibid., pp 172–3; M. Ó Siochrú, *Confederate Ireland, 1642–1649: a constitutional and political analysis* (Dublin, 1999), p. 25.   [12] Clarke, *Old English*, pp 162–3.

were actively working for the extirpation of Irish Catholicism. This suspicion, which had also been advertised by the Ulster insurgents as a reason for their actions, was moving the Old English closer to alliance with their traditional enemies.

Their principal causes for complaint were the activities of Sir Charles Coote who had first come to Ireland during the latter, and most brutal, stages of the Nine Years War.[13] He afterwards settled in Jamestown, Co. Leitrim, and was appointed provost-marshal of Connacht, the first in a succession of offices that eventually included the vice-presidency of the province, a seat on the commission for defective titles, and membership of the Irish Privy Council.[14] As provost-marshal and administrator of martial law in the western province, Coote had opportunities to inflict summary justice on malcontents and potential rebels and this experience undoubtedly influenced his response to events in 1641–2.[15] During the 1620s and 1630s, however, his greatest efforts were directed towards extending his patrimony; he was viewed even by some of his fellow New English settlers as an unseemly land-grabber. By the 1630s he had accumulated estates, using a variety of often-underhand means, all over Ireland. He was a member of the commission for defective titles, a prime means for the extension of settler landholding at the expense of their Old English or Gaelic Irish neighbours, and he urged the plantation of Connacht.[16] Thus Coote was, even before the war, a thorn in the side of many Catholic proprietors. In many ways, Coote was representative of a specifically Protestant New English interest, one that, as time went by, was prepared to oppose any English government that threatened their interests in Ireland through leniency towards Irish Catholicism, still Protestant Ireland's most dangerous rival. This New English grouping was dominated by the earl of Cork and advocated a thoroughgoing plantation of Ireland that would leave the settler interest dominant in every part of the island, and they also urged punitive measures against the Catholic church.[17] Although

---

13 P. Lenihan, 'Coote, Sir Charles, first baronet (*d.* 1642)', *Oxford Dictionary of National Biography*, http://www.oxforddnb.com/view/article/6239, accessed 21 April 2006.   14 V. Treadwell, *Buckingham and Ireland, 1616–1628. A study in Anglo-Irish politics* (Dublin, 1998), pp 200–1.   15 My thanks to David Edwards and Clodagh Tait for these points. For a further discussion of the use of martial law by New English administrators see David Edwards, 'Spenser's *View* and martial law in Ireland', in Hiram Morgan (ed.), *Political ideology in Ireland, 1541–1641* (Dublin, 1999), pp 127–57.   16 Clarke, *Old English*, pp 64, 108; H. Kearney, *Strafford in Ireland* (Cambridge, 1989), pp 88–9.   17 N. Canny, *The upstart earl: a study of the social and mental world of Richard Boyle, first earl of Cork* (Cambridge, 1992); Canny, *Making Ireland British*, passim; Patrick Little, *Lord Broghill and the Cromwellian union with Ireland and Scotland* (Woodbridge, 2004), pp 11–58. The position of the Scots in Ireland was compromised by their non-conformity with the established Church of Ireland; for more on this see R. Armstrong, 'Ireland's puritan revolution? The emergence of Ulster Presbyterianism reconsidered', *English Historical Review*, 121 (2006), 1048–74; K. Forkan, 'Scottish-Protestant Ulster and the crisis of the three kingdoms, 1637–1651' (unpublished

the New English lost some power during the governorship of Thomas Wentworth from 1633 to 1640, the appointment of men such as William Parsons, Adam Loftus and William Borlase to the government in 1640–1 signalled their return to prominence.

The actions of Sir Charles Coote in late 1641 and early 1642 have been blamed by generations of historians for helping to foment over a decade of total war, and ultimately the defeat and expropriation of the Irish Catholic interest during the Cromwellian period. Apparently in Dublin at the outbreak of the rebellion, the sexagenarian Coote was appointed military governor of the city in November 1641.[18] The capital being threatened by incursions from Wicklow to the south, Coote led an expedition to clear the area and relieve some besieged castles. The mission was a military success, but a political disaster. Although legally entitled to administer summary justice under martial law, Coote's previous experience in Connacht seems to have made him, at best, profligate in the use of such powers. Alternatively, his actions could be, and soon were, construed as state-sponsored murder on a major scale, designed to goad Catholics into rebellion. One of his English officers noted that after the relief of Wicklow town on 29 November, Coote ordered the execution of several Irishmen and women for unspecified crimes.[19] During a scouting mission that evening, two more 'of the enemie' were apprehended and hanged, while Coote personally despatched a third 'with his owne pistoll', although whether this occurred before or after the unfortunate's capture is unspecified.[20] Irish Catholic commentators quickly supplied more gruesome details. Coote had allegedly hanged 'a gentlewoman great with child' in whose possession some plundered goods had been found, ignoring her pleas that she had purchased them legitimately. Afterwards, he was said to have called a local peasant from his plough and ordered him to blow the smoke from his pistol; upon obeying the 'simple man' was shot in the mouth and killed, apparently for sport.[21] A more vehement author accused Coote and his men of having:

> killed all that came in their way, both man, woman and child, nay would murther the women in their verie travel, where one of his troupers carried on the pointe of his speeare the head of a little babe, which he cutt off in the verie instant of his delivery, and killed the poor mother, which Coote obsearving, said that he was mightie pleased with many such frolicks.[22]

These gorily embellished actions occurred at the same time as another government force sent to relieve Drogheda had been defeated at Julianstown by the insurgents, helping to convince the Palesmen both of the malice and the

---

PhD thesis, NUI, Galway, 2003), passim. 18 W. Harris, *The history and antiquities of the city of Dublin* (London, 1776), p. 334. 19 Gilbert, *History of the Irish Confederation*, 1, p. xxxii. 20 Ibid. 21 Ibid., p. 34 22 Gilbert, *Contemporary history*, 1, p. 13.

weakness of the government. A few days later, a rumour emerged from Dublin Castle that Coote had threatened to massacre all the Catholics in Ireland.[23] This was quickly denied by the Lords Justices, but the damage was compounded by an expedition led by Coote to Clontarf in north Co. Dublin on 15 December. More civilians were murdered in this attack, and the house of George King, a prominent local Old Englishman who was engaged in the attempts by the Old English to defuse the situation, was destroyed.[24] King had been among those invited by government under protection to Dublin to discuss their grievances. This affront, seemingly intended as a deliberate attack on any nascent peace moves, led local Catholics to band together to defend themselves.[25] It was then a matter of days before the Old English of the Pale and the Ulster Irish leaders united.[26] From now on, the gloves were off in a war of religion, and Sir Charles Coote became Protestant Ireland's most vigorous defender, winning a string of victories against the as yet disorganized Irish Catholic forces. These successes were achieved with unusual ferocity, as Coote's men rampaged throughout Dublin and Kildare, firing villages, massacring civilians and slaughtering garrisons that had surrendered on terms, in a blood-soaked prelude to the decade of warfare to follow.

Such has been the standard reading of Sir Charles Coote's brief wartime career. This legend of a murderous, blood-crazed, and essentially irrational madman was quickly created by Irish Catholic authors who wished to emphasize how the actions of Coote and the Dublin government had forced them to provide for their own defence in the early 1640s. As early as 1646, a play, entitled *A tragedy of Cola's furie*, was published in Kilkenny that depicted Coote, the said Cola, as an 'inexplicably deranged villain', causing havoc in a fictional Ireland, and who had to be stopped at all costs.[27] Later, Coote's alleged barbarism was used as a deliberate counterpoint to the massacres allegedly perpetrated by the Ulster Catholics in the first weeks of the rising, thereby justifying the defensive rebellion of the Old English against the Dublin government. The outbreak of the English civil war then allowed the Confederate Catholics to portray themselves as the king's loyal Irish subjects, opposed to the 'puritan party' in the three kingdoms that apparently sought to extirpate them as well as to defeat the king. This image was propounded by the early Catholic historians of the 1640s, the Old Englishman Richard Bellings, and the

---

23 Clarke, *Old English*, p. 182.   24 R. S., *A Collection of some of the murthers and massacres committed on the Irish in Ireland* (London, 1662), pp 8–9. My thanks to Pádraig Lenihan for this reference. Maighréad Ní Murchadha, *Fingal 1603–60: contending neighbours in north Dublin* (Dublin, 2005), pp 264–5.   25 Clarke, *Old English*, p. 186.   26 Ó Siochrú, *Confederate Ireland*, p. 25.   27 H. Burkhead, *A tragedy of Cola's furie, or, Lirenda's miserie* (Kilkenny, 1646); P. Coghlan, '"The model of its sad afflictions": Henry Burkhead's *Tragedy of Cola's furie*', in M. Ó Siochrú (ed.), *Kingdoms in crisis. Ireland in the 1640s* (Dublin, 2001), pp 192–211. The quote is from ibid., p. 205.

anonymous author of the *Aphorismical discovery of treasonable faction*, the latter describing Coote as a 'human bloodsucker'.[28] These authors also provide the descriptions of Coote's Wicklow expedition as quoted above. The exiled Catholic cleric John Lynch portrayed him similarly, 'a bad crow from a bad egg, [who] perpetrated horrible massacres in several parts of Meath and Leinster, before either had been involved in the flame of war'.[29] The memoirs of Bishop Nicholas French and the earl of Castlehaven, written in the later seventeenth century, emphasized the violent actions of the Dublin government in Leinster; while neither mentioned Coote by name the import was clear.[30] Thomas Carte's biography of James Butler, duke of Ormond, written in the first half of the eighteenth century, specifically noted 'the inhumanities complained of, as committed by Sir C. Coote in Wicklow', as vital in encouraging Old English opposition to the government.[31] Later in the eighteenth century, as Catholic Ireland regained some confidence, writers such as John Curry further emphasized the behaviour of Coote and the lords justices and minimized events in Ulster, a trend even copied by some Protestant authors.[32] The rise of Irish Catholic nationalism in the nineteenth century prompted an attempt by Protestant or unionist writers to reemphasize the 1641 massacres.[33] In more recent years most Irish historians of the 1640s have continued to blame Coote's activities, along with the Julianstown defeat, for the alliance of the Old English and the Ulster Irish.[34] Micheál Ó Siochrú, for instance, labelled Coote 'a notorious anti-Catholic bigot', and condemned his activities as 'murderous'.[35]

There is, however, another representation of Sir Charles Coote that was created contemporaneous with his brief wartime career and in the years immediately following his controversial death in 1642. This was the story of a Protestant hero, bravely confounding age and infirmity to destroy those who

---

28 Bellings's history is printed in Gilbert, *History of the Irish Confederation*, and the 'Aphorismical Discovery', in J.T. Gilbert (ed.), *A contemporary history of affairs in Ireland from 1641–1652* (3 vols, Dublin, 1879). Both of these edited volumes also include a vast quantity of previously unprinted manuscript material.   29 Quoted in J. Ohlmeyer, 'Introduction: for God, king or country?', in Jane Ohlmeyer (ed.), *Political thought in seventeenth-century Ireland* (Cambridge, 2000), p. 7.   30 N. French, *The bleeding Iphigenia* (Louvain, 1674); J. Touchet, earl of Castlehaven, *The earl of Castlehaven's review or his memoirs* (London, 1684). 31 T. Carte, *An history of the life of James, first duke of Ormonde* (3 vols, London, 1735–6), 1, p. 253.   32 J. Curry, *An historical and critical review of the civil wars in Ireland* (Dublin, 1775), pp 239–41; W. Crawford, *A history of Ireland from the earliest period, to the present time* (2 vols, Strabane, 1783), 2, 386.   33 For example, M. Hickson, *Ireland in the seventeenth century, or, The Irish massacres of 1641–2* (2 vols, London, 1884).   34 Clarke, *Old English*; Perceval Maxwell, *Outbreak*; Ó Siochrú, *Confederate Ireland*; and T. Ó hAnnracháin, *Catholic Counter-Reformation in Ireland: the mission of Rinuccini, 1645–1649* (Oxford, 2002), p. 22, all agree that Coote bore a large amount of the blame in propelling the Old English into rebellion. Armstrong, *Protestant war*, pp 19–22, places Coote's activities within the context of the imposition of martial law in Leinster and the government's attempts to comprehend the insurrection within the existing legal framework.   35 Ó Siochrú, *Confederate Ireland*, pp 24, 37.

had rebelled against the king's authority in Ireland, while refusing to countenance compromise with these 'bloody rebels'. Such an image was created and popularized in a series of pamphlets, based on letters sent from Dublin and published in London, celebrating Coote and his exploits from January 1642 until his death in action the following May. In most cases, the publishers of the pamphlets also printed much material for the English parliament, leading to the conclusion that the letters were, in the main, sent to members of that parliament, or their associates, and several were published by explicit order of the parliament.[36] In them, the acclaim for Coote rises to a crescendo, until he is portrayed in terms of God's righteous anger bearing down on the Irish rebels. The series begins with a pamphlet, *A true and good relation, of the valliant exploits and victorious enterprises of Sir Simon Harcourt, and Sir Charles Coote*, based on a letter sent from Dublin on 20 January 1642.[37] It describes Coote's actions in north Co. Dublin, the very ones that helped finally to alienate the Old English from the government. It was admitted that Coote hanged some Irish and that towns were pillaged and burnt, but these were deliberately contextualized against descriptions of the Ulster massacres. Protestant violence was presented as being against unnamed and universalized 'enemies', undefined, except for their Irishness. The author also contrasts Coote's ardour in attacking the Irish Catholics to the lacklustre response of his commander, James Butler, earl of Ormond. Although a Protestant, Ormond was of Old English stock and related to many of those now in rebellion. He quickly became an object of suspicion amongst many Protestants from an English settler background, the pamphlet's author making the point, 'There are 4 Lords, whose names are Butler, that are rebels, I pray God the fift ... may never ... violate the trust reposed in him'.[38] This first pamphlet identifies all of Catholic Ireland as 'the enemy' and harbours deep suspicion of anyone who might be tempted to treat them with anything other than total ruthlessness.

The next, from 19 February, brings in another theme.[39] After recounting more of Coote's successes, the idea of a new and thorough plantation of Ireland after the inevitable Protestant victory was mooted, as the defeated rebels would

---

[36] Jason Peacey has emphasized the way in which news of the 1641 rising and associated atrocity stories were deliberately published by John Pym's oppositional faction in the English parliament, in order to further inflame public opinion against Charles I's alleged connivance in a popish plot and gain support for the inevitable civil war in England: Peacey, *Politicians and pamphleteers*, pp 240–2; see also Shagan, 'Constructing discord'. The pamphlets described in this piece, however, were produced after the initial rush of rebellion/atrocity literature, and are part of a more proactive attempt by the Protestants of Ireland themselves to influence opinion in England.   [37] *A true and good relation, of the valliant exploits and victorious enterprises of Sir Simon Harcourt, and Sir Charles Coote* (London, 1642).   [38] Ibid., p. 5.   [39] *Two famous battels fought in Ireland: wherein the Protestants under the command of the Earle of Ormond, Sr. Charles Coote, and Sr. Simon Harcourt, slew great numbers of the rebels*

forfeit 'land enough to plant a better, and a more permanent generation'.[40] This was connected to the passage of the Adventurer's act through the English parliament at the time, which offered forfeited Irish lands to those who would contribute money towards the reconquest of Ireland. Another pamphlet, dated 29 February, resembled a prayer that 'the heaven-guided parliament', whose 'worthy members that are now fathers of our country', would aid the Protestants of Ireland in pursuing their war to victory.[41] Thus by late February 1642, Sir Charles Coote's apparently heroic exploits had been used both to articulate the wartime aspirations of the Protestant settler interest, and to advertise them to their most likely ally, the English parliament. The goal was a new conquest and a complete plantation of the island, to the benefit of the settlers and their allies in England, and the complete extirpation of Irish Catholicism as a political and landed force.

Coote continued to be extolled in the London press. In a printed letter of 20 March he was applauded for shooting one of his own soldiers who had attempted to desert to the Irish, while on 6 April he was commended for his role in the storm of the castle of Carrickmines in south Dublin.[42] After the battle of Kilrush on 15 April, the London press usurped credit for the Protestant victory from the earl of Ormond in favour of Coote, whose apparent blood-lust was described approvingly; he 'scoured about the field, crying Kill, Kill, and with his hand gave the example'.[43] Coote was then sent to garrison Naas, Co. Kildare, where he hanged some Irish civilians, and banished the rest on pain of similar treatment, introducing in their stead Protestant refugee families from Dublin; an example in practice of the war-accelerated plantation sought by his propagandists.[44]

In late April 1642, after relieving several castles in Queen's County, Coote was called to aid the Protestant forces in Trim, Co. Meath. He relieved the town on 1 May, narrowly escaping death when a bullet 'past within three inches of his throat'.[45] His delight at the victory was evident; as he prepared to banish the native inhabitants of Trim as he had at Naas, it was noted that 'it makes the old Sir Charles young again to see God so blesse him in his exercises'.[46] However, Trim was again attacked by the Irish on 7 May, and in the confused fighting Coote was shot dead while apparently leading the charge that routed them.[47]

(London, 1642). **40** Ibid., p. 2. **41** *The truest, most happy, and joyfull newes that ever came from Ireland* (London, 1642). **42** Both of these letters were printed in *New and true newes from Ireland: relating these particulars following several overthrows given to the rebels by Sir Charles Coote* (London, 1642). Recent archaeological evidence has indicated that the storm of Carrickmines was followed by a massacre of soldiers and civilians sheltering in the castle. See M. Clinton, D. Shiels and L. Fibiger in this volume. **43** *Captaine Yarner's relation of the battaile fought at Kilrush upon the 15th day of Aprill* (London, 1642), p. 3. **44** Ibid., p. 5. **45** *Admirable, good, true and joyfull newes from Ireland* (London, 1642), p. 3. **46** Ibid., p. 5. **47** Bodleian Library, Carte MSS 3, f. 124, Richard Grenville to Ormond, 8 May 1642.

The fatal shot was almost certainly an accident, discharged by an English lieutenant who was reportedly so distressed as to be restrained from committing suicide immediately afterwards.[48] On 17 and 18 May, two London pamphlets reprinted a letter written in Dublin on 11 May and reported Coote's death as accidental.[49] The report to the House of Commons in London also confirmed that he had been killed by 'an unfortunate shot from one of his own men'.[50] Irish Catholic writers, of course, attributed Coote's death to a divine miracle, noting that just before it his son had destroyed a wooden image of the Virgin Mary in order to provide firewood for his father.[51] However, the death, as the life, of Sir Charles Coote would be used in order to further the goals of the Protestants of Ireland.

Coote was buried in Christchurch Cathedral in Dublin on 14 May 1642, 'with much lamentations to all Protestants', while an elegy described him as 'England's honour, Scotland's wonder, Ireland's terror'.[52] In the weeks following his death his former subordinates tried to live up to the latter epithet, and the pamphlet material reaches new heights of viciousness, openly rejoicing in the killing of 'men, women and children, giving no quarter, no not to such as were protected', or the fate of '18 or 20 men, besides women and children', captured at Newcastle, Co. Dublin, 'who dyed the common death of rebels'.[53] Another pamphlet describes the hanging of priests and mutilation of enemy corpses, while again reminding readers of the potential profitability of the Irish lands that would accrue to the Protestant victors of the war, the latter point becoming more relevant as the civil war looming in England threatened to seriously reduce military aid from thence.[54] Other pamphlets produced during the summer of 1642 recounted the barbarity of the 1641 rebellion and presented plans for the reform of Ireland, one in particular foreseeing the penal laws of the late seventeenth and early eighteenth century with an uncanny accuracy.[55]

Coote's funeral sermon was given by the minister Faithful Teate, a puritan-inclined preacher who would come to greater prominence in the Cromwellian

---

48 *A most certain and true relation of the severall victories and overthrows given to the rebels in Ireland ... as also the certain death of Sir Charles Coote, and the manner thereof* (London, 1642), p. 6.   49 Ibid.; *A remonstrance of divers passages and proceedings of our army in the kingdome of Ireland* (London, 1642).   50 *Commons Journal*, 2, p. 57.   51 Gilbert, *Contemporary history*, 1, p. 32; R. O'Farrell and R. O'Connell, *Commentarius Rinuccinianus, de sedis apostolicae legatione ad foederatos Hiberniae catholicios per annos 1645–9*, ed. S. Kavanagh (6 vols, Dublin, 1932–49), 1, p. 305.   52 *A perfect relation of the proceedings of the English army against the rebels in Ireland, from May 12 to the 23 1642* (London, 1642); *Calendar of the manuscripts of the Marquess of Ormonde* (11 vols, London, 1895–1920), n.s., p. 108.   53 *A perfect relation of the proceedings of the English army.*   54 *A trve relation of such passages and proceedings of the army of Dublin in the kingdome of Ireland, as have happened since the death of Sir Charles Coote to this present* (London, 1642).   55 *A discovrse concerning the rebellion in Ireland* (London, 1642); *The teares of Ireland wherein is lively presented as in a map, a list of the unheard of cruelties and perfidious treacheries of bloud-thirsty Jesuits and the Popish faction* (London, 1642).

period. It only found its way into print in 1658; Teate declared that he had been prevented from publishing it in 1642 because of the politically sensitive assertions it contained.[56] The sermon consisted of a biblical exegesis legitimizing the war against the Catholic Irish, and illustrating God's approval for 'an extirpation of Nation and name'.[57] In a hint of the rewards that victory in this just war would bring, Teate reminded his audience that 'David's house was surely founded in the blood of the enemies of the lord'.[58] He also gave the first intimation that Coote may have been killed, 'by treachery'.[59] Such a controversial assertion was made in the context of political developments within Ireland and Britain. In England, relations between Charles I and his parliament would degenerate into open warfare by the end of August 1642. Determined that Protestant Ireland should be under his control, the king increasingly relied upon Ormond, whose loyalty was by him unquestioned. Ormond, however, was an object of suspicion for many in the New English community; not only was it felt that he was not fully committed to the war against the Confederates, but they feared that through his offices some sort of compromise might be found that would frustrate plans for a compete destruction of Catholic Ireland as a political and landed force. In the event, such fears were justified. Within a year Charles would order Ormond to negotiate first a cessation of arms, and then a full-scale peace treaty with the Irish Confederate Catholics, as part of his plans to seek their support in his war against his parliament.

Coote's death now took on a new meaning: his vigorous and uncompromising conduct of the war could be represented as blocking a royalist scheme to ally with Catholic Ireland in the conflict engulfing the three kingdoms of England, Scotland and Ireland. In the months after Coote's death, Ormond gained effective control over the Irish government in Dublin, imprisoning such as were most vociferous in their support for the continuance of the war with the support of the English parliament, men such as William Parsons, John Temple and Adam Loftus.[60] In London, the alleged treachery hinted at by Faithful Teate could now be fully unveiled. In March 1644 one of Coote's younger sons, Chidley, penned a pamphlet describing the cessation as 'a trap to catch Protestants'.[61] The same year another pamphlet accused Ormond of deliberately wasting supplies during 1643 so the cessation would appear a necessity and the English parliament would be blamed for not supplying Dublin.[62] By 1646, with a peace treaty between Ormond, now a marquis and lord lieutenant of Ireland, and the Confederate Catholics at an advanced stage of completion, the dominant Irish Protestant interest launched a two-pronged attack on the royalist policy of

---

56 F. Teate, *The souldiers commission, charge, & reward ... opened in a sermon ... upon the occasion of the interring of Sir Charles Coote* (London, 1658).   57 Ibid., p. 14.   58 Ibid., p. 2.   59 Ibid., p. 10.   60 Armstrong, *Protestant war*, pp 92–3.   61 Chidley Coote, *Irelands lamentation for the late destructive cessation, or, a trap to catch Protestants* (London, 1644). 62 *The plott and progresse of the Irish Rebellion* (London, 1644), p. 8.

alliance with the Catholic Irish. Most of the main figures from the early 1640s administration were now in London, men such as Loftus, Parsons and Temple, who joined with other exiles such as Robert Meredith, and John Borlase. Around this time, parliament had also sent several such exiles back to Ireland to act on behalf of its, and their own, interests, men such as Arthur Annesley, Robert King, and Coote's eldest son, Charles, who would distinguish himself in the war against the Confederates in Ulster and Connacht. The Protestant settlers of Ireland were now represented by a coherent lobby group at Westminster, and their agenda had been co-opted by the English parliament, now close to victory against the king.[63] Accordingly, a Protestant history of recent events had to be produced. To this end, John Temple's *Irish rebellion*, appeared in April 1646, which demonized the Irish Catholics and prepared an English audience for the scorched earth campaign deemed necessary against such devilish rebels, and the concomitant transfer of their landed wealth to the sufferers in their rebellion.[64] In the autumn of 1646, Temple's volume was followed up by a lengthy pamphlet, *Ormond's curtain drawn*, almost certainly written by the son of Robert Meredith, who was part of the same London-based Irish Protestant grouping.[65] Shifting the focus of attack from Irish Catholics, whom Temple had demonized sufficiently, Meredith sought to ensure that the ideology of his group was accepted as the true voice of Protestant Ireland. This meant destroying the reputation of any Protestant, such as Ormond, who would deign to compromise with the Irish Catholics. Where Temple's work ends, in late 1641, *Ormond's curtain drawn* takes up, illustrating the victories of the Protestants in early 1642, 'the Rebels running continually before us; five chasing a hundred, and ten putting a thousand to flight' led by Sir Charles Coote, 'by a speciall providence being sent'.[66] Following on from the suspicions voiced by Teate in 1642, it was now asserted that 'there was something more than faire play in the businesse' of Coote's

---

63 Little, 'Irish "Independents"', pp 951–4; Armstrong, *Protestant war*, pp 161–4, 169–70.
64 J. Temple, *The Irish rebellion* (London, 1646). 65 *Ormond's curtain drawn: in a short discourse concerning Ireland* (London, 1646). Only 32 pages of the tract are in the surviving printed version. There is then a lacuna, and the rest of the tract, in manuscript form, is to be found at British Library, Additional MSS 4189, ff 320–332. There is also a manuscript version of the printed section, at British Library, Additional MSS 4763, ff 4–6 (pp 1–6), and British Library, Additional MSS 4819, ff 333–344 (pp 7–32). While Adam Meredith is acknowledged as the author on British Library, Additional MSS 4763, f. 4, the first page of the printed pamphlet has the note 'By Sr John Temple; but not ffinished'. It is likely that the tract was a joint effort by several members or associates of the anti-Ormond faction on the council at Dublin from 1641–43, given the huge amount of evidently eyewitness information included therein. For further debates on the authorship, content and significance of this tract, see J. Adamson, 'Strafford's ghost: the British context of Viscount Lisle's lieutenancy of Ireland', in Ohlmeyer, *Independence to occupation*, p. 140n; Little, 'Irish "Independents"', pp 953–4; Armstrong, *Protestant war*, pp 182–3. 66 *Ormond's curtain drawn*, p. 11.

death, and that 'there was so good use made of his death, as may make a man believe he was taken out of the way'.[67] The culprit was obvious. Coote's death proved the turning point in Protestant affairs, 'from that time every thing began to look new', and Ormond began to fill the council with his creatures, removing what Meredith consistently refers to as the 'honnest party', and weakening the army and state so that peace with the Confederates would become a necessity.[68] These two works by Temple and Meredith were produced in collaboration, and served the same end: to promote the aims and aspirations of a set of people, mainly English and exclusively Protestant, who had settled in Ireland prior to the 1641 rising, and who now saw in the war there and the unsettled conditions of the Stuart archipelago their opportunity for hegemony in the kingdom. This goal, while existing from the early seventeenth century, had been redefined and tempered in the heat of vicious conflict in 1641–2, and Sir Charles Coote had been their standard-bearer, obligingly performing all that was expected by them on the battlefield, while his death was used to obliterate any alternative view of the war in Ireland.

Concluding, this article has attempted to retrieve an alternative contemporaneous history of Ireland in the early 1640s, one created for a specific ideological purpose. What was thus produced was propaganda, within a framework already familiar to English pamphleteers through their coverage of the Thirty Years War: a battle between antichristian Catholics and godly Protestants, the sufferings of an afflicted people, and the emergence of a Protestant hero. The Irish war was the first real chance for the London pamphleteers to test their new-found freedom by describing a conflict within the Stuart kingdoms, and in doing so they found ready-made 'correspondents' in the Protestant settler interest, creating a symbiotic relationship whereby news from Ireland was used to sell pamphlets, to comment on English and Scottish events, and, most importantly, to further the agenda of the settlers. All the goals of the Protestants of Ireland, enunciated in the series of pamphlets here described, eventually came to fruition; the Cromwellian conquest and confiscation destroyed Catholic Ireland as a serious rival in the kingdom, and the deft switch of most of them to Royalism in 1660 ensured that they kept almost of what they had gained thereby.

Yet the reading of 1640s Ireland as given here, that of Protestants vigorously and successfully waging an uncompromising war against the Catholic Irish was airbrushed out of history by its original creators. It is, however, easy to see why this might be so. To celebrate the victories of 1641–2 would downplay the dangers, as insisted on by Protestant Ireland after the Restoration, that Catholic Ireland still posed. It was more politic to remember victimhood and 1641.

---

67 Ibid., p. 12. 68 Ibid.

Furthermore, most of their 1640s pamphlets were blatantly pro-parliament and anti-Royalist, and they were best forgotten after the restoration of the Stuarts and the return of Ormond to his post as lord lieutenant. The brief and bloody war of the early 1640s in Leinster could be forgotten, since the victors had gained the spoils of the kingdom. It was left to apologists of Catholic Ireland to emphasize Coote's role in widening the war, but this could always be trumped by the assertion that it was the Irish rebellion that had begun the cycle of violence.[69]

Finally, it may be asked whether or not Sir Charles Coote did really shoot a harmless ploughman in the mouth for amusement, laugh as his soldiers hanged a heavily pregnant woman and piked her premature offspring, and threaten to kill every Catholic in Ireland?[70] That extreme violence occurred in Wicklow and Clontarf is well enough attested to by both sides to be accepted; it is less clear whether it occurred because of the over-zealous application of martial law, as part of a cynical attempt to goad the Palesmen into further rebellion in order to seize their lands, or simply because Coote, who was an elderly man, had lost control of his soldiers. Interestingly, Coote's actions during the first half of 1642, those celebrated in the London pamphlets, did not seem to generate as much interest within Ireland at the time. A note of the services performed by various Protestant commanders during 1641–2 only mentions his movements in Wicklow and north Dublin.[71] He is not mentioned at all in Sir James Ware's diary of events during this period.[72] A later Catholic source notes, in passing, atrocities Coote was alleged to have carried out during his time in Trim, and he was specifically linked with the death of the Catholic martyr Peter Higgins.[73] Furthermore, there is almost no correspondence between Coote and his commander, the earl of Ormond during this time.[74] For a man whose actions were celebrated and maligned by so many, and for such differing purposes, we are left with almost nothing from his own pen during the vital period from December 1641 to May 1642, six months that created his enduring reputation. In one of the few letters that survive from Sir Charles Coote during his active service in the spring of 1642, he wrote to Ormond from Naas about prisoners

---

69 T. Barnard, '1641: a bibliographical essay', in B. Mac Cuarta (ed.), *Ulster 1641. Aspects of the Rising* (Belfast, 1997), pp 177–9; T. Barnard, '"Parlour entertainment in an evening"? Histories of the 1640s', in Ó Siochrú, *Kingdoms in crisis*, pp 23–32.   **70** Gilbert, *History of the Confederation*, 1, p. 35; Gilbert, *Contemporary history*, 1, p. 13; Clarke, *Old English*, p. 182.   **71** Bodleian Library, Carte MSS 59, f. 374 (Notes of services done, [18 Sept. 1642]). My thanks to David Edwards for this reference.   **72** Dublin City Library and Archive, Gilbert MS 169, pp 224–5. My thanks again to David Edwards for this reference.   **73** *A collection of some of the murthers*, p. 12; Augustine Valkenburg, 'Peter Higgins, OP', in P. Corish & B. Millett (eds), *The Irish martyrs* (Dublin, 2005), pp 148–64. Higgins was captured by Ormond's men in Naas and extra-judicially hanged by Coote in Dublin.   **74** Bodleian Library, Carte MSS 2 & 3.

he had taken: 'I cannot p[er]swade my selfe to p[er]mit men to be killed in could blood'.⁷⁵ Whether this statement is truth, hypocrisy, or Coote's own perception of his conduct in the war that he was fighting, may be left to one side; the object of this essay has been to explore representation. His last written words, however, may allow us to reflect on how men of action are used by men of letters for their own purposes, both in life and beyond the grave.

---

75 Bodleian Library, Carte MSS 3, f. 88 (Coote to Ormond, 23 April 1642).

'Escaping massacre': refugees in Scotland in the aftermath of the 1641 Ulster Rebellion

JOHN R. YOUNG

Gryte crueltie in Ireland, and mekill blood spilt of the English and Scottis puritane protestantis; fyre and suord went also throw the haill land but mercie of sex or kynd, young or auld man, woman, or chyld, all put to death, and ther goodis spolzeit.[1]

Such were the comments of John Spalding, the contemporary historian and north-eastern Royalist in Scotland, with regard to the bloodshed in the aftermath of the 1641 Ulster Rebellion. For obvious reasons the rebellion has been a controversial event in the history of Ireland. Given the wider British context of the wars for the three kingdoms, the rebellion clearly impacted on England and Scotland. In terms of refugees and victims of warfare, Keith Lindley's seminal article assessed the impact of the rebellion upon England and Wales.[2] In terms of the historiography of the covenanting movement of the 1640s in Scotland and the 1641 rebellion, however, the main emphasis has been on the covenanting army which was sent to Ulster in 1642, its presence there, and the problems of adequately supplying and funding that army.[3] What has not been fully explored is the extent and impact of refugees and victims of warfare escaping from the rebellion to Scotland. The reaction of Charles I, still in Edinburgh when the rebellion broke out in October 1641, and the diplomatic, political and military initiatives which resulted in covenanting military intervention in Ulster in 1642, have been well-charted by scholars such as David Stevenson, Nicholas Canny and Michael Perceval-Maxwell.[4] The latter two

---

1 J. Spalding, *Memorialls of the trubles in Scotland and England, 1624–1645* (2 vols, Aberdeen, 1850–1), 2, p. 99.   2 K. Lindley, 'The impact of the 1641 Rebellion upon England and Wales, 1641–5', *IHS*, 18 (1972), 143–76.   3 D. Stevenson, *Scottish Covenanters and Irish Confederates* (Belfast, 1981). Refugees are briefly discussed here on pp 53–4.   4 Ibid.; N. Canny, *Making Ireland British, 1580–1650* (Oxford, 2003); M. Perceval-Maxwell, *The outbreak of the Irish Rebellion of 1641* (London, 1994). For the latest three-kingdom overviews of the period, see A. Woolrych, *Britain in Revolution, 1625–1660* (Oxford, 2002); D. Scott, *Politics and war in the three Stuart Kingdoms, 1637–49* (Basingstoke, 2003); and A.I. Macinnes, *The British Revolution, 1629–1660* (Basingstoke, 2005).

scholars in particular have also examined the dynamics of the rebellion in the ways that the Scottish settlers in Ulster were regarded and treated by the native Irish as the rebellion progressed.

This article explores a different historical perspective on the impact of the rebellion on Scotland. In doing so, it will examine several key issues. First, the administrative structure developed by the covenanting regime for the provision of humanitarian aid for refugees who had escaped the rebellion is examined. Second, different categories of those refugees on Scottish soil are identified by recourse to the examination of sample synod, presbytery and kirk session records of the Church of Scotland. The tales or accounts therein of what had happened to individual refugees are also considered. This represents the most 'human' part of the article whereby the 'voices' of those refugees can be heard through the historical records.

THE STRUCTURE OF ADMINISTRATIVE RELIEF

The Scottish Privy Council first discussed the problem of refugees on 1 February 1642. The covenanting parliament of 1639–41 was no longer in session, having ended on 17 November 1641, and the administration of the country under the covenanting regime was based on parliamentary interval committees (which convened after the end of that parliament) and the Privy Council. During 1642 the Council played an important role in preparing and then undertaking in supplying and provisioning the covenanting army in Ulster. In 1643 the Council raised voluntary contributions to provide money for that army. On 1 February it was noted that because of 'the crueltie of the rebels in Ireland great nombers of his Majesties good subjects and our own countrey men thair are daylie forced to flee out of Ireland to those parts in the west countrey quhair they find best occasion of landing'. This suggests that refugees had been flooding in to the west coast of Scotland in the months after the rebellion. As a result, 'the multitude of whiche poor people is become so great and thair necessities and wants so pressing', that the western parishes where refugees had landed could not cope. Parish funds for distribution to the poor had been 'exhausted', as had informal collections in the parishes. In light of this growing human and financial crisis, it was becoming impossible to help the refugees 'who in that regarde as lyke to be in worse condition heere, quhair they looked for succour and refreshment, in so farre as be flight having escaped the sword of the enemie, by famine they will miserablie perish if they be not tymouslie supplied'. Accordingly, the Privy Council stated that it was obliged to help these people, as 'the cause for which they suffer, being loyaltie and religion, will be powerful motives for all good subjects and true hairted christians liberallie to contribut of thair best meanes for the refreshment and comfort of so manie christian soules, especiallie being our owne countrey men'.[5]

Financial aid was to be raised through the institutional structure and mechanisms of the Church of Scotland in a 'bottom up' approach from individual parishes to presbyteries. Ministers were instructed to 'use all the powerfull and persuasive wayes they can, in thair sermons and other wayes, to stirre up their flocks liberallie and cheirfullie to contribut in this erand'. The minister of every parish was to collect a 'christian benevolence' and take it to the moderator of his presbytery, who was then to forward it to designated merchants for specified geographic areas. Two organizational divisions were created. Presbyteries for the areas of Stirling, Glasgow, Ayr, Argyll, Dumfries and Galloway were to forward their contributions to John Osburne and Robert Gordon, burgesses of Ayr. Presbyteries for Fife, Angus, Aberdeen, Ross and Moray, Lothian, Peebles and Tweeddale were to forward their contribution to three Edinburgh burgesses, James Stewart, Samuel Lockhart and John Meyn (Mean). These merchants were described as 'men of approven credit and honestie'. They were to act in accordance with any Council orders for the distribution of financial aid among the refugees.[6] Three days after the Council meeting of 1 February, Edinburgh burgh council responded to the Council's initiative on 4 February 1642. It asked the Edinburgh residents to comply with the policy and it noted 'the lamentable and deplorable estate of the many good Christians within the kingdom of Ireland who were being forced to flee to this country from the barbarous cruelty of the natives'. Accordingly, it was ordered that a 'voluntary subscription' was to be raised in the churches of the city on the following Sunday.[7]

Further developments took place towards the end of the month. On 23 February, Edinburgh burgh council ordered the collectors of the contribution 'gathered at the Kirk doores upon Sunday last for reliefe of the poor distressed Irishe flieing to this country' to deliver the money raised to George Suttie, an Edinburgh merchant. The following day, the Privy Council established a committee to advise on answers to be given to petitions that had been submitted for a proportion of the collections gathered for 'the poor people of Ireland'.[8] Four days later, the Council dealt specifically with the presbyteries of Ayr and

---

5 P. Hume Brown (ed.), *The register of the Privy Council of Scotland*, second series, vol. 7, 1638–43 (Edinburgh, 1906), pp 189–90.   6 Ibid., pp 190–1. All sums of money in this article are given in Scottish currency. The pound sterling was worth 12 pounds Scots in the seventeenth century. The merk is the Scottish merk worth 13 shillings (s) 4 pence (d) Scots. The merk was valued at two-thirds of the pound Scots. One dollar was equivalent to *c*.two pounds and 18 shillings. See M. Todd, *The culture of Protestantism in early modern Scotland* (New Haven and London, 2002), p. xiii; H.M. Dingwall, *Late seventeenth century Edinburgh. A demographic study* (Aldershot, 1994), p. xi.   7 M. Wood (ed.), *Extracts from the Records of the Burgh of Edinburgh, 1642–55* (Edinburgh, 1938), pp 3–4. Cited in Canny, *Making Ireland British*, p. 561.   8 *The register of the Privy Council of Scotland*, 7, 1638–43, p. 208.

Irvine. It had heard at length from commissioners from these two presbyteries who wanted 'some proportion of the collections gathered for releiffe of the poor people in Ireland'. The commissioners had asked for priority treatment for 'the supplie of great nombers of the saids poore people in thair bounds'. Accordingly, the Council instructed George Suttie to transfer £4,000 out of the collections to John Kennedy, bailie of Ayr, and Mr John Rosse, indweller in Irvine, for distribution to the refugees in these areas. Suttie had previously been involved in the collection of financial aid for exiled Protestant ministers in the Palatinate in the late 1620s and early 1630s.[9] In this respect, a link can be identified between victims of the Thirty Years War and victims of the 1641 Ulster Rebellion.

Despite these initiatives, the system experienced teething troubles at best and corrupt activities at worst. On 25 March, restructuring took place to speed up the process of considering refugees' petitions and to expand the provisions of 1 and 24 February. A formal Privy Council commission was issued to receive and consider petitions.[10] By this time, growing centralization at the Edinburgh level was taking place with regard to the refugees' petitions. Furthermore, the Council was aware that collections were not being forwarded to collectors as per the intended system. Additional fears had emerged by 13 April. Commissioners appointed for the distribution of aid were instructed only to give out money to those who could produce testimonials subscribed by the western collectors stating that they had not received money there, but had been recommended to do so in Edinburgh. A Council proclamation issued on 23 April hinted at corruption in areas of Fife, the north-east, Lothian, and the Borders. Collections had been taken by people who had not been warranted to do so. Money collected was not being forwarded to moderators of presbyteries nor by moderators to the designated collectors in Edinburgh.[11]

The problem of raising money had not been resolved by 9 June when the Council noted that several unidentified presbyteries within the provinces of Stirling, Glasgow, Ayr, Argyll, Dumfries, and Galloway had not forwarded collections. As a result of this reluctance or negligence, 'the multituds of these poore people resideing in the presbiteries of Air and Irwing, being above foure thousand persons, are lyke to sterve'.[12] This estimate of over 4,000 refugees in the presbyteries of Ayr and Irvine represents the most significant piece of

---

[9] Suttie was a member of Edinburgh burgh council. See M. Wood (ed.), *Extracts from the records of the Burgh of Edinburgh, 1626–1641* (Edinburgh, 1936), pp 1, 244; and *Extracts from the records of the Burgh of Edinburgh 1642–1655*, pp ix–x, 1, 13, 35. For details of the Privy Council's efforts to raise money for the ministers of the Palatinate and their families, see P. Hume Brown (ed.), *The register of the Privy Council of Scotland*, second series, vol. 3, 1629–30 (Edinburgh, 1901), pp 275–6, 291; and vol. 4 (Edinburgh, 1902), pp xlii–xliii, 118, 131–4, 277, 307, 357–8, 492–3, 537–9, 569. [10] *The register of the Privy Council of Scotland*, 7, 1638–43, pp 231, 264. [11] Ibid., pp 231, 237, 254. [12] Ibid., p. 267.

contemporary information concerning the number of refugees in Scotland. It may have been an exaggeration, but it does suggest a concentration of refugees within these two presbyteries. Furthermore, as David Stevenson has pointed out, 'it is clear that a significant proportion of the Protestant population of Ulster had fled to Scotland'.[13] Based on the estimated figures of the numbers of Scots in Ulster at the time of the 1641 Rebellion, 4,000 refugees corresponds with a figure of between thirteen and twenty per cent of the total number of the Scottish population in Ulster (20,000–30,000).[14] The geographic concentration of refugees in the west of Scotland, especially in the presbyteries of Ayr and Irvine, is confirmed by the writings of John Livingstone, the former minister at Killinchy in County Down (1630–4) and the minister at Stranraer from 1638 to 1648. According to Livingstone, in the winter following the rebellion 'many came flieing over to Scotland, sundry came to Ayr and Irvine, and other places of the West, by sea; but the greatest number came by Portpatrick and Stranrawer, and were for the most part in a very destitute condition'. Hence the western and south-western ports of Ayr, Irvine, Portpatrick and Stranraer were the main points of entry for refugees, with the bulk of refugees entering through the two south-western ports of Portpatrick and Stranraer.[15]

Livingstone was not the only minister with a charge in the south-west at this time who had previously served in Ireland, but had been forced to flee due to persecution. John McClellan, the former schoolmaster at Newtonards in Co. Down, who had been licensed, deposed and then excommunicated in Ireland, was now the minister at Kirkcudbright.[16] As has been well documented, both men were closely associated with non-conformism and conventicles in south-west Scotland and Ulster in the 1620s and 1630s. Livingstone, along with Robert Blair, minister at Bangor, 1622–34, and other Scottish ministers in the area 'established what was a presbyterian system in all but name'.[17] Livingstone was part of the dissident group of ministers who had crossed back and forward over the North Channel and who had close links with south-west Scotland.[18]

13 Stevenson, *Scottish Covenanters and Irish Confederates*, p. 54.   14 T.C. Smout, N.C. Landsman, and T.M. Devine, 'Scottish emigration in the seventeenth and eighteenth centuries', in N. Canny (ed.), *Europeans on the move: studies on European migration, 1500–1800* (Cambridge, 1994), p. 78.   15 'A brief historical relation of the life of Mr John Livingstone', in W.K. Tweedie, *Select Biographies* (2 volumes, Wodrow Society, 1845–7), 1, p. 166; H. Scott, *Fasti Ecclesiae Scoticanae, volume II. Synods of Merse and Teviotdale, Dumfries and Galloway* (Edinburgh, 1917), p. 356; J. McConnell, *Fasti of the Irish Presbyterian Church* (Belfast, 1936), p. 10.   16 Scott, *Fasti Ecclesiae Scoticanae, volume II*, p. 417.   17 D. Stevenson, 'Conventicles in the Kirk, 1619–1637: the emergence of a Radical party', *Records of the Scottish Church History Society*, 18 (1972–4), 107. Printed in D. Stevenson, *Union, revolution and religion in 17th century Scotland* (Aldershot, 1997).   18 Ibid., 105–11. John Mean, the Edinburgh burgess named on 1 February as one of the collectors of contributions for the presbyteries of Fife, Angus, Aberdeen, Ross and Moray, Lothian, Peebles and Tweeddale, was married to Barbara Hamilton. Their son, John Hamilton, became minister at Anwoth.

It would appear that the total amount of money raised by June 1642 was inadequate to deal with the refugee problem and funds were coming in slowly.[19] By 8 October, the burgh of Glasgow had received just over £1,099 from the Irish contribution for distribution by those appointed for this purpose.[20] Sampling of local church records indicates that refugees were not exclusive to the south-west as they can also be found in records of the north-east, such as the kirk session of Elgin. This would appear to confirm the view of Nicholas Canny that 'impoverished survivors of the insurrection first descended upon the towns of the west of Scotland, but concern soon became country-wide'.[21]

By the time the 1642 General Assembly of the Church of Scotland met at St Andrews on 27 July, the administrative structure for the collection and distribution of aid for refugees had been drawn up. The cases of refugees that were considered by kirk sessions, presbyteries and synods indicate that the General Assembly played an important role in vetting or approving aid to be given to appropriate individuals. The Assembly, as indicated in specific examples that follow throughout this article, appears to have sanctioned recommendations for aid, based on testimonials. Individual refugee cases indicate that this was taking place in the 1642 General Assembly, which met at St Andrews between 27 July and 6 August. The problem of surviving records makes this difficult to say for certain, but the 1642 Assembly approved an 'Act anent delivery of the Irish contribution to the receivers appointed by the Secret Councell'.[22] It also dealt with issues related to the situation in the north of Ireland in 1642 and 1646.[23]

Evidence from Lothian and Tweeddale synod on 3 November 1642 indicates that the policy devised by the Privy Council at a centralized level in Edinburgh was facing difficulties in implementation at the local level. Andrew Kerr, deputy clerk of the 1642 General Assembly, appeared before the synod and presented a letter from Robert Douglas, the current moderator. His letter stated that the Assembly commissioners had received 'divers complaints and regraits' that the Irish contribution was not being sent to the collector in Edinburgh. Accordingly, Douglas's letter reminded the synod of the acts ordaining this contribution and, 'in respect of the poor distressed people of Ireland here', that the synod should require their presbyteries to 'send in the several collections with all

---

One of her sisters married Robert Blair, and John McClellan and John Livingstone married two of her nieces (ibid., 105). **19** Stevenson, *Scottish Covenanters and Irish Confederates*, p. 54. **20** J.D. Marwick (ed.), *Extracts from the records of the Burgh of Glasgow, 1630–62* (Glasgow, 1881), p. 51. **21** Canny, *Making Ireland British*, p. 561. **22** A. Peterkin (ed.), *Records of the Kirk of Scotland, containing the acts and proceedings of the General Assemblies, from the year 1638 downwards, as authenticated by the Clerks of the General Assembly with notes and historical illustrations* (Edinburgh, 1838), 1, p. 333. **23** Ibid., pp 331–2, 354, 360–1, 431–4, 452–454, 480–3, 517–20, 555–9; *Acts of the General Assembly of the Church of Scotland, 1638–1842* (Edinburgh, 1843), pp 69–71, 74–5, 87, 97–8.

diligence'.[24] Almost seven weeks earlier, on 15 September 1642, the presbytery of Kirkcaldy had received correspondence from Robert Douglas. As well as informing the presbytery that those who were members of 'the committee appoyntit be the Generall Assemblie' (those appointed to the 1642 commission of the kirk) were to be present in Edinburgh on 21 September, the letter also 'desyred that a contributioun for Irland may be expede'. Yet the presbytery had decided at an earlier meeting at Dysart on 13 July that there should be a collection for 'the distressed people of Irland' and at its next meeting on 10 August it did consider the case of one 'Mistress Stewart come from Irland' who was to 'get some support'.[25]

The structure and procedure for recommendations and testimonials relating to the provision of aid can be discerned from details relating to refugees as they are described in sample surviving records. On 10 September 1643, for example, Elgin kirk session dealt with the cases of Elizabeth Cuming, spouse of Robert Smith, both of whom were described as 'distressed Irishes'. Elizabeth had a testimonial direct from 'the Commitie and Generall Assembly to the Sinod in Murray'. On 6 October the kirk session instructed one Andrew Annand to give money to five 'distressed people come from Ireland that hade testimonialls from the Comity of Estates and Generall Assembly'.[26] Likewise, Kirkcaldy presbytery noted on 17 July 1644 the cases of four refugees who all had recommendations from the General Assembly.[27] In order to secure financial aid from the Irish contributions, it would therefore appear that testimonials were required from the General Assembly and the committee of estates. Examination of individual cases also indicates that refugees could be entitled to aid on a national basis, with the General Assembly issuing a general recommendation to all the presbyteries in the kingdom for a charitable supply to be provided.

CHURCH RECORDS AND THE 'VOICES' OF THE REFUGEES

Sampling of local case studies provides a useful insight into the operation of charitable aid for refugees. Church records contain details of refugees, although some cases are more detailed than others. Consideration of refugees in this article is drawn primarily from the Elgin kirk session in the north-east of Scotland, Kirkcaldy presbytery in Fife, the presbytery of Lanark in Lanarkshire and Lothian and Tweeddale synod in the Edinburgh-Borders area. Evidence from other areas and sources is included where appropriate information has been found.

24 J. Kirk (ed.), *The records of the Synod of Lothian and Tweeddale, 1589–1596, 1640–1649* (Edinburgh, 1977), p. 136.   25 W. Stevenson (ed.), *The Presbytrie Booke of Kirkcaldie being the record of the proceedings of that Presbytery from the 15th day of April 1630 to the 14th day of September 1653* (Kirkcaldy, 1900), pp 236, 240.   26 S. Ree (ed.), *The records of Elgin 1234–1800* (2 vols, Aberdeen, 1908), 2, pp 245–6.   27 *The Presbytrie Booke of Kirkcaldie*, p. 272.

Lothian and Tweeddale synod met in Edinburgh during the first four days of November 1641. At its first meeting, Archibald Johnston of Wariston, clerk to the General Assembly and one of the leading covenanters, appeared with instructions from Charles I, parliament and commissioners of the kirk attending parliament. The assembly was asked to elect brethren to assist these commissioners to 'think upon the causes, time and advertisement of a ffast, craved of his majestie for the rebellion in Ireland'. In addition, the nominees were to assist the church commissioners attending parliament for the duration of the sitting. Twelve ministers and three ruling elders were accordingly chosen by the synod meeting for this task.[28] The first case of a refugee from Ireland was considered by the synod on 4 November. A petition was given in by the unnamed widow of one John Trewman on behalf of herself and her children. It was 'credibly reported' that Trewman had been 'cruelly put to death for avowing of the Scots covenant': interestingly, this implies he had been killed before the outbreak of the rebellion. 'Having at length seen and considered' this petition, the synod recommended the case to the consideration of the presbyteries for a 'charitable and tymous contribution' to help support the fatherless family.[29] The last piece of business undertaken by the synod on 4 November was to set out the details for a 'ffast for the troubles of Ireland'.[30] The Trewman example may highlight two issues: the potential for manipulation of stories of persecution in Ireland, and a problem with the correct recording of the names of refugees. Lassade parish in Fife allocated money to 'a minister's wife from Ireland, who had her husband cruelly execute by the rebels'. Trewman was 'martyred and quartered by the deputie in Ireland ... for our Scottis cause'.[31] His case was thus seemingly being conflated with the outbreak of the rebellion: presumably to gain extra sympathy. The kirk session of 'Tyninghame' dealt with the case of the widow of one James Freeman on 5 December 1641. A collection was to be made for 'ane pure honest woman', spouse to James Freeman who had been 'slain in Ireland and quartered, as is allegit, for maintaining the Scottis Covenant'.[32] The information contained in both testaments is remarkably similar and there is a close chronological link. John Trewman and James Freeman may well have been the same person.

---

[28] *The records of the Synod of Lothian and Tweeddale*, p. 117. Wariston had played an active role in the drafting of the 1638 National Covenant. He was appointed procurator for the kirk in November 1638 and was one of the commissioners at the Pacification of Berwick on 18 June 1639. He was knighted by Charles I on 15 Nov. 1641 as part of the king's policy of attempting to pacify the covenanters. As the 1640s progressed, he had a high profile role in the movement and was closely associated with Archibald Campbell, eighth earl and first marquis of Argyll. See M. Young (ed.), *The parliaments of Scotland. Burgh and Shire Commissioners* (2 vols, Edinburgh, 1992–3), 1, pp 381–2.   [29] *The records of the Synod of Lothian and Tweeddale*, p. 121.   [30] Ibid., p. 123.   [31] Cited in J.K. Hewison, *The Covenanters* (2 vols, Glasgow, 1913), 1, p. 364.   [32] Cited in ibid., p. 494.

Elgin kirk session first noted the Irish situation on Sunday 28 November 1641 when it intimated that a fast was to be held on the following Sunday (5 December) for 'the troubles of Irland'.[33] John Spalding noted that a fast was also held in Aberdeen on Sunday 12 December 'for the trubles in Ireland betuixt the papistis and protestanes'.[34] Two-and-a-half months later, on Sunday 27 February 1642, William Strachan, minister at Old Machar parish, Aberdeen, preached to the people there 'showing the estait of our protestantis in Ireland and how thay, thair wyves and barnes [bairns], wes miserablie baneshit, and forsit to flie into the wast [west] pairtis of Scotland for refuge, and the land not able to sustene thame'. Accordingly, it was 'found expedient' that each parish in the kingdom was to receive a collection of 'ilk manis charetie' (each man's charity) for the help and support of these people. Spalding noted that eighty pounds was collected in Old Machar parish.[35] The information conveyed by William Strachan has a close similarity to that contained in the Privy Council records for 1 February 1642. Moreover, the information provided by John Spalding indicates that the financial structure devised by the Privy Council for the collection of money via the parishes was indeed being implemented in an efficient manner in Old Machar parish. In Elgin, however, on the same date (Sunday 27 February 1642) the kirk session noted that 'the contribution for the distressed that cam out of Irland was intimat to be gathered', indicating that a collection had not yet being made in the parish.[36]

On 13 December 1641, Dunoon presbytery had appealed to the Privy Council, via a supplication, that it could be 'relieved from the support of the great numbers of poor from Ireland who have settled in their bounds'.[37] The moderator and brethren of the presbytery pleaded that they were 'ower chargit with a great multiude of poore people quha are laitlie cum from the keingdome of Ireland'. These people were concentrated in two parishes of the presbytery, especially the Isle of Bute. John Kennedy and Robert Gordon, collectors in Ayr, were ordered to pay out 1,000 merks for the relief of these poor people, but Robert Gordon had declared that the contributions from his own district had not been received and that 'theis parts ar owerlaid with the poore of Ireland already, sua that thair can be no hoip for any supplie from them'. As per December 1641, over 500 poor people from Ireland were estimated to be on Bute and 'a great many more have since come'. As no help could be expected from Ayr, the Council ordered that the supplication be recommended to the collectors appointed for giving out contributions for the supply of those poor people who had come from Ireland.[38] The Council received a further

---

33 *The records of Elgin*, 2, p. 241.   34 Spalding, *Memorialls*, 2, p. 88.   35 Ibid., pp 107–8.
36 *The records of Elgin*, 2, p. 242.   37 *The register of the Privy Council of Scotland*, 7, 1638–43, p. 500.   38 Ibid., pp 500–1. See also, Stevenson, *Scottish Covenanters and Irish Confederates*, p. 53.

supplication from Dunoon presbytery on 13 April 1642. This supplication was specifically concerned with 'ministers who have been driven from Ireland by the rebellion', their families and 'others persons of good qualitie, quho, although they had good means in Irland, yit now are in equall condition with the poorest, having brocht nothing with them, either cloaths or moneys, that could helpe or sustain them bot a verie few dayes'. The ministers of the Isle of Bute were 'daylie ane eye witness of there distressed condition'. In common with the decision of 13 December 1641, John Kennedy and Robert Gordon, the Ayr collectors, were instructed to forward 1000 merks for the relief of those who had fled from Ireland.[39]

Argyll synod, held at Inverary in the heartland of the territory of Archibald Campbell, eighth earl and first marquis of Argyll, dealt with refugees in 1643 and 1644. The synod meeting of 7 October 1643 allocated 50 pounds to John Allan, provost of Dungannon. Later, on 2 May 1644, Argyll synod stated that the sum of 20 pounds was to be paid to James Campbell, 'now indwelling in Dunoone with four motherless children'. Campbell was identified as 'one of the number of these who escaped for safetie of their lyves from the rebells'. Duncan Campbell, described as being 'on of the same conditionne', was to receive a payment of 16 pounds. Both sums of money were to come out of the contribution 'which is collected for the supplie of the distressed people fled out of Ireland'.[40]

Lothian and Tweeddale synod dealt with refugees between 4 and 8 November 1644.[41] The majority of these cases were concentrated in 1644 and different categories of refugees can be identified. Refugees in Lothian and Tweeddale synod were predominantly widows and daughters. More specifically, they were widows of ministers, widows of soldiers killed in military action, widows whose husbands had been killed by the Irish rebels, and daughters of ministers. Often these widows had a large number of dependents. In addition, ministers represented a distinct male category of refugee. Refugees' supplication for charitable aid often told tales of murder, mutilation, loss of goods and property and robbery. These categories of refugees in Lothian and Tweeddale are also discernible in Elgin, Kirkcaldy and Lanark.

Refugees were often returning migrants coming back to Scotland in the aftermath of the 1641 Ulster Rebellion. The widows of ministers formed part of this group. For example, on 15 February 1643, Kirkcaldy presbytery authorized its 'support' for Agnes Stewart, widow of one John Malcolm, a minister who 'was killed in Irland'. No further details about her circumstances were

---

39 *The register of the Privy Council of Scotland*, 7, 1638–43, pp 546–7.   40 D.C. Mactavish (ed.), *Minutes of the Synod of Argyll, 1639–1651* (Scottish History Society, third series, 37, Edinburgh, 1943), pp 82, 90.   41 *The records of the Synod of Lothian and Tweeddale*, pp 116–302.

given and at the next meeting of the presbytery one week later on 22 February the brethern 'supported' Agnes Stewart according to their 'promeise'. This suggests that she received aid, although no exact details are given. At the same meeting, Frederick Carmichael, minister, presented a 'note' (receipt) of three hundred merks received by John Milne, receiver of the Irish contribution, from Carmichael.[42] This does suggest that financial contributions from Kirkcaldy presbytery were indeed being forwarded to the appropriate receiver at the central level by the early months of 1643.

The supplication of Anna Stewart was heard by Lothian and Tweeddale synod on 8 November 1643. Anna was the wife of one Mr John Mader, minister at 'Donochmoir in Ireland'. The synod was informed that her husband was 'most treatcherouslie drawne furth of his bed from hir and murthrered'. Her six children had been 'scattered abroad', she herself had been taken captive and 'keiped a long space'. In addition, her husband's books had been burned and their money taken away. After 'hir delyverance' she had 'come to this hir native cuntrey'. She presented herself, her six children and 'their afflictiones' to 'the compassionat kirk of this kingdome' as 'the trew object of commizeration'. She begged that 'some cure be given to swettine these waters of her afflictioun that schee and hirs drink not to their bodilie destructioun': the synod instructed all its presbyteries to provide help 'with all diligence'.[43]

Christiane Grahame was another returning Scottish migrant whose supplication was also considered by Lothian and Tweeddale synod on 8 November 1643. She was the widow of Mr John Murray, 'minister of Gods word at Ochir in Ireland'. She had 11 children and her husband and eldest son were 'killed by the enemie'. Their estate was taken away from them and 'schee with her ellevin children, ten boyes and ane girdle chyld' were 'stript very naked'. By God's providence she had escaped to 'this her native countery for succour and releiff'. She entreated the assembly to give her and her fatherless children 'ane recommendatioun to all churches and presbyteries wher they sall happin to com that schee and hir children maybe relieved'. Her supplication further stated that this would be a great work of charity 'whilk God almightie will not let be unrecompensed'. After consideration and approval, her case was recommended to the presbyteries in the synod.[44] The daughters of ministers also appear in the records. On 17 February 1643, Elgin kirk session approved the payment of two dollars to one Marjory Hay, whose father had been killed in Ireland.[45] Other female relations of ministers can be identified. The supplication of Barbara and Grissel Stewart was considered by Lothian and

---

42 *The Presbytrie Booke of Kirkcaldie*, pp 247–8.   43 *The records of the Synod of Lothian and Tweeddale*, 149. See also p. 159, this volume.   44 Ibid., p. 150. This was probably Augher in County Tyrone. I am grateful to Dr William Kelly of the Institute of Ulster-Scots Studies at the University of Ulster for this piece of information.   45 *The records of Elgin*, 2, p. 244.

Tweeddale synod on 3 May 1643. Through the 'common calamity of Gods people in Ireland', they had sustained 'great loss both of their children and of their goods'. This suggests that both women had children, but no mention is made of the fate of their husbands. Both women had been reduced to 'such extremity' that they were forced to 'have recourse to the charity of compassionate Christians' for the maintenance of themselves and their children. They had 'clear evidence of the reality of their miseries', witnessed by a testimonial, and they also noted their 'near relation' to an uncle, Mr Robert Bog (described as a 'reverand servant of God to this kirk'), and to Mr Harie Bog, their kinsman. The Stewarts' supplication was read and verified and they were recommended for a charitable contribution. Additional details provided in the synod records for 30 April 1644 indicate that Barbara and Grissel Stewart were sisters of Mr Robert Rollock, minister at Edinburgh.[46]

In Carnock parish in Fife, the kirk session meeting of 3 September 1644 considered the harrowing case of Geils Donaldson, widow of James Hamilton 'a minister in Irland'. Her husband was 'pitifullie murderit and cuttit in pieces be the Erische rebellis'. Geils had 'two bairnes brunt quick', she herself was 'borne out of the house quhen it wes burning' and she had to 'baire hir bairne in the feildis, being naked, and had no clothes to cover hir with'. Furthermore, she, 'knowing of the deathe of hir husband and children, became distracted in hir wittes'. This particular case was documented by John Row, the minister of Carnock. Geils Donaldson had come personally to Row with letters from his son, John Row, minister at Aberdeen, and the high-profile covenanting minister Robert Blair of St Andrews. Blair also 'intertened ane of her living bairnes', due to the fact that he was 'acquentit with the bairnes father and mother'. Thus personal contact and knowledge, in this case Blair's knowledge of and acquaintance with Geils Donaldson and James Hamilton, could result in the provision of aid. In this instance Carnock kirk session gave Geils Donaldson a payment of 30 shillings.[47]

Ministers who had been ousted from their parishes formed an important category of refugee. On 3 May 1642, for example, Lothian and Tweeddale synod considered the supplication of Mr Thomas Hogg, minister at Dungannon in Co. Tyrone for the previous ten years. He had 'lived in a good and plentiful

---

46 *The records of the Synod of Lothian and Tweeddale*, pp 144, 153. The Robert Rollock in question may have been Robert Rollock (1555–99), a prominent Edinburgh minister in the 1580s and 1590s. His Edinburgh parishes included Greyfriars and St Giles. He was principal of the college of Edinburgh, 1587–9, and moderator of the General Assembly in 1597. Both Barbara and Grissel Stewart would appear to have been elderly women, if the 1642 reference to Robert Rollock applied to the man who died in 1599. See H. Scott, *Fasti Ecclesiae Scoticane. Volume I. Synod of Lothian and Tweeddale* (Edinburgh, 1915), p. 37.   47 J. Row, *The history of the Kirk of Scotland, 1558–1637*, ed. D. Laing (Edinburgh, 1842), p. xxviii. The Kirk Session entry is for 8 September 1644, but the case details refer to 3 September.

condition even till the lamentable rebellion in Ireland' when he was 'spoiled' of over 200 pounds English money 'ever since for the space of eleven monaths'. He and his wife, two children, two younger brothers and a maid servant had since lived in the castle of 'Mincha' by 'the goodness of God and sheriff of the county'. At Mincha he was kept and defended by the sheriff, but they and over 400 people 'have lived in great misery and preserved hithertill from the bloody sword of the merciless rebels'. Within the previous month, Sir Robert Stewart of Kilmoir had been passing the castle with an army and Hogg had escaped 'to the Darie' [Derry] from where he fled to Scotland. Hogg was seeking more than mere charitable aid: 'if God shall offer the occasion' he wanted 'any place for exercising of his calling in the ministry whereby he and his family may live without being chargeable'.[48] The supplication proceeded to state that Hogg was 'of the intention presently to return to Ireland to use all means possible for the safe transporting of his wife and children which he cannot conveniently do unless he had some means to maintain them'. Hogg entreated that some means could be found by the synod for the 'charitable supply for maintaining and supporting them'. His supplication clearly stated that Hogg thought 'himself bound in conscience rather to live in Ireland for the comfort of that distressed people there'. Moreover, he asked if he could be recommended to the brethern in 'Clandiboues' that 'some place may be provided for him' where he could serve 'in less danger'. The ministers of Edinburgh were instructed to take note of his supplication, to ensure that he subscribed the National Covenant, and were thereafter to assist him for obtaining support out of 'the general contribution for Ireland'.[49]

A supplication from a Mr James Mirke was heard by Lothian and Tweeddale synod on 2 November 1642. Mirke had lived in Ireland as 'an actual minister in very good account and estimation of the very best' for a period of seven years before 'the common calamity moved be the Irish rebells'. The rebels had 'spoiled' him of the value of almost 8,000 merks ($c.£5,333$ Scots) worth of goods. His life 'by Gods providence being miraculously preserved', he was now unable to maintain himself and his family 'until it shall please God to oppen a door for him for the use of his talent' and he 'humbly desired' the assembly to 'take to consideration and find out a way for his present supply and of any occasion now vacant' within the province. His supplication was heard at length and considered: no vacancy appears to have been forthcoming but he was recommended to receive charity from the presbyteries.[50]

The supplication of a Mr Robert Colden was heard on 8 November 1643. His parish was not identified, although his supplication stated that 'by Gods

---

48 *The records of the Synod of Lothian and Tweeddale*, p. 130. On Stewart, see Stevenson, *Scottish Covenanters and Irish Confederates*, pp 51–2, 98; D. Stevenson, *Highland warrior. Alasdair MacColla and the Civil Wars* (Edinburgh, 1994), pp 86–7.   **49** *The records of the Synod of Lothian and Tweeddale*, p. 130.   **50** Ibid., pp 133–4.

providence he is redacted to extream necessitie by the crueltie of the Irish rebelllis and driven fra his holy ministrie he had in that kingdome'. Colden, his wife and children had fled to Scotland. Had the presbyteries of Dunbar and Haddington not 'communicatted to his necessities since he came', he and his family would have 'sterved'. Accordingly, Colden sought 'godlie and charitable support' from the assembly 'in what manner and measour they pleis'. His plight was recommended to the charity of the presbyteries in the synod.[51]

The onset of disease as a result of the Irish rebellion impacted upon one Mr James Bannerman, 'sumtyme minister at Baltimure in Ireland', whose case was considered by Lothian and Tweeddale synod on 8 November 1643. He was robbed of 'his goods and geir' by 'the cruell rebellious Irishes' and 'put fra his chairge ther'. As a result of 'divers diseases' he 'did lose his rycht eye', and as a result of lack of maintenance he was forced to come to Scotland. The assembly was asked to consider his 'distressed, aged, weak and impotent estate' and to grant him help and relief. He was to receive aid from the 'severall presbytreis' within the synod.[52] Later, on 20 December, the presbytery of Kirkcaldy, meeting at Dysart in Fife, heard the case of Mr James Bannerman, 'ane Irish minister'. He was granted limited financial support at the presbytery's next meeting at Kirkcaldy one week later. Bannerman was also receiving support from the presbytery as late as 3 and 17 July 1644.[53] This evidence suggests that Bannerman was in the Lothian and Fife areas in the winter of 1643 and was back in Fife by early July 1644.

The Lothian and Tweeddale synod diet of 8 November 1643 dealt with the case of another minister, Mr Patrick Weddell (Waddell), of Enniskillen, Co. Fermanagh. Waddell's supplication stated that he had been a minister at Enniskillen for 16 years. He was taken by the rebels and 'keiped by them prisoner a long space, robbed of his goods and nothing left him whereupone to live till at lenth he was relived with great hazard of his lyfe'. Waddell's supplication was also approved and he was recommended to the charity of the presbyteries in the synod.[54] Refugee ministers may have been receiving support as late as 1646, although this may have been on an individual basis. One David Colt, 'sometime minister of Ireland,' gave in a petition for 'support' to Kirkcaldy presbytery on 4 November 1646. The presbytery brethren promised to provide him with support and a small amount of money was given to him, provided by various parishes, at the presbytery meetings of 18 and 25 November 1646.[55]

Other male refugees apart from ministers received charitable aid. The supplication of Thomas Fleming was heard by Lothian and Tweeddale synod

---

51 Ibid., p. 148. 52 Ibid., p. 150. 53 *The Presbytrie Booke of Kirkcaldie*, pp 262–3, 272.
54 *The records of the Synod of Lothian and Tweeddale*, p. 151. 55 *The Presbytrie Booke of Kirkcaldie*, p. 305.

on 3 May 1643. Fleming had harboured 'godlie and well affected of the ministry' and 'other godlie Christians' who had been troubled by Thomas Wentworth, first earl of Strafford and Lord Deputy of Ireland. When any of these people came along, 'he did take them into him and convoy their business the best way it pleased God to direct him'. As a result of this he was 'put to daily trouble', he had been imprisoned three times and fined. He was 'forced either to hazard his life or forsake all means to his utter undoing'. The 'Irish rebellion' had exacerbated these problems. The rebellion had 'frustrate him altogether of any recovery', he had an 'aged wife' and both of them were 'infirm of sight'. The supplication was read, considered and 'verefied by famous testimonies' and he was to receive aid from the charitable contribution from the churches within the province.[56] Lothian and Tweeddale synod granted charitable aid to one Alexander Boyd on 3 November 1642 and one 'Doctor Oneil' and his family on 3 May 1643 respectively. Boyd's supplication stated that he had performed 'good service for the kirk of Scotland' by apprehending 'ane Jesuit Anderson, a Jesuit of great respect in the kingdome'. Boyd had 'performed this service' by his own cost and charges and he performed that task 'coming out of Ireland for that same business only'. Now he was subject to the 'common calamity of Gods people there in that kingdome' and was forced to have recourse to 'godlie and well disposed Christians' in Scotland. He requested that he be granted an act 'that he may have way throw the presbyteries' and churches of the province and that he 'receive such releif as they shall bestow'. Boyd's supplication was recommended to the presbyteries.[57] The case of 'Doctor Oneil' attracted particular attention and received high priority. A 'well grounded report of the reverend brethern of the ministry of Edinburgh and certain others' was considered by the assembly, and the 'distressed estate' of Oneil, his wife and family was noted. Oneil had 'fled Ireland for the love of the reformed Protestant religion'. The report noted his 'worthie gifts in the ministrie' and his 'pious life' and the assembly, 'in ane most singular way', recommended the brethern 'in ane honest and fair manner' to contribute a supply for him and his company. The moderators were required to collect and send a supply to the presbytery of Edinburgh in order that it could be delivered to Oneil. Furthermore, they were instructed to 'prefer him to all other persons recommended'.[58]

Soldiers' widows and families also constituted an element of the female refugee population. The supplication of Janet Houston was heard by Lothian and Tweeddale synod on 3 May 1643. She had been born and lived in Ireland all her life until her father, Captain Alexander Houston, had been killed by the Irish rebels at 'Aulra'. Her mother was already deceased and Janet was now in

---

56 *The records of the Synod of Lothian and Tweeddale*, p. 144.   57 Ibid., p. 131.   58 Ibid., p. 144.

charge of seven brothers and sisters. They were all in the town of Ayr and had 'nothing to maintain her nor them with'. The synod recommended that the Houston family be 'timeously helped' out of the charitable contribution of the presbyteries.[59] On 8 November 1643, the same synod dealt with the supplication of 'Phennel McConnell', wife of one Matthew 'Hummiel'. Along with their six children they had lived in Ireland until of late they 'were surpryzed by the rebels'. Their goods had been taken from them and their house burnt. Her mother-in-law and several of their family had been killed. By the providence of God they had come to Scotland for 'some releiff', although her husband had remained in Ireland 'in service against the rebels'. As a result of this they were reduced to 'extream povertie'. In line with other cases, the synod recommended aid from the presbyteries within the synod.[60]

Other widows can be identified in the records. On 25 August 1643, for example, Elgin kirk session granted 40 shillings to 'tuo women who hade young bairnes and come from Irland'.[61] On 10 September 1643, Elgin kirk session awarded one Margaret Sime two dollars. She was described as 'ane uther Scottis Irish gentlewoman who hade tuo or three bairnes' and her unnamed husband had been killed by 'the Irish rebels'.[62] Of specific interest here is the description accorded her by Elgin kirk session. It is notable that she is described as 'ane uther Scottis Irish gentlewoman' because the same kirk session meeting of 10 September dealt with the cases of Elizabeth Cuming, spouse to Robert Smith, 'distressed Irishes' who were awarded four pounds by the session. These descriptions suggest that the ethnic descriptions of 'distressed Irish' and 'Scottis Irish' were being used in an interchangeable manner by Elgin kirk session.[63] Lothian and Tweeddale synod considered the supplication of one Dorothy Kennedy, alias Watson, on 8 November 1643. Her husband, Oliver Kennedy, 'wes killed by the Irische rebels' and she was left with eight children. Her financial resources were exhausted and three of her children were 'deid throw hard usage'. She had been 'sustained' by her friends, but they were now 'overchairged' and therefore she sought 'such measaur of cherritie upon her for maintenance of hir and her fyve children as God shall move their hartes to bestow'. The synod decided that she was to receive aid from the presbyteries 'with all diligence'.[64]

Local records also contain evidence of refugees who do not fall into the categories listed above, primarily due to the lack of detail in the records. Some examples can be given from Elgin kirk session records. The kirk session dealt with cases of refugees with testimonials from the General Assembly and committee of estates on 10 September and 6 October 1643. Two cases were considered on 10 September 1643, namely Elizabeth Cuming and her husband

---

59 Ibid., pp 143–4.   60 Ibid., pp 150–1.   61 *The records of Elgin*, 2, p. 245.   62 Ibid., p. 246.
63 Ibid.   64 *The records of the Synod of Lothian and Tweeddale*, p. 149.

Robert Smith who have been discussed earlier in a different context, but in this respect they were husband and wife refugees.⁶⁵ On 6 October Elgin kirk session dealt with five cases of 'distressed people come from Ireland that hade testimonialls' – Elizabeth Fairlie, Elizabeth Weims, Elspeth Cuming, Margaret Ross and 'ane dumb man caled John Sincklair'. No further details are given apart from the payments they received, but it is noticeable that Elspeth (Elizabeth) Cuming received another, but smaller payment (two merks), and that her husband, Robert Smith, was not mentioned.⁶⁶ After the elders of Elgin kirk session subscribed the Solemn League and Covenant on Sunday 5 November 1643, the session proceeded to grant 12 shillings of the 'Irish money' to William Craighead, 'ane distressed man that come out of Ireland'⁶⁷. On 17 November it also granted twelve shillings to William Dalgardno, 'a poor man that came out of Ireland'. This trend continued in Elgin in the first three months of 1644.⁶⁸ On 9 February the session dealt with four 'distrest people that cam out of Ireland. All shared the same surname suggesting a family link or unit (James Hay, Francie Hay, Margaret Hay and Jean Hay) and all had testimonials.⁶⁹ The case of Margaret Duncan was dealt with on 29 March. She was described as 'ane poore woman who was creple of both hands be the rebells in Ireland'.⁷⁰ At the next diet on 2 April aid was given to 'ane distressed woman … that cam out of Ireland'. Her name was Jonnet (Janet) Forbes and she had 'tuo or thrie bairnes'.⁷¹ On 3 May 'ane Irish woman', Isobel Graham, received aid of five merks.⁷² Carnock kirk session in Fife dealt with the case of one Alexander Drummond and his unnamed wife on 25 August 1644. They were 'spoiled in Irland of all that they had' and were in possession of testimonials. Drummond's wife received 10 shillings from the kirk session.⁷³ In this case it would appear that the wife and not the husband received financial aid.

Evidence from the Elgin kirk session records also provides specific examples of the Irish fund being raided for purposes other than the provision of aid for refugees. There are three examples of this, although this does not necessarily indicate widespread corruption. On 31 January 1643 one dollar was to be paid out of the Irish contribution to an unnamed 'dumb man that was ane ministers son'.⁷⁴ On 16 April 1643, the session authorized the payment of 16 merks 'to be givin out of the contribution for Ireland' to six shipwrecked Englishmen and soldiers.⁷⁵ On 9 January 1644, payment out of the Irish contribution was authorized to be paid to one David Livingstone, 'ane distrest man that cam out of Pol.' (Poland).⁷⁶ Given the vast numbers of Scots who had migrated to Poland by the 1640s and that many of those Scots had their origins in the north-east of Scotland, Livingstone may well have been a returning migrant.⁷⁷ The

65 *The records of Elgin*, 2, pp 245–6.   66 Ibid., p. 246.   67 Ibid., p. 247.   68 Ibid.   69 Ibid., p. 248.   70 Ibid., p. 249.   71 Ibid.   72 Ibid.   73 Row, *History of the Kirk of Scotland*, p. xxvii.   74 *The records of Elgin*, 2, p. 244.   75 Ibid., p. 245.   76 Ibid., p. 248.   77 A. Biegańska, 'A note

total payment given to the seven individuals mentioned above only amounted to 24 merks, but this was more than individual refugees from Ireland could receive in Elgin. Janet Forbes (2 April 1644) only received two merks, despite having two or three children, and Isobel Graham (3 May 1644) only received five merks. Furthermore, at the next diet on 16 January 1644, more money was given out of the Irish contribution to three individuals (Donald Roxburgh received four pounds, Cuthbert Bar two merks and John Wilson eight shillings) and it is not clear if they were 'distressed Irish' or not.[78] There is a possibility that the Irish contribution was being raided to give money to these three men for other purposes.

Evidence exists of refugees receiving charitable aid in different parts of Scotland, although this was probably sanctioned by the General Assembly. Refugees were neither confined to a specific geographic location nor restricted to charitable aid in the form of a single, one-off financial payment. Seven examples of refugees claiming aid in different parts of Scotland can be cited. The first two examples relate to Barbara and Grissel Stewart, discussed earlier in the context of female relations of ministers. Lothian and Tweeddale synod considered their supplications on 3 May 1643 and the two women were recommended for a charitable contribution.[79] On 17 July 1644, their names appear in a list of supplications recommended by the General Assembly that was considered by Kirkcaldy presbytery, and on 31 July they were granted 48 pounds.[80] This was part of a wider scheme of payments to refugees as per the presbytery records for this date. Analysis of these payments reveals a further example of a refugee seeking financial aid in different areas. On 6 May 1644, the Synod of Lothian and Tweeddale considered supplications and referred individual cases to specified presbyteries. Elizabeth Kinross and Jean Lawder were described as widows and their cases were referred to Haddington presbytery. The name of Elizabeth Kinross appears in the records of Kirkcaldy presbytery for 31 July 1644. In these records she was not described as a widow although it was noted that she had five children. She was awarded 24 pounds by Kirkcaldy presbytery.[81]

---

on the Scots in Poland, 1550–1800', in T.C. Smout (ed.), *Scotland and Europe, 1200–1850* (Edinburgh, 1986), pp 157–163; M. Bogucka, 'Scots in Gdansk (Danzig) in the seventeenth century', in A.I. Macinnes, T. Riis and F.G. Pedersen (eds), *Ships, guns and bibles in the North Sea and the Baltic states, c.1350–c.1700* (East Linton, 2000), pp 39–46; T.M. Devine, *Scotland's empire, 1600–1815* (London, 2004), pp 10–13; A.F. Steuart, *Papers relating to the Scots in Poland, 1576–1793* (Edinburgh, 1915). For the most recent research on Scots in Poland, see W. Kowalski, 'The placement of urbanized Scots in the Polish crown during the sixteenth and seventeenth centuries', in A. Grosjean and S. Murdoch (eds), *Scottish communities abroad in the early modern period* (Leiden, 2005), pp 53–103.   **78** *The records of Elgin*, 2, pp 244, 245, 248, 249.   **79** *The records of the Synod of Lothian and Tweeddale*, p. 144.   **80** *The Presbytrie Booke of Kirkcaldie*, pp 272–3.   **81** Ibid., p. 273; *The records of the Synod of Lothian and Tweeddale*, pp 157–8.

Anna Griffith also received aid in different parts of Scotland. Kirkcaldy presbytery, meeting at Dysart in Fife on 21 September 1642, considered the case of 'One Anna Griffith, craveing support'. She had 'ane warrand from the Generall Assemblie to that effect' and her case was 'supported' by the presbytery.[82] On 18 March 1643 she appeared personally before Elgin kirk session. She was described as 'ane distressed Irisch woman' and was the 'sometyme spous' to one Mr William Murray, a minister in Ireland, 'whom the rebels there, as hir testimoniall declared, hade crucified', and was paid a sum of five dollars out of the Irish contribution.[83] Nearly 18 months later, on 7 November 1644, Lothian and Tweeddale synod (meeting in Edinburgh) considered a supplication given by Anna Griffith. These more detailed records described Griffith as a 'relict' (widow) of a Mr Thomas Murray (not William as per the Elgin record), the minister of Killyleagh in Ireland. According to Griffith, Murray was 'cruellie murderit and hanged on a trie betuix tuo uther gentlemen by the cruell rebellis in Ireland and hir tuo sonnes cutt in pieces before hir eyes and her awne body maimed and woundit, the marks whereof ar yet to be sein as hir famous testimonialls doth testifie.'[84] Largo kirk session in Fife gave four pounds to 'the wife of one Mr Thomas Murray, a minister in Ireland, who, she said, was crucified for the religion'.[85] This suggests that Thomas was the more accurate Christian name. The records of Lothian and Tweeddale synod indicate that the Griffith case can be traced back to the 1642 General Assembly. The synod understood that the 1642 assembly granted Griffith 'ane generall recommendatioun to the hail presbytreis of this kingdome for their charitable supplie'.[86] This perhaps indicates that the Assembly could order aid to be given to specified refugees on a national basis. Indeed, the *Fasti of the Irish Presbyterian Church* indicates that Anna Griffith, the widow of Thomas Murray, minister of Killyleagh, petitioned the Assembly for assistance in 1642. The language and content of the extract from her petition as printed in the *Fasti* is slightly different from that printed in the Elgin records, stating that:

> her husband was most cruelly crucified on a tree, by the most unchristian rebels with two other gentlemen hanged with him, the one on the right hand, the other on the left; her two sons killed and cut to pieces before her eyes; her own body frightfully cut and maimed in sundry parts; and that she was kept in prison and inhumanly used by the rebels, from whom at last by God's merciful providence she escaped.[87]

---

82 *The Presbytrie Booke of Kirkcaldie*, p. 240.   83 *The records of Elgin*, 2, p. 245.   84 *The records of the Synod of Lothian and Tweeddale*, pp 166–7.   85 Quoted in Hewison, *The Covenanters*, 1, p. 364. This is Largo in Fife and not Largs in Ayrshire. McConnell incorrectly cites Largs. See *Fasti of the Irish Presbyterian Church*, p. 11.   86 *The records of the Synod of Lothian and Tweeddale*, p. 167.   87 McConnell, *Fasti of the Irish Presbyterian*

On 7 November 1644 Lothian and Tweeddale synod further noted with regard to Anna Griffith's case that 'manie of the presbytreis within this province hes at yet collectit nothing for the supplicant'. The synod therefore recommended her case to the 'charitie' of all those presbyteries in the synod who were deficient in payment. Furthermore, due to the lack of payment Anna Griffith was 'not able to travell this winter season' and moderators of presbyteries were to send in their contributions to the synod's clerk, James Murray.[88]

The 7 November diet of Lothian and Tweeddale synod also considered the supplications of other 'distressed persons' from Ireland. Individual cases were thereafter referred to the charity of specific presbyteries. Four of the five supplicants considered were described as 'gentlemen' (John Thomson, Robert Houston, David Nairn and James Penycook [Penicuik]), and the other was Susanna Forbes, the daughter of a minister named Mr William Forbes. Forbes and Thomson were to receive charity from all presbyteries in the synod, whereas Nairn was to receive charity from the presbyteries of Peebles and Biggar, Houston from the presbyteries of Linlithgow, Peebles and Biggar and Penicuik was to receive charity from all the synod's presbyteries except those of Edinburgh, Dalkeith and the church of Dunbar.[89] Robert Houston appears in the records of Lanark presbytery on 22 May 1645, another example of a refugee seeking aid in different parts of the country. Houston presented 'ane recommendation from the General Assemblie, to the severall presbyteries, for some charitable supplie to his present necessities'.[90] This appears to confirm the procedure suggested by the Griffith case, whereby the General Assembly acted as a centralizing agency for providing recommendations for presbyteries to provide charity for refugees. Houston's recommendation stated that he had been 'spoiled and robbed in Ireland, by the cruell and mercilesse Irishes'.[91] Roughly 18 months later, on 6 November 1646, Lothian and Tweeddale synod recommended Houston's supplication to the presbyteries of Haddington, Dunbar, Peebles and Biggar. Houston was described as 'lately come from Irland and wracked by the rebells ther'. The synod had already recommended his case to the presbyteries of Linlithgow, Peebles and Biggar on 7 November 1644. Now in 1646 two additional presbyteries were expected to contribute.[92]

David Nairn also received aid in more than one area of Scotland. At Lothian and Tweeddale synod on 7 November 1644, no specific details were given,

---

Church, p. 11. **88** *The records of the Synod of Lothian and Tweeddale*, p. 167. **89** Ibid. **90** J. Robertson (ed.), *Ecclesiastical records. Selections from the registers of the Presbytery of Lanark, 1623–1809* (Edinburgh, 1839), p. 43. **91** Ibid. **92** *The records of the Synod of Lothian and Tweeddale*, pp 167, 211–12. The printed extracts on p. 211 are listed under 'Edinburgh 30 *Augusti* 1644 *ante meridiem*', but they appear chronologically in the synod records for Nov. 1646 and the printed records thereafter state that the next synod was to meet in Nov. 1647 (although the first date of meeting was on 26 May 1647). Thus, I have taken the date of the synod's consideration of Houston's supplication to have been 6 Nov. 1646.

although he was to receive charity from the presbyteries of Peebles and Biggar.[93] Several months earlier on 31 July 1644, however, Kirkcaldy presbytery had authorized the payment of 50 merks to David Nairn as part of a wider scheme of payment to specified individuals.[94] One of the individuals listed in the Kirkcaldy records on 31 July 1644 was Christian Balfour who was to receive 20 pounds.[95] Evidence from various records indicates that she was a proactive refugee who received aid in different parts of Scotland. Christian Sharp or Balfour was the widow of a minister at Drumbo in Ireland, Mr Peter Sharp. A supplication from her was considered by Lothian and Tweeddale synod on 8 November 1643 and by Lanark presbytery on 29 May 1645. The Lanark records indicate that she presented a recommendation from the General Assembly. According to her account in the Lanark records, her husband had died in prison, 'under the persecution of the Bishope', and she herself had been 'spoiled by the cruell enemies.'[96] Lothian and Tweeddale records indicate that her husband had been cited to Dublin for censure by the bishops but had died before appearing. She had been pursued 'so hard' by the rebels that 'of all her estate they left hir nothing quhairby schee was necessitat to come to her native cuntrey'.[97] She was receiving aid as late as 12 November 1645, when one Mr John Chalmer, a minister in Kirkcaldy presbytery, provided 24 shillings at the presbytery meeting for 'the releif of Cristian Balfour a ministers wyff'.[98]

As well as charting cases as they appeared in the records on an individual basis, evidence also exists of cases being dealt with and/or payments being made to several individuals at specific meetings. This is what happened at the meetings of Lothian and Tweeddale synod on 6 May 1644 and Kirkcaldy presbytery on 31 July 1644. Nine cases were referred to the presbyteries within Lothian and Tweeddale synod on 6 May 1644. Six of these eight cases were widows, two of whom were widows of ministers.[99] More detailed financial data is given in the Kirkcaldy records of 31 July 1644. At the presbytery meeting of that date, it was noted that ten parishes had contributed a total of £133 and 58 merks.[1] Ten individuals were listed with the amount of money that they were to receive. Five of these (Barbara and Grissel Stewart, Elizabeth Kinross, David Nairn, and Christian Balfour) have been discussed already in the context of refugees seeking and/or receiving aid in different parts of the country. The two Stewart women received the largest payment, 48 pounds.[2]

By the late 1640s it would appear that abuse of the system taking place, with individuals travelling to different parts of Scotland claiming financial aid on the basis that they were refugees from Ireland. This problem was noted at the

93 Ibid., p. 167.   94 *The Presbytrie Booke of Kirkcaldie*, p. 273.   95 Ibid.   96 *Selections from the registers of the Presbytery of Lanark*, p. 43.   97 *The records of the Synod of Lothian and Tweeddale*, p. 150.   98 *The Presbytrie Booke of Kirkcaldie*, p. 291.   99 *The records of the Synod of Lothian and Tweeddale*, p. 158.   1 *The Presbytrie Booke of Kirkcaldie*, p. 273.   2 Ibid.

meeting of Lothian and Tweeddale synod which in 1649 established a committee to consider how the parliamentary act anent the poor of 28 February should be implemented (this was part of the drive to create a purified godly society by the radical covenanting regime of 1649).[3] This committee reported its findings back to the synod on 7 November. The sixth item of the report noted that the provision for the poor was 'exceidinglie exhaustit by contributions to strangeris who travel from place to place under pretence they were harried in Ireland or in some distresit pairtis of this kingdome'. It was therefore recommended that 'sufficient testimonialls' be provided by the moderator or clerk register of the presbytery from whence such strangers had travelled which bore witness to the sufferings those strangers had experienced. These testimonials were to be presented directly to the minister and elders of the areas to which these 'strangers' had travelled. The testimonials were required to be dated from the point of travel in order that 'it may be knowne how long they linger' by the date of 7 May. It was noted that 'some pretend to com from Ireland to ther freindis in Scotland and under pretence theroff have gottin larg recommendations from the preceiding generall assemblies wherby a great deale of collections is given to the prejudice of the puir of every paroch'.[4] In essence, fraudulent behaviour had taken place and it was the native poor who had suffered due to the raiding of the poor fund. The committee therefore recommended that it should be represented to the next General Assembly that none be recommended by the assembly or synods except where people were returning to the parish of their birth where they would 'abyd either labouring for ther living or manteined as ther puir'. This was in line with the ethos of Scottish poor law legislation which stated that the provision of poor relief was based on the locality in the form of the parish unit and that each parish looked after its own poor. Returning migrants from Ireland (warfare in 1649–50 had resulted in a new wave of refugees coming to Scotland in light of the royalist triumph in Ulster) were to be incorporated within this structure.[5]

---

[3] *The records of the Synod of Lothian and Tweeddale*, pp 291–2. For the wider dimension of the drive for a godly society, see John R. Young, 'Scottish Covenanting radicalism, the Commission of the Kirk and the establishment of the parliamentary radical regime of 1648–9', *Records of the Scottish Church History Society*, 25 (1995), 342–375 and idem, 'The Covenanters and the Scottish Parliament, 1639–51. The rule of the godly and the second Scottish Reformation', in E.A. Boran and C. Gribben (eds), *Enforcing Reformation. Ireland and Scotland, 1560–1690* (Aldershot, 2006), pp 131–58.   [4] *The records of the Synod of Lothian and Tweeddale*, p. 292.   [5] Ibid. See Stevenson, *Scottish Covenanters and Irish Confederates*, pp 280–3.

CONCLUSION

The presence of refugees from the 1641 Ulster Rebellion in Scotland remains a relatively unexplored area of investigation in the historiography of both the Covenanting movement and the relationship between Scotland and Ireland during the early modern period. This theme needs to be placed within the British context of war widows, refugees, and victims of warfare during the wars for the three kingdoms and within the wider European context of the Thirty Years War. The covenanters set up an administrative structure for the provision of charitable aid for refugees, although this was not without problems in terms of policy implementation. Systematic analysis of surviving records on a national basis and the examination of surviving financial accounts is required in order to provide an authoritative picture of the refugee problem, but important trends and categories of refugees have been identified here. In terms of the human experience of the settler community in Ulster of the 1641 Rebellion, the church records of Scotland also bring to life the tales and tribulations of those who fled Ireland shocked, bereaved, despairing, and impoverished.

The Drogheda massacre in Cromwellian context[1]

JOHN MORRILL

Surprisingly enough, Oliver Cromwell was capable of understatement. This is how he demanded the surrender of one of places he besieged:

> I summon you to deliver into my hands the House wherein you are, and your ammunition, with all things else there, together with your persons, to be disposed of as Parliament shall appoint, which if you refuse to do, you are to expect the utmost extremity of war.[2]

When the Governor failed to take the hint, he became less euphemistic: 'if God give you into my hands, I will not spare a man of you, if you put me to a storm.'[3]

This is not Cromwell writing to the Irish Governor of an Irish town. It is Cromwell writing to the English Governor of an English town. And this is not 1649 but the spring of 1645, in the dog days between Cromwell's resignation as Lieutenant General of the Army of the Eastern Association and before his commissioning into the New Model. He was working out his notice and besieging Faringdon, a market town on the main road from Oxford to Swindon and Bristol. Lieutenant Colonel Burges, commander of the garrison, called his bluff and Cromwell, lacking artillery to open up a breach, stormed the walls but was driven back with 14 casualties. He was then recalled and could not make a second attempt. So we do not know whether Cromwell was bluffing or whether he intended to anticipate the Drogheda Massacre in England.

The English phase of the War of the Three Kingdoms is usually seen as remarkable for the restraint of all participants. Killings in cold blood are almost unheard of; killings of civilians in hot blood rare and limited. There is no evidence of prisoners being killed at the end of battles. Officers were exchanged – John

---

1 I am grateful to Jason McElligott, Micheál Ó Siochrú, Rory Rapple, David Smith, and the editors of this book for their perceptive comments on drafts of this article. 2 S.C. Lomas (ed.), *The letters and speeches of Oliver Cromwell with elucidations by Thomas Carlyle* [henceforth L&S] (3 vols, London, 1904), 1, p. 195. 3 Ibid.

Lilburne was the beneficiary of one such exchange arranged by Cromwell himself[4] – or ransomed in the traditional way, or were released on a pledge not to return to fighting.[5] Rank-and-file soldiers were either disarmed and sent home or were offered an opportunity to change sides. So great was the royalist take up of the offer of positions in the New Model that when at the Putney Debates it was proposed to enfranchise every soldier who had served Parliament in the 'late wars', the offer was restricted to those who had served before 'Naseby fight'.[6] A vast majority of the sieges in the English sector were settled by negotiation and surrender, and on such occasions both sides always extended a guarantee of security of personal safety and always honoured terms made. When towns were stormed, there could be loss of life, and civilians killed in the cross-fire; and stormed towns could be plundered. But Rupert's sack of Bolton and Leicester were notorious because they were so unrepresentative, and even there it was plunder, not rape and murder, that his men were intent on.[7]

It is clear, however, that there was a hardening of attitudes over time. When Fairfax took the surrender of Colchester in early September 1648, he granted 'fair quarter' to all civilians and to the rank and file, but insisted that the 300 officers surrender on 'mercy'.[8] Tellingly, the garrison asked for definitions and were told by Fairfax that 'fair quarter' meant 'to be free from wounding and beating and to be provided with adequate clothing and food while in custody', while 'mercy' meant that they had to surrender their lives into his hands and that he would decide their fate. In the event, he put three leaders on trial before a military tribunal and had two of them shot.[9] So the principle of executing those held culpable for delaying a surrender and causing loss of life preceded Cromwell's arrival in Ireland.

---

4 M. Gibb, *John Lilburne the Leveller* (London, 1949), pp 91–3.   5 See especially the important sequence of articles by Barbara Donagan: 'Atrocity, war crime and treason in the English Civil War', *American Historical Review*, 99:4 (1994), 1137–66; 'Codes and conduct in the English Civil War', *Past and Present*, 118 (1988), 65–95; and 'The web of honour: soldiers, Christians and gentlemen in the English Civil War', *Historical Journal*, 44:2 (2001), 465–89.   6 C.H. Firth (ed.), *The Clarke Papers* (4 vols, Camden Society, 1891–7), 1, pp 365–7.   7 The best account of Rupert's sack of Bolton is G. Pendlebury, *Aspects of the English Civil War in Bolton and its neighbourhood* (Bolton, 1983), pp 9–17; and for the sack of Leicester, see J.E.O. Wilshere and S. Green, *The siege of Leicester, 1645* (Leicester, 1970). All the general military histories, from Gardiner onwards, describe these as atypical examples of plunder; but all accounts are surprisingly vague on the number of people killed.   8 See the discussion in Edward Hyde, earl of Clarendon, *History of the Great Rebellion* (6 vols in 3 parts, 1839), 6, p. 250. For the clearly understood distinctions between surrender on quarter and on mercy, see Donagan, 'Atrocity, war crime and treason in the English Civil War', 1150–2.   9 A. Kingston, *East Anglia and the Great Civil War* (London, 1902), pp 281–3; and see the discussion in J. Burke, 'The New Model Army and the problems of siege warfare', *IHS*, 27 (1990), 6–8; Firth, *The Clarke Papers* 2, pp xi–xiv.

II

The nearest thing to a Drogheda-in-England in the First Civil War was Cromwell's sack of Basing House in October 1645.[10] Basing House was a vast medieval house upgraded by successive marquises of Winchester on the spoils of office – 380 rooms were added during the reign of Henry VIII alone. The defensive earthwork enclosed an area of more than 14 acres, and the Old and New Houses were protected by walls eight feet thick with regular towers. Three times in 1643–4 Sir William Waller had stormed it and been driven back. In 1645 Cromwell spent many weeks trying to starve out the garrison of 300–400 men, only for a relief column to break through with several weeks' supplies. Cromwell believed that not only the marquis but most of the defenders were Papists. It took six weeks of the play of cannon on those massive earthworks for a breach wide enough to permit a storm to be made. At 6 [?]a.m. on 16 October 1645, 6,000 New Model soldiers stormed the House, facing stern resistance, taking heavy casualties especially from nail bombs lobbed from windows. Full and clear reports suggest that between a quarter and a third of the defenders were killed in hot blood. Most of those not bearing arms or who surrendered were spared, although there is reliable evidence that six Catholic priests were killed in cold blood, and less reliable testimony that a few others, including the daughter of a Protestant chaplain who went to her father's aid, were also killed. Some of those who surrendered were stripped naked and plundered, but they do not otherwise seem to have been harmed. The worst that the royalist press could claim is that Inigo Jones was stripped and had to be carried out in a blanket. The words of Cromwell's soldier-chaplain Hugh Peters seem accurate enough: the Ironsides treated prisoners, he said, 'somewhat coarsely but not uncivilly'.[11]

This is an account that would be accepted by all the historians who have studied it. Let us now see how Cromwell wrote about it, when he sent his account to the Speaker of the House of Commons. He begin with a very matter-of-fact account of the storm of the House, noting that when Colonel Pickering had taken the New House and came to the Old House, the defenders 'summoned a parley; which our men would not hear'. At the end of the storm 'we have little loss: many of the enemy our men put to the sword; and some officers of quality; most of the rest we have prisoners, amongst whome the Marquis of Winchester himself and Sir Robert Peak. With divers other officers, whom I have ordered to be sent up to you'.[12] He clearly did not want to practice

---

10 The fullest discussions are in W. Emberton, *The close and perilous siege of Basing House* (Basingstoke, 1972); G. French, *The siege of Basing House* (Hove, 1970); and the admirable J. Adair, *They saw it happen: contemporary accounts of the siege of Basing House* (London, 1961). 11 H. Peters, *The full and last relation of all things concerning Basing House* (London, 1645). 12 L&S 1, pp 223–5.

summary justice on them, but to give Parliament the opportunity of show trials if it wished. He then called 'for the place to be utterly slighted' and indeed it was. It was burnt to the ground and the blackened stone and brick offered to the local communities for their own purposes. Within weeks it was reduced to what we see today, the outline of a medieval earthwork. Cromwell speaks of the 'good encouragement of his men', a euphemism for booty. He asks for fresh infantrymen to be conscripted and 'a course to be taken to pay the army', perhaps a reference to proposals to sell off the bishops' lands. And he concludes: 'The Lord grant that these mercies may be acknowledged with all thankfulness: God exceedingly abounds in His goodness to us, and will not be weary until righeousness and peace meet; and until He hath brought forth a glorious work for the happiness of this poor kingdom.'[13]

Faced by an especially defiant and apparently Catholic garrison, Cromwell was not especially concerned to save life, let alone safeguard property. He was willing literally to dismantle one of the three or four largest houses in England, to kill those he held most responsible, to hand over the key leaders for condign punishment, and to feel utterly confident he was doing God's work. Given the coarsening effect of war on all those involved, of becoming used to piles of bodies, it is not a huge distance from Basing to Drogheda.

III

Cromwell spent just 40 weeks in Ireland in between mid-August 1649 and late May 1650. In that time, he captured 25 fortified towns and castles (and visited 5 more already in English hands) on a progress that began in Co. Louth and moved through counties Dublin, Wicklow, Wexford, Waterford, Cork, Kilkenny, Tipperary and (the east tip of) Co. Limerick. In other words, he travelled through east Leinster, but spent 34 of his 40 weeks clearing Munster of royalist garrisons.[14] He never moved north of Drogheda, or south of Kinsale, or west of Mallow and Dunmanway. He killed most of the garrisons at Drogheda and Wexford, many in cold blood hours or days after they had surrendered, and in each case a significant number of civilians were killed, either caught in the cross-

---

13 Ibid.   14 The following are in my view sound and clear general accounts: J. Scott Wheeler, *Cromwell in Ireland* (Dublin, 1999); A. Woolrych, *Britain in revolution, 1625–1660* (Oxford, 2002), pp 461–80; P. Corish, 'The Cromwellian conquest', in T.W. Moody, F.X. Martin and F.J. Byrne (eds), *A new history of Ireland: iii Early modern Ireland, 1534–1691* (Oxford, 1976, 1991), pp 336–85. The Irish context is fully and admirably explored by P. Lenihan, *Confederate Ireland at war, 1641–1649* (Cork, 2001). There is still much to be said for the calm authority of S.R. Gardiner, who retraced Cromwell's footsteps on a cycling holiday that took him to Drogheda as far south as Cork. See his *History of the Commonwealth and Protectorate* (4 vols, London, 1903), 1, pp 80–159.

fire or at least in the heat of action, albeit often vindictively. We will examine what happened in more detail shortly. But we need to remember that he followed up the ferocity at Drogheda and Wexford by startlingly generous surrender articles (as at Mallow, Fethard and Kilkenny), and blood was shed on only five occasions even though several towns defied him for days or weeks (he was even forced by the weather and disease to abandon a siege of Waterford). The nearest thing to a further massacre was at Gowran which he took on 21 March 1650. Cromwell had offered quarter; it was refused until after the artillery had breached the walls. At that point Cromwell declined further negotiation but granted quarter to the common soldiers and mercy to the officers for an immediate surrender. The garrison included, significantly, some renegade officers from the 1648 Kentish rebellion. Cromwell shot the commissioned officers, including the English ones, hanged the priest to the garrison and released the rest.[15] More dramatically and revealingly, although he lost 2,000 men at Clonmel in a spectacular ambush in May 1650, he offered and honoured generous terms to both town and garrison.[16] If we leave aside Drogheda and Wexford (which of course we won't!) the laws of war as understood in England were as strictly observed by Cromwell in Ireland as they had been in England.[17] The same cannot be said for other English commanders, but that is another part of the context for making sense of what happened at Drogheda and Wexford.

IV

Cromwell was not amongst the most anti-Catholic and probably not amongst the most anti-Irish of Englishmen in the 1640s and 1650s. He was anti-Catholic and anti-Irish, but he was less so than many of those he served alongside in the army and the Long Parliament. This might seem very surprising, and it will take more space than is available here to make this case convincingly.[18] Nonetheless let us adumbrate it.

Cromwell's letters and speeches are surprisingly short of strong anti-Catholic rhetoric. He does not make the same intimate connection between Laudian bishops and Popery that one finds in Pym or Prynne, for example. One

---

15 L&S 2, pp 46–7. 16 The number of casualties suffered by the English varies in the different accounts, but the careful Scott Wheeler, *Cromwell in Ireland* p. 156 and n. 65 gives 2,000. 17 See the precise discussion in Jason McElligott, 'Cromwell, Drogheda and the abuse of Irish history', *Bullán*, 6:1 (2001), 123–5. More generally, and excellent, see Donagan, 'Codes and Conduct', 76ff. 18 The fourth of my Ford Lectures in Oxford in 2006, entitled '*Ubi Solitudinem Faciunt, pacem appellant*. War and "peace" in Ireland, 1650–1655', explored this theme, and will be published in a book provisionally entitled *Living with revolution: the peoples of Britain and Ireland and the legacies of war, 1646–1670*.

looks in vain for repeated references to the papal antichrist.[19] There is no reference in his letter from Basing House to those he has killed and taken prisoner being Papists. The Heads of the Proposals, with which he is closely associated, offered the Catholics the prospect of an easier time in the future than in the past.[20] His defense of indemnity acts in the Rump would have spared Papists in arms from the penalties of the Acts of Sale.[21] No Catholic priest in England was tried and executed while he was Lord Protector.[22] In a letter bearing his name to Cardinal Mazarin, he wrote that:

> although I believe that under my government your Eminency, in the behalf of the Catholics, has less reason for complaint as to rigour upon men's consciences than under the Parliament. Truly ... I have made a difference; and as Jude speaks, plucked many out of the fire,[23] the raging fire of persecution, which did tyrannize over their consciences and encroached by an arbitrariness of power upon their estates. And herein it is my purpose, as soon as I can remove impediments, and some weights that press me down to make further progress, and discharge my promise to your Eminency in relation to that.[24]

His speeches as Lord Protector were equally silent on the special culpability of the Catholics. His foreign policy was based on an utter conviction that 'the Spaniard is your enemy'. That gave rise to some strong language about the international Catholic conspiracy to overthrow Protestantism, and he does refer there to his belief that the 'Spaniard have an enemy in your bowels' – the English Catholic community – but he does not press for any new measures against them.[25] His purpose was to get Parliament's financial support for the

---

[19] The nearest he comes is in his opening speech to the second Protectorate Parliament on 17 September 1656: see below. [20] S.R. Gardiner (ed.), *Constitutional documents of the Puritan Revolution 1625–1660* (3rd edn, Oxford, 1906), pp 316–26, at art.XII, which repeals all the penal laws and speaks (mildly) of 'some other provision to be made for discovering of papists and popish recusants, and the disabling of them from disturbing the State'. [21] A.B. Worden, *The Rump Parliament* (Cambridge, 1974), pp 267–8. [22] One priest was executed, but he had been convicted of treason in 1628 and permanently exiled on pain of death if he returned to England. He was given every opportunity to avoid execution in 1654 but embraced it. See John Morrill, 'John Southworth 1592–1654', *New Oxford Dictionary of National Biography* (2004), http://www.oxforddnb.com/view/article67460, accessed 25 January 2005. [23] A reference to *Jude* 1: 22–23: 'And of some have compassion, making a difference. And others save with fear, pulling them out of the fire; hating even the garment spotted by the flesh.' [24] T. Birch (ed.), *A collection of state papers of John Thurloe, esq* (7 vols, London, 1742), 5, p. 735; L&S 3, pp 5–6; W.C. Abbott, *Writings and speeches of Oliver Cromwell* (4 vols, Cambridge, MA, 1937–47), 4, pp 368–9. There is some doubt as to the authenticity of this document (drawn to my attention by Blair Worden), but most of those who have studied it are happy to treat it as genuine. [25] L&S 3, pp 511–17.

Spanish War. All laws penalizing Catholics for absenting themselves from Protestant worship were repealed, and penalties for attending Catholic worship largely unenforced. In terms of freedom of religious practice, the 1650s were the easiest decade for English Catholics between the accession of Elizabeth I and the accession of George I. Cromwell disliked Catholics; he had friends who were open about their yearning for the return of the Book of Common Prayer and bishops, indeed he was a friend to past (Ussher) and future (Wilkins) bishops, as well as to supporters of the Presbyterian order, the Congregational way, to born-again Baptists and to Quakers. He was friends with all those with 'the root of the matter in them', all who were seekers after God's truth, for he did not believe that any one church had a monopoly of truth,[26] though we cannot find any sign that he found the root of the matter in any Catholic. But persecution was not a route to conversion. Cromwell would give liberty to evangelize to all those who sought truth through the sovereign authority of Scripture; and he would give a de facto liberty to practise any other form in private.[27]

Cromwell was an extreme erastian. He hated priestcraft, the claims of the clergy to a monopoly on preaching and to a custodianship of the truth. His earlier spleen against the English bishops (in 1636 he called them 'the enemies of God His Truth',[28] and he was outspoken in his denunciations of them in the early days of the Long Parliament)[29] was equaled, if not surpassed, by his loathing of Scottish Presbyterian ministers. This is what he wrote to the Commissioners of the Kirk on 3 August 1650, just days before the Battle of Dunbar:

> There may be a spiritual fullness, which the World may call drunkenness ... There may be as well a carnal confidence upon misunderstood and misapplied precepts ... I pray you read the twenty eighth of Isaiah, from the fifth to the fifteenth verse.[30]

That reference is to the desecration of the Temple by drunken priests vomiting over the altar of the Lord. He is accusing the Presbyterian clergy of spiritual drunkenness and of spiritual arrogance. There is a spitting contempt in this passage that he reserved for a self-important clergy. And he says to these Scottish clergy: 'There may be a covenant with death and hell'.[31] He had used that phrase once before, in a document with a chilling title: 'The Declaration of the Lord Lieutenant of Ireland for the undeceiving of deluded and seduced people ... in answer to certaine late declarations and acts framed by the Irish Popish Prelates and clergy in conventicler at Clonmacnoise'. And addressing

---

[26] The best of the many discussions of how he wrestled with these issues is J.C. Davis, *Oliver Cromwell* (London, 2001), pp 112–37. [27] John Morrill, 'Oliver Cromwell 1599–1658', *Oxford Dictionary of National Biography* (2004), http://www.oxforddnb.com/view/article6765, accessed 25 January 2005. [28] L&S 1, p. 79. [29] Morrill, 'Oliver Cromwell 1599–1658'. [30] L&S 2, pp 79–80. [31] Ibid.

those clergy, *not the Irish people*, he writes 'your covenant if you understood it, is with death and hell! Your union is like that of Simeon and Levi'.[32] And this is our link from Cromwell's contained anti-Catholicism to his contained anti-Irishness.

The *Declaration* is withering in its contempt for the Irish clergy and deserves a fuller study than is possible here.[33] It lays the blame for the 1641 Rebellion on the clergy: 'you put the English to the most unheard of & most barbarous massacre (without respect of sex or age) that ever the sun beheld'. He accuses them of exercising an ecclesiastical tyranny and superstition, of terrorizing people into handing over their property with a false promise of helping them to Heaven in return, of mystifying the people and withholding the truth from them:

> you cannot feed them [with the word of God] but instead poison them with your false abominable and Antichristian doctrine and practices; you keep the word of God from them, and instead thereof you give them your senseless orders and traditions.[34]

He thus portrays the Irish as *held in ignorance*. He has no doubt that the English have brought civility and sound economy amongst them, and that they enjoyed peace and prosperity because of it until the clergy corrupted them into rebellion. He is deeply prejudiced. But there is a large gap between prejudice and a will to exterminate. His scorn turns to anger as he examines the charge of the Clonmacnoise Declaration[35] that his purpose was 'to extirpate the Catholic religion' and 'the distruction of the lives of the inhabitants of this nation'.[36] To the first he makes clear that he will strike out against all public (as against private) Catholic worship or evangelization; but

> as for the people what thoughts they have in matters of religion in their own breasts I cannot reach, but thinke it my duty if they walk honestly and peaceably, not to cause them in the least to suffer them to suffer for the same, but shall endeavour to walk patiently and in love towards them to see if at any time it shall please God to give them another or a better minde.[37]

This is entirely consistent with his policy in England: persecution doesn't work, so permit those outside the circle of truth to worship privately but not to evangelize.

---

32 L&S 2, pp 5–23, at p. 7. The reference to Simeon and Levi is to Genesis 34, where these sons of Jacob became the embodiment of fanaticism and bad faith to those who had come amongst them to right a terrible wrong done to their sister Dinah.   33 See note 18.   34 L&S 2, p. 14.   35 For the text to which he is replying, see Denis Murphy, *Cromwell in Ireland* (Dublin, 1902), pp 406–10. ('Declaration of the bishops and clergy assembled at Clonmacnoise, 4 December 1649').   36 L&S 2, pp 15, 17.   37 L&S 2, p. 17.

He is even more emphatic on his plans for a civil settlement: 'I shall not willingly take or suffer to be taken away the life of any man not in arms, but by trial to which the people of this nation are subject by law for offences against the same'. Banishment would only be used to commute the sentences of those guilty of capital offences. Estates would be confiscated only from those who had taken part in the massacres or taken up arms in defence of the rebellion, and those laying down their arms would be given 'merciful consideration'.[38] This is of course a far cry from the language of the Act of Settlement of 1652;[39] but it is close to the policies he advocated for royalist-Catholics in England, and it is close to the policy of the Protectorate in Ireland. I will demonstrate elsewhere that Cromwell was strongly opposed to the Act of Settlement. For the moment, I will rest on the categorical statement of S.R.Gardiner after his careful examination of the evidence: 'as far as the act of 1652 is concerned, there is no evidence whatever to connect it with Cromwell.'[40]

Cromwell came to Ireland full of disinformation about the nature and extent of the massacres of 1641–2.[41] He came full of contempt for priestcraft in general and Catholic priestcraft in particular. He came believing the English to be God's chosen people and the Irish an ignorant, backward people needing English civility. He came to Ireland knowing that he had to divide and rule if he was to succeed. He came knowing that his most inveterate enemies were those whose loyalty to the House of Stuart was even greater than their loyalty to the Church of Rome, and knowing that he could do business with those whose loyalty to the Church of Rome was greater than their loyalty to the House of Stuart. And so he sanctioned George Monck's pacification with O'Neill;[42] he made his own accommodation with the marquis of Antrim – a pardon in exchange for the use of the latter's boats as transports;[43] and he also sanctioned exploratory discussions with leading Catholic clergy to see if he could secure political obedience in return for minimal rights of religious practice.[44] His personal dealings with liberal Catholics like Sir Kenelm Digby were perfectly amicable throughout the 1650s. Even at an individual level, he could exercise acts of compassion for Catholics. When he discovered that Bishop David Rothe was dying, he rescinded the order banishing from Ireland clergy whom he had taken prisoner at Kilkenny, so that the old man could die amongst his own people.[45]

38 Ibid., pp 18–20.   39 Gardiner, *Constitutional documents*, pp 394–400.   40 S.R. Gardiner, 'The transplantation to Connaught', *English Historical Review*, 14 (1899), 707.   41 For a brilliant reconstruction of the impact of press discussion of the 1641 massacres, see Ethan Shagan, 'Constructing discord: ideology, propaganda and English responses to the Irish Rebellion of 1641', *Journal of British Studies*, 36 (1997), 4–34.   42 Gentles, *New Model*, pp 355–6 and n. 39.   43 J. Ohlmeyer, *Civil War and Restoration in the three Stuart Kingdoms: the career of Randal MacDonnell, Marquis of Antrim 1609–1683* (Cambridge, 1993), pp 230–40.   44 J. Collins, 'Thomas Hobbes and the Blackloist Conspiracy' *Historical Journal*, 45:2 (2002), 305–31; A. Brown, 'Anglo-Irish Gallicanism, 1635–1675', (unpublished PhD thesis, University of Cambridge, 2004), chapter 4   45 M. Tanner, *Ireland's Holy Wars* (New

Cromwell came to Ireland because:

> England hath had experience of the blessing of God in prosecuting just and righteous causes, whatever the cost and hazard be! ... We are come to ask an account of the innocent blood that hath been shed; and to endeavour to bring to an account ... all who by appearing in arms, seek to justify the same. We come, by the assistance of God to hold forth and maintain the lustre and glory of English liberty in a nation where we have an undoubted right to do it; wherein the people of Ireland ... may equally participate in all the benefits; to use their liberty and fortune equally with Englishmen, if they keep out of arms.[46]

He came to Ireland with a sense of ethnic superiority but not of ethnic hatred.

V

We can now turn to events at Drogheda in September 1649 and in Wexford in October 1649. In both those towns there were massacres. In both those towns the greater part of the garrison was killed in hot blood or in cold blood, and in the former the survivors were sent to indentured servitude in Barbados.[47] In both towns there were significant levels of civilian casualties, killed or molested in hot blood. The evidence that civilians (other than priests and friars) were killed in cold blood is of a limited and inconclusive form. But Cromwell himself confessed that significant numbers of civilians were killed. In total, there seems no reason to doubt an official New Model report that 3500+ were killed at Drogheda, and there is now fairly general agreement that about 1500–2000 were killed in Wexford.

The above paragraph already pins my colours to the mast. There are more than enough accounts of the massacres and excellent accounts of the historiography, especially of the massacre at Drogheda. Jason McElligott has given us an outstanding summary of the nationalist and revisionist cases,[48] and

Haven, 2003), p. 145. **46** *Declaration*, L&S 2, p. 21. For the present the reader has to take it on trust that this is not a Machiavellian tract, designed to pretend to a settlement he had no intention of honouring. I have no space within the limits set for this essay to say more than I have about the consistency of his thinking. The question of Cromwell's Machiavellianism is explored in John Morrill, 'How Oliver Cromwell Thought', forthcoming in a festschrift. **47** It is important to note that transportation of large numbers of English, Scots and Irish political prisoners took place in the 1650s, the single largest group being Scots after the battles of Dunbar and Worcester. See Sean O'Callaghan, *To Hell or Barbados* (Dingle, 2000). Chapters 1 and 2 deal specifically with the transportations after the massacres of Drogheda and Wexford. See more generally C. Carlton, *Going to the wars* (London, 1992), pp 332–6 and n. 79. **48** McElligott, 'Cromwell, Drogheda and the abuse of Irish history', 109–32.

LETTERS FROM IRELAND,

Relating the several great Successes it hath pleased God to give unto the

Parliaments Forces

there, in the Taking of *Drogheda, Trym, Dundalk, Carlingford,* and the *Nury.*

Together with a LIST of the Chief Commanders, and the Number of the Officers and Soldiers slain in *Drogheda.*

Die Martis, 2 *Octobr.* 1649.

Ordered by the *Commons assembled in Parliament, That the several Letters from the Lord Lieutenant of* Ireland, *together with so much of Colonel* Venables *Letter as concerns the Successes in* Ireland, *be forthwith printed and published.*

Hen: Scobell, Cleric. Parliamenti.

London, Printed by *John Field* for *Edward Husband,* Printer to the Parliament of *England.* 1649.

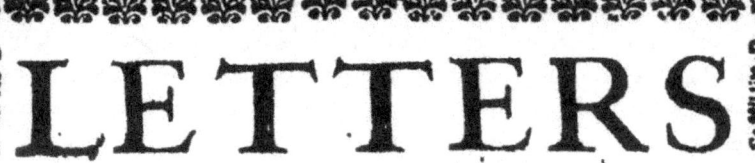

9 Anon., *Letters from Ireland* (London, 1649), title page.

a totally convincing and necessary explanation of why Tom Reilly's claim that there was no civilian massacre at Drogheda is not to be trusted.[49] In essence, Reilly fails the test of source criticism at almost every turn. He argues a case and unreasonably privileges second- and third-hand evidence that supports his presupposition and unreasonably dismisses contrary evidence.[50] When it comes to first-hand evidence, he reasserts an already discredited attempt to deny that Cromwell confessed to the deaths of civilians. This is so central that I will rehearse McElligott's arguments here by reference to the original printed version. Figure 9 is the title page of the pamphlet in which Cromwell's main account of the taking of Drogheda (dispatched on 17 September) was printed together with the follow-up to events following the storm and massacre (dispatched 27 September). The first contains a list of royalist regiments (totalling 2,700) and their commanders and the second contains 'a list of the officers and soldiers slain at the storming of Drogheda', naming eight of the dead officers. It makes clear that it is published with the authority of the Parliament itself, and the printer (John Field) had been the regular printer of 'official' print for several years and was to remain so even after Cromwell became Lord Protector.[51] It is unthinkable that he (for commercial or any other reason) would falsify a report from the Lord Lieutenant of Ireland, especially so soon after the new Licensing Act[52] under which all the printers had been called in, put on tough bail bonds of £300 not to publish without a license and not to publish anything detrimental to the regime (like a false report of a civilian massacre). Figure 10 gives us the end of Cromwell's second letter to Lenthall and the appendix listing those killed at Drogheda. There is nothing typographically or otherwise to suggest that this is not part of Cromwell's letter. Indeed it is clearly the list referred to in the Commons order to the printer: 'A letter from the Lord Lieutenant of Ireland, from Dublin, of the twenty seventh day of September *together with a list of the officers and soldiers slain at the storming of Drogheda* was this day read ... and be forthwith printed and published.'[53] And what does this appendix tell us? It tells us that at Drogheda, Cromwell's army killed 60 royalist officers 220 troopers, and 2,500 infantry, surgeons, 'and many inhabitants'. There is no getting round those words.[54] Hugh Peter, close to

---

49 T. Reilly, *Cromwell: an honourable enemy* (Dingle, 1999).   **50** McElligott, 'Cromwell, Drogheda and the abuse of Irish history', 120–7.   **51** Ibid., p. 121; Anon., *Letters from Ireland* (London, 1649).   **52** For a discussion, see Jason McElligott, 'Propaganda and censorship: the underground Royalist newsbooks, 1647–1650' (PhD thesis, University of Cambridge, 2000), pp 166–85. It is perhaps also worth stressing that John Field, printer of Cromwell's letter from Drogheda, was also the printer of this Act. See *An act against unlicensed and scandalous books and pamphlets, and for better regulating of printing* (20 September 1649).   **53** *Journal of the House of Commons* 6, 2 October 1649, http://www.british-history.ac.uk, accessed 30 January 2005.   **54** Reilly tries to do so (*Cromwell: an honourable enemy*), pp 96 and 119 n. 19, by drawing attention to Carlyle's false claim in the first edition of L&S that the appendix is an eighteenth-century addition. As

> **A List of the Officers and Soldiers slain at the storming of Droghed*a*.**
>
> Sir *Arthur Aston* Governor.
> Sir *Edmond Verney* Lieutenant Col: to *Ormonds* Regiment.
> Col: *Fleming*, of Horse.
> Lieutenant Col: *Finglass*, of Horse.
> Major *Fitzgerald*, of Horse.
> Eight { Captains / Lieutenants / Cornets } of Horse.
> Col: { *Warren*, / *Walls*, / *Byrne*, } of Foot, with their Lieutenants, Majors, &c.
> The Lord *Taaffs* brother, an *Augustine* Fryer.
> Forty four Captains, and all their Lieutenants, Ensigns, &c.
> Two hundred and twenty Reformado's and Troopers.
> Two thousand Five hundred Foot Soldiers, besides Staff-Officers, Chyrurgeons, &c. and many Inhabitants.

10 'A list of the Officers and Soldiers slain at the storming of Drogheda', from *Letters from Ireland*.

Cromwell and on his council of war,[55] suggested that the total number killed was 3,552, and he gives the number of military survivors amongst the defenders as 400. Cromwell thinks there were 2,782 killed apart from 'the many inhabitants' (although his 2,500 infantrymen and support service men is clearly a rounded number).[56] The implication of both Cromwell and Peter is that about 700–800 civilians died and I see no reason to doubt that figure. After all, several thousand soldiers climbing over the corpses of colleagues to clear a town full of effective

figure 10 reveals this claim was simply incorrect. This is in itself fatal to Reilly's thesis and it is disgraceful that so many reviewers have not checked this.   55 Anon, *A Letter from Ireland, read in the House of Commons from Mr Hugh Peter, minister of God's Word* (London, 1649), title page and p. 4.   56 My arithmetic from the figures given in figure 10 and is very close to that of Gentles, *New Model*, p. 361.

snipers, and clearing it street by street and house by house, are not going to ask questions about the status of those they encounter. What is not clear is how many civilians, as against how many combatants, died in cold blood. The sources that discuss this are amongst the least reliable and nothing is to be gained by revisiting that debate. What is clear from Cromwell's own pen is that there was a significant but not enormous level of killing of disarmed combatants, and possibly others, in cold blood.

As to the precise sequence of events, we have a completely satisfactory description and analysis by James Burke, no element of which has been challenged by any of the more recent military historians to study it.[57] The main elements in the story are these. First, Cromwell summonsed the town and threatened to withhold quarter if there was no surrender on his terms.[58] Second, his initial storm of the town was repulsed with considerable loss of life – enough for the successful storm to be assisted by the heaped pile of their comrade's corpses that they could scramble over so as to effect an entry through a breach that did not come down to ground level. Third, it was the sight of fallen comrades that was the occasion of Cromwell issuing the order for no quarter to be given 'to any in arms in the town'. Fourth, the New Model stormed through Drogheda across the Boyne Bridge killing all that opposed them in any way. Fifth, this left significant numbers of defenders and civilians holed up in the castellated Towers around the walls, in the tower of St Peter's Church, and on Millmount. According to a letter from 'an eminent person in the army' published in London on 8 October, Colonel Axtell was detached to take Millmount, and (daunted by the steep rise and the sturdy stockade that protected it), he offered to spare the lives of the governor and the 200 men with him if they surrendered on the promise of their lives, which they did.[59] But the same letter tells us that the disarmed men were moved to a windmill 'where they were later slain', implying a delay; and Ormond wrote to a fellow royalist that 'they were butchered an hour after quarter was given them.'[60] Those who took refuge in St Peter's Church died after the pews were ignited beneath them, dying in the flames or by jumping from the Tower. It is not clear if those in the church included civilians; it seems perfectly possible. Those who took refuge

---

57 James Burke, 'The New Model Army and the problems of siege warfare, 1648–1651', *IHS* 105 (1990), 1–29 – see especially 8–15. For more recent accounts that follow Burke, see Scott Wheeler, *Cromwell in Ireland*, pp 83–90 or Gentles, *New Model*, pp 357–63. Burke covers all the important points about Cromwell's 'massacres' far more thoroughly than anyone else, including the widely cited, but evidentially very thin, Robin Clifton, 'An indiscriminate blackness? Massacre, counter-massacre and ethnic cleansing in Ireland, 1640–1660', in M. Levene and P. Roberts (eds), *The massacre in history* (Oxford, 1999), pp 107–26, especially pp 108–10, 117–22.   58 Murphy, *Cromwell in Ireland*, p. 92.   59 The letter was published in a diurnal strictly licensed by the Houses, *Perfect Diurnal* (London, 8 October 1649).   60 J.T. Gilbert, *A contemporary history of affairs in Ireland* (6 vols, Dublin, 1880), 2, pp 271–2. See below, n. 67.

in the turrets around the walls surrendered the following day, and we know that the officers and every tenth man (Roman-style decimation) were clubbed to death and the rest sent to the Tobacco Islands.[61] Some royalist reports speak of summary executions spread over several days – in the case of Sir Edmund Verney three days after the taking of the town, and although this is from a second-or third-hand account, it is consistent with the reports of New Model officers.[62] As a final act of vindictiveness, the heads of 16 royalist officers were sent to Dublin and stuck on pikes on the approach roads.[63] (Slightly odd: why not leave them at Drogheda?)[64]

The key evidence remains Cromwell's own reports to John Bradshaw and William Lenthall, dispatched on 16 and 17 September once the Lord Lieutenant had returned to Dublin. The first was about 400 words long and the second more than 2,000 words, one of his longest letters. The former gives no detail of the storming of the town, but reports the main facts: that 'being entered, we refused them quarter'; that almost all the defenders were killed and the rest already en route to the Barbados; that some 3,000 were slain; and that his next target was Wexford.[65] Two other things in the letter are worthy of note: the first is the statement that God had given the defenders strength to resist, the more to 'give new courage to our men' – this is clearly linked to the refusal of quarter. The second is the justification that 'this bitterness will save much effusion of blood, through the goodness of God'. Although he also hopes 'that all honest hearts may give the glory of this to God alone, to whom indeed the praise of this mercy belongs', he stops short of saying whether 'this mercy' is the low number of English casualties or the large number of defenders killed as a punishment for their misdeeds.[66] The emphasis is that this is an act done *in terrorem*.

Cromwell's much longer and more considered letter, written the next day,[67] gives more precise detail of this military operation than any of his other battlefield letters, with the possible exception of the letter after the battle of Preston. Cromwell's willingness to admit in writing of the killing of those who surrendered on Millmount ('they were ordered by me to be put to the sword'[68]

---

61 We know this from Cromwell's account, see below p. 257.   62 It is a near contemporary account, from one of Ormond's officers to the family back home at Claydon, Bucks. See F.P. Verney (ed.), *Memoirs of the Verney family during the Civil War* (4 vols, London, 1892), 2, pp 344–5.   63 Anon., *Two letters of a bloody fight in Ireland* (London, 22 September 1649). The display of heads had not been part of the English (or Irish) experience of war (as against judicial execution for treason) over the previous half century, although some of the reports of the 1641 Rebellion had spoken of the display of Protestant heads at Kilkenny (I am grateful to Clodagh Tait for this reference). Above all it was not part of *Cromwell's* experience.   64 For a possible explanation, see below, pp 258–9.   65 He refers to it as 'the southern design – you know what' – an intriguing message.   66 L&S 2, pp 464–5.   67 L&S 1, pp 466–72.   68 Thus overruling Axtell who had granted quarter. What remains an insoluble problem is whether Axtell knew that Cromwell had forbidden any to be spared and cynically offered it knowing that he would be overruled, or whether Axtell believed that he

he says, adding 'being in the heat of action, I forbade them to spare any that were in arms in the town').[69] This is carefully vague about the fact that they had surrendered before they were killed, although it is implied.[70] A statement that when those holed up in the turrets surrendered, 'their officers were knocked on the head, and every tenth man of the soldiers killed' is more explicit about what happened,[71] as is the statement that 'all the friars were knocked on the head promiscuously but two', along with Fr Peter Taaffe, brother of Lord Taaffe.[72] Perhaps grimmest of all his account of the roasting of those sheltering in the Tower of St Peter's Church 'where one was heard to say in the midst of the flames: 'God damn me, God confound me, I burn, I burn.'[73] It is hard to believe that in the general confusion and screaming from within a locked Tower, these words could be made out. Cromwell is here putting words into the mouth of a dying man, words which describe and prescribe his agony now and in the life to come (in bleak Calvinist mode). There is an edgy bravado here, which suggests that Cromwell is not really content with his *in terrorem* argument. He wants also to strengthen the case for that extraordinary use of the discretionary power that lay in him as the general of an army denied entry to a town.

And in this letter to the Speaker of the House of Commons, a letter he could anticipate would be published, he made a double justification of what had happened:

> I am persuaded that this is a righteous judgment of God upon these barbarous wretches, who have imbrued their hands with so much innocent blood; and that it will tend to prevent the effusion of blood for the future, which are the satisfactory grounds to such actions, which otherwise cannot but work remorse and regret.[74]

We have seen that the second of these reasons is the one he also used in the letter to John Bradshaw that he did not expect to be published.[75] It was followed up immediately by letters in his summons to the Governors of Trim and Dundalk ('I offered mercy to the garrison at Tredagh[76] ... which being refused brought their evil upon them ... if you, being warned thereby, shall surrender your garrison to

---

had the authority to grant quarter only to find his superior officer had forbidden it and countermanded it. Given the chaos as the third storm began and the evidence that the order to deny quarter was given after the assault had started, the latter is at least as likely as the former. 69 L&S 1, pp 468–9. 70 At the battle of Philiphaugh, General Leslie granted quarter to several hundred of Montrose's men, but was subsequently overruled by his council of war and the men were executed: see below, p. 264. 71 L&S 1, p. 469. 72 Ibid., p. 471. 73 Ibid., p. 469. 74 Ibid., p. 469. 75 In the past his letters to the Speaker of the Commons following a military engagement were ordered to be published, his letters to the executive committees of the Parliament never were. 76 Cromwell always refers to Drogheda as Tredagh (the English spelling of the Irish Droichead Átha). I am grateful to Rory Rapple for this

the use of the Parliament of England, ... you may thereby prevent effusion of blood').[77] The towns were surrendered and all lives were spared. As we have seen, it set the pattern: surrender and be spared; resist and be massacred. Although several towns held out for weeks on end, eventually all but Wexford surrendered on terms and were spared. The same cannot be said for all the commanders under the authority of the Parliament.[78] But it held true for Cromwell.

But what of that chilling phrase 'this is a righteous judgment of God upon these barbarous wretches, who have imbrued their hands with so much innocent blood'? It has generally been assumed by all who have written about it that it referred to the 1641 massacres, and it has often enough been said that he knew he was lying – that he knew perfectly well that the garrison consisted of English and Ormondist troops, none of whom could have taken any part in the 1641–2 massacres.[79] Drogheda had *never* been a Confederate town. So why do we assume that he was referring to the 1641 rebellion? In the course of his post-Drogheda letters Cromwell only mentions by name *English* officers and members of Irish noble families. In that list of those killed, he privileges the names of English officers along with those from Irish noble families – the earl of Westmeath and Sir James Dillon, brother of the earl of Roscommon.[80] Is it not possible that Cromwell's reference is to the blood guilt of those who refused to accept the judgment of God in the first Civil War, those who committed sacrilege by renewing the war and carried a culpability far higher than that of those who fought to establish God's judgment in that first war, the culpability for shedding innocent blood that brought Charles I to the scaffold?[81] It was a reference to that same rage which overtook him throughout 1648 and led to the summary trials and death sentences on the leaders after the sieges and battles of Pembroke, Preston and Pontefract. It was a rage that had allowed him to refer to those English rebels who obstructed the Lord's work as acting 'barbarously'; so this was not a term he held back to use of the Irish.[82] Is this why the heads

explanation. 77 L&S 1, pp 463–4, Letter from Drogheda, 12 September 1649. 78 It was broadly true of his successors as senior commander, but it certainly not true of the New English set on vengeance for 1641 – notably Sir Charles Coote, whose own father had been killed during a skirmish with the Irish. 79 See, e.g., Gentles, *New Model*, p. 362; Woolrych, *Britain in revolution*, p. 469; Morrill, 'Oliver Cromwell 1599–1658'. 80 Above, p. 254, figure 10. 81 See P. Crawford, 'Charles Stuart, that man of blood', *Journal of British History*, 16:2 (1977), 41–61. 82 For example, Cromwell to Fairfax, 4 August 1645, referring to his defeat of the very English Clubmen at Sherborne: 'they have taken divers of the Parliament soldiers prisoners, besides Colonel Fienes and his men; and used them most barbarously' (L&S 1, p. 210); for other uses by Englishmen about Englishmen, see Donagan, 'Codes and conduct', 90–1. I also entered the word 'barbarous' and the period 1641–49 into the long title search on Early English Books Online. There were 103 hits. Only one quarter of them applied to the actions of Irish Catholics, far fewer than the number that applied to the action of English royalists (above all Prince Rupert). Smaller number of entries related to Scottish Royalists, foreign Catholics, Parliamentarian soldiers, non-Christians, and there were six Leveller

of the English officers like Sir Edmund Verney were sent to be put on spikes in Dublin? Is this why he singled out English officers to be denied mercy at Gowran? And was the concern to highlight the English officers intended to send a clear message to royalists amongst the English readership of the letter not to cross to Ireland to continue the struggle?

My suggestion is, then, that there was a massacre at Drogheda, but that we must be careful not to make that the emblem of a focused and blind hatred of the Irish on Cromwell's part. Cromwell went to Ireland as a calloused army veteran hardened to the sight of blood. He went with a distaste for the Catholics in general and Irish Catholics in particular, though a distaste tempered by his sense of them as the victims of priestly obfuscation, and he went to do a job of work. The letter to Speaker Lenthall ended with a 300-word plea for supplies:

> that a consideration may be had of them ... such as may give a speedy issue to this work, to which there seems to be a marvelous fair opportunity offered by God. And although it may seem very chargeable to the State of England to maintain so great a force, yet surely stretch a little for the present, in following God's providence, in hope the charge will not be long.[83]

That's the rub. He was well aware how much every army had been rendered unfit by the lack of political will to do unpopular things to requisition men, money and supplies, and that throughout the last nine years (and, he might have known, the last 100 years) it had been the bane of generals in Ireland. He was nervous about being left without money or reinforcements. The whole letter can also be seen as a vindication of this postlude.[84] Give me the tools and I will do the job, with God visibly on my side. I will use terror where it is needed, mercy where it is prudent. For 'if God please to finish it here as He hath done in England, the war is like to pay itself'.[85]

VI

The sack of Wexford is too often seen as the logical next step after the sack of Drogheda. In fact, it was a disaster for Cromwell's policy. He had threatened

---

accusations of 'barbarous' behaviour by the Long Parliament. 83 L&S 1, p. 471. 84 This is also how I would read his speech to the General Council of the Army in Whitehall on 23 March 1648 on whether or not he would accept the invitation to command the army that was being assembled for the Irish campaign. Although he calls the Irish interest 'the most dangerous' and says that 'all the world knows their barbarism' (L&S 3, pp 403–4), the main thrust of his speech is that he cannot undertake the task unless he is guaranteed a sufficient supply of men, munitions and cash (see the comments either side of the intervention of Hardress Waller on ibid., 3, p. 405). 85 Ibid.

his way into five fortified towns since taking Drogheda and had treated well those who surrendered to him. He clearly intended to talk his way into Wexford and to use it as his winter headquarters. But – by common consent – he lost control of the situation and an unauthorized massacre took place.

The following facts are not in dispute. Cromwell arrived before the gates with only 60 per cent of the force that he had at Drogheda (because, as he put it on 27 September, 'it's easily conceived what [numbers of men] the garrisons already drink up, what our field armies will come to, if God shall give more garrisons into your hands').[86] He could afford to wait a little while to negotiate the surrender, for his artillery was coming by sea and he could not plan an attack until it arrived. On the other hand, there was an outbreak of the 'bloody flux' (dysentery) amongst his men, and that was all too likely to reduce their fighting effectiveness.[87] Furthermore, he could not readily prevent the Governor, David Synott, from receiving reinforcements. The latter already had more men in the garrison (around 3,000) than Aston had had at Drogheda, and by all accounts far more armed townsmen at his disposal, perhaps as many as 4,500 men in all.[88] So while he was less peremptory in the early exchanges with Synott, time was not on his side and once his artillery was in place, he began to apply pressure.

Although most of the town walls were reinforced with 15-foot earthworks, there was a vulnerable area at the southern end, and Cromwell's guns quickly made a breach there. Synott decided to surrender at this, but given the civilized nature of their previous exchanges (which included a cart laden with 'sack, strong waters and strong beer' as a gift to Cromwell from the town),[89] he opted to attempt one more round of negotiation first. He was generally satisfied with the terms offered to the garrison (freedom for the common soldiers to return home, disarmed; the officers to surrender on the promise of their lives but not their liberty; the townsmen to be free from plunder). Nonetheless, he hoped one last round of negotiations might improve those terms, both to protect his officers' freedom and especially to protect the lives and liberties of the Catholic clergy and religious. As he haggled, his subordinate, in charge of the Castle at the southern corner, unilaterally accepted the terms Synott was seeking to refine. Cromwell's troops poured into the Castle and started bombarding the town from the high castle walls. The defenders retreated from the town walls, allowing Cromwell's men (without awaiting orders from their field officers, and certainly without an order to deny mercy) to swarm over the walls and rampage through the town, killing at will. English and Irish sources agree that at least 1,500 and probably nearer 2,000 people were killed, including two overloaded boatloads of escapees, many (most?) of whom were civilians. There was indis-

---

86 L&S 1, pp 471–2. 87 Gentles, *New Model*, pp 364–5 is especially good on this aspect.
88 Scott Wheeler, *Cromwell in Ireland*, p. 97; Reilly, *Cromwell: an honourable enemy*, p. 155.
89 Reilly, *Cromwell: an honourable enemy*, p. 148.

criminate pillage, although it does not seem to have continued beyond nightfall on the day of the storm – that is, a few hours. There is much less evidence of killing in cold blood, but much more suggestion that civilians as well as soldiers were killed in hot blood.[90]

The level of killing was less both absolutely and proportionately. There was no systematic summary execution of prisoners. According to one English report sent back to London by Richard Lawrence, 1,300 prisoners were taken.[91] This is compatible with Cromwell's report, but it is odd that it is not spelled out. Nonetheless, even the Irish sources do not speak of calculated killing of the kind that had been an instrument of policy at Drogheda. They do speak, however, of sadistic mistreatment and slaughter of civilians during the sack of the town.

Fr Denis Murphy offers the fullest account of later Catholic sources, and he had no doubt that there was much gratuitous targeting of civilians, including women. Tom Reilly in contrast thinks none of the Catholic sources can be trusted and that (those capsized boats apart) there were few civilian deaths.[92] The truth here can be fairly safely put in the middle. Reilly seeks to discredit all the Catholic sources by criticizing those written in the aftermath of the Land Settlement. So he fails to give proper weight to the near-contemporary testimony of, for example, Bishop Lynch, who was writing within months that 'many priests, not a few religious, many more townspeople and two thousand soldiers were killed'.[93] In general, I see no reason to doubt that civilians were killed in significant numbers in Wexford.

It is important to bear in mind that there was a great deal of friction between the inhabitants and the recently arrived and none-too-welcome garrison. Wexford was a Confederate town and most of the leading townsmen had backed the radical Confederate line adopted by Cardinal Rinuccini – to put loyalty to

90 There is an especially clear account in Woolrych, *Britain in revolution*, pp 468–72, followed by Gentles, *New Model*, pp 366–72, Corish, 'The Cromwellian conquest', pp 340–3 and Scott Wheeler, *Cromwell in Ireland*, pp 96–100. The account in Reilly, *Cromwell: an honourable enemy* (pp 131–67), as against the tendentious commentary (pp 169–96), is sound. Gardiner, *Commonwealth and Protectorate* 1, 127–33 is, as ever, brilliant in his source evaluation, but on this occasion a bit weak on his claim that Cromwell was not in breach of the laws of war. 91 R.L., *The taking of Wexford. A letter from an eminent officer of the Army* (London, 1649). 92 Murphy, *Cromwell in Ireland*, pp 161ff; Reilly, *Cromwell: an honourable enemy*, pp 169–96, both refer to and discuss all the main sources, from both sides.   93 'Multi sacerdotes, nonnulli religiosi, plurimi cives et duo millia militum', in P.F. Moran (ed.), *Spicilegium Ossoriense* (3 vols, Dublin, 1875), 1, p. 341. Reilly fails to spot that this is written in 1650 not in the 1670s (and indeed refers to it is as by 'Fr' Lynch not by a Bishop). He does not seem to have read the compelling discussion of the Irish Catholic sources that does distinguish the probably unreliable from the probably reliable in Gardiner, *Commonweath*, 1, pp 131–2 and nn. In any case, there is a much more reliable exact contemporary source whose veracity simply cannot be impugned: Bodleian Library, Carte MSS 25, f. 720, Commissioners of Trust [viz Richard Bellings, Nicholas French, Gerald Fennell] to Ormond, written from Kilkenny, reported the fall of the town 'and all put to the sword'. I am grateful to Micheál

the Church first and to the King second. Furthermore, the town had been a haven for pirates who had long preyed on Parliamentarian supply lines to its friends and supporters in Munster, and Cromwell himself commented on atrocities committed by the townsmen rather than by the garrison (the starving to death of Protestant prisoners in a locked chapel, and the drowning of about 150 other prisoners in a leaking hulk in the harbour).[94] The composition of the garrison inserted by Ormond under the agreement between himself and the more pragmatic Confederates caused a lot of friction, and Ormond had to agree to complement it with regiments of impeccable Confederate pedigree. This garrison was solidly Irish and Catholic. These were not people he could be expected to wish to treat mercifully. Yet all the evidence is that while there was a massacre, there was no deliberation about it. When I – like others – have called Drogheda Cromwell's Hiroshima and Wexford his Nagasaki, we were wrong. He was shamefaced about what happened at Wexford, and brought things back under control as soon as he could.

Despite Tom Reilly's attempt to minimize the number of civilian deaths, there can be no doubt that they took place. Whatever the reliability of the specific stories told later in Catholic sources, the correspondence emanating from the army is quite clear. What Cromwell does own up to is the deaths of many townspeople: 'of the former inhabitants, I believe scarce one in twenty can challenge any property in their houses. Most of them are run away and many of them killed in this service.'[95] Cromwell knew the garrison to be overwhelmingly 'outsiders', so this must be a reference to the deaths of civilians. This is also implied by his statement that many of the deaths were 'a just judgment upon them, causing them to become a prey to the soldier, who in their piracies had made preys of so many families, and made their bloods to answer the cruelties which they had exercised upon the lives of divers poor Protestants.'[96] These again are references not to the garrison, almost all of whom had arrived in the past few weeks (as Cromwell well knew), but to the inhabitants of the town who had been notoriously involved in piracy, and probably to alleged atrocities in which Protestant prisoners were starved and drowned years before.

All the letters and newsbooks on the Cromwellian side that reported the sack of the town acknowledged that when the defenders abandoned the battlements, the troops (presumably under their captains) scaled the walls and stormed through the town. Cromwell never says whether he attempted to restrain them, or whether he allowed events to take their course, although his silence is eloquent. All the other English accounts are silent on that too (again I do not think this silence is neutral). So although army sources claimed that many more were spared death at Wexford, the number killed in the first assault would

Ó Siochrú for this reference.   94 L&S 1, pp 486–7. He does not make clear that these incidents had happened in 1641–2.   95 L&S 1, p. 487.   96 L&S 1, p. 486.

appear to be indiscriminately soldiers and civilians as one would expect with an army out of control.

Cromwell's letter home is edgy and defensive, with long digressions aimed to lay the blame on Synott for stalling the surrender, and particularly for dragging things out on the day of the assault. And Cromwell distances himself – although, significantly, not God – from what ensued.

> We intending better to this place than so great a ruin, hoping the town might be of more use to you and your army, yet God would not have it so; but by an unexpected providence in his righteous justice, brought a just judgment upon them ... I could have wished for their own good and the good of the garrison that they had been more moderate ... Thus it has pleased God to give into your hands this other mercy, for which, as for all, we pray God may have all the glory. Indeed your instruments are poor and weak and do nothing but through believing and that is the gift of God also.[97]

That the intention had been to secure the town by surrender on terms, that the storm and sack of the town were uncontrolled by the senior officers, that they needed to make clear that the Governor was to blame for not surrendering while he could, were confirmed, or at any rate reiterated, by all the English reports from Wexford back to London.

VII

The Drogheda massacre was a massacre. It was without straightforward parallel in seventeenth-century British and Irish history. There were occasions when 3,000 or more combatants were killed in a single engagement; there were occasions when a comparably high *proportion* of those on the losing side were killed. There were a few examples of the defeated being killed in cold blood, but probably not on the scale of Drogheda, and there were even fewer occasions when it would seem that significant numbers of civilians were killed. But there was nothing which matched it in scale or in the range of its brutalities.

Charles Carlton has tabulated deaths during the English Civil Wars. He says that there are nine battles in which more than 1,000 participants were killed, but in none of these was the death rate on either side above 25 per cent. Much the same is true of towns taken by storm. Even at Basing, the proportion of the defenders killed was around one quarter – 100 out of 300–400. Civilians were clearly killed in significant numbers (80 or so at Bolton by Rupert's soldiers probably the largest number) or in cold blood (as again by Rupert's men at

---

[97] L&S 1, pp 486–8.

Leicester in late May 1645).⁹⁸ In Scotland, higher proportions of the defeated army were killed during and especially in the immediate hot aftermath of battle (one in three Covenanters at the battle of Aberdeen in September 1644; one in two at Auldearn on 9 May 1645;⁹⁹ and the Covenanters took their revenge at Philiphaugh on 13 September 1645 where half of Montrose's men were killed in hot blood and many more in cold blood, after General Leslie's undertaking of quarter was overruled by his council of war).¹ None of the numbers or percentages on these occasions reached the total killed at Drogheda.

Death-rates in the major battles in Ireland were comparable to those in Scotland,² although the slaughter of Lord Preston's Army at Dungan's Hill (8 August 1647) was certainly the highest proportionately (probably over 60 per cent) and perhaps absolutely of all the battles of the Wars of the Three Kingdoms.³ The average death rate in all the set-piece battles in Ireland was roughly three times the rate in England (30 per cent as against 10 per cent). This was very much in line with the sixteenth-century wars in Ireland where bad faith and killings in cold blood had been commonplace in the early 1540s as in the last quarter of the sixteenth century, although the English did not return to the system of martial law and provost marshals described elsewhere in this volume for that earlier period.⁴ No storm of an Irish town in the 1640s led to more than 100 deaths.

So the Drogheda massacre does stand out for its mercilessness, for its combination of ruthlessness and calculation, for its combination of hot- and

98 Carlton, *Going to the wars*, chapter 9 ('To slay and be slain'); though c.f. W. Coster, 'Massacre and codes of conduct in the English Civil Wars', in Levene and Roberts, *Massacre in History*, pp 92, 96, 98–100, who puts the number slain at Bolton at '78+'. He gives the largest number slain in cold blood in one place as the 120 soldiers who surrendered to Waller at the end of the battle of Cheriton (29 March 1644), most of whom were (or were thought to be) Irish. However, this figure is not sustained or justified in the only source Coster cites (J. Adair, *Roundhead General: a military biography of Sir William Waller* (London, 1969), p. 148). 99 E. Furgol, 'The civil wars in Scotland', in John Kenyon and Jane Ohlmeyer (eds), *The Civil Wars: a military history of England, Scotland and Ireland, 1638–1660* (Oxford, 1998), pp 58–9. 1 C.V. Wedgwood, *Montrose* (London, 1952, 1998), pp 110–15. For a context for Scottish massacres, see A. Macinnes, '"Slaughter under trust": clan massacres and British state formation', in Levene and Roberts, *Massacre in history*, pp 127–48 2 Lenihan, *Confederate Catholics at war, 1641–49*, chapters 5–6 and appendix 8. See index entries. 3 Scott Wheeler, *Cromwell in Ireland*, pp 34–5, thinks 3,000 out of 5,000 men in Preston's army were killed at Dungan's Hill, and that 'the English put to the sword all prisoners who were "formerly of our side, and all English"'. See also, P. Lenihan, 'The army of Leinster and the battle of Dungan's Hill', *Irish Sword*, 18 (1991), 139–53; A.W.M. Kerr, *Ironside in Ireland: the remarkable career of Lieutenant General Michael Jones* (London, 1923), pp 69–75 4 Probably the best introduction to martial law as it was (brutally and corruptly) used in Ireland is D. Edwards, 'Ideology and experience: Spencer's *View* and martial law in Ireland' in H. Morgan (ed.), *Political ideology in Ireland, 1541–1641* (Dublin, 1999), pp 127–57, or, in a more focused way, in D. Edwards, 'Beyond reform: martial law and the Tudor reconquest of Ireland', *History Ireland*, 5:2 (1997), 16–21.

cold-bloodiness. With as much bloodstained ink having already been spilt about it, this essay adds nothing to what we know about what happened – except for a reproof to those who continue to misrepresent the plain facts. It simply says that we need to be careful not to exaggerate the blind anger and prejudice of the man responsible for it, Oliver Cromwell. Cromwell had, in my view, been building up to an explosion of anger against anyone who defied God's judgment in the wars of 1642–7. Those who, in the wake of what he took to be a conflict resolved, continued to fight for the family and the office God had blasted – be they English, Anglo-Irish or Irish – must be punished for the innocent blood they had shed. At Drogheda, he killed English, Anglo-Irish and Irish indiscriminately, if anything singling out the English for severity: their heads were the ones which against the custom of those wars were displayed on pikes; those who were spared death and transported to slave-conditions in Barbados were Irish. In establishing that Cromwell was content to undertake an *in terrorem* massacre at Drogheda, we should distance ourselves from too easily making him the scapegoat for the bigotry of others in the English conquest and miscalled Cromwellian Settlement. Paradoxically, by blaming Cromwell for the much more lasting horrors of the Commonwealth period in Ireland, we let those really responsible off the hook.

Propaganda, rumour and myth: Oliver Cromwell and the massacre at Drogheda

MICHEÁL Ó SIOCHRÚ

De English steal our hoart of Usqquebagh,
Dey put us to de Sword all in Dewguedagh[1]

On 11 September 1649, the New Model Army, commanded by Oliver Cromwell, stormed the town of Drogheda. The ensuing massacre helped establish his name as the primary scourge of Irish Catholics. However, in a fascinating article on the historical perceptions of Cromwell, Toby Barnard argues that this malignant reputation, in literary tradition at least, was largely a nineteenth-century construct.[2] It is certainly true that the subsequent disillusionment of the Catholic Irish with the duke of Ormond and the Restoration land settlement, followed by the trauma of defeat in the Jacobite Wars, eclipsed in the minds of many the horrors of the 1640s. Nonetheless, the misdeeds of Cromwell feature prominently, and consistently, in Irish language poetry from the mid-seventeenth century. For example, the poet Dáibhí Cúndún, writing in the 1650s, refers directly to Cromwell's complicity in the massacre at Drogheda, in which he claims that civilians, as well as soldiers, were killed.[3]

---

* I would like to thank the Leverhulme Trust for the two-year research fellowship, which enabled me to complete my work on this article. Thanks also to Professor Jane Ohlmeyer for commenting on an earlier draft.

1 This quote is from a contemporary poem, 'A medley of the nations [the Irish]', c.1655, in Andrew Carpenter, *Verse in English from Tudor and Stuart Ireland* (Cork, 2003), p. 312.
2 Toby Barnard, 'Irish images of Cromwell', in R.C. Richardson (ed.), *Images of Oliver Cromwell* (Manchester, 1993), pp 180–8. The dating of folklore is particularly difficult, but the sheer bulk of surviving material suggests that many of these stories may have been in circulation long before the nineteenth century. The case, however, remains unproven. See Dáithí Ó hÓgáin, 'Nótaí ar Chromail i mbéaloideas na hÉireann', *Sinsear*, 2 (1980), 73–83; Seán Ó Súilleabháin, 'Oliver Cromwell in Irish oral tradition', in L. Dégh, H. Glassie and F. Joinas (eds), *Folklore today: essays in honour of Richard Dorson* (Bloomington, 1976), pp 473–83; Alan Smith, 'The image of Cromwell in folklore and tradition', *Folklore*, 79 (1968), 17–39. 3 The relevant lines in *Aiste Dáibhí Cúndún* are '"S ón lá fuair Cromuil an chonair 'na slaodaibh/ 'nar sgaoil fá chumas an brusgar so an Bhéarla/ ar fuaid chupaird is chláir an

This tragic event had a profound and immediate impact on opinion in Ireland, which not only influenced the course of the war, but also the nature of that conflict. Arguments have raged for centuries over what exactly happened, but the emergence of the massacre story in late 1649, whether through private letters, published works or oral rendition, has received little attention. Uncovering this hitherto hidden trail should help resolve some of the disputes regarding one of the most controversial episodes in Irish history.

I

Despite the advent of printing in the mid-fifteenth century, the channels for the propagation of news across much of Europe, including England and Ireland changed little over the next 150 years. As Richard Cust explains, early seventeenth-century England was still only a partially literate society, and so 'the commonest method of passing on news remained word of mouth'.[4] Official or private correspondence sometimes provided additional information to supplement a vibrant oral culture, creating a potent cocktail of rumour, gossip and genuine fact. Adam Fox has shown how a casual remark by a traveller at an inn about events at the English royal court could quickly spread panic across several neighbouring counties.[5] According to Ethan Shagan, this oral network provided an unofficial forum for the dissemination and interpretation of ideas, which proved impossible for the authorities to control.[6] Thus, while rumours might indeed be wildly exaggerated or totally inaccurate, they often represented the only source of uncensored news.

The outbreak of the Thirty Years War in 1618 increased the demand in England for regular printed reports from the continent. The first official 'Corantoes' appeared in the 1620s. Tightly controlled by the English Privy Council, they dealt solely with foreign news. However, more independent newsletters and 'separates' circulated in manuscript form, thus managing for

---

t-ár 's a' t-éirleach/ is tug i nDroithead Átha an t-ármhach créachtach/ ar mhnáibh, ar leinbh, ar fhearaibh is ar laochra'. See Cecile O'Rahilly, *Five seventeenth-century political poems* (Dublin, 1977), p. 47. [It was then that Cromwell went his deadly way/ to let loose the power of the English rabble/ spreading havoc and slaughter throughout the land/ and in Drogheda released his bloody army/ to strike the women, the children, the men and the troops.] Thanks to my father, Oisín Ó Siochrú, for his assistance with the translation. **4** Richard Cust, 'News and politics in early seventeenth-century England', *Past and Present*, 112 (1986), 65. **5** Adam Fox, *Oral and literate culture in England, 1500–1700* (Oxford, 2000), p. 353. **6** Ethan Shagan, 'Rumour and popular politics in the reign of Henry VIII', in Tim Harris (ed.), *The politics of the excluded, c.1500–1800* (Basingstoke, 2001), p. 58. Tim Harris believes that the lower social orders in seventeenth-century England had a higher degree of political awareness, and a more important political role, than is normally conceded. Tim Harris, *London crowds in the reign of Charles II* (Cambridge, 1987), p. 15.

the most part to avoid governmental censorship. The newsletters, forerunners of the more well known newssheets of the 1640s, reported on both foreign and domestic issues, while the 'separates' provided transcripts of trials, parliamentary proceedings and military campaigns.[7] With the deterioration in relations between King Charles I and parliament from 1640 onwards, the apparatus of censorship ceased to function, which resulted in an explosion of print. In 1640 no uncensored printed news books existed in England, but over the next 20 years 350 separate titles appeared.[8] These cheap, weekly pamphlets, with a print-run probably numbering no more than a few hundred, were widely circulated and read. They ranged in style from bland, factual narratives to wild diatribes, filled with invective, in which news was often manufactured, mixing fact and fiction much like the tabloid press today.[9]

According to Joad Raymond, the first recognisable printed news-book appeared on 29 November 1641. Entitled *The heads of several proceedings in this present parliament*, it contained reports of a rebellion which had broken out in Ireland a month earlier.[10] Within a few weeks the trickle of information became a flood, and the news books and pamphlets played a crucial role in whipping up anti-Irish and anti-Catholic sentiment, with a series of lurid tales (often illustrated) on the massacre of innocent Protestant settlers by bloodthirsty Irish Catholics.[11] The oral testimony of Protestant refugees, fleeing from rural areas to the city of Dublin, provided ample material for the London publishers.[12] A gullible public, horrified yet titillated by the gruesome tales emanating from Ireland, accepted uncritically these wildly exaggerated stories of death and mutilation. For the next six months increasingly hysterical reports from Ireland rolled off the presses, although the focus gradually shifted from the victims of terror to the alleged perpetrators of these heinous crimes, as all shades of political opinion in England demanded revenge. One account railed against 'these bloody Papists', who were guilty of 'cruelties and tortures exceeding all parallel, unheard of among Pagans, Turks, or Barbarians'.[13] There is a long

---

7 Cust, 'News and politics', p. 62; Fox, *Oral and literate culture*, p. 394.   8 Fox, *Oral and literate culture*, p. 394.   9 Joad Raymond, *Making the news: an anthology of the newsbooks of revolutionary England, 1641–1660* (Gloucester, 1993), p. 19.   10 Joad Raymond, *The invention of the newspaper: English newsbooks, 1641–1649* (Oxford, 1996), p. 13.   11 Iain Donovan provides an extensive list of the pamphlet literature in England dealing with events in Ireland during the early 1640s. Iain Donovan, 'Bloody news from Ireland: The pamphlet literature of the Irish massacres of the 1640s' (unpublished M. Litt thesis, TCD, 1995). According to Ethan Shagan, English publishers in 1641–2 condemned the Irish both for their popery and their disloyalty. See Ethan Shagan, 'Constructing discord: ideology, propaganda and English responses to the Irish rebellion of 1641', *Journal of British Studies*, 36:1 (1997), 7.   12 33 volumes of these depositions (including some miscellaneous documents) survive in the library at Trinity College, Dublin. TCD, MSS 809–41.   13 James Cranford, *The tears of Ireland. Wherein is lively presented as in a map, a list of the unheard of cruelties and perfidious treacheries of blood-thirsty Jesuits and the Popish faction* (London, 1642), p. 3.

tradition of virulent anti-Irish prejudice in English political and historical writings, dating back to Giraldus Cambrensis in the twelfth century.[14] The production, however, of cheap news books in the early 1640s made this material available to a much wider audience than had hitherto been possible.

In Ireland, as in England, a strong oral tradition continued to flourish. Whereas English was the language of the administration, parliament and the professional classes, and Latin the *lingua franca* among clerics and many scholars, the majority of the population still spoke Irish.[15] Determining the levels of literacy in early modern Ireland, however, has proved difficult due to lack of evidence. Nonetheless, by the mid-seventeenth century Raymond Gillespie estimates that a significant reading public existed, be it in English, Latin or Irish.[16] Manuscript copies of histories, genealogies, saints' lives and bardic poetry circulated widely in the first half of the seventeenth century, including large numbers of Geoffrey Keating's bulky history, *Foras Feasa ar Éirinn*.[17] Printing in Ireland was restricted to the city of Dublin, where the colonial authorities closely monitored the output, at least until the 1641 revolt.[18] Most books were imported from England, though clerics and traders also smuggled Catholic tracts into the country from the continent.[19] In addition to books in English and Latin, the authorities in Dublin published a number of Protestant texts in Irish during the first decade of the seventeenth century, while the Irish college at Louvain acquired a Gaelic language press in 1611.[20]

[14] Kathleen Noonan contends that Sir John Temple's hugely influential book, *The Irish rebellion*, first published in 1646, played a key role in developing the notion that the Irish were racially distinct, Kathleen Noonan, '"The cruell pressure of an enraged, barbarous people": Irish and English identity in seventeenth-century policy and propaganda', *Historical Journal*, 41:1 (1998), 152. For an analysis of the early modern discourse in England on Irish 'barbarism', see Clare Carroll, *Circe's cup: cultural transformations in early modern Ireland* (Cork, 2001), pp 11–27.   [15] Brian Ó Cuív estimates that while Irish was the dominant language in 1600, the seventeenth century marked the beginning of a real decline. See Brian Ó Cuív, 'The Irish language in the early modern period', in T.W. Moody, F.X. Martin and F.J. Byrne (eds), *A new history of Ireland*, iii, *Early modern Ireland, 1534–1691* (Oxford, 1991), pp 509–13. There are a number of excellent studies of literary developments in Ireland during the early modern period. Breandán Ó Buachalla, *Aisling ghéar: na Stíobhartaigh agus an t-aos léinn, 1603–1788* (B.Á.C., 1996); Joep Leerssen, *Mere Irish and Fíor-Ghael* (Cork, 1996); Éamonn Ó Ciardha, *Ireland and the Jacobite cause, 1685–1766* (Dublin, 2002); Patricia Palmer, *Language and conquest in early modern Ireland: English Renaissance literature and Elizabethan imperial expansion* (Cambridge, 2001).   [16] Gillespie argues that the seventeenth century marked an important shift in the balance between oral and written cultures. See Raymond Gillespie, 'Political ideas and their social contexts in seventeenth-century Ireland', in Jane Ohlmeyer (ed.), *Political thought in seventeenth-century Ireland* (Cambridge, 2000), p. 112.   [17] Bernadette Cunningham, 'Representations of king, parliament and the Irish people in Geoffrey Keating's *Foras feasa ar Éirinn* and John Lynch's *Cambrensis Eversus*', in Ohlmeyer, *Political thought*, p. 132.   [18] The first recorded printer, Humphrey Powell, set up business in Dublin as early as 1550. W.K. Sessions, *The first printers in Waterford, Cork and Kilkenny, pre-1700* (York, 1990), pp 2–5.   [19] Introduction to Ohlmeyer, *Political thought*, p. 29.   [20] Ó Cuív, 'Irish language in the early

Despite the limited development of printing in Ireland, the Catholic Confederates fully appreciated the importance of print propaganda. Shortly after establishing their association at Kilkenny in October 1642, they imported a printing press, probably from Flanders, operated by Thomas Bourke in Waterford. Propaganda or political works, such as edicts from the confederate Supreme Council or military instructions for confederate forces, constituted the vast bulk of Bourke's publications. However, his output appears to have been very limited, certainly by English standards, with fewer than thirty accredited titles still surviving.[21] Desperate for a peace treaty with Charles I, the Confederates avoided responding in print to the more lurid excesses of the London press, and rarely criticized English or Protestant interests in Ireland. In fact, they proved every bit as vigilant as the authorities in Dublin in regulating and monitoring the activities of printers and booksellers, and the Supreme Council in Kilkenny ruthlessly suppressed any independent publications which threatened a rapprochement with the king.[22]

In 1645, the arrival in Ireland of a papal nuncio, Giovanni Battista Rinuccini, archbishop of Fermo, challenged Bourke's printing monopoly in confederate territory. A Jesuit, Bryan MacDavitt, accompanied the nuncio to Ireland, bringing with him a printing press from France. Assembled in Kilkenny, the Jesuit press produced a number of religious tracts, as well as one of the first plays published in Ireland, *Cola's furie*, based on the life and violent death of the Protestant planter, Sir Charles Coote.[23] An internal Confederate crisis in August 1646, over a peace treaty with the Royalist marquis of Ormond, abruptly shattered the peaceful co-existence of the Waterford and Kilkenny printers. Clerical opponents of the treaty skilfully exploited the medium of

---

modern period', p. 533.   **21** Sessions lists eight imprints for 1643, seven for 1644, two for 1645, and then one for 1648 before Bourke disappears completely. Sessions, *First printers in Waterford, Cork and Kilkenny*, p. 11. McClintok Dix believes that thirty items survive from the Waterford press of Bourke, though concedes that the origins of some of them are doubtful. E.R. McClintok Dix, 'Printing in the city of Waterford in the seventeenth century', *Proceedings of the Royal Irish Academy*, 32c (1914–6), 333.   **22** The most spectacular example of this occurred in 1645, when an Irish Jesuit, Conor O'Mahony, resident in Portugal, published his *Disputatio Apolegetica* in Lisbon. O'Mahony called for the expulsion of all non-Catholics from Ireland and the rejection of the authority of the heretical Charles I. The book was banned by the Confederate authorities, and burned by the public hangman in Galway and elsewhere. Galway Corporation records, Book A, f. 191b; Peter Walsh, *The history and vindication of the loyal formulary or Irish remonstrance* (1674), pp 736–9. The king of Portugal also issued two orders in 1647, censuring the book, under pressure from the English Royalist ambassador. Bodl. Clarendon MSS 30, f. 198.   **23** Sessions, *First printers in Waterford, Cork and Kilkenny*, p. 182; E.R. McClintok Dix, 'Printing in the city of Kilkenny in the seventeenth century', *Proceedings of the Royal Irish Academy*, 32c (1914–6), 125–37. For information on 'Cola's Furie', see Patricia Coughlan, '"The modell of its sad afflictions": Henry Burkhead's *Tragedy of Cola's Furie*', in Micheál Ó Siochrú (ed.), *Kingdoms in crisis: Ireland in the seventeenth century* (Dublin, 2001), pp 192–211.

print to mobilize the mass of confederate opinion against the agreement and seize power. By 1648, however, with Royalist sympathizers once again in the ascendancy in Kilkenny, the Confederate press loyally supported the new peace treaty with Ormond.[24] The Royalist/Confederate alliance, however, proved less successful in controlling the spread of rumours, allegations and gossip through word of mouth, as Ormond subsequently discovered to his cost.

II

Following the execution of Charles I in January 1649, preparations got underway in England for an invasion of Ireland, led by Oliver Cromwell. In anticipation, English propagandists worked themselves into a frenzy of invective, denouncing the Catholic Irish in numerous publications. One commentator, in an earlier attempt to convince reluctant English soldiers to campaign in Ireland, could barely contain his excitement at the prospect of slaughtering thousands of Irish Papists. 'Cursed be he that holdeth back his sword from blood!!!' the author foamed, 'Yea, cursed be he that maketh not his sword stark drunk with Irish blood!!!'[25] In the summer of 1649, the authorities at Westminster authorized Thomas Waring, formerly clerk of the commission taking statements from Protestant refugees in Ireland, to revisit in print the alleged massacre of settlers at the outbreak of the Irish rebellion.[26] Basing his account on the depositions of the survivors, he described the Catholic Irish as 'savages', 'cannibals', and argued that there could be 'no safety in cohabitation with them'. Therefore, Waring concluded, parliament could 'warrantably and righteously endeavour the extirpation of them'.[27] As William Hickman later wrote to Cromwell, 'God hath marked out that people for destruction'.[28] In this increasingly hate-filled atmosphere, the subsequent behaviour of Cromwell's troops in Ireland should have surprised nobody.

Arriving in Dublin towards the end of the campaign season in late August, with an army totalling 12,000 men, Cromwell desperately needed a cooperative local population to provide food and other vital supplies to his forces. From the

---

24 See Micheál Ó Siochrú, *Confederate Ireland, 1642–1649: a constitutional and political analysis* (Dublin, 1999), p. 183. **25** Theodore De la Guard, *The simple cobbles of Aggavam in America* (London, 1647), quoted in Denis Murphy, *Cromwell in Ireland: a history of Cromwell's Irish campaign* (Dublin, 1883), p. 45. **26** 9 May, 1649, Day's proceedings of the Council of State, *Cal. S.P. Domestic, 1649–50* (London, 1875), pp 131–2. **27** Thomas Waring, *A brief narration of the plotting, beginning & carrying on of that execrable rebellion and butcherie in Ireland* (London, 1650), pp 30, 41–2, 64. The poet and Commonwealth official, John Milton, helped arrange a speedy publication of Waring's work, *Cal. S.P. Domestic, 1649–50*, p. 474. **28** John Nickolls (ed.), *Original letters and papers of state addressed to Oliver Cromwell* (London, 1743), p. 29.

outset of his campaign in Ireland, therefore, he developed a sophisticated propaganda strategy. While he condemned those 'barbarous and bloodthirsty Irish' who had planned and taken part in the rebellion, he publicly assured the lower social orders that he had no quarrel with them.[29] Cromwell hanged a handful of his troops for unlicensed pillaging, and where possible insisted that his army pay for whatever goods they took.[30] This drive to win the hearts and minds of the local population initially proved successful and unsettled Cromwell's opponents. Sir Edmond Butler, governor of County Wexford, wrote to Ormond complaining that he had difficulty in preventing the country people from making terms with the Parliamentarians, as 'the rouges allure them by speaking that they are for the liberty of commoners, and that they will have no contribution of them if they [hold] their market at the camp'.[31] Unlike the Royalists, as Sir Lewis Dyve noted wearily, the parliamentarians 'had money to pay for what they took'.[32]

The storming of Drogheda, however, and the massacre which ensued, severely tested Cromwell's communication and propaganda skills. He wasted little time in relating an official version of events to both John Bradshaw, President of the Council of State, and William Lenthall, Speaker of the House of Commons. On 16 September, Cromwell admitted frankly to Bradshaw that as the town had refused a summons, the defenders received no quarter. He argued that this harsh approach would, in the long run, 'save much effusion of blood', terrorizing the Royalists and their allies into an early submission.[33] Cromwell repeated this justification in a letter the following day to Lenthall, but added the powerful motive of revenge for the massacre of Protestants in late 1641/early 1642. 'I am persuaded', Cromwell wrote, 'that this is the righteous judgement of God upon those barbarous wretches, who have imbrued their hands in so much innocent blood'.[34] Drogheda's defenders, however, included English Royalists, as well as many Irish Protestants, while the Catholic Confederates did not control the town at any stage during the 1640s. Therefore, the inhabitants and most of the garrison could not have taken part in the attacks on Protestant settlers.

Ten days later, Cromwell sent Lenthall an update of military developments in Ireland, along with details of enemy losses at Drogheda. Apart from the 3,000

---

29 W.C. Abbott (ed.), *The writings and speeches of Oliver Cromwell* (4 vols, Oxford, 1939, rep. 1988) 2, pp 107, 111–12.   30 The Parliamentary expedition was well furnished with cash, which Ormond believed was 'more formidable' then any military strength they possessed: 22 Aug. 1649, Ormond to Clanricarde, Bodl. Carte MSS, vol. 25, f. 321. For detailed information on Parliamentary financial preparations for the invasion of Ireland, see James Scott Wheeler, *Cromwell in Ireland* (Dublin, 1999), pp 67–71.   31 29 September 1649, Sir Edmond Butler to Ormond, in P.H. Hore (ed.), *The history of the town and county of Wexford*, (6 vols, London, 1906), 5, pp 278–9.   32 Both quotes are from, *A letter from Sir Lewis Dyve to the lord marquis of Newcastle ... September 1648–July 1650* (Hague, 1650), p. 28.   33 Abbott, *Writings and speeches of Oliver Cromwell*, 2, pp 124–5.   34 Ibid., pp 125–8.

military casualties, the list also included the phrase 'and many inhabitants' (figure 10, p. 254). Unfortunately, the original letter does not appear to have survived, but parliament ordered a copy to be published on 2 October.[35] Writing in the mid-nineteenth century, Thomas Carlyle claimed, without any evidence whatsoever, that the offending phrase must have been added in a later printed compilation, while C.H. Firth suggested that the printers in 1649 may have simply tagged the entire casualty list onto Cromwell's original letter, perhaps at the orders of parliament.[36] Carlyle's supposition is easy to dismiss, as the original pamphlet from October 1649, complete with the incriminating phrase, still exists. As for Firth's theory, the Parliamentary regime in England took a close interest in printing, and passed an act in late September to control output.[37] John Field and Edward Husband, official printers to the parliament, risked losing their positions if they tampered with official documents in any way. Moreover, why parliament might have added something so important to one of Cromwell's letters, without his approval, has never been explained.[38] Oftentimes, the most straightforward answer is the correct one. In his report, Cromwell, who witnessed the attack on Drogheda at close quarters, simply acknowledged that the casualties included a number of civilians.

In deciding to publish Cromwell's dispatches from Ireland, parliament publicly signalled its support for his conduct at Drogheda. Cromwell received a letter of thanks, 'taking notice that the House approve of the execution done at Drogheda as an act both of justice to them and mercy to others who may be warned by it'.[39] The Parliamentarians fully realized the importance of this victory over the Royalists, and ordered it to be proclaimed in churches across London.[40] In Ireland, Cromwell proved eager to exploit the psychological advantage the slaughter at Drogheda gave him over his adversaries. On 12 September, the day after taking the town, he demanded that the nearest Royalist garrison, at Dundalk, capitulate immediately to avoid a similar fate.[41] The

---

35 *Letters from Ireland ... together with a list of the chief commanders, and the number of officers and soldiers slain at Drogheda* (London, 1649).   36 Thomas Carlyle (ed.), *The letters and speeches of Oliver Cromwell* (3 vols, London, 1904), 1, pp 474–5.   37 *An act against unlicensed and scandalous books and pamphlets, and for the better regulating of printing*, Bodl. Carte MSS, vol. 207, pp 1–10.   38 Although parliament did on occasion, much earlier in Cromwell's military career, remove certain potentially controversial sections from his letters before printing them, there is no example of any material ever being added to his printed correspondence. Peter Gaunt, *Oliver Cromwell* (Oxford, 1997), p. 63.   39 Order in Parliament, 2 October 1649, PRO, SP 25/87, f. 89. Being the bearer of good news was also a lucrative business. The Committee on Irish Affairs of the Council of State ordered that Captain Samuel Porter be paid £100 'for his pains and charges in his journey bringing the news of taking Drogheda'. Warrant book of the Committee of Irish Affairs, PRO, SP 21/29, f. 146.   40 Proceedings of the Council of State, *Cal. S.P. Domestic, 1649–50*, pp 327–8.   41 J.T. Gilbert (ed.), *A contemporary history of affairs in Ireland from 1641–52* (3 vols, Dublin, 1879), 2:2, p. 267.

defenders, however, had already fled, while Carlingford and Newry subsequently surrendered without a fight. As news of Cromwell's severity at Drogheda spread, through word of mouth and written correspondence, it appeared as if his harsh policy might indeed pay immediate military dividends.

III

Shortly before Cromwell's arrival in Ireland, Ormond had issued a defiant declaration, forbidding any commander to capitulate to the enemy 'upon any terms save in the language of the sword, but upon all occasions to fight it out to the last man'.[42] However, following the defeats at Drogheda and elsewhere, he admitted in a letter to Charles II that it was 'not to be imagined how great the terror is that those successes and the power of the rebels have struck into this people'.[43] Both Ormond and Lord Inchiquin received first-hand accounts of the events at Drogheda from soldiers who fled the doomed town. Captain Arthur Dillon, having escaped the carnage, reported directly to Ormond, and told of the 'putting to the sword of all the garrison'.[44] Captain Tadhg O'Connor's men suffered a similar fate, 'put to the slaughter, until after the fall of night'. Left for dead, the wounded captain slipped over the walls under the cover of darkness, 'the rest of his men being all killed'.[45] Inchiquin received a particularly detailed account from Garrett Dungan and others, which he relayed to Ormond on 15 September, just four days after the assault on the town. They all agreed that killings had taken place, despite the promise of quarter, and 'yet many were privately saved' by sympathetic parliamentary officers and soldiers.[46]

Ormond, a voluminous correspondent, quickly put his pen to work, denouncing the actions of Cromwell and the New Model Army. On 18 September, he informed Prince Rupert of the fall of the town, with the 'bloody execution of almost all that were within it'.[47] The following week, in a letter to the king, Ormond accused Cromwell of 'much more than anything I ever heard in breach of faith and bloody inhumanity'.[48] In an appeal to the religious and nationalistic prejudices of the English Royalist, Lord Byron, he wrote that Cromwell's deeds 'would make as many several pictures of

---

[42] *The loyal declaration of his Excellency the right honourable, James Marquesse of Ormond* (London, 1649), p. 5. Fine rhetoric from a man who subsequently avoided battle with the Parliamentarians at all costs!   [43] [Sept] 1649, Ormond to Charles II, in Gilbert, *Contemporary history*, 2:2, pp 306–7.   [44] Narrative of military operations during 1649, Bodl. Carte MSS, vol. 26, f.441v.   [45] Petition of Captain Teague Connor, Bodl. Carte MSS, vol. 156, f. 272; King's Inn Library, Dublin, Prendergast Papers, vol.10, ff 151–2.   [46] 15 Sept. 1649, Inchiquin to Ormond, Bodl. Clarendon MSS, vol. 38, f. 24.   [47] 18 Sept. 1649, Ormond to Prince Rupert, Bodl. Carte MSS, vol. 25, f. 553.   [48] 27 Sept. 1649, Ormond to the King, Bodl. Carte MSS, vol. 25, ff 596–8.

inhumanity as are to be found in the Book of Martyrs or in the relation of Amboyne'.[49] He compared the behaviour of the Parliamentarians unfavourably to that of the Royalists, giving as an example the storming of a small fortification outside Dublin the previous July. The Royalists took the entire garrison at Rathfarnham prisoner on that occasion, 'and though 500 soldiers had entered the castle before any officer of note yet not one creature was killed, which I tell you by the way to observe the difference ours and the rebels making use of a victory'.[50]

While unreserved in condemning the massacre at Drogheda to Royalist leaders abroad, Ormond proved uncertain on how best to exploit the affair in Ireland itself. Cromwell's severe tactics had clearly unnerved his opponents in the field. As the parliamentary army approached Trim, the panicked garrison fled, failing to burn the town and castle, as ordered by Ormond.[51] The commander of Wexford, Cromwell's next main target, warned Ormond of the townsmen's inclination to surrender, 'such impression they have of Drogheda'. Interestingly, the governor of Co. Wexford urged Ormond to reveal if there had been a breach of quarter at Drogheda, in order 'to settle the hearts of the commonality', and stiffen their resolve to oppose Cromwell.[52] The governor's plea suggests that Ormond played down the horrors of Drogheda, so as not to alarm his supporters. Indeed, the Royalists printed few items of consequence after Cromwell's arrival in Ireland, and by early 1650, following the fall of Cork and Kilkenny, Ormond no longer had access to a printing press.[53]

Despite the reservations of the inhabitants, Wexford did resist Cromwell, and suffered a similar fate to Drogheda when Parliamentary troops stormed the town on 11 October. Over 2,000 soldiers and civilians died as the English 'put all to the sword that came in their way'.[54] According to the one eyewitness account, the Parliamentarians spared more soldiers at Wexford than at Drogheda, but severely damaged the town itself, much to Cromwell's dismay.[55]

---

49 29 Sept. 1649, Ormond to Lord Byron, Bodl. Carte MSS, vol. 25, ff 628–30. The murder of English merchants by the Dutch at Amboyna in the East Indies almost 30 years earlier had caused outrage in England. See, for example, *A true relation of the unjust, cruel, and barbarous proceedings against the English at Amboyna in the east Indies, by the Netherlandish governor and council there* (London, 1632).   **50** 29 Sept. 1649, Ormond to Lord Byron, Bodl. Carte MSS, vol. 25, ff 628–30.   **51** Narrative of David Galbraith, Bodl. Carte MSS, vol. 25, f. 526.   **52** [30] Sept. 1649, Sir Edmund Butler to Ormond, Bodl. Carte MSS, vol. 25, f. 638. The letter from the commander of Wexford, Col. Sinnott, is in Gilbert, *Contemporary history*, 2:2, p. 282.   **53** Burke's printing press at Waterford was moved to Cork, *c*.1648. Sessions, *First printers in Waterford, Cork and Kilkenny*, pp 186–9. The Parliamentarians gained control of Cork in October 1649, and Kilkenny fell the following March, thus denying the Royalists access to a printing press.   **54** Abbott, *Writings and speeches of Oliver Cromwell*, 2, pp 140–3.   **55** Cromwell had hoped to use the town of Wexford to quarter his troops for the winter. Abbott, *Writings and speeches of Cromwell*, 2, pp 140–3. A contemporary account of the assault on Wexford can be found in NLI, MS 9696, ff 15–29.

Worryingly for the Parliamentarians, as winter approached, the persistent rumours of breach of quarter and the murder of civilians had begun to generate a backlash. When Cromwell approached the strategic fort of Duncannon in late October, the commander, Thomas Roche, rejected a summons to surrender, as 'I and those under my command are sensible of your cruel and tyrannical quarter'.[56] Shortly afterwards, when the Royalists attempted to retake the town of Carrick, recently seized by the Parliamentarians, the attackers cried out to the besieged 'that they would soon give them Tredagh [Drogheda] Quarters'.[57]

In December 1649, the Catholic bishops assembled at Clonmacnoise, in an effort to rally support for the Royalist cause 'and the good of this nation in general'. The prelates claimed that the Parliamentarians intended 'to extirpate the Catholic religion out of all his Majesties dominions', and they condemned Cromwell's 'tyrannical resolution', so brutally displayed at Drogheda and elsewhere.[58] Stung by this attack, Cromwell replied in early January with a savage broadside against the bishops, who he denounced as 'hypocrites', misleading the 'poor laity' to destruction. As for his conduct of the war, he defied anybody 'to give us an instance of one man since my coming into Ireland, not in arms, massacred, destroyed or banished', though he concluded, 'concerning the two first of which justice hath not been done *or endeavoured to be done* [my emphasis]'.[59] This crucial caveat allowed him to justify his actions, by claiming that he had at least tried (if not always successfully) to do the right thing. Cromwell, unlike his most blatant apologists, was clearly troubled by some of what he had seen at Drogheda and Wexford.

Despite the best efforts of the Catholic bishops to direct Irish anger against Cromwell and his troops, it had already become apparent that many blamed Ormond for the depressing litany of military disasters. In mid-October an English Royalist news sheet, *Mercurius Elenecticus*, focused on Ormond's failure to attempt a relief of Drogheda, 'to the wonder and amazement of his friends'.[60] The following month, John Walsh, a leading confederate and ardent Royalist, described an encounter with the marquis of Antrim, a long-time adversary of Ormond. According to Antrim, admittedly a notoriously unreliable witness, 'it was the opinion of many a considerable man though not of the

---

56 [25 Oct.] 1649, Thomas Roche to Cromwell, BL Add MSS 4769B, f. 4.   57 Copies of letters relating to Ireland, 1649–50, with narrative, BL Add MSS 4769B, f. 8v.   58 The declaration by the bishops was one of the few items produced by the Kilkenny press in 1649. *Certain acts and declarations made by the ecclesiastical congregation at Clonmacnoise* (Kilkenny, 1649).   59 *A declaration of the Lord Lieutenant of Ireland, for the undeceiving of deluded and seduced people: which may be satisfactory to all that doe not wilfully shut their eyes against the light. In answer to certaine late declarations and acts, framed by the Irish Popish Prelates and clergy, in a conventicler at Clonmacnoise*, in Abbott, *Writings and speeches of Oliver Cromwell*, 2, p. 203.   60 *Mercurius Elenecticus* (no. 24), 8–15 Oct. 1649. Ormond had anticipated such a criticism in a letter to Lord Byron in late September, and promised to provide a rebuttal at a later stage. 29 Sept. 1649, Ormond to Lord Byron, Bodl. Carte MS 25, ff 628–30.

common sort' that the Irish had been betrayed.[61] The following day, however, the earl of Castlehaven, writing from the recently besieged city of Waterford, confirmed the existence of widespread discontent with Ormond's leadership.[62] The Lord Lieutenant professed to be unperturbed by the rumours and allegations, having already informed Viscount Muskerry that 'want of [military] success is always accompanied with the dislike of the people and that with calumny'. In a stoical mood, he reflected how 'when things go well every body approves the conduct how improper soever to attain so good an end, and when things fall cross, the conduct is blamed though never so good'.[63]

Despite his tempered philosophical musings on human inconsistency, Ormond adopted an aggressive pro-active strategy to deflect any blame from himself. Shortly after the fall of Drogheda, he wrote to the king, claiming that he had provided supplies and ammunition to the town 'for a much longer time than it held out'.[64] Criticism of the defenders, implied in the case of Drogheda, was more overt following the storming of Wexford. Two days after the Parliamentarians seized the town, Ormond informed Owen Roe O'Neill that Cromwell's success was due to the 'cowardice of the soldiery and treachery of the townsmen and inhabitants, and not for the things necessary for the defence thereof for a much longer time'.[65] In a further letter to the king at the end of November, Ormond admitted that the military defeats had occasioned 'a jealousy in the Irish of the English [Royalists]', but he still refused to accept his own shortcomings had in any way contributed to the disastrous state of affairs.[66] He complained bitterly about the lies spread by 'the ever disloyal party of the Irish [Catholic] clergy', for whom 'lying was as natural as rebellion'.[67]

His close associates on the continent similarly went to great pains to defend his reputation at the expense of incompetent officers or duplicitous Catholic clergy. Shortly after arriving in Holland from Ireland, Sir Robert Stewart wrote to Charles II, blaming the fall of Drogheda on the over-confidence of the governor, Sir Arthur Aston, who otherwise would have been relieved by Ormond.[68] A few months later, another close colleague, Sir Lewis Dyve, published a book in The Hague, which gave a detailed account of what he termed 'the massacre at Drogheda'. According to Dyve, 'there were butchered near 3,000 soldiers, and those truly reputed the best that kingdom afforded'. He roundly criticized Catholic bishops and priests in Ireland, and accused them of

---

61 16 Nov. 1649, John Walsh to Ormond, Bodl. Carte MS 26, f. 219. 62 Castlehaven related how rumours abounded that Ormond had made a deal with Parliament and betrayed Ireland, 17 Nov. 1649, Castlehaven to Ormond, Bodl. Carte MS 26, f. 223. 63 30 Oct. 1649, Ormond to Muskerry, Bodl. Carte MS 26, f. 55. 64 Sept. 1649, Ormond to Charles II, Gilbert, *Contemporary History*, 2:2, p. 270. 65 13 Oct. 1649, Ormond to Owen Roe O'Neill, Gilbert, *Contemporary History*, 2:2, p. 297. 66 30 Nov. 1649, Ormond to Charles II, Gilbert, *Contemporary History*, 2:2, pp 329–30. 67 26 June 1650, Ormond to King, Bodl. Carte MS 28, f. 54. 68 4 Nov., 1649, Sir Robert Stewart to Charles II, Bodl. Carte MS 130, f. 94.

fomenting internal dissent in Royalist ranks. In Dyve's opinion, they had effectively undermined Ormond's leadership, as well as his ability to wage war on Cromwell and the New Model Army.[69] This version of events played well at the Stuart court-in-exile, and has dominated the subsequent historiography of the Cromwellian Wars, but it failed to impress the bulk of those fighting for the king in Ireland. Discontent continued to grow, and the main cities under Royalist control, Limerick, Galway and Waterford, proved reluctant to admit Ormond or any troops under his command. On 12 August 1650, the Catholic bishops gathered at Jamestown issued a declaration against the continuance of his government, accusing him, among other things, of failing to relieve the siege of Drogheda the previous September.[70] Ormond may have won the propaganda battle at court, but he could not control the spread of rumour and gossip. A change of fortunes on the battlefield might have enabled him to hang on, but the continued lack of military success eventually forced him to leave the country at the end of 1650.

IV

Outside of Ireland, apart from official declarations by the Parliamentarians, news of the massacre at Drogheda spread through oral and written communications. In the weeks following the fall of Drogheda letters flooded back to England, a number of which were subsequently published. According to Bulstrode Whitelocke, a leading figure in the new regime, while they might have provided different details and perspectives on events, 'they all agreed in the not giving of quarter' at Drogheda.[71] Sailors working on the Irish Sea, or soldiers returning home from service in Ireland, were another obvious source of news. Thomas à Wood, for example, fought at Drogheda, and regaled his family in England the following year with colourful and lurid stories about the massacre of civilians, which his brother later published.[72] As early as November 1649, however, Royalists circulated detailed accounts of the killing of officers after quarter had been given. James Buck, for example, wrote to Sir Ralph Verney describing the murder of his younger brother, Sir Edmund, at Drogheda as he walked alongside Cromwell, and the execution of Colonel Boyle, allegedly summoned away to his death while dining with Lady More.[73]

---

69 *A letter from Sir Lewis Dyve*, pp 24, 34–6.   **70** 12 Aug. 1650, A declaration by the bishops at Jamestown, Bodl. Carte MS 28, ff 300–2.   **71** Bulstrode Whitelocke, *Memorials of the English affairs or an historical account* (London, 1682), pp 411–12. For examples of published letters, see *Two letters from Dublin in Ireland and the other from Liverpoole* (London, 1649). **72** Anthony Wood, *The life of Anthony à Wood from the year 1632 to 1672* (Oxford, 1772), pp 68–9.   **73** 18 Nov. 1649, James Buck to Sir Ralph Verney, *HMC, Report 7, appendix* (London, 1879), p. 457.

In early October 1649, news reached the continent of Cromwell's bloody victory in Ireland. The Venetian ambassador in Paris received a report from England (dated late September 1649), which told of 'a sanguinary encounter' at Drogheda.[74] 'Came newes of Droghedas been taken by the Rebells', the Royalist, John Evelyn, noted in his diary, 'and all put to the sword, which makes us very sad, forerunning the losse of all Ireland'.[75] Shortly afterwards, Charles II's secretary, Sir Edward Nicholas, wrote to Ormond from Paris about Drogheda, 'and the cruelty used by those inhumane rebels that took it, which had made a great impression of grief in his Majesty'.[76] Those in exile on the continent, however, remained constantly wary of any news from home. Another Royalist, Charles Parker, later wrote to Nicholas about 'a strong rumour of good news from Ireland but we have been so often deceived that I will suspend troubling you with the particulars of it until we have it confirmed'.[77]

In addition to the increasingly detailed and graphic oral and written communications about Drogheda in the latter months of 1649, a bitter war of words also erupted in print. Despite the best efforts of the Parliamentarian regime, Royalist newssheets continued to appear regularly throughout 1649, publishing bitter diatribes against the new political order. The London press had become increasingly preoccupied with the affairs of Ireland as the preparations for Cromwell's invasion force continued apace during the summer of 1649. By mid-September the focus had shifted specifically to the town of Drogheda, which the Royalist newssheets proclaimed confidently was an 'impregnable town'. Confident that the Parliamentarians would suffer defeat and humiliation in Ireland, they gave details of alleged setbacks suffered by Cromwell on his march from Dublin.[78] Such bravado was misplaced, as the recent capture of Drogheda by the Royalists had proved that the town was far from impregnable. On 22 September, a vessel from Ireland brought news that Drogheda had fallen to Cromwell, with the loss of 3,000 defenders. *The Moderate Messenger*, a Parliamentary publication, wanted to believe the news, 'but reports are commonly accompanied with such incredible stories, that it diminisheth that credit which otherwise would be given thereto'.[79]

The Royalist press also responded cautiously, with the editor of *Mercurius Elenecticus* declaring that he would not render himself 'so ridiculous as others

---

74 Like most major European powers, Venice refused to recognize the English Commonwealth at first, and did not send an official representative to London until 1652. *Calendar of State Papers, Venice*, vol. 28 (London, 1927), p. 121.   75 E.S. De Beer (ed.), *Diary of John Evelyn* (Oxford, 1955), 2, p. 565.   76 16/26 Oct. 1649, Secretary Nicholas to Ormond, Bodl. Carte MS 25, ff 747–8.   77 3/13 Aug. 1650, Charles Parker to Secretary Nicholas, BL, Egerton MS 2534, f. 34.   78 *Mercurius Pragmaticus*, 10–17 Sept. 1649; *The Man in the Moon*, (no. 22), 12–19 Sept. 1649.   79 The news from the Dublin vessel was published in *A modest narrative of intelligence*, 15–22 Sept. 1649; See also *The moderate messenger* (no. 22), 17–24 Sept. 1649.

have done, in reporting falsities improbable, nay impossible things, to please the credulous readers'.[80] Other newssheets simply denied the veracity of the reports from Ireland, claiming as late as the first week in October that Drogheda still held out against Cromwell.[81] The publication of letters from Hugh Peters and Cromwell on 2 October, provided details of the siege and assault on the town, though one news-sheet poked fun at Peters' precise figure of 3,552 enemy losses, 'not a man more or less'.[82] Casualty lists, notoriously inaccurate in the early modern period, were a particular bone of contention with the Royalists. Following the rout of Ormond's army by Colonel Michael Jones at Rathmines in early August, *Mercurius Elenecticus* claimed that the Parliamentarians tampered with a letter from Dublin giving details of the battle, doubling the number of Royalist casualties 'with an ink of a blacker temper than the letter was written in'.[83] *The Man in the Moon* questioned the news from Drogheda, and declared that the besiegers themselves had lost 3,000 men.[84] In an effort to convince a sceptical public, some Parliamentary newssheets published Cromwell's account of events, including his full casualty list with the phrase 'and many inhabitants'. A number of others, however, no doubt conscious that the killing of civilians, even those suspected of massacring Protestant settlers, would reflect badly on Parliamentary forces, chose to omit these controversial words when reproducing the letter for publication.[85]

Parliamentary newssheets accepted Cromwell's justification that the slaughter at Drogheda would hasten an end to the conflict in Ireland. An official government publication insisted that the sacking of the town had so terrified the enemy, 'that they scarce can make a defensive war against us, but leave us everywhere masters of the field'.[86] According to another news sheet, 'though

---

80 *Mercurius Elenecticus* (no. 22), 17–24 Sept. 1649.   81 See for example *Mercurius Pragmaticus*, 10–17 Sept. 1649. The Parliamentarian press mocked the unwillingness of Royalists to accept reports from Drogheda, until confirmed not only by public news, but also by letters from their friends, 'although some of them would faine discredit still the truth thereof upon some trifling conjecture'. *A brief relation of some affairs and transactions* (no. 3), 16 Oct. 1649   82 *Mercurius Pragmaticus*, 25 Sept.–2 Oct. 1649. The Reverend Hugh Peters, from the safety of Dublin, almost certainly based his estimate on the defenders' muster rolls, plus the 1,000 Cromwell believed had perished fleeing to St Peter's church for safety. Cromwell thought that upwards of 3,000 had died in the attack, 'but some say near four thousand'. *A letter from Ireland read in the House of Commons on Friday September 28 from Mr Hugh Peters* (London, 1649), pp 4–5; Abbott, *Writings and speeches of Oliver Cromwell*, 2, pp 125–8.   83 *Mercurius Elenecticus* (no. 21), 10–17 Sept. 1649. Ormond, while admitting to the defeat in a letter to king, also claimed that Jones grossly exaggerated the number of Royalist casualties, 27 Sept. 1649, Ormond to Charles II, Bodl. Carte, MS 25, ff 596–8.   84 *The Man in the Moon* (no. 24), 26 Sept.–10 Oct. 1649.   85 *The Kingdomes weekly intelligencer* (no. 331), 25 Sept.–2 Oct. 1649, and *Perfect occurrences of every daie journal of the parliaments* (no. 144), 28 Sept.–4 Oct. 1649 included the phrase, while *The perfect weekly account*, 26 Sept.–3 Oct. 1649, *Several proceedings in Parliament* (no. 1), 25 Sept.–9 Oct. 1649 and *A perfect diurnall of some passages in Parliament* (no. 323), 1–8 Oct. 1649, did not.   86 *A brief relation of some*

some are of the opinion, that the enemy's rage will be the greater, by the slaughter at Tredagh, yet we find the terror great, that is upon them'.[87] Unable any longer to refute the evidence concerning the fall of Drogheda, the Royalist press began to focus on the 'inhuman cruelty' of the Parliamentary forces, and for the first time stories about a wholesale massacre of civilians began to emerge.[88] In early October, the *Mercurius Elenecticus*, until then the most moderate of the Royalist newssheets (at least in its Irish coverage), made a number of specific and lurid allegations. The dead at Drogheda included women and children, while many officers died after quarter had been promised them, 'in the most cruel manner they could invent, cutting off their members, and pieces of their flesh, which they wore in their hats triumphantly two days after'.[89] *The Man in the Moon* picked up on the allegations of civilian deaths the following week, claiming that of the 3,000 dead, 2,000 were women and children. It concluded damningly that the 'barbarous cruelty in that abhorrid act [was] not to be paralleled by any of the former massacres of the Irish'.[90] Whether based on first-hand accounts from Ireland, gleaned from rumours circulating around London, or simply invented, these stories added to Cromwell's growing reputation for cruelty in Ireland.

Within a matter of weeks, the attention of the London press had shifted from Drogheda to Wexford and elsewhere. For the next nine months, the public continued to have access to newssheets hostile to the Commonwealth regime, despite the strict regulations controlling printing.[91] As their war effort began to collapse, however, Royalist reports on Ireland became increasingly far-fetched, seizing on any slight piece of good news as evidence of a major setback for the Parliamentarians. Fictitious Royalist armies marched on Dublin, while Cromwell suffered defeats wherever he went, 'himself hardly escaping, a sad farewell for him to leave Ireland on such conditions'.[92] Shortly after Cromwell's return to England in late May 1650, the Council of State took steps to suppress all unofficial news publications. Mr Ellis, the printer of *Mercurius Pragmaticus*, was incarcerated in Newgate, and shortly afterwards, his paper, along with *The Man in the Moon* and *Mercurius Elenecticus* ceased to appear.[93] The Royalist press had finally been silenced and, in England at least, uncensored news from Ireland became increasingly difficult to obtain.

---

affaires and transactions, civil and military, both forraigne and domestique (no. 1), 2 Oct. 1649. 87 *The moderate intelligencer*, 27 Sept.–4 Oct. 1649.   88 *The Man in the Moon* (no. 24), 26 Sept.–10 Oct. 1649; A second Royalist news sheet talks of enemy reports of 'another Utopian victory', *Mercurius Pragmaticus*, 9–16 Oct. 1649.   89 *Mercurius Elenecticus* (no. 24), 8–15 Oct. 1649.   90 *The Man in the Moon* (no. 26), 17–24 Oct. 1649.   91 *Mercurius Pragmaticus*, 9–16 Oct. 1649 complained about the act, while *Mercurius Elenecticus* (no. 23), 24 Sept.–1 Oct. 1649, revelled in openly flouting the new law.   92 *The Man in the Moon* (no. 53), 1–9 May 1650.   93 Abbott, *Writings and speeches of Oliver Cromwell*, 2, p. 262.

VI

Writing in the 1680s, the duke of Ormond described pen and paper as 'dangerous tools', yet the seventeenth-century explosion in printing had helped create an even more potent weapon, the popular press.[94] During the 1640s, however, the Confederate Irish came off second best in the propaganda war against their adversaries. Hampered by limited printing facilities, and constrained by the desire not to alienate their monarch, their most effective literary broadsides were often directed not against the Parliamentarians but, ironically, against their own comrades in a series of internal disputes. Similarly, in late 1649, following the storming of Drogheda, the Royalist/Confederate alliance did little to counter Parliamentary propaganda, except through word of mouth or private correspondence. Only in England, where the maverick editors of Royalist newssheets defied efforts by Westminster to regulate publishing, did an alternative view to Cromwell's official account appear in print. Nonetheless, Cromwell's reputation for cruelty towards the Irish, clearly well established by the early 1650s, was consolidated over the next two centuries, particularly in popular culture.[95] Vincent Morley, Breandán Ó Buachalla, Toby Barnard, Raymond Gillespie, Michael Perceval-Maxwell, and Jane Ohlmeyer have already begun to uncover the complex relationship between contemporary writings and the histories of the 1640s, but the role of propaganda during the course of the war itself, whether in oral, written or printed form, is deserving of more attention than it has hitherto received.[96] Only then can we begin to disentangle myth from reality in what the seventeenth-century Kerry poet, Seán Ó Conaill, described as 'an coga do chríochnaig Éire [the war that destroyed Ireland]'.[97]

---

[94] *A letter from His Grace, James, duke of Ormond, Lord Lieutenant of Ireland, in answer to the Right Honourable Arthur, earl of Anglesey, Lord Privy Seal* (London, 1682), p. 4. Thanks to Jane Ohlmeyer for bringing this reference to my attention. [95] In a paper delivered at the 'Unity and diversity in European culture' conference, hosted by the British Academy in September 2003, Vincent Morley identified a number of poets, including among others Seán Ó Gadhra, Aodh Buí Mac Cruitín, Art Mac Cumhaigh and Antaine Raiftearaí, from the seventeenth to the nineteenth centuries, who included Cromwell as a principal figure in their 'rogues' gallery' (article forthcoming). [96] In addition to those works already referenced, see Toby Barnard, '"Parlour entertainment in an evening"? Histories of the 1640s', and Michael Perceval-Maxwell, 'Robert Southwell and the duke of Ormond's reflections on the 1640s', both in Ó Siochrú (ed.), *Kingdoms in crisis*, pp 20–43, 229–47. [97] Seán Ó Conaill's 'Tuireamh na hÉireann' in O'Rahilly (ed.), *Five seventeenth-century political poems*, p. 75.

The laws of war in seventeenth-century Europe and their application during the Jacobite War in Ireland, 1688–91

JOHN CHILDS

Although a literature exists on the historical and philosophical evolution of the laws of war during the seventeenth century, little attempt has been made to evaluate their impact upon the conduct of hostilities in the field.[1] 'Laws' of war is a misnomer. These were not laws that had been approved by a ruling prince or representative assembly, agreed codification was entirely absent, and there were no courts or agencies of enforcement. They resembled voluntary codes of practice and conduct, usually unwritten, which governments and soldiers chose to follow, adjust or ignore depending upon the nature of their opponents and the imperatives of reciprocity. 'Customs of war' is a more accurate description. Because it is a more common usage, 'laws of war' will be employed throughout.

First, what were the origins and nature of those laws that attempted to modify and restrain the practice of war during the seventeenth century? According to Geoffrey Parker most of the modern conventions appeared in Europe between 1550 and 1700, 'both in theory and, rather more slowly, in practice'. He has identified five principal components.[2] The law of nature and nations suggested behaviour that might normally be expected from reasonable, moral Christians. Based on the Bible, Roman Law, Canon Law and the works of St Augustine and the *Summae* of St Thomas Aquinas, this code was assumed

1 R. Tuck, *The rights of war and peace: political thought and the international order from Grotius to Kant* (Oxford, 1999); J.J. Johnson, *Ideology, reason and the limitation of war: religious and secular concepts, 1200–1740* (Princeton NJ, 1975); J.J. Johnson, *Just war tradition and the restraint of war* (Princeton NJ, 1981). This paper is concerned with laws governing the conduct of war and the behaviour of military personnel towards each other and civilians. Laws that regulated relations between states (*jus inter gentes*), later defined by Jeremy Bentham as international law, and laws that might have enjoyed more universal application (*jus gentium*) are not under consideration. 2 G. Parker, 'Early modern Europe', in M. Howard, G.J. Andreopoulos and M.R. Shulman (eds), *The laws of war: constraints on warfare in the western world* (New Haven & London, 1994), pp 41–2; G. Parker, 'The etiquette of atrocity: the laws of war in early modern Europe', *Empire, war and faith* (London, 2003), pp 143–68.

to be universal amongst Christians. Secondly, the Peace of God movement during the eleventh century established, *inter alia*, the enduring principle that those who could do no harm should not be harmed. Thirdly, there was Military Law, the internal legal codes through which armies sought to organize and discipline their men to create and retain military effectiveness. Fourthly, there were the laws and customs of war, frequently prefixed by the adjective 'ancient', which had accumulated through practice, precedent and common sense. Although subject to local variations, these were international and self-evident to logical and rational minds. Fifthly, there was reciprocity – 'do as you would be done by' – resulting in codes of conduct that were always unwritten, varied widely, and tended to be theatre-specific. As well as these legal factors, the hard practicalities of logistics, financial cost, weapons, tactics, institutional structures, ritual and ceremony also influenced the conduct of war.

Gradually, during the later sixteenth and seventeenth centuries, two complications greatly reduced the efficacy of the laws of war: the failure to establish a supra-national agency of enforcement and the split in the Western Church. On 24 October 1648, the Thirty Years War ended. The peace treaties at Osnabrück and Münster established an international system that was to colour and shape West European inter-state relations until 1789. There is no evidence that Hugo de Groot's *De Juri Belli ac Pacis* (1625) directly influenced the plenipotentiaries but his ideas had reached a wide audience by 1648. Perhaps his advocacy of order, system and honour in warfare and international relations, within a framework of natural law, had a subliminal effect.[3] The notion of collective security was raised during the negotiations but only partly implemented through the appointment of Sweden and France, the two most obvious beneficiaries of the Peace, as guarantors.[4] Recent historical thinking interprets the Peace of Westphalia as conservative and backward-looking rather than the harbinger of future international 'systems'.[5] Yet, there was a discernible sense amongst the negotiators that such a destructive war must not be allowed to reoccur and it was incumbent upon them to create a comprehensive and durable peace. By and large their successes were greater than their failures: there was no return to general European war until Napoleon finally unravelled the remaining skeins of Westphalia; religion diminished as a major *casus belli* within Central and Western Europe; and the Westphalian settlement became a benchmark against which later French attempts at territorial expansion were measured and partially contained. However, Westphalia encouraged rather than discouraged international conflict because it demonstrated that war, even if

---

3 See D. Croxton, *Peacemaking in early modern Europe: Cardinal Mazarin and the Congress of Westphalia, 1643–1648* (London, 1999).   4 G. Symcox (ed.), *War, diplomacy and imperialism, 1618–1763* (London, 1974), pp 39–62.   5 R. Asch, *The Thirty Years War: the Holy Roman Empire and Europe, 1618–1648* (Basingstoke, 1997), pp 141–9.

unsuccessful in achieving its political ends, strengthened the nation state and absolute monarchy. Those German principalities that did not acquire additional territory at Westphalia still secured the right to raise and maintain their own armed forces and increased their political independence from the Holy Roman Emperor, in both domestic and foreign affairs. Their increasingly absolutist governments, bolstered by the new standing armies, allowed the major German princes to exercise augmented power within the Empire and sell their favours to the principal external players in Imperial affairs: France, Sweden, Spain, Austria and the Netherlands.

Generally, the laws of war applied to conflicts between Christians and were more likely to be observed in hostilities between those of the same branch of that confession. Turks, Muslims and devotees of the numerous deities found by European explorers and colonists in Asia, Africa and the Americas were, naturally, excluded. Laws governing conflict between Christians belonging to the Western Church broke down in the face of the Protestant Reformations of the sixteenth century. Not only did the split in the Western Church introduce elements of extreme emotion and ideology into warfare but the demarcation between soldier and civilian became indistinct. Even worse, plebeian soldiers or infantrymen grew more numerous than cavalrymen, who were usually drawn from higher social orders. Foot soldiers were much cheaper to raise and maintain than mounted men and, in the new age of gunpowder weapons, more effective. Laws that functioned within the international brotherhood of chivalrous gentlemen and aristocrats could not possibly be expected to extend to peasant pikemen and musketeers.[6] Following the schism in the Western Church the laws of war within Europe underwent little basic change but were frequently ignored as the religious clashes induced massacre, vengeance, self-interest, bigotry and conversion through violence.

Most armed contests over religion contained elements of civil war. As Barbara Donagan has pointed out, during the English Civil War the worst excesses were often avoided because participants knew that when conflict ended they would have to live side-by-side with former enemies.[7] The English Civil War was also paradoxical because, although it was basically caused by differences in religion, it was a contest between Protestants rather than the usual European line-up of Protestant versus Catholic. Donagan also places emphasis on the fact that the three English Civil Wars were short: the longer a war, the more likely that restraint would break down because violence and animosity became institutionalized and socially acceptable to generations that grew up knowing nothing else.

---

[6] Blaise de Monluc, *The Habsburg–Valois Wars and the French Wars of Religion*, ed. I. Roy (London, 1971), p. 41. [7] B. Donagan, 'Codes and conduct in the English Civil War', *Past and Present*, 118 (1988), 65–95.

In order for laws, customs, common practices, and ritual to function, they had to serve mutual interests. When mutuality ceased adherence faltered. Reciprocity, the fear of reprisals, has always been the basic coercion obliging soldiers, civilians and politicians to follow codes of conduct in the fighting of wars. Whether it was the extraction of contributions during the Thirty Years War; the unwritten agreement to avoid chemical weapons during the Second World War; or the power of nuclear deterrence between 1945 and 1991, reciprocity has been the effective determinant. Perhaps the prime reciprocal factors encouraging restraint in seventeenth-century warfare were expense and logistics. For instance, it was cheaper and more convenient to exchange prisoners than incarcerate them.[8] No participant wanted to be burdened with the care of redundant enemy combatants and so arrangements for the regular and frequent exchange of prisoners were often amongst the first diplomatic contacts between antagonists. Failing this, every effort was made to persuade prisoners to accept service with the captor's own army. The financial and economic costs of war were high. In the protracted wars of the seventeenth century states needed to minimize their martial expenditure, so it was preferable to fight on enemy soil in order to pay and supply troops from an opponent's resources. Sweden campaigned for over a century on the premise that, ideally, war should be self-financing. Campaigns were normally offensive aiming at the occupation of territory possessing sufficient agricultural and economic value to support troops. This restricted campaigning to certain parts of Europe, for instance the Netherlands, the Rhine and Po valleys, coastal margins and river lines. Because of the ever-present threat and frequent reality of war, these theatres developed infrastructures capable of dealing with and profiting from war.[9] Constraint imposed by logistics was a great operational leveller, controlling the size of field armies.

Both the tactical capabilities of armies and advances in military engineering further restrained the conduct of war. With rare exceptions, seventeenth-century armies, and navies, were unable to destroy their opponents. Most battles, although sometimes tactically decisive, were usually operationally and strategically indecisive. Breitenfeld in 1631, Aughrim in 1691, Blenheim in 1704 and Ramillies in 1706 were exceptions that proved the rule. Even then, none of these battles brought an end to the war. Sweden fought on for another seventeen years after Breitenfeld, whilst Marlborough's initial victories failed to terminate the War of the Spanish Succession. Even after Aughrim, success at Limerick was no foregone conclusion for Ginkel's army. Indecisiveness was a major characteristic of the politico-military system. In the first place, most

---

8 *Cal. S.P. Dom. 1690–1*, p. 393, Lords Justices of Ireland and General Ginkel to the earl of Nottingham, 28 May 1691.   9 M.P. Gutmann, *War and rural life in the early modern Low Countries* (Princeton, NJ, 1980).

wars involved coalitions leading to half-hearted campaigning and a multiplicity of, usually, conflicting war aims resulting in complicated peace negotiations. Secondly, armies employed the same weapons and tactics. Advantages, when they occurred, were fleeting: Sweden's shock value in Germany lasted less than two years. Thirdly, war was territorial and, in an age of poor road networks and dependence upon water communications, the fixed fortification, built according to the *trace italienne*, was dominant. Armies could only progress by the systematic siege and capture of enemy fortresses in order to clear lines of communications and occupy hostile territory from which the conquering troops could be supplied. So, to a great extent, the conduct of war was governed by the demands of practicality, reciprocity and the deterrence of mutual weakness rather than abstract laws. It was not that contemporary generals did not wish to thrash their opponent's army and occupy his territory – French plans for the dismantling of the Dutch Republic in 1672 offer sufficient witness – but they lacked the means. Limited methods of fighting led to wars fought for limited political ends because the politicians were dependent upon what their soldiers could deliver. Wars could rarely be fought to natural, strategic conclusion. Instead, negotiations induced by attrition and war weariness resulted in compromise, negotiated peace settlements that contained the seedlings of the next war. In this sense, the Jacobite War in Ireland was atypical. Although its conclusion resulted from negotiation, Ginkel had effectively eliminated the Jacobite field army at Aughrim and taken the two remaining, viable fortresses at Galway and Limerick. Ginkel thus recaptured the entirety of Ireland for the English and Protestant interest. In seventeenth-century terms, it was a complete and decisive victory.

Dr Mortimer's evidence suggests that the material and human damage caused by the Thirty Years War, which has so traumatized European memory, resulted principally from the demands of military supply.[10] Confessional differences and gratuitous violence certainly did not harmonize civil-military relations but the deterioration was mostly caused by the expectation of the military that they could live off the land and the inability of local economies to provide for this on more than a *pro tem* basis. Quite when the system of organized contributions became the basis for military supply in Western Europe is not clear, but probably it matured during the first half of the Eighty Years War between Spain and the rebellious Netherlands.[11] By the time of Wallenstein it was a well-established and practised art. When an area of enemy, or even neutral, territory was occupied, every town and village was assessed and ordered to pay a sum in cash or kind. Failure to deliver by the deadline saw the execution

---

[10] G. Mortimer, *Eyewitness accounts of the Thirty Years War, 1618–48* (Basingstoke, 2002). See also G. Benecke, *Germany in the Thirty Years War* (London, 1986), pp 22–42.   [11] G. Parker, *The army of Flanders and the Spanish Road, 1567–1659* (Cambridge, 1972), p. 142.

of hostages and houses torched, 'brandschatzen'.[12] When an area was exhausted, the troops moved on. Gustav II Adolf marched through central and southern Germany in 1631 and 1632 perhaps in pursuit of vague political objectives, but certainly searching for productive areas to place under contribution.[13] Contributions demanded by the myriad armies steadily devoured Germany: food production diminished, swathes of land were depopulated, and starving soldiers committed atrocities upon civilians in their desperation for sustenance. Peasants resisted, formed their own armed bands and took revenge upon the soldiers. To hold down contribution and supply areas, local small-scale wars of garrisons, posts and ambuscades were common.[14] The final stages of the Thirty Years War were dominated by self-perpetuating campaigns as armies, having evolved into almost autonomous, mobile mini-states, struggled for food and cash. During the Franco-Dutch War, 1672–78, the campaigns along the Middle Rhine and Mosel followed a similar pattern.[15]

The standing army was re-invented in Western Europe between 1648 and 1700 partly in response to the excesses of the Thirty Years War. In tandem, because war continued to be hugely expensive, the bogey of contributions was institutionalized. French and Spanish delegates met at Deynze, south of Ghent, between September 1676 and February 1678, to improve mechanisms for controlling the levying of contributions. Although no official concord emerged from the Deynze Conference, early in February 1677 Louis XIV decided to abide by the spirit of the proceedings and the Spaniards concurred in the following year. Total contributions from an affected area were not to exceed the yield from peacetime taxation levied in the base-year of 1669. Occupying armies were enjoined to negotiate contributions across wide geographical areas rather than victimize individual towns and villages. If the required sums could not be paid, then there was to be no retaliatory damage to property but an orderly exchange of hostages until arrangements were completed: the demon of *brandschatzen* was outlawed. Deynze was a brave attempt. Foreign occupation would always prove more onerous than the exactions of peacetime government but some of the gratuitous violence practised by soldiers on civilians was theoretically excised.[16] Although the Deynze Conference was probably motivated by the need to maintain military discipline, soldiers had begun to appreciate that there was more to gain from the systematic exploitation of a region than by its destruction. The conference also recognized that resources

---

12 For examples see Benecke, *Germany in the Thirty Years War*, pp 25–7.   13 P. D. Lockhart, *Sweden in the seventeenth century* (Basingstoke, 2004), pp 49–55.   14 See Benecke, *Germany in the Thirty Years War*, pp 61–71.   15 J. Childs, 'Captain Henry Herbert's narrative of his journey through France with his regiment, 1671–3', *Camden Miscellany*, 30 (Camden Society, London, 1990), pp 340–9.   16 H. van Houtte, 'Les conférences Franco-Espagnoles de Deynze, 1676–1678', *Revue d'Histoire Moderne*, 2 (1927), 191–215; J. Childs, *The Nine Years War and the British army, 1688–1697* (Manchester, 1991), pp 34–6.

were finite. Unfortunately, during the Nine Years War, 1688–97, most of the fine words spoken at Deynze were forgotten. The inhabitants of the Spanish Netherlands, the bishopric of Liège, Luxembourg and, in particular, Savoy-Piedmont, the Palatinate and Württemberg, suffered from requisitioning, commandeering, *brandschatzen*, plunder and pillage.[17]

Dr Lynn has suggested that fortifications, especially those of the field variety, had dual usage: one specifically military and the other to command and define areas that could be exploited through contributions.[18] So well organized had the levying of contributions become that, by the time of the War of the Spanish Succession, quartermasters were armed with printed, blank *pro formas* which they presented to the magistrates of towns and villages placed under contribution. Tired of marauding troops marching over his lands to use the Maas bridges, in 1690 the Prince-Bishop of Liège appointed a military commissioner to liaise with all foreign troops crossing his principality. He co-operated with the 'visiting' officers to ensure that the billeting and feeding of their men was executed with minimum disruption to the civilian population. In 1691, Louis XIV, the Circle of Swabia and the Duchy of Württemberg concluded a convention stipulating that only parties of more than 19 infantrymen or 15 cavalrymen, accompanied by an officer, might collect contributions; smaller groups would be treated as robbers.[19] There was no altruism in this. Pillage and marauding were deemed injurious to military discipline and effectiveness, although that did not prevent ruthlessness comprising a major element in the contemporary conduct of war. Burning and destroying standing forage as a means of denying an area or route of march to the enemy was routine. Villages and towns were burned if their occupation by an opponent was likely to yield him an advantage. Stores of provisions or other resources were seized or destroyed in order to deny them to the opposition, even if this had the most adverse effect upon the civilian population. The Second Ravaging of the Palatinate by the French during the winter of 1688–9 was the most egregious example of such tactics.[20] The *cordon sanitaire* – 'glacis' was Louvois's euphemism – which it created along the middle and upper Rhine and southwest Germany was so effective that large-scale operations in this theatre were impossible for the remainder of the Nine Years War. Also of note were the First Devastation of the Palatinate by Turenne in 1674 and the ferocious campaigns in Savoy-Piedmont between 1690 and 1696.[21] From Caesar, through Sherman,

---

17 On the war in Savoy-Piedmont see G. Rowlands, 'Louis XIV, Vittorio Amadeo II and French military failure in Italy, 1689–96', *English Historical Review*, 115 (2000), 534–69.
18 J.A. Lynn, 'Food, funds and fortresses: resource mobilization and positional warfare in the campaigns of Louis XIV', John A. Lynn (ed.), *Feeding Mars* (Boulder, CO, 1993), p. 150.
19 Childs, *Nine Years War*, pp 36–7. 20 See, K. von Raumer, *Die Zerstörung der Pfalz von 1689* (Munich, 1930). 21 G. Symcox, *Victor Amadeus II: Absolutism in the Savoyard State, 1675–1730* (London, 1983), pp 106–17; C. Storrs, *War, diplomacy and the rise of Savoy,*

to Bomber Harris, practitioners of terror have defended what they did by the plea that it would save time and lives in the longer term. The burning of towns, villages, and country houses; driving off cattle; the ruination of agriculture; and the destruction of forage during the Jacobite War in Ireland were entirely congruent with the conduct of war on the mainland of Europe.

To some extent, the evolution of the standing army in Western Europe between 1650 and 1700 lessened the impact of the military upon civilians. Magazine systems and the employment of private victualling contractors provided the basics for men and horses encouraging a partial reduction in naked plunder, whilst more effective central administrations, corps of professional officers and reasonably regular pay, produced an improvement in discipline. The introduction of militias mitigated the worst excesses of popular involvement in warfare by channelling civilian martial energies into local defence and support for the standing army. Standing armies and militias adopted uniform, which also helped by clearly distinguishing soldiers from civilians. However, benefits deriving from these developments should not be over-stated: armies continued to rely upon local resources for the majority of their daily requirements. Where possible, assuming the men had been paid, local markets were established close to military camps but these took time to create and were only viable if an army remained in a locality for some time, perhaps if undertaking a siege. Even then, locals took advantage of a captive market and raised their prices. Generals responded by trying to fix rates so the locals ceased bringing their produce to market resulting in a return to requisitioning, robbery and plundering. In Ireland, these problems were tackled, unsuccessfully, by Schomberg in 1689 and Ginkel in 1691.[22] The Danish troops were amongst the worst offenders, largely because their pay was substantially in arrears. Some of the native Irish thought that the soldiers from Denmark were Viking invaders reincarnate.[23]

To what extent was the Jacobite War in Ireland, 1688–91, conducted according to the various laws and rules, both theoretical and real? In the first place, it was that most vicious and uncontrollable of wars, a civil war fuelled by religion, ethnicity, two centuries of antagonism, vengeance, and external intervention.

1690–1720 (Cambridge, 1999), pp 20–73; Rowlands, 'Louis XIV, Vittorio Amadeo II and French Military Failure in Italy', pp 534–69. **22** *An order published by the command of the Duke of Schonberg, in the camp at Dundalk, for establishing the rates and prizes of provisions in the army* (London, 1689), 3 October 1689; G. Story, *A true and impartial history of the most material occurrences in the kingdom of Ireland during the last two years* (London, 1691), p. 48; G. Story, *A continuation of the impartial history of the wars of Ireland, from the time that the Duke Schonberg landed with an army in that Kingdom, to the 23d of March 1691/2 when their Majesties' proclamation was published, declaring the war to be ended* (London, 1693), pp 185–6; HMC, *Ormonde MSS*, old series, 2, p. 415. **23** K. Danaher and J.G. Simms (eds), *The Danish force in Ireland, 1690–1691* (IMC, Dublin, 1962), pp 15–23.

To the internal religious and ethnic ferment were added invasions by troops from England, Scotland, France (both Catholic and Huguenot), the Netherlands, Brandenburg and Denmark, each importing differing codes of martial conduct. Some common ground existed amongst the most senior officers, many of whom were well known to one another from either previous employment in the armies of Restoration Britain or those on the continent. The widespread internationalism of the European officer class probably also assisted in the establishment and maintenance of norms for military behaviour as did the remnants of chivalric values that still lurked amongst the landed classes of Western Europe, mostly encompassed within the vague concept of honour. However, this argument can be pressed too far. If an officer served in a number of theatres in each of which different standards of reciprocal behaviour were tolerated, there was a tendency for the lowest common denominator to become that man's point of reference. Conrad von Rosen brought his rough, impatient, Lithuanian manners to the Siege of Derry in 1689, introducing a level of intensity to the siege that both James II and Lieutenant-General Richard Hamilton were probably anxious to avoid.

Generally, officers learned their trade in the field allowing, presumably, acceptable standards of military behaviour to be inculcated from generation to generation. There were private military academies where young gentlemen might learn some rudiments of the soldier's art but their contribution to officer education was informal. They were more akin to the riding and fencing academies of the Renaissance.[24] In 1626, Turenne, when aged 15, studied at such a private academy. State-sponsored military schools had appeared towards the end of the sixteenth century in Tübingen and Kassel, whilst the Duc de Bouillon opened an academy at Sedan in 1606. Its most famous graduate was Hermann von Schomberg, the future marshal of France and commander of William III's army in Ireland during 1689.[25] The heightened political and religious tensions in Germany in the years immediately preceding the Thirty Years War encouraged further experimentation with specialist colleges, notably the *Schola Militaris* at Siegen, founded by Johann VII of Nassau in 1616 and opened in the following year. Its first, and last, director was Johann Jacobi von Wallhausen, a disciple of the new Dutch tactical methodology which he adumbrated in numerous treatises. Highly selective, it graduated a mere 20 students before locking its doors in 1623.[26] Wallenstein seems to have possessed an officer-training school at Gilschin within his duchy of Friedland, Bohemia.

---

24 W.H. Manchée, 'The Fouberts and their Royal Academy', *Proceedings of the Huguenot Society of London*, 16 (1938–41), 77–97; Sydney Anglo, *The martial arts of Renaissance Europe* (New Haven, 2000), pp 7–18. G. Hanlon, *The twilight of a military tradition: Italian aristocrats and European conflicts, 1560–1800* (London, 1998), pp 342–7, suggests that, in Italy, the principal function of the academies was to civilize the unruly aristocracy.   25 J. Childs, 'A patriot for whom? "For God and for honour": Marshal Schomberg', *History Today*, 38 (1988), p. 46.   26 G. Parker, *The Thirty Years War* (London, 1984), pp 12, 205–6, 278 n.33.

In 1626 the Assembly of Notables of France advocated a state-run military college to educate young noblemen, which Richelieu translated into a project for an academy housing 1,000 students, 400 to be trained for the church and 600 for the army. The attenuated result, in 1629, was the *Académie royale des exercises militaires* for 20 young aristocrats who were admitted when aged between 14 and 15: the young Condé attended in 1637. For two years they pursued a curriculum including morals, mathematics, fortification, logic, physics, geography, history, the French language, equine management, and the handling of weapons. The college, which cost the government 20,000 livres *per annum*, closed soon after Richelieu's death in 1642 and Mazarin's attempt to revive it failed before the jealous opposition of the Sorbonne.

Most aspiring officers joined regiments as teenage cadets, effectively military apprenctices, relying for their instruction upon emulating the example of their fellow officers and senior NCOs. After 1648, the guards and household regiments in the new standing armies often served as training units for aspiring officers. Many young officers, with the active encouragement of the state, served in foreign armies in order to gain experience of the latest methods of warfare employed by eminent practitioners. In 1653, Frederick I, the Great Elector of Brandenburg, gathered all cadets serving with regiments into a single company attached to the Knights' College at Kolberg (now Kolobrzeg in Poland). Louvois copied the Brandenburg scheme, establishing nine cadet companies in 1682, a total of 4,275 young gentlemen rising to 7,000 in 1688, but the scheme proved expensive and, after his death in 1691, it lost impetus and was abolished in 1696. The cadet companies were educationally ineffective: many of the cadets were illiterate, the syllabus was undemanding and badly designed, and discipline poorly maintained. The French army then reverted to the earlier practice of placing youngsters directly into field regiments as officer-cadets. The technical branches were better served. A French artillery school was opened in Douai in 1679, moving later to Metz and Strasbourg, whilst, in 1700, Vauban advocated the opening of a similar institution to instruct engineering officers. These colleges and cadet companies taught the rudiments of practical soldiering rather than the niceties of the laws of war. Certainly no mention of them is to be found amongst their various curricula.[27]

Self-education was, of course, always possible. The discerning reader, and probably rather few of the British, Dutch, Danish and Irish officers who fought

---

27 F.B. Artz, *The development of technical education in France, 1500–1850* (Cambridge, MA, 1966), pp 43–51; J.R. Hale, 'The military education of the officer class in early modern Europe', in C.H. Clough (ed.), *Cultural aspects of the Italian Renaissance: essays in honour of Paul Oskar Kristeller* (Manchester, 1976), pp 440–61, also in J.R. Hale, *Renaissance war studies* (London, 1983), pp 225–46; D. Parrott, *Richelieu's army: war, government and society in France, 1624–1642* (Cambridge, 2001), pp 38–44; G. Rowlands, *The dynastic state and the army under Louis XIV* (Cambridge, 2002), pp 178–88; J.A. Lynn, *Giant of the Grand Siècle*

in the Jacobite War fell into this category, could have extracted a great deal of information about the contemporary conduct of war from the leading memoir-histories. Amongst the most important were the volumes of Henry Hexham, Robert Monro, Richard Elton, Thomas Venn, Sir James Turner, and, especially for the Irish context, the earl of Orrery.[28] During the first part of the seventeenth century, a significant number of military books were published in England, reflecting both interest in the course of the Thirty Years War and a revival of domestic martial activity.[29] Those blessed with sufficient wealth and social standing to undertake the continental grand tour, often included in their itinerary attendance at a formal siege.[30] More common were the printed textbooks devoted to military discipline, tactics, drill, weapons' handling and field craft. Jacob de Gheyn's publication at the beginning of the century was rapidly followed by a host of imitators taking advantage of the market created by the Thirty Years War and the Eighty Years War between the Dutch and Spanish.[31] The English Civil Wars naturally threw up many military textbooks, both official and unofficial: Charles I published a drill manual for his army at Oxford during the winter of 1642–3, based on the *Directions for musters* of 1638. Perhaps the most influential was that by Henry Hexham.[32]

The Williamite and Jacobite armies in Ireland had common origins in the armed forces of Charles II and James II. Codes of military discipline, usually referred to as Articles of War, first issued in Restoration England on 17 March 1663 and periodically refined thereafter, were based on the model of the

(Cambridge, 1997), pp 268–75. 28 H. Hexham, *A historicall relation of the ... siege of Busse, and the surprising of Wesell* (London, 1630); *A journal of the taking of Venlo, Raermont, Syrale, the memorable siege of Mastricht, the towne & castle of Limburch under ... the Prince of Orange* (London, 1633); and *A briefe and true relation of the famous siege of Breda: besieged and taken in under the able and victorious conduct of His Highness the Prince of Orange* (London, 1637); R. Monro, *Monro, his expedition with the worthy Scots regiment called Mac-Keys* (London, 1637), new edition ed. William S. Brocklington (London, 1999); R. Monro, *The Scotch military discipline learned from the valiant Swede* (London, 1644); R. Elton, *The compleat body of the art military* (London, 1650); T. Venn, *Military & maritine discipline in three books* (London, 1672); Sir James Turner, *Pallas armata: military essays of the ancient Greek, Roman, and modern art of war* (London, 1683); R. Boyle, earl of Orrery, *A treatise of the art of war* (London, 1677). 29 M.J.D. Cockle, *A bibliography of the English military books up to 1642* (London, 1900 and 1957). 30 Attendance at the Siege of 's-Hertogenbosch in 1629 constituted Thomas Fairfax's only experience of warfare prior to the outbreak of the English Civil War. J.Wilson, *Fairfax* (London, 1985), pp 7–8. 31 J. de Gheyn, *Wapenhandling van roers, musquetten ende spiessen* (Amsterdam, 1607); J.J. von Wallhausen, *Kriegskunst zu Fuss* (Oppenheim, 1615); and *Manuale militare, oder Krieggs Manual* (Frankfurt-am-Main, 1616); J. *Militarie instructions for the cavallerie* (Cambridge, 1632); J. Bingham, *The tactiks of Aelian* (London, 1616); and *The art of embattailing an Army, or the second part of Aelians tactiks* (London, 1629); W. Barriffe, *Militarie discipline: or the young artillery-man* (London, 1635). 32 H. Hexham, *The principles of the art militaire; practised in the warres of the United Netherlands* (London, 1637 and 1642).

'Martial Laws' used by the Cromwellian garrison of Dunkirk.[33] They were revised in 1686 and 1688 and then reissued in 1692.[34] These were the codes of military law by which the army governed and disciplined its soldiers. They extended to questions of obedience to orders, uniform, health and hygiene, religious observance, musters, bearing and manner, misdemeanours against civilians, conduct in camp and quarters, offences committed by one soldier against another, and all matters pertaining to the internal organization and administration of the army. If a soldier failed to contravene one of the 130 clauses, then he was bound to fall foul of the catchall whereby, 'all other faults, disorders, and offences not mentioned in these Articles, shall be punished according to the general custom and laws of war.'[35] Offenders were tried before a court martial, which did not enjoy the right to impose punishments that might endanger the limbs or life of an offender because soldiers remained subject to the common law of England. All cases in which a soldier was accused of an offence against a civilian, or *vice versa*, automatically came before the common law courts. Apart from on active service abroad, when the Articles of War formed the sole legal code and the court martial was empowered to impose the full range of punishments, including death, the Articles of War were toothless and soldiers, by and large, had to be tried before common law courts for specifically military offences. During the emergency created by the mutiny of the Royal Scots in 1689, the Mutiny Act recognized that not only did the military require its own code of law within the British Isles but also needed courts that could impose effective and exemplary punishment. Courts martial were therefore allowed to try cases according to the Articles of War and inflict physical and capital punishment. Both the Jacobite and Williamite armies thus went to war in Ireland equipped with fairly comprehensive codes of military law, governing both intra-military behaviour and conduct by the military towards civilians, plus courts martial to enforce these regulations.

The rival armies also enjoyed a common tactical doctrine enshrined in *The abridgement of English military discipline*, first issued in 1675. A second edition was published in 1678, followed by a revision in 1682. The lessons learned from Monmouth's Rebellion in 1685 were incorporated in a revised edition in 1686: this was republished without alteration in 1686. The regulations relating to the infantry were extracted into a separate publication, *The exercise of the Foot*, in 1690. *Exercises of the Horse, Grenadiers of Horse and Dragoons* were added in 1701.[36] In effect, both armies fought the Jacobite War according to the drill and tactics laid down in the 1686 edition of the *Abridgement*, which favoured French

---

33 J. Childs, *The army of Charles II* (London, 1976), pp 98–9, 254–5.   34 J. Childs, *The British army of William III* (Manchester, 1987), pp 84–5.   35 Childs, *Army of Charles II*, p. 99.   36 Childs, *Army of Charles II*, p. 64; J.A. Houlding, *Fit for service: the training of the British Army, 1715–1795* (Oxford, 1981), p. 173n.

practices over those of the Dutch. All officers and soldiers should have been aware of the contents of both the Articles of War and the *Abridgement*. The latter was printed and, presumably, the majority of army officers must have had access to it even if they were not formally issued with a copy. The Articles of War were read periodically at the head of each troop, company and battalion by its commanding officer. Despite this, discipline amongst both officers and men was hard to enforce. In Ireland, there were regular hangings of deserters and other malefactors by the roadside *pour décourager les autres* but, throughout 1691, Ginkel's army was abominably behaved. Its soldiers plundered, pillaged, raped, assaulted and murdered. Robbery was routine, both from the enemy and their own comrades. Lack of regular pay was partly to blame but the greatest culprit was the failure of the Williamite government to provide its soldiers with a regular and decent supply of food and necessities. With men often close to starvation, no code of military law, however draconian its enforcement, was sufficient to maintain military discipline. In May 1691, Dr Robert George, who had acted as secretary to Schomberg during the campaign of 1689, sent a memorandum to the government in Whitehall listing the reforms required for 'the better management of the Irish War'. From the back bearings to this document, it is possible to discern the major disciplinary problems facing Ginkel in 1691. The officers and men failed to observe their religious obligations; did not pay for their billets; ate and drank to excess; dragoon and cavalry mounts were allowed to waste pasture; horse feed was seized without payment; there was misbehaviour in billets to the extent that every battalion needed a weekly tribunal of investigation to hear complaints; they robbed and plundered 'on pretence of nationality and religion'; straggled from the camp and column of march without leave or permission; seized and requisitioned horses; employed army horses for private purposes; destroyed corn; hindered ploughing; interfered with the smooth running of markets; took billets without reference to the quartermaster; and failed to keep their persons, clothes and arms clean.[37] Apart from bestiality with turkeys, a habit beloved of certain elements within the old Tangier garrison, imagination would struggle to add to the list.

There was, generally speaking, attention to some of the ritual and ceremonial aspects of conflict although there was no formal declaration of hostilities. Ireland drifted into war between December 1688 and February 1689, in much the same way that England had gradually descended into civil war during the first six months of 1642. Who was responsible remains unclear: the Protestants blamed the Catholics and *vice versa*.[38] Conversely, the war was concluded by a

[37] *Cal. S.P. Dom. 1690–1*, pp 398–402.   [38] For contrasting views on culpability for starting the Jacobite War see C. Leslie, *An answer to a book, inituled, the state of the Protestants in Ireland under the late King James's government* (London, 1692); *A faithful history of the northern affairs of Ireland from the late K. James accession to the crown, to the siege of Londonderry ... By a person who bore a great share in those transactions* (London, 1690).

proper peace treaty that, by the rather loose standards of the time, just about brought an end to the violence.³⁹ Prisoner exchanges occurred, although not as frequently as in the principal theatres of the Nine Years War. Jacobite garrisons that chose to surrender as prisoners of war rather than submit when summoned, were harshly treated. Those captured at Ballymore on 9 June 1691 were sent to Lambay Island off the coast of County Dublin where they endured miserable conditions. Even so, the hope was that they would volunteer for service in the armies of the Grand Alliance in Flanders under the command of Williamite officers.⁴⁰

Ritual was most closely associated with siege warfare. Sieges were theatre. Probably before, and most certainly after, Vauban's introduction of the three parallels at Maastricht in 1673, sieges were conducted according to a predictable and well-known pattern, similar to a stylized play or opera. Everyone knew what was coming, roughly when it would happen and what the dénouement would be. It was said that the great Vauban could predict almost to a day how long a siege would last. Because war was concerned with the capture of territory, the fortified town and city represented the key to strategy. Successful sieges offered solid and tangible gains whereas victory in battle was often ephemeral and could only be turned to political and strategic advantage if its exploitation could lead to the capture of important towns and cities. Many battles were fought when an army attempting to relieve a besieged place ran into the 'covering army' of the besiegers. When an important city in the Low Countries was besieged, Louis XIV often left Versailles with his court and ladies and took up temporary residence in the army camp. From here he could 'command' and observe from a suitable vantage point the unstoppable progress of his great army as it moved through the pre-ordained sequence of scenes and acts towards the surrounded city according to the carefully staged theatrical devices of the Vauban 'siege in form'. When the inevitable occurred, the Sun King was present in person to receive the keys from the defeated governor.⁴¹

However, a siege in form was the exception rather than the rule. The vast majority of towns in Europe and Ireland situated in strategically important areas or at nodal points on transport routes did not suffer formal sieges. An attacking army issued a summons to surrender and most had the good sense to comply. Only if the fortifications were strong and reasonably modern, and the town had been adequately garrisoned and provisioned, did a 'siege in form' occur. In other words, sieges only took place where the defender expected and

---

39 Rapparee activity, particularly in Cork and Kerry, continued throughout the decade of the 1690s. See É. Ó Ciardha, *Ireland and the Jacobite cause, 1685–1766* (Dublin, 2002), pp 87–111.
40 *Cal. S.P. Dom. 1690–1*, p. 418, Sir Charles Porter to Lord Henry Sydney, 17 June 1691.
41 The best summary of the rules governing siege warfare remains J.W. Wright, 'Sieges and customs of war at the opening of the eighteenth century', *American Historical Review*, 39 (1933–4).

wished for such an outcome: military initiative thus rested with the defending army rather than the attacker. The major sieges in Ireland – Derry, Cork, Kinsale, Athlone, First and Second Limerick, and Galway – were conducted according to the well-known but unwritten rules of siege warfare. At Charlemont in 1690, even the subtle distinctions between blockade and siege were observed.[42] However, it was one thing to agree the terms of a surrender but quite another to carry them out in the face of hostile, victorious troops. The Jacobite defenders of Carrickfergus in 1689 were grossly abused, mostly by the local Ulster Protestants, as they marched from the castle and town.[43] Neither was the Siege of Derry always conducted according to the rules, because James regarded the Derry men as rebels rather than regular troops.

Apparently, formal contributions were levied although the surviving records suggest that this was infrequent.[44] Schomberg's, William's and Ginkel's armies lived off the land, established local markets when in prolonged camp, and, particularly in 1691, drew supplies from depots in Dublin and Cork. The Jacobite armies, operating mostly amongst a sympathetic population, were supplied via local markets or directly from the countryside. However, in the aftermath of the first Siege of Limerick when the Jacobites were confined behind the line of the Shannon, pressure on supplies in Connaught and northern Munster became intense and the troops were forced to plunder and requisition from amongst their own supporters. A major problem for the Jacobites was the host of camp followers and refugees that the army attracted as the Williamite forces occupied larger and larger areas of Ireland. This was not just a problem for the Jacobites. Numerous 'Scots-Irish' followed William's army to the Boyne in 1690 where they distinguished themselves by the speed and rapacity of their battlefield pillaging.[45] Both armies plundered and robbed to reward their own soldiers and to deny resources to the enemy. It was rare for an army to quit a town under pressure and not reduce it to ashes before departure. Country houses were routinely stripped and burned and, towards the end of the war, neither side bothered to distinguish between friend and foe when an opportunity for plunder occurred. Forage and standing crops were devoured or burned, sometimes with strategic objectives in mind, often not. It was a vicious war in which material depredation was considerable and widespread. The only major city to escape substantial physical damage was Dublin. Yet, none of this was at variance with the conduct of operations in

---

42 *Cal. S.P. Dom. 1690–1*, p. 5, Schomberg to William III, 5 May 1690.   43 Story, *True and impartial history*, p. 10; Leslie, *An answer*, p. 161; *A full and true account of the besieging and taking of Carrickfergus by the Duke of Schomberg* (London, 1689), pp 1–2.   44 *A true and impartial account of their Majesties army in Ireland* (London, 1690), p. 3.   45 *The history of the wars in Ireland, betwixt their Majesties army and the forces of the late King James, by an officer in the Royal Army* (London, 1691), p. 18; Story, *True and impartial history*, pp 62, 82; *True and impartial account of their Majesties army in Ireland*, p. 2.

other theatres of the Nine Years War in the Low Countries, Italy, Germany and Spain.

The real problem in Ireland was the lack of clear distinction between soldier and civilian. William's soldiers treated all Catholic Irish with the greatest suspicion and rarely granted the benefit of the doubt. In the motion picture, *Full Metal Jacket*, as a U.S. Marine Corps helicopter skims the ground its machine gunner fires indiscriminately at everybody in sight, despite the fact that they are all obviously civilian, drawling, 'if they run they're V.C.; if they stand still they're disciplined V.C.' That exactly summarized the attitude of William's English, Dutch, French and Danish Protestant soldiers towards the native Irish: that of his Irish Protestant troops, principally the Enniskilleners, was a good deal more extreme. The issue was confused by the widespread guerrilla conflict and the employment of civilians in overtly military roles. Ulster, Derry and Enniskillen were defended in 1689 by their Protestant civilians converted into temporary soldiers. During the latter part of 1690 and the winter of 1690–1, militias commanded by regular army officers were organized in those counties firmly under Williamite control.[46] Again, these Protestant civilians under arms showed great enthusiasm for killing Irish irregulars. Then there were the rapparees. James II permitted the association between the Jacobite regular army and the irregular bands of armed pike men [a *rápaire* was a half-pike] in 1689, although he did try to make a distinction between freebooting robbers and Jacobite partisans. The Protestants failed to appreciate this nicety and hunted them all down like wild animals, killing as many in the field as possible and hanging those captured. The 'body count' of rapparees grew to be a measure of Williamite progress towards victory, similar to the later American obsession with the numbers of Viet Cong dead in Vietnam. In return, the rapparees, sometimes operating in conjunction with regular units, harried small Williamite garrisons, murdered stragglers and deserters, and passed intelligence to the main field army. Even the fearsome Danes were supposed to have been scared of the rapparees. In a predictable escalation, William's soldiers viewed all Catholic Irish as either rapparees or the natural supporters of rapparees. In effect, the activities of the rapparees ensured that the war in Ireland involved virtually the entire population and blurred the boundaries between civilian and military. If there was a conflict that demonstrated the utter wrong-headedness of believing that warfare in late seventeenth-century Europe was a business conducted by professional soldiers without involving the civilian population, it was to be found in Ireland. Similar 'total wars' were fought in the Balkans during the Austrian offensives after 1683, in Catalonia during the French

---

46 J. Mitchelburne, *An account of the transactions in the north of Ireland, anno domini, 1691* (London, 1692), pp 19–20; J.C. O'Callaghan, *History of the Irish Brigades in the service of France* (Shannon, 1969), pp 6–7; Story, *True and impartial history*, p. 148.

invasions between 1689 and 1697, and in Savoy-Piedmont from 1690 to 1696. 'Guerrilla' activity occurred in the wars between Denmark and Sweden, 1657–8 and 1674–9, when the Scanian peasants, driven to desperation by the harshness of the Swedish forces of occupation, joined local bands of irregulars. Popular, religiously-inspired resistance against the insensitive and Protestant Swedes also broke out in Poland in 1656.[47]

Historians are often insufficiently down-to-earth in their approach, hasty in forming moral judgements and unrealistic in their expectations of human behaviour. Most people have sufficient knowledge and experience to understand how everyday affairs function but war is different. It is very difficult for a non-soldier to appreciate how wars are fought, what the methodology involves, even to picture how a small unit fights. There is something to be said for recognizing that only practitioners can have a true understanding of warfare. Even then, an army is riddled with paradoxes in what it expects from its own soldiers: the men are required to be violent yet disciplined; obedient but able to demonstrate initiative; humane and compassionate whilst involved in killing; and do their duty under a system of laws and rules whilst undertaking an activity that militates against any form of control. Historians also need to be very clear in their definitions. The mass killing of soldiers as they broke from their formations and ran in panic from the field of battle, was not an atrocity. The unburied corpses littering the Aughrim countryside mostly died during the course of the battle and its aftermath, the pursuit. Defeated armies are pursued and their men killed – no victorious general would expect anything less from his command – but where the battlefield ends and the region of gratuitous and unnecessary butchery begins is unclear and cannot, in all probability, ever be defined. Even if it was definable, such distinctions could never be enforced. During the battle, the Jacobites killed Colonel Charles Herbert after he had been taken prisoner, and the Williamites similarly disposed of Colonel Charles Moore and Lord Galway. Although both actions were contrary to the laws of war, they were understandable given that soldiers could not guard prisoners in the heat of action.[48] The Reverend George Story blamed no-one but drew comparison with Henry V's massacre of French prisoners at Agincourt.[49] Again, neither historians, nor indeed lawyers, appreciate the absurdity of expecting a frightened soldier who is firing, hitting, stabbing, wounding and killing, to take a copy of the *Laws of war or Rules of engagement* from his back pocket and calmly consult the relevant chapter when the enemy soldier in front of him suddenly throws down his weapon and yells 'Quarter!' It has long been recognized that the raising of hands is the most dangerous point for a soldier seeking to surrender. He is as likely to be promptly bayoneted as arrested,

---

47 Ó Ciardha, *Ireland and the Jacobite cause*, p. 72, n.97; R.I. Frost, *The Northern Wars, 1558–1721* (London, 2000), pp 169–72.   48 Leslie, *An answer*, pp 162–3.   49 Story, *Continuation*, pp 135–6.

11 Nicolas Chevalier, *Historie de Guillaume III* (Amsterdam, 1692), p. 232.

especially if he has been actively fighting up to the moment before submission. The definition of an atrocity that breaks the laws of war is obvious: a premeditated act in which killing or destruction is committed in cold blood rather than the warmer variety. In siege warfare it was accepted that the refusal of a garrison to surrender when the outcome had become inevitable, forfeited the right to honourable terms. If resistance was further prolonged obliging the besiegers to lose lives unnecessarily by storming of fortress, then the garrison lost all rights and was subject to massacre and pillage.

By contemporary standards, the conduct of the Jacobite War in Ireland was neither outstandingly ferocious nor especially benign. As Eric Carlton reminded us, wars nearly always give rise to massacres but there was no Wexford, no Drogheda.[50] Nobody expected much in the way of decent behaviour from seventeenth-century soldiers. All that laws of war could achieve was to seek to restrain the worst excesses of violence and try to limit the damage inflicted by the armed soldier upon the unarmed civilian and establish a framework within which war can be waged to achieve a political purpose: a war in which the violence of the means undermines the political ends is counter-productive.

Of course the laws of war were only partially observed: they still are. Of course victors got away with much more than the defeated: they still do. Of course rebels against a legitimate government were treated more harshly than the armed forces of another state: they still are. Of course, when military discipline broke down because of weak leadership, the blood lust of victory, starvation or lack of pay the laws of war were instantly forgotten: that is still the case. Of course, when religion and ethnicity became involved, powerful emotive and ideological forces overrode the laws of war: they still do today.

50 E. Carlton, *War and ideology* (London, 1990), p. 174.

Contributors

VINCENT P. CAREY teaches Early Modern European history at SUNY Plattsburgh in upstate New York. He has written and edited a number of books, including *Surviving the Tudors: Gerald the 'Wizard' earl of Kildare and English rule in Ireland, 1537–1586* (Dublin, 2000) and *Taking sides? Colonial and confessional mentalités in early modern Ireland* (Dublin, 2002), and is currently working on a book on atrocity and history in Early Modern Ireland.

JOHN CHILDS is Professor of Military History and Director of the Centre for Military History in the University of Leeds and chairs the English Heritage Battlefields Panel and the Royal Armouries Development Trust. Author of a series of books on armies and warfare in Early Modern Europe, his most recent title is *The Williamite War in Ireland, 1688–1691* (London, 2007).

MARK CLINTON holds a degree in Early and Medieval Irish history and archaeology (UCD) and a PhD in archaeology (UCG). He was the Excavation Director at the Carrickmines Castle site and is the author of numerous articles and papers, including the standard reference book on Irish souterrains.

DAVID EDWARDS is a senior lecturer in the Dept. of History, UCC, and a Director of the Irish Manuscripts Commission. He has written and edited a number of books, including *The Ormond lordship in county Kilkenny, 1515–1642: the rise and fall of Butler feudal power* (Dublin, 2003), *Gaelic Ireland, c.1250–c.1650: land, lordship and settlement* (Dublin, 2001), and *British sources for Irish history, 1485–1641* (Dublin, 1997).

LINDA FIBIGER holds an MSc in osteology and palaeopathology from the University of Bradford and has been working as a freelance osteoarchaeologist since 2001. She has completed numerous specialist reports for commercial and research projects thoughout Ireland, been involved in third level and CPD teaching, and is currently carrying out DPhil research into violence and conflict in Neolithic northwest Europe at the University of Oxford.

KEVIN FORKAN received his PhD from NUI Galway in 2003, and held an Irish Research Council for the Humanities and Social Sciences fellowship at Trinity College Dublin. He has published several articles on the Protestant interest in Ulster and Ireland during the 1640s.

PÁDRAIG LENIHAN is a lecturer in history at the University of Limerick. He has a special interest in early modern military history and his publications include *Catholic Confederates at War, 1642–49* (Cork, 2001) and *1690: Battle of the Boyne* (Stroud, 2003). He has also edited a collection of essays *Conquest and resistance: Irish warfare in the seventeenth century* (Leiden, 2001).

BRIAN MAC CUARTA SJ has edited *Ulster 1641: aspects of the rising* (Belfast, 1993) and is the author of *Catholic revival in the north of Ireland, 1603–41* (Dublin, 2007).

JOHN McGURK is retired head of history at Liverpool Hope University and has lectured widely on the Elizabethan wars in Ireland. He is the author of *The Elizabethan conquest of Ireland* (Manchester, 1997) and *Sir Henry Docwra, 1564–1631: Derry's second founder* (Dublin, 2005).

HIRAM MORGAN teaches history at University College Cork. He has authored *Tyrone's rebellion* (Woodbridge, 1993), and edited *Political ideology in Ireland, 1541–1641* (Dublin, 1999), and *The battle of Kinsale* (Bray, 2004). He is currently chairman of the Royal Irish Academy Committee for Historical Sciences.

KENNETH NICHOLLS was for many years Statutory Lecturer in the History Department, UCC. As well as many articles, he has written the seminal work *Gaelic and Gaelicised Ireland in the Middle Ages* (Dublin, 2003), and *Land, law and society in sixteenth-century Ireland* (Dublin, 1976). Now retired, he continues to contribute to research, and is involved in the Early Modern Project in the Department.

JOHN MORRILL is Professor of British and Irish History at the University of Cambridge. His biography of Oliver Cromwell (originally in the Oxford Dictionary of National Biography) has just been published by Oxford University Press and his Ford Lectures, entitled *Living with revolution*, and dealing with England, Ireland and Scotland in the period 1646–60, are being revised for publication.

MICHEÁL Ó SIOCHRÚ is a lecturer in history at the University of Aberdeen. He is the author of *Confederate Ireland, 1641–1649: a constitutional and political analysis* (Dublin, 1998), and his latest book, *God's executioner: Oliver Cromwell and the conquest of Ireland*, will be published by Faber in 2008.

DAMIAN SHIELS holds an MA in archaeology and heritage from the University of Leicester and is currently the Post Excavation Manager with Headland Archaeology Ltd. He was formerly a Senior Site Supervisor on the Carrickmines Castle excavation and an Assistant Keeper II working on the

National Museum of Ireland's 'Soldiers & Chiefs' exhibition; his principal research interest is conflict archaeology, a topic on which he has published several papers.

CLODAGH TAIT is a lecturer in history in the University of Essex. She is the author of *Death, burial and commemoration in Ireland, 1550–1650* (Basingstoke, 2002) and of several articles on martyrdom, iconography, childbirth, baptism, and naming in early modern Ireland, and is completing a book on the social history of Britain and Ireland in the sixteenth and seventeenth centuries for Polity press.

JOHN R. YOUNG is a senior lecturer in history at the University of Strathclyde. He is a specialist in early modern Scottish history. His main areas of interest are the pre-1707 Scottish Parliament, the Covenanting movement, 1637–51, and Scotland's relations with Ulster. He is currently writing a book for Edinburgh University Press on *The Scottish Covenanters and the British Civil Wars* and he is one of the editors of *The transactions of the Scots Army in Ireland from 1643 to 1648* (Four Courts Press, forthcoming).

Index

Aberdeen, 227, 230
Abridgement of English Military Discipline, 294–5
Adventurer's Act, 212
agriculture, 41
Aldrich, William, Protestant minister, 158, 159–60n
Alen, John, archbishop of Dublin, 55, 57
Alva, duke of, 125
Americas: *see* New World
Amussen, Susan, historian, 20
Anglicization, 11, 63, 74
Anglo-Irish (Old English) population, 49, 55, 61, 66, 71, 81, 155
  lordships, 37, 39, 41, 46, 48, 50, 53–4, 62, 116; *see also* Warfare, conduct of
Annesley, Arthur, 215
anthropology and anthropologists, 24, 29, 31
anti-Catholicism, 20–1, 87–94, 120–1, 142, 155–6, 191, 205, 209–10, 216, 246–50, 268, 295–6, 298; *see also* Martyrs
Antichrist, the, belief in, 22, 28, 87, 89–93, 141–2, 145, 148, 169–71, 247
anti-English attitudes, 11, 154
anti-Irish attitudes, 11, 27–8, 81, 96, 249, 268
anti-Protestantism, 20–1, 154–5, 158–75 passim, 295–6
Antrim, 51, 64, 77, 176
Aphorismical Discovery of Treasonable Faction, Catholic narrative, 142, 199, 210
Archbold family, 181

Ardee, 162
Ardglass, massacre at (1562), 73
Argyll, lords of: *see* Campbell
Arklow, 52
Armagh, archdiocese and province of, 159n
Armagh city, 64, 76, 124, 159, 171; Cathedral 148
Armagh, County, 97, 155–6, 158, 160, 165–8, 170, 172, 176
Arms trade, 52
Askeaton, 134
assassinations, 47, 95–6, 101–10 passim, 112–4
Athlone, 64–5, 77, siege of, 297
Athy, Co. Kildare, 70
atrocity literature: *see* pamphlet literature
Augher, Co. Tyrone, 14, 229
Aughrim, Co. Galway, battle of (1691), 11, 22, 286–7, 299
A View of the Present State of Ireland (Spenser), 80, 81, 83
Axtell, Daniel, colonel, 255, 256n
Aylmer, Sir Andrew, of Donadea, 184
Ayr, 221–3, 227, 234

Bagenal, Sir Henry, 100, 106, 108–15
Bagenal, Mabel, countess of Tyrone, 110
Bagenal, Sir Nicholas, 68, 112
Baldongan Castle, Co. Dublin, 186
Bale, John, bishop of Ossory, 71
Ballydavey, massacre at (1641), 180
Ballymore, 296
Baltimore, 232
bandits and banditry, 31, 296n, 298
Bangor, 223

305

Bann, river, 109, 112
Baptists, 248
Barbados, 251, 256, 265
Barnard, Toby, historian, 266, 282
Barnewall family, 184
Barrow, river, 41
Basing House, Hampshire, 140
Bath, John, Tyrone servant, 114
Beacon, Richard, 119
Beard, Thomas, 132, 149
Beckett, Thomas, martyr archbishop, 150
Bective, Co. Meath, 186
Bedell, William, bishop of Kilmore, 159n, 165
Beheadings, 21, 47, 56–7, 101, 125, 137, 140, 158, 256, 258–9, 265
Belfast, 34, 52n, 112–3
Bellahoe, battle of, 60
Bellings, Richard, 190, 209–10
Belturbet, 171
Berners, John, 199
Berry, John, serjeant major, 197–9
Bible, the, 120, 149–50, 157–8, 171–2, 283–4
Bingham, Sir Richard, governor of Connacht, 84, 90n, 100
Blackwater fort, 99, 114, 124, 128
Blackwood Castle, Co. Kildare, 182–3
Blair, Robert, Presbyterian minister, 223–4, 230
Blanco, Pedro, Tyrone servant, 101
Blaney, Sir Edward, 126
Blaney, Richard, 170
Blennerhassett, Thomas, 126
Blount, Charles, Lord Mountjoy, earl of Devonshire, 20, 25–6, 28, 79, 118, 120, 123–5, 127–9
Boine, Henry, Protestant minister, 160
Bolles, Sir John, captain, 121, 123
Book of Common Prayer, 248
Borlase, Edmund, 178, 190, 197, 198–9, 203

Borlase, Sir John, lord justice, 184, 186, 195, 206, 208
Bourke, Thomas, printer, 270
Bowen family, of Ballyadams, 180
Boyle, Richard, earl of Cork, 180, 207
Boyle, Robert, Protestant minister, 160
Boyle, Roger, earl of Orrery, 293
Boyne, river, 115, 196 battle of (1690), 17, 297
Brabazon, Sir William, lord justice, 67, 70, 74
Brackland Castle, Co. Offaly, massacre at (1537), 59
Bradshaw, Brendan, historian, 17–8, 115–6, 119
Bradshaw, Henry, 140
Bradshaw, John, 256–7, 272
Bramhall, John, bishop of Derry, 159
Brereton, Andrew, 68, 72–3
Brereton, Randal, of the Dufferin, 113
Brodie, Captain, 61n
Brooke, Sir Calisthenes, 125–6
Brouncker, Sir Henry, lord president of Munster, 20–1, 27, 30, 132, 144–51, 153
burials, 134–6, 139–40, 167–9, 173–4, 192, 200–2
Burke, James, historian, 255
Burke, John, of Brittas, martyr, 144, 147
Burke, Ulick-na-gceann, 47
Burkes of Clanricarde, family, 47, 51–2
Burkhead, Henry, playwright, 142, 209
Burghley, Lord: *see* Cecil
Butlers of Cahir, 43n
Butlers of Ormond, 41, 52–3, 62, 63, 66
Butler, Sir Edmund, of Cloghgrenan, 71
Butler, Sir Edmund, confederate governor, 272
Butler, Eleanor, countess of Desmond, 134

Index

Butler, James, twelfth earl, first marquis and duke of Ormond, 29, 147, 181n, 182, 185–6, 189, 195–6, 210–12, 214–7, 255, 262, 266, 270–1, 275, 277–9, 282
Butler, Piers Ruadh, eighth earl of Ormond, earl of Ossory, 43n, 45n, 50–1, 52, 55n
Butler, Richard, third Viscount Mountgarret, 183
Butler, Thomas, seventh earl of Ormond, 49, 50
Butler, ('Black') Thomas, tenth earl of Ormond, 72

Caesar, Julius, his *Gallic Wars*, 123, 127
Calvinism: *see* Puritans
Camden, William, his *Annales*, 94, 95, 116
Campbell, Archibald, eighth earl and first marquis of Argyll, 226n, 228
Campion, Edmund, 92, 94
cannibalism, 123–4
Canny, Nicholas, historian, 15, 119–20, 154n, 178, 219, 224
Carbery, Co. Kildare, 67
Cardinall family, of Donadea, 184, 188
Carew, Sir George, lord president of Munster, 79, 120, 123, 124n, 127
    Irish genealogies kept by 102
Carew, Sir Peter, 135n
Carlingford, 274
Carlow, County, 63, 64
Carlton, Charles, historian, 263
Carrick Castle, Co. Tipperary, 276
Carrickfergus, 40, 112–3, 297
Carrickmacross, 158, 162, 165, 179n
Carrickmines Castle, Co. Dublin, 193, 196–7 massacre at (1642), 23, 25, 186, 190, 192, 194, 196–203 passim, 212
Carrickmore (Termonmagurk), 122
Carrickogunnell Castle, Co. Limerick, massacre at (1536), 59

Castlehaven, lord: see Tuchet
Castlereagh, 112
Catholics and Catholicism, 10, 15, 28, 137, 147, 156–7; *see also* anti-Catholicism
Catholic clergy, 28–30, 85–6, 115, 121, 123, 126, 129, 130–1, 133, 137, 142, 144, 145, 147, 149, 152, 154n, 156, 157n, 160–3, 165–70, 173–4, 184, 244, 247n, 251, 270–1, 276–8; *see also* Dominicans, Franciscans, Jesuits
Catholic historiography, 12, 16, 86, 149, 152
Catholic rebellion (1641), 20, 21, 29, 141, 154–75 passim
Caulfield, Sir Toby, Lord Charlemont, 125–6, 179, 190
cavalry, 98, 102, 285, 295
Cavan, County, 111, 152, 154–6, 158, 161–5, 166n, 167–8, 169n, 170–3
Cavan town, 115, 164 abbey in 115
Cecil, Sir Robert, earl of Salisbury, 123, 125, 128, 145, 193
Cecil, Sir Thomas, 104
Cecil, Sir William, Lord Burghley, 104, 109
Celbridge, 185
Champion, Arthur, 188n
Charlemont, siege of (1690), 297
Charles I, 138, 140, 156n, 204, 211n, 214, 219, 226, 258, 268, 270–1, 293
Charles II, 138, 156n, 274, 277, 279, 293
Charles V, Holy Roman emperor, 54
Cheeke, John, soldier, 88–9, 92, 93–4
Chichester, Sir Arthur, army officer and lord deputy, 25, 120, 125, 128–9
Chichester, Sir John, 125
Children, as victims of violence, 20, 26, 59, 71, 85, 104, 124–6, 128–9, 143, 164, 166, 169n, 176–81, 183–90, 192, 199, 203, 228–32, 234–7, 281

chivalry: *see* honour
Church of Ireland: *see* Protestants and Protestantism
civilians, 20, 26–7, 44, 70, 74, 76–8, 120, 123, 127–8, 242–3, 245, 251, 253, 255, 260–3, 266, 273, 275–6, 280–1, 286–90, 294, 298, 300
Clandeboy, territory, 64, 112–3, 231
Clare, County, 139
Clifford, John, 193
Clogher diocese, 160
Cloghlea Castle, Co. Cork, 190
Clones, 111, 164, 166, 172n
Clongoeswood, Co. Kildare, massacre at (1642), 180–1, 183–4, 186–8
Clonmacnoise, 47 Declaration of, 248–9, 276
Clontarf, massacre at (1641), 209, 217
Clontibret, battle of (1595), 115, 128
Coleraine, 124
Commentarius Rinuccinianus, 181, 189
common law, 35, 68, 105, 120, 127, 294
Confederate Catholics, 10, 12, 137, 141, 180, 184, 190, 198, 209, 214, 217, 258, 270, 272, 282
Connacht, 40, 47, 52, 63, 98, 139, 174, 207–8, 215, 297
conversion, 121, 163n, 164–6, 174, 179, 248, 285
Cook, John, chief justice of Munster, 139
Cooke, Richard, lieutenant, 198
Coote, Sir Charles, the elder, 20–1, 22, 26, 28, 30, 132, 136, 141–4, 147–8, 150–3, 188, 195–6, 205, 207–18 passim, 270
Coote, Sir Charles, the younger, 213, 215, 258n
Coote, Chidley, 214
Coppinger, John, 86, 131, 147, 149
Cork city, 139, 146, 179n, 275, 297; siege of, 297
Cork, County, 63, 245, 296n

Cornwall, 21
Coshering, 109
Coughlan, Patricia, scholar, 142
courts martial, 56, 137, 294
Cowley, Sir Henry, captain, 67
Cranford, James, 148
crannogs, 108, 113
Crawford, Jon, historian, 69n
Crawford, Patricia, historian, 24
creaghts, 109–10, 127
Creichton, George, Protestant minister, 158
Cromwell, Oliver, 17, 21, 24, 25–6, 28–30, 136, 140, 151, 242–65 passim, 266–7, 271–82 passim
Cromwellian government 136–7, 139, 180–1, 191, 213–4 land settlement, 11, 178, 216, 250
Cuellar, Francisco de, 117
Cullen, Paul, cardinal, 12
Cumber, 123

Dalton family, 62, 77
Dangan Castle, Co. Offaly; massacre at (1537), 59
Danish troops in Ireland, 290, 298
Davies, Sir John, 119, 126
Deansgrange, Co. Dublin, 196
debt, 154, 160–2, 172
decimation, 256–7
De Gheyn, Jacob, 293
De Groot, Hugo, 284
Denny, Sir Edward, 87, 88
Depositions (1641), the, 11, 13–14, 155, 171n, 173, 180, 271
Derricke, John, 125
Derry, 47, 121, 123, 127, 147, 298; prior of, 123; siege of (1689), 291, 297
deserters, 295
Desmond, earls of: *see* Fitzgerald
Devereux, Robert, second earl of Essex, lord lieutenant, 121–2

Index

Devereux, Walter, first earl of Essex, 15
Devon, 123
Digby, Sir Kenelm, 250
Dillon, Arthur, captain, 274
Dillon family, 67n, 70n, 77, 155
Dillon, Sir James, 258
Dillon, Robert, lord of Kilkenny-west, earl of Roscommon, 155, 258
Dingle, Co. Kerry, 83, 88
Docwra, Sir Henry, 121–3, 124, 125–6, 127–9
Doherty, Gabriel, historian, 16
Dominicans, 147
Donagan, Barbara, historian, 285
Donaghmore, 124, 229
Donegal, County, 40, 70, 100
Dowdall, George, archbishop of Armagh, 45n, 72n, 76–8
Down Priory, 64
Drogheda, 61n, 98, 101, 103, 115, 123, 184, 186; siege of (1641–2), 196, 208; massacre at (1649), 21–2, 23, 24, 26, 29–30, 242, 245–6, 251, 253–9, 260–4, 266, 273–82, 300
Drury, Sir William, lord justice, 28, 130–1, 133–6, 147, 150–3
Dublin city, 23, 28, 53, 57, 61n, 70, 72, 74, 77, 99, 103–4, 113, 121, 128, 135, 140, 146, 161, 164, 183, 195, 211, 239, 256, 268–9, 280, 297; places in: Christchurch cathedral, 213; Dublin Castle, 34, 100, 102, 107, 125, 205–6; St Patrick's cathedral, 134–5, 136
Dublin, County, 167n, 196, 206, 245
Dufferin, the, territory, 64, 113
Duffy, Eugene, friar, 162, 169
Duke, Sir Henry, 111, 115
Dún an Óir: *see* Smerwick
Dunbar, battle of (1650), 248, 251n
Dunbar, Mr, Protestant minister of Donoghenry, 158n
Dunboy, Co. Cork, massacre at (1602), 34, 124n
Duncannon fort, 276
Dundalk, 109–12, 115, 190, 257, 273
Dungan, Garret, 274
Dungan, Sir John, of Castletown, 185
Dungan's Hill, battle of (1647), 22, 198, 264
Dungannon, 98–9, 101, 104, 111, 122, 124, 128, 157, 160; minister of, 230–1; provost of, 228
Dungarvan, 52
Dunlop, Robert, historian, 13
Dunshaughlin, 186
dysentery, 260
Dyve, Sir Lewis, 272, 277–8

East Breifne, territory of, 45, 65
East Indies, 275
Edinburgh, 219, 221, 224, 233
Edward VI, 78
Edwards, David, historian, 18–19, 120n, 127–8, 188
Elizabeth I, 37, 76, 78, 86, 87–8, 106, 121–2, 133
Ellis, Steven, historian, 54–5
Elton, Richard, 293
Ely, territory of, 65
England, 9, 21, 23, 28, 34, 50, 54, 60, 67, 68, 74, 79, 80, 93, 104, 112, 115, 119–20, 125, 127, 136–7, 155–6, 178, 195, 205n, 242–5, 247, 281, 293
English Catholics, 23, 85, 181, 247, 250 settled in Ireland, 177n, 184–5
English Civil War, 24, 32, 19, 244, 256–8, 263–4, 285, 293
English Parliament, 13, 205, 211–2, 214–5, 242, 244, 246–8, 253, 258, 272–3
English Privy Council, 105–6, 121, 127–8, 135
English royal court, 104–6

English ('New English') settlers, 9, 11, 25, 28, 63, 70–1, 81, 141–2, 148, 157–9, 163–5, 167, 180, 195, 205–6, 211, 280
Enniscorthy, Co. Wexford, massacre at (1569), 71–2
Enniskillen, 115, 232, 298
Europe, conditions in, 23, 27–8, 85, 96, 115–6, 118, 177; support of Irish rebellion in, 11–12, 23, 29, 133
Eusebius, writings of, 150
Eustace family, of Craddockstown, 185
excommunication, 137, 167

Faerie Queene, epic poem, 79–83
famine and dearth, 34, 44–5, 76–8, 80, 81, 120, 122–4, 128–9, 176
Farmer, William, surgeon, 123–4
Farrer, Sir Robert, 196
Fenton, Sir Geoffrey, secretary of state, 88n, 90, 111, 114
Fercall, territory of, 65
Ferdinand II, Holy Roman emperor, 197
Fermanagh, territory and County, 45n, 46, 49, 108, 111, 126n, 155, 159n, 160n, 165, 170–1, 172n
Fethard-on-sea, Co. Wexford, 41
Fews, the, territory of, 111
Fingal, Lord: *see* Plunkett
Fingall, territory of, 184, 186
Fitzgerald, Garret Mór, eighth earl of Kildare, 43, 49
Fitzgerald, Garret Óg, ninth earl of Kildare, 48
Fitzgerald, Gerald, fifteenth earl of Desmond, 134
Fitzgerald, Henry, 48
Fitzgerald, James, eleventh earl of Desmond, 51
Fitzgerald, James Fitzmaurice, of Carrigaline, Co. Cork, 71, 83, 133–4

Fitzgerald, Maurice Bacach, tenth earl of Desmond, 49, 51
Fitzgerald, Piers MacThomas, 183n
Fitzgerald, Thomas 'the Bald', of Desmond, 51
Fitzgerald, Thomas ('Silken'), Lord Offaly, tenth earl of Kildare, 58, 62
Fitzgerald, Rev. William, minister, 148
Fitzgeralds of the Decies, 42
Fitzgeralds of Desmond, 41, 43, 51, 53n, 66; revolt (1579), 10, 12, 37, 96, 133–4
Fitzgeralds of Kildare, 41, 50, 52–3, 63, 180; Great revolt (1534), 10, 34, 54–62 passim; Lesser revolt (1546–7), 72
FitzPatrick, Elizabeth, archaeologist, 31
Fitzpatrick family: *see* MacGiollapadraig
Fitzpatrick, Thomas, historian, 14, 178
Fitzsimons, Fiona, historian, 31
Fitzwilliam, William, Lord Merrion, 199
Fitzwilliam, Sir William, lord deputy, 99–101, 103, 104, 106, 108, 110, 113
Flattesbury, Christopher, lawyer, 188n
Flemings of Slane, family, 115, 189
Flight of the Earls, 10, 125
Florida, 97, 117
folklore accounts, 30, 144
fosterage, 31, 102, 103, 108–9, 187
Fox, Adam, historian, 148
Foxe's *Book of Martyrs*, 132, 275
France, 34, 63, 115, 136, 142, 270, 279, 285
Franciscans, 25, 60, 101, 130–1, 134, 157–8, 173, 251n, 257, 269
Frederick V, prince of the Palatinate, 204
French, Nicholas, bishop of Ferns, 27, 210

Index 311

Froude, J.A., historian, 13
Fullerton, William, Protestant minister, 160 his widow 160n

Gaelic Irish: society, 31, 74, 81, 126, 179; lordships, 37, 39, 41, 46, 48–9, 63, 104–6, 116; annals 39–40, 40n, 45–6, 47n, 48, 52n, 56, 58, 115, 118, 130; poetry 41, 44, 266, 282; *see also* Warfare, conduct of
Gaelic language, 98, 121, 126, 269
Galloglasses, 15, 52–3, 122
Galway city, 278, 287 siege of, 297
George, Dr Robert, Ginkel's secretary, 295
Geraldine League, 10
Germany, 116
Gerrard, Sir William, lord chancellor, 90, 134
Gilbert, Sir Humphrey, 127
Gilbert, Sir John, historian, 14
Gillespie, Raymond, historian, 131, 269, 282
Ginkel, Godard van Reede, Baron von, 286–7, 290, 295, 297
Giraldus Cambrensis, 96, 119, 269
Glasgow, Tom, historian, 84
Glenmalure, Co. Wicklow, battle of (1580), 93
Glenshane Pass, 124
Glinns, the, territory, 64
Gottfried, Rudolf, scholar, 87
Gowran, Co. Kilkenny, 259
Greames, Richard, 180, 184, 186–7
Gregory XIII, pope, 83, 87, 94
Gregorian calendar, 103n
Greenblatt, Stephen, scholar, 79–80
Grenville, Sir Richard, 196
Grey, Arthur, fourteenth Baron de Wilton, lord deputy, 23, 25, 29, 79, 81–4, 86–91, 93–4, 97
Grey, Leonard, Viscount Grane, lord deputy, 54, 58–62

Guns and gunpowder, 52, 66, 98, 100, 109–10, 185, 196–9, 202, 244, 260, 285
Gustavus Adolphus, king of Sweden, 204, 288

Hadfield, Andrew, scholar, 80, 83
Hadsor, John, of Cappoge, 189
Hadsor, Richard, lawyer, 189
Hamilton, Sir Frederick, 26
Hamilton, Richard, general, 291
Harcourt, Sir Simon 23, 185–6, 195–200, 202, 211
Hayes-McCoy, G.A., historian, 15, 117
Heath, James, 138
Henrietta Maria, queen, 156, 173
Henry VII, 53
Henry VIII, 37, 53–5, 58–9, 61, 117
Herbert, Charles, colonel, 299
Hetherington family, 180
Hexham, Henry, 293
Hickman, William, 271
Hickson, Mary, historian, 13
Holinshed, Raphael, his *Chronicles*, 93–4
honour, concepts of, 27, 31, 46, 48, 58, 59, 71–2, 114, 125–6, 135, 291, 300
Hooker (alias Vowell), John, 84–5, 93
hostage-taking: *see* prisoners
Hostings, 75
Houston, Alexander, captain, 233
Hovendon, Henry, 98–101, 102, 114
Hovendon, Richard 98, 101
Howling, John, 86
Hume, David, writer, 13

iconoclasm, 147, 173
Inch Island, Lough Swilly, 122
Inishowen, massacre at (1588), 97–101, 117
Intermarriage, 126, 163n
Ireland, government of: *see* Cromwellian government, Stuart monarchy, and Tudor monarchy

Ireton, Henry, lord deputy, 28, 132–3, 136–40, 147, 150–3
Irish Historical Studies, journal, 14
Irish Sword, journal, 15
Irvine, 223
Islandmagee, massacre at (1641), 176, 180–1
Italy, 79, 116
Italian soldiers, 79, 82–3, 84, 89–90, 91–2, 93
Iveagh, territory, 64, 112

Jacobite
James II, king, 9, 291, 293, 298
James VI and I, king, 204
Jamestown, Co. Leitrim, 207
Jefferies, Samuel, 141
Jenkins, Raymond, scholar, 87
Jesuits, 86, 92, 145, 233, 270
Jones, Henry, dean of Kilmore, 159n
Jones, Inigo, 244
Jones, Michael, colonel, 280
Joyce, John, constable, 199
Judson, Alexander, scholar, 87
Julianstown, battle of (1641), 195, 208, 210

Kavanagh (MacMurrough), family, 41, 63, 68, 71
Kavanagh, Art Boy, king of Leinster, 50
Kavanagh, Gerald, king of Leinster, 50
Kavanagh, Murrough, chieftain, 70, 72
Kavanagh, Murrough Ballach, king of Leinster, 49–50
Keating, Geoffrey, 269
Kells, Co. Meath, 115, 163
Kelly, John, lieutenant, 98, 100
Kerry, County, 12, 79, 87, 296n
Kildare, County, 61–2, 64, 177, 181–5, 187–8, 206
Kildare, dean of, 56
Kildare, earls of: *see* Fitzgerald

Kilkenny city, 184, 209, 250, 270–1, 275
Kilkenny, County, 41, 52, 62, 245, 250
Killetra, territory of, 109
Killultagh, territory of, 112, 114
Kilmallock, 130, 151
Kilrush, battle of (1642), 188, 212
Kilsallaghan Castle, siege of (1642), 196
Kilwarlin, territory of, 112–3, 114n
Killybegs, Co. Donegal, 40, 45
Kinelarty, territory of, 68
King, George, 209
King, Henry, 199
King, Robert, 215
King, William, archbishop, 9
Kinsale, 245, 297 battle of, 12, 34, 79, 118, 121, 124
Kingsmill, William, 189
Knock Castle, Co. Meath, 183–4
Knockboy, battle of, 51–2
Knockdoe, Co. Galway, battle of, 43
Knockrath Castle, Co. Wicklow, 188

Lagan valley, 112
Lambay Island, 296
Lambert, Lord Charles, 196
Lane, Parr, 145–6, 148, 153
language, 154, 162, 170, 184, 269
Laois, County (Queen's County), 42, 63, 71, 75–6
Laois-Offaly plantation, 11, 67, 70–1
Latin, 98, 121, 133, 269
Leap Castle, Co. Offaly, 52n
Lecale, territory, 64
Lecky, W.E.H., historian, 13
Lee, Thomas, captain, 104, 105–6
Leigh, Edward, captain, 122
Leinster, kingdom of, 50
Leinster province, 25, 40, 52–3, 63, 77, 175, 176–7, 188
Lenthall, William, speaker of the Commons, 256, 259, 272

Levittstown, Co. Kildare, 52
Lewis, C.S., author, 82, 87
Limerick city, 137–8, 146, 278 siege of (1691), 286–7, 297
Limerick, County, 63, 64, 245
Limerick, diocese of, 115
Literacy, 267, 269
Livingstone, John, Presbyterian minister, 223, 224n
Loftus, Adam, chancellor-archbishop, lord justice, 104
Loftus, Sir Adam, 208, 214–5
Loftus, Sir Arthur, 185
Lombard, Peter, Catholic primate of Ireland, 86
London, 23, 50, 58, 86, 90, 92, 102, 121, 141, 156, 157n, 211, 215, 261, 273; places in: Somerset House, 139; Tyburn, 58, 140; Westminster abbey, 139–40
Longford, County, 65, 190
Lough Foyle, 127
Loughgall, 160–1
Lough Neagh, 108, 110, 122
Lough Swilly, 122
Louis XIV, 288–9, 296
Louth, County, 49, 76–7, 111, 113–14, 186, 189, 245
Louvain, Irish college at, 269
Lucas, Sir Thomas, 196
Ludlow, Edmund, 137, 139
Lydon, James, historian, 116
Lynch, John, 27, 138, 142–3, 144–5, 149, 181, 189, 210
Lynch, Catholic bishop, 261

McBride, Lawrence, historian, 16
MacCartan family, 68, 112
MacCarthy Mór, Donal, earl of Clancarty, 71
MacCarthy, Donough, Viscount Muskerry, 77
MacCarthy family, 41, 47, 51, 63

McClellan, John, schoolmaster, 223, 224n
MacCoghlan family, 47
MacCoghlan, Seamus, chieftain, 47
MacCoghlan, Sir John (Shane Óg), 188n
MacDavitt, Hugh Boy, 121
MacDermott Ruadh, chieftain, 40n
MacDonnell, Alasdair, chieftain, 73
MacDonnell, Catherine, 102
MacDonnell, Sir Randall, marquis of Antrim, 250, 276
MacDonnells of Antrim and the Isles, 51, 63, 72, 95; MacRanaldboy sept, 73
McElligott, Jason, historian, 251, 253
McEvagh, Donal Óg, 109
MacGiollapadraig, Barnaby, fifth baron of Upper Ossory, 189
MacGiollapadraigs (Fitzpatricks) of Upper Ossory, 42
Machiavelli, Niccolo, and Machiavellianism, 116–17, 251n
Mackworth, Humphrey, captain, 84–5, 88
McLean, Catherine, 102
McLeans of Duart, family, 99, 101–2
MacMahon, Art McBrian Lavagh, 170
MacMahon, Brian McHugh Og, 110
MacMahon, Coll McBrian, 169n
MacMahon family, 45, 49, 60, 107, 110–1, 112, 179n; Farney sept, 76
MacMahon, Felim, chieftain, 60n
MacMahon, Sir Ross, 108
MacMahon, Rossa, chieftain, 49
McMurrehy family, 104
MacQuillan, Cormac, chieftain, 40
MacQuillan family, 45
MacSweeney, Eugene, Catholic bishop, 163, 165
MacSweeney family, 40; Fanad sept 122
Madder, John, Presbyterian minister, 159n, 229

Maddern, P.C., historian, 20
Magee, Rory, 112
Magennis, Ever McRory, 113, 114n
Magennis, Sir Hugh, of Iveagh, 112
Mageoghegan family, 67
Magrath, Miler, archbishop of Cashel, 102
Maguire, Donn Carrach, 188n
Maguire, Donough, chieftain, 46
Maguire family, 44n, 46, 49, 103
Maguire, Hugh, 108–9, 111, 114–5
Maguire, Hugh MacAdegane (Mac O Degan), priest, 165, 167
Maguire, Rory, captain, 171
Maguire, Shane Óg, chieftain, 102
Maguire, Turlough Moyle, 188n
Maley, Willy, scholar, 17–18
martial law, 19, 25, 56, 60–1n, 69, 74, 97, 100, 105–6, 117, 120, 127, 130, 134, 144, 178, 179n, 184, 207–8, 210n, 217, 264
Martin, Colin, archaeologist, 84
martyrs and martyrdom, 30, 85–6, 89, 130–1, 132–3, 137, 143, 147–9, 152–3, 217
Mary I, 78
Matchett, Ellen, 172n
Maynooth Castle, Co. Kildare massacre at (1535), 24, 34, 55–7, 60
Mazarin, Jules, cardinal, 247, 292
Meath, County, 61–2, 111, 186, 206, 210
Meelick Castle, massacre at (1557), 73
Mellifont, 169n
Meredith, Robert, 215–6
Midlands, the, 42, 47, 50, 53, 56, 64–5, 74, 77, 117–8, 190
Milton, John, 27, 271
Monaghan, County, 97, 107, 128, 155–8, 161–2, 164–5, 169n, 171n
Monaghan town, 170 priory in 60
Monck, George, military commander, later duke of Albemarle, 181n, 183, 190, 196, 199, 250

Monroe, Robert, colonel, 189–90, 293
Montgomery, James, parson, 161–2
Monmouth's Rebellion, 294
Moore, Charles, Jacobite colonel, 299
Moore, Charles, Viscount Drogheda, 169n, 186
Moore, Fr Lawrence, martyr, 85–6
Moran, P.F., cardinal archbishop, 12
Morice, John, major, 181
More, St Thomas, 119
Moryson, Fynes, 123–4
Mountjoy, Lord: *see* Blount
Mourne Abbey, Co. Cork, battle of, 51, 52n
Mullaghmast, Co. Kildare, massacre at, 14, 34
Munday, Anthony, 27, 91–4
Munster, 40, 41, 43, 52–3, 63, 64–5, 71, 72n, 81, 96, 118, 123, 148, 176, 177, 262, 297 Plantation of, 24
Muskerry, Lord: *see* MacCarthy
Mutiny Act (1689), 294

Naas, Co. Kildare, 141, 185, 212, 217; massacre at (1535), 55
Nalson, John, 178
Naples, 98
Navy and naval forces (English), 88, 91, 286
Nenagh, 77
Netherlands, the, 34, 89, 125, 195, 277, 285–7, 289
Netterfield, James, proctor, 165–6
Netterville, Luke, 196
New History of Ireland, 15
New Model Army, 242–4, 255, 266, 274, 278
New World, the, 43, 97, 120, 126, 129, 285
Newry, 64, 107, 111, 123, 190
newsbooks: *see* pamphlet literature
Newtownards, 223
Newtownbutler, 171

Index

Nicholls, Kenneth, historian, 69
Nugent, Richard, second earl of Westmeath, 258
Nugents of Delvin and Westmeath, family, 67, 171

O'Brien family, 41
O'Brien, Murrough, Lord Inchiquin, 180, 274
O'Brien, Terence Albert, Catholic bishop, 137, 140
O'Byrne, Feagh McHugh, chieftain, 115
O'Byrne, Hugh McPhelim, 196
O'Byrne, Walter, of Newrath, 199
O'Cahan (O'Kane), Donal, 47
O'Cahan family, 124
O'Carrolls of Ely, family, 50, 75
O'Connolly, Turlough, priest, 167n
O'Connor Faly, Cahir, chieftain, 49
O'Connor Faly, family, 59, 67, 70–1, 74–5, 76–7
O'Connor Ruadh, chieftain, 40n
O'Connor Sligo, Phelim, chieftain, 49
O'Connor, Tadhg, captain, 274
O'Daly, Dominic, 27, 137–8
O'Daly, Loghlin Oge, bard, 41
O'Doherty family, of Inishowen, 98, 100; rebellion (1608) 125
O'Donnell, Calvagh, 70, 147
O'Donnell, Donough, 47
O'Donnell, 'Red' Hugh, chieftain, 99, 107, 118, 122, 128
O'Donnell, Niall Garbh, 128
O'Donnells of Tirconaill (Donegal), family, 40, 41, 45, 46n, 49, 51, 63, 98, 100–1, 105
O'Donnelly family, marshals of Tyrone, 102, 103
O'Dowd, Mary, historian, 46, 178
O'Driscoll family, 123
O'Duffy, Owen, 111
O'Dunne, Barnaby (Brian Óg), of Brittas, 180

O'Dunne, Charles, 180
O'Dwyer, Edmund, Catholic bishop of Limerick, 137
Offaly, County, 64, 75–6
O'Gallagher, Raymond, Catholic bishop of Derry, 98, 121, 123
O'Gallagher family, 109
O'Hagan family, 95n, 108, 109–11, 114, 124
O'Hallaghan, James, priest, 167
O'Hanlon family, 112
O'Hanlon, Patrick, 106
O'Hanlon, Phelim, 109
O'Healy, Patrick, Catholic bishop, martyr, 130–1, 134, 150–2
O'Heyne, John, 138
O'Higgins, Peter, Dominican martyr, 147, 217
Ohlmeyer, Jane, historian, 282
O'Kearney, David, Catholic archbishop, 145
O'Kearney, Fr Brian, Jesuit, 145
O'Kellys of Hy Many, family, 52n
O'Kennedys of Ormond, family, 50
Old English population: *see* Anglo-Irish
O'Madden family, 67
Omagh, 122, 128
O'Malley family, 45
O'Melaghlin family, 67
O'Melaghlin, Kedagh, chieftain, 47
O'Molloy family, 75, 77
O'More, Lewis, 188
O'More, Rory, rebel leader (1641), 187
O'Mores (O'Moores) of Laois, family, 42, 50, 67, 70–2, 75–7
O'Neill, Art, captain, 164, 166n
O'Neill, Art McBaron, 99, 115
O'Neill, Art McShane, 102
O'Neill, Art Óg, chieftain, 51
O'Neill, Brian (d. 1562), 95
O'Neill, Brian Ballagh, chieftain, 40
O'Neill, Brian McArt McBaron, 112–13

O'Neill, Brian McHugh boy, 148
O'Neill, Brian McShane, 102, 104
O'Neill, Collo McFerdoragh, 109
O'Neill, Con Bacach, first earl of Tyrone, 51, 67–8
O'Neill, Con Mac an Íarla, 110–11
O'Neill, Con McNeill Óg, of Clandeboy, 112
O'Neill, Con McShane, 102, 104, 106, 124
O'Neill, Cormac McBaron, 108, 110–11, 115
O'Neill, Dr, Presbyterian minister, 233
O'Neill, Edmund McShane, 102, 106
O'Neill, Ever, 95n, 109
O'Neill, Henry Óg, 111, 114, 124
O'Neills of Clandeboy, 108, 112
O'Neills of Tyrone, 20, 49, 67, 72, 106, 107, 112; Slioght Airt sept of, 43n, 51
O'Neill, Hugh, baron of Dungannon, second earl of Tyrone, 95–107, 115–7 passim; Revolt (1594), 10, 12, 23, 26, 31, 37, 86, 106–15, 117–8, 122, 124–5, 128
O'Neill, Hugh Balbh, 43n
O'Neill, Hugh Gavelach McShane, 101–7, 128
O'Neill, Matthew, baron of Dungannon, 95
O'Neill, Neill McBrian, lord of South Clandeboy, 112–13
O'Neill, Neil McHugh, 112–13
O'Neill, Niall, 43n
O'Neill, Niall Mor, chieftain, 49
O'Neill, Owen Roe, 250, 277
O'Neill, Sir Phelim, 148, 156–7, 159, 163, 166, 171, 179, 190
O'Neill, Phelim McTurlough, of Killetra, 95n, 108–10, 114
O'Neill, Shane, chieftain, 9, 68, 70, 77, 95–6, 147; sons of (the McShanes), 102, 103, 110, 128

O'Neill, Shane McBrian, 113
O'Neill, Turlough Luineach, chieftain, 95, 96–7, 99, 100–4, 107, 114, 115
O'Neill, Turlough McHenry, of the Fews, 111
O'Neill, Turlough Óg, 163
O'Queely, Malachy, Catholic archbishop, 174
O'Quinn family, 111, 128
O'Quinn, Patrick, 122
O'Rahilly, Alfred, historian, 15
Oral culture, 267, 278–9
O'Reilly family, 44n, 45, 143
O'Reilly, Hugh McMulmory, 161
O'Reilly, M., writer, 12
O'Reilly, Mulmory, sheriff of Cavan, 163n, 172
O'Reilly, Owen McDonnell, 163n
O'Reilly, Philip, 115
O'Reilly, Philip McHugh McShane, 172
Ormond, earls, marquises and dukes of: see Butler
Ormond's Curtain Drawn, pamphlet, 215
O'Rourke, Conn, friar and martyr, 130–1, 133–4, 147, 151
Ó Siochrú, Micheál, historian, 210
O'Sullivan Beare, Philip, 27, 147
O'Sullivan family, 123
O'Toole, Brian, 72
O'Toole family, 72
O'Toole, Luke, 188
Owen, William, 197–8

Pale, the, 39, 53n, 55–6, 62, 63, 66, 67, 76–7, 96–7, 106, 115, 129, 186, 203, 206, 209, 217
Palmer, Patricia, scholar, 21
pamphlet literature, 90–2, 141, 143, 182–3, 189, 197–8, 204–5, 211–4, 215–6, 244, 262–3, 267–9, 270, 276, 279–82, 295–6n

Index

Papacy, the, 12, 54, 87, 89–90, 117, 130, 155, 164
Paris, Christopher, constable of Maynooth, 56–7
Parker, Geoffrey, historian, 84, 283
Parker, Sir John, 72n
Parliamentarians, 137, 242, 272–3, 275–6, 278–81; *see also* Cromwellian forces, and New Model Army
Parsons, Sir William, lord justice, 195, 206, 208, 214
Peasants and plebeians, 27, 46, 70, 74–5, 114, 127, 155, 169, 184, 190, 208, 217, 285, 288, 299
Pelham, Sir William, lord justice, 96, 135
Perceval-Maxwell, Michael, historian, 219, 282
Percival, Sir Philip, 189
Perrot, Sir James, 106
Perrot, Sir John, lord deputy, 36n, 97, 103, 112
Peters, Hugh, soldier-chaplain, 244, 253–4, 280
Philip II, 97, 121
Pilgrimage of Grace, the, 60–1
Piracy, 262
placenames, 154
Plague, 77, 137–9, 192
Plantations, 10, 14, 70, 75, 173, 207, 211
Plunkett, Luke, earl of Fingal, 141
Portadown, 161
Portglenone, 109
Portpatrick, 223
Portugal, 92, 270n
Power, Ellen, Lady Fermoy, 179n
Power family, of Curraghmore, 42
Powerscourt Castle, Co. Wicklow, 72
Presbyterians, in Ireland, 223, 228–30, 232–3, 238–9 ministers, 223, 224n, 228, 230–2, 238–9 ministers killed (1641–2), 228–30, 237

Preston, Thomas, Confederate general, 198, 264
prisoners, 22–3, 24, 43, 55–8, 59, 61n, 96, 99–101, 177, 242, 261–2, 275, 286, 288, 296, 299
propaganda, 87, 90–4, 133, 147–8, 271–2, 278
prophesy, 144, 152
protection, promise of: *see* safe conduct
Protestants and Protestantism, 9, 12, 15, 28, 121, 133, 138, 146, 148, 152, 154, 177, 184, 187, 215–6, 297 clergy 115, 143, 146; *see* also anti-Protestantism
Protestant historiography, 13, 16, 149
Providentialism, 87–8, 92–4, 130, 131–3, 137–8, 142, 149, 152
Purcell, Patrick, Confederate general, 137
Puritans and Puritanism, 88n, 89, 120–1, 155–6, 158, 166, 180, 191, 209, 257
Pym, John, 211n, 246

Quakers, 248
quarter, promise of, 137, 176, 178, 181–2, 184, 186, 190, 213, 243, 255–6, 264, 272, 274–6, 278, 281
Quinn, D.B., historian, 15, 34, 85n, 119

Radcliffe, Sir Henry, 75
Radcliffe, Thomas, third earl of Sussex, viceroy, 69, 72–7 passim
Raleigh, Sir Walter, 23, 29, 84, 85n, 94
Rambuss, Richard, scholar, 81
rape, 71, 237, 295
rapparees: *see* bandits and banditry
Rathcoffey, massacre at (1642), 181, 183
Rathfarnham, 275
Rathlin Island, 64; massacre at, 34
Rathmines, battle of (1649), 280

Reade, Fr Peter, Jesuit, 186
Redshanks (mercenaries), the, 52
refugees, 27, 76, 186n, 212, 219–41 passim, 268, 271, 297
Reilly, Tom, historian, 253, 261
religious persecution, 132, 144, 147, 149–50, 152–3, 156, 226, 233
Renwick, W.L., scholar, 82–3
Restoration land settlement, 266
Rich, Barnaby, 27, 119, 121, 135–6
Richelieu, Armand Jean du Plessis de, cardinal, 292
Rinuccini, Giovanni Battista, archbishop, 12, 261–2, 270
Roche, Thomas, Confederate commander, 276
Roches of Fermoy, family, 179n
Rome, 12, 54, 101, 123, 250
Roscommon, County, 152
Rosen, Conrad von, general, 291
Rothe, David, Catholic bishop, 150, 250
Route, the, territory, 64
Royalists and royalist forces, 133, 182, 219, 240, 243, 250, 256, 259, 271–3, 275, 277–9, 281
Royal Society of Antiquaries of Ireland, journal of, 15, 140
'R.S.', author, 176, 181
Rupert of the Rhine, prince, 243, 258n, 274
Russell, Sir William, lord deputy, 113

safe conducts, 103, 114, 147
St Leger, Sir William, lord president of Munster, 177, 180, 189
Sanders, Dr Nicholas, papal envoy, 130, 133
Sarsfield, William, of Lucan, 184
Schomberg, Friedrich Herman, duke of, 290–1, 295
scorched earth, 45, 52, 55, 61–2, 74–7, 79, 120, 122, 125–6, 185–6, 190, 194, 230, 234, 288–90, 297–8

Scotland, 9, 23, 27–8, 63, 98, 101, 155–6, 179, 195, 205, 214, 219–41 passim, 248, 251n, 264, 291
Scotland, Church of, 220–2, 224, 257n; general assembly of, 224–6, 240; kirk sessions of, 225, 227, 230, 234–5, 237; synods of 226, 228–9, 231, 232–3, 238–40
Scottish Catholics, 191, 233
Scottish Covenanters, 219–20, 226, 231, 235, 241, 257n, 264 forces of in Ireland, 181, 189–90, 220, 233–4
Scottish Presbyterians, 248; *see also* Presbyterians in Ireland
Scottish Privy Council, 220, 222, 224, 227
Scottish settlers in Ireland, 9, 28, 52–3, 148, 165–7, 180–1, 207n, 220, 223; *see also* Presbyterians in Ireland
Scurlock, Patrick, of Rathcredan, 185
sectarianism, 11–12
Sexton, Edmund, 146
Shakespeare, William, 18
Shannon, river, 47, 65, 72, 297
sieges, 52n, 55–7, 59, 72–3, 83–4, 88, 287, 290, 296, 300; *see also* warfare, conduct of
Sidney, Sir Henry, lord deputy, 73, 74–6
Sidney, John, captain, 125
Sidney, Sir Philip, 89
Sidney Sussex College, Cambridge, 140
Simms, Hilary, historian, 177
Simpson, Nicholas, MP, 163–4
Shillelagh, Co. Wicklow, 64, 71
Skeffington, Sir William, lord deputy, 24, 54–8, 59
Slaney, river, 71
Sligo, County, 108
Smerwick, Co. Kerry, massacre at, 15, 22, 34, 79–80, 82–94 passim, 96–7, 117, 134

snipers, 110, 199, 254–5
Southampton, earl of: *see* Wriothesley
Spain, 79, 89, 94, 119, 121, 123, 285
Spanish Armada, 93, 97–8
Spanish soldiers, 79, 82, 84, 86, 89, 92, 97–101, 128
Spenser, Edmund, 18, 25, 27, 79–83, 86, 87, 121
Stanley, Sir George, marshal, 72
Stationers' Register (London), 80, 94
Stephens, John, captain, 182–3
Stevenson, David, historian, 219, 223
Stewart, Sir Robert, 231, 277
Strabane, 95
Strafford, earl of: *see* Wentworth
Stranraer, 223
Streedagh strand, Co. Sligo, 101
Stuart monarchy, 14, 23, 205, 250; court-in-exile 277–8
surrender and regrant, policy of, 114
Sussex, earls of: *see* Radcliffe
Swords, Co. Dublin, battle of (1642), 196
Synnott, David, colonel, 260, 263, 275n

Taaffe, Fr Peter, martyr, 257
Taaffe, Theobald, Viscount Taaffe, 257
Teate, Faithfull, Protestant minister, 143, 158, 161, 172, 213–5
Temple, Sir John, 13, 178, 214–6, 269
Termonfeckin, 76
The True Reporte of the Prosperous Successe which God gave unto our English souldiers ... (1581), 90–2
Thomond, territory of, 41, 64
Three Castles, Co. Wicklow, battle of (1547), 72
Timolin, Co. Kildare, 181, massacre at (1642), 181–3
Tipperary, County, 64, 177, 189, 245
Tichbourne, Sir Henry, military governor, 186
Tobacco Islands, 256

Toome Castle, 108
torture, 85
transplantation, 81
transportation, 251n
treason, laws of, 55, 57–8, 61n, 74, 120
Trim Castle, 61n, 141, 212, 257
Tuchet, James, third earl of Castlehaven, 142, 185, 190, 210, 277
Tudor monarchy, 12, 14, 23, 34, 60–1; government of Ireland, 35–6, 39, 53–4, 69n, 74, 100, 102, 104–6, 119–20, 127–9; lexicon of, 111–12; conquest policy, 10, 15, 17, 36–7, 53, 63, 68–9, 78, 79, 119, 121–2, 129
Tullyhogue, Co. Tyrone, 20
Tullow, Co. Carlow, 52, 55n
Turks, 28, 93, 128, 285
Turner, Sir James, 293
Tyrone, County, 64–5, 75n, 76, 103, 108, 110, 158
Tyrrell family, 62

Ukraine, 191
Ulster, 15, 52, 104, 107, 120, 188n, 226; plantation of 126; violence in, 25, 49, 51, 64–5, 70, 73, 110, 112, 122, 154–75 passim, 176–7, 180–1, 189–90, 195, 205–7, 209, 219–20, 222–3, 227, 228–35, 237–40
Upper Ossory, barons of: *see* MacGiollapadraig (Fitzpatrick)

Vavasour, Sir Charles, 190
Venetian diplomats, 279
Venn, Thomas, 293
Verney, Sir Edmund, 256, 259
Verney, Sir Raplh, 278
Virginia, Co. Cavan, 163, 184n

Wadding, Luke, 142
Wales, 35

Waller, Sir William, 244
Wallop, Sir Henry, vice-treasurer, 134–5
Walsh family, of Carrickmines, 196–7, 200–1
Walsh, Fr., priest, 56
Walsh, John, Confederate leader, 276
Walsham, Alexandra, historian, 131–2
Walsingham, Sir Francis, secretary of state, 135
War of the Two Kings (1688–91), 10, 23, 266
Ware, Sir James, 217
warfare, conduct of, 38, 63, 69–70, 85, 97–8, 116–18, 126, 283–90, 291–2, 300; by native forces, 37–8, 39–48, 55, 62, 63, 70–2, 76–7, 96–7, 98–101, 102–3, 107–10, 111, 112–5, 126, 128, 163–5, 166–7, 170, 180, 188; by English crown forces, 35–6, 37, 38, 54–62 passim, 63–9 passim, 72–6, 78, 79, 81, 83–5, 88–90, 92–3, 97–8, 121–5, 127–9, 177–8, 180–90 passim, 195–6, 197–200, 207–9; by Cromwellian forces, 26–7, 151, 176, 242–65 passim, 272, 275–6, 294; by Jacobite and Williamite forces, 286–7, 290–1, 293–300
Waring, Thomas, 27, 271
Warwick, Philip, 138
Waterford city, 131, 134–5, 145, 270, 277–8
Waterford, County, 42, 245
Welsh people, 21, 70–1, 167
Wentworth, Sir Thomas, earl of Strafford, 159, 174, 181n, 208, 226, 233

Western Isles, 51–2
Westmeath, County, 61–2, 190
Wexford, County, 41, 63, 64, 196, 245, 272
Wexford town, 24; massacre at (1649), 22, 23, 26, 246, 251, 258, 259–63, 275–7, 300
Whitelocke, Bulstrode, 278
Wicklow, County, 23, 25, 64–5, 141, 195–6, 217, 245
Wicklow town, 208
William III, 291
Williamite regime, 295, 298
Williams, Margery, Lady Thame, 135
Willis, Humphrey, captain, 108
Wilson, Thomas, royal secretary, 135
Winter, Sir William, admiral, 83–4, 88
Wise, Fr, priest, 145
Wollick, William, martyr, 85
Wolsey, Thomas, cardinal archbishop, 53
women, 102, 136, 180; as victims of violence 20, 26, 33, 34, 59, 71, 85–6, 104, 125–6, 128–9, 141, 164, 172n, 176–7, 179, 181, 183–7, 189–90, 192, 199, 201–3, 208, 217, 225–40 passim, 244, 261, 281
Wood, Owen, 103
Wood, Thomas a, 278
Wriothesley, Henry, third earl of Southampton, 194

Yeats, W.B., 82, 87
Yellow Ford, battle of, 122
York, 181n
Youghal, 147

Zouche, John, captain, 88